D1711344

Out of the Woods

Out of the Woods

The Origins of the Literary Fairy Tale
in Italy and France

NANCY L. CANEPA, EDITOR

Introduction by
Nancy L. Canepa and Antonella Ansani

WAYNE STATE UNIVERSITY PRESS   DETROIT

Library of Congress Cataloging-in-Publication Data

Out of the woods : the origins of the literary fairy tale in Italy and

France / Nancy L. Canepa, editor ; introduction by Nancy L. Canepa

and Antonella Ansani.

        p.   cm.

    Includes bibliographical references and index.

    ISBN 0-8143-2687-0 (pbk. : alk. paper)

    1. Romance literature—History and criticism.   2. Fairy tales—

France—History and criticism.   3. Fairy tales—Italy—History and

criticism.   I. Canepa, Nancy L., 1957–

PN808.097   1997

843'.409—dc21   97-20652

                                                        CIP

Contents

Contents

Preface

THE ESSAYS collected here are in large part the end product of a two-day workshop that was held at Dartmouth College in the spring of 1995 on the topic of "Literary Fairy Tales of the Seventeenth and Eighteenth Centuries in France and Italy." This workshop had the important purpose of bringing together scholars who share an interest in the early history of the European fairy tale, in the literary and sociohistorical contexts by which the early tales were informed, and in the role that the tales themselves had in expressing and revising the cultural concerns of their age. The workshop was an exciting opportunity to share ideas across the boundaries of national literatures and academic disciplines, and by the end of our time together we had decided to expand and make public our discussions in the form of an anthology of essays. We are convinced that this volume will prove to be a valuable aid in the study and teaching of literary fairy tales, both activities that have gained in vigor over the past few decades. These studies of the origins of a genre that is just as healthy today as it was at its inception four hundred years ago not only provide a piece of literary history that has been largely missing until now, but also help us to appreciate the magical power that fairy tales continue to wield today.

I would like to thank my colleague Stephanie Hull for her help in co-organizing the workshop and to express my deep gratitude to Jack Zipes for his precious suggestions and guidance in all phases of the project. The Ramon and Marguerite Guthrie Fund of Dartmouth College both made the workshop possible and provided me with an additional subsidy to cover publication costs; without such generous help this volume probably would never have come into being.

Introduction

Nancy L. Canepa and Antonella Ansani

To be reminded of the vitality of the literary fairy tale, one need look no further than bookstore display cases, where explicitly satirical manipulations of fairy tales such as Garner's *Politically Correct Bedtime Stories* vie for space with anthologies of contemporary tales such as *The Oxford Book of Modern Fairy Tales* and *The Outspoken Princess and the Gentle Knight*.[1] That all of these sorts of collections contain tales addressed as much to adults as to children should not come as a surprise, for the earliest literary fairy tales comprised an exclusively adult genre, written for privileged court audiences and conspicuously colored with references to the cultures of their times. But, notwithstanding the blossoming of interest in the fairy tale today, its origins as a literary genre have been all but forgotten. Whereas later collections by the Grimms and Hans Christian Andersen (and to a certain degree, Perrault) have in the Anglo-American context acquired a "classic" status, the importance and influence of the first literary fairy tales born in the seventeenth-century court and salon cultures of Italy and France have assumed, over the centuries, the role of Cinderellas.[2]

The essays included in this volume focus on the early history and development of this genre, whose birth should be considered in the context of the many shifts in literary culture that occurred in the seventeenth and eighteenth centuries. The contemporary rise of the novel, the commedia dell'arte, the opera and the mock epic, as well as significant transformations of traditional genres, have all tended, however, to overshadow the early history of the literary fairy tale. The texts and authors treated here range from the Italian Giovan Francesco Straparola's *Le piacevoli notti* (1550–53), one of the first novella collections to include numerous fairy tales; to his countryman Giambattista Basile's *Lo cunto de li cunti* (1634–36), the first framed collection of literary fairy tales by a single author in Europe and the "foundation stone of the modern literary tale";[3] through the extraordinarily intense "first wave" of

9

fairy-tale production in the late-seventeenth- and early-eighteenth-century France of Louis XIV, that included works by Charles Perrault and Marie-Catherine d'Aulnoy, among others; up to the various manipulations and transformations of the genre later in the eighteenth century, by authors such as Antoine Hamilton, Carlo Gozzi, and Giacomo Casanova. One of the principal aims of this volume is, indeed, to rescue the Italian and French ancestors of better-known collections from the relative oblivion in which they lie. The authors of these essays, far from considering these tales as anomalous or minor works, foreground their important role in questioning and revising the contours of the cultural history of their times.

All of the contributors to this volume, though adopting various critical methodologies and investigating different phases of the genre's evolution, share an interest in exploring the literary, sociohistorical, and ideological contexts by which the early tales were informed. Where this approach departs from others, which dominated fairy-tale scholarship well into the 1970s—principally, the structuralist, the folklorist, and the psychoanalytic[4]—is in its refusal to embrace any sort of universalization of its subject and in its affirmation of the need to move beyond a consideration of the fairy tale as a monolithic genre to the recognition that it is a vital, changing form, firmly entrenched in cultural history. Although a number of the authors and works treated here have been analyzed from this perspective in recent years, the panoramic and multidisciplinary view of the early history of the genre that emerges from this volume is entirely unique.

The literary fairy tale first appeared in Europe in Italy in the sixteenth century. Of course, at this time the fairy tale was anything but a new genre: oral tales had already been in circulation for thousands of years and had left traces in works ranging from Apuleius's *Golden Ass* to medieval romances to Boccaccio's *Decameron*. As Jack Zipes has aptly summarized, in the period immediately preceding the re-creation of the fairy tale as a literary genre

> folk tales were told by non-literate peasants among themselves at the hearth, in spinning rooms, or in the fields. They were told by priests in the vernacular as part of their sermons to reach out to the peasantry. Literate merchants and travelers transmitted them to people of all classes in inns and taverns. They were told to children of the upper class by nurses and governesses. They were remembered and passed on in different forms and versions by all members of society and told to suit particular occasions—*as talk*.[5]

Zipes has also claimed, persuasively, that the initial appearance of the literary fairy tale in Italy was due in part to the pivotal role that many Italian cities had in international commerce (thereby facilitating contacts, mercantile and cultural, with other geographical areas, especially the Middle East, which had rich and highly developed tale traditions), and in part to the intense cultural activity and high literacy rates that Italy enjoyed at that time.[6] After a number of extremely suggestive experimentations with the genre, of which Basile's masterpiece is the culminating point, by the middle of the seventeenth century the fairy tale had begun to elicit less interest in Italy and was virtually left by the literary wayside.[7] Yet even if Basile's work was more of a milestone than a literary model, the use that he made of the fairy tale in some way set the tone for its subsequent developments. The tales of *Lo cunto*, effervescent and often racy, not only thrill the reader with their dizzying playfulness but engage him equally intensely with a series of social and literary concerns pertaining to the culture in which they were produced. This heritage was to be fully exploited by the first generation of French tale-writers (especially female authors such as Marie-Catherine d'Aulnoy), who skillfully manipulated the various marginalities associated with the fairy-tale genre to address their own issues of marginality, as well as by, in the Italian tradition, the late-eighteenth-century playwright Carlo Gozzi.[8]

By the end of the seventeenth century, with the boom of tale-writing that occurred in France, the fairy tale had begun its journey toward canonization as a literary genre (the term *fairy tale* [*conte de fées*] was first coined during this period). The reasons adduced for the remarkable success of this genre include the primary importance of France as a political power and the emerging role of French as a transnational courtly language, the fact that developments in printing allowed for greater diversity in the types of literature that were published, and the general atmosphere of "cultural creativity and innovation" that characterized the French literary world of this period.[9] D'Aulnoy, one of the most prolific fairy-tale writers of her generation, initiated the vogue with the publication of the fairy tale "L'Isle de la Félicité" (which was embedded in the novel *L'Histoire d'Hippolyte, comte de Duglas*) in 1690, and from 1696 to 1698 published several volumes of tales. Charles Perrault, perhaps the best-known member of this generation, in 1697 published his *Histoires ou contes du temps passé*, which included what would later become the "classic" tales of "Little Red Riding Hood," "Puss in Boots," "Bluebeard," and others. The authors—and audiences—of the first French tales, as of the earlier Italian tales, were the elite frequenters of courts and salons, and these authors lost no opportunity to use the tales to air their views on prevailing social and political conditions, sexuality, and mores—in short, on the "civilizing process." The extraordinarily rich and voluminous corpus of tales that was produced during this "first wave" of fairy-tale production in France (1690–1703) was comprised above all of "salon fairy tales," so named because many of them had their origins in the literary circles or salons organized and attended by women in the later years of Louis XIV's reign.[10]

Many of the authors of fairy tales treated here will be unfamiliar to the general scholarly public. The only one who is universally recognized, is, in fact, Perrault. Perhaps the reasons for the canonical status of Perrault lie in the fact that he was well positioned in the political and literary circles of Louis XIV's reign.[11] But, as is made clear by many of the contributors to this volume, he was only one member of a generation of many writers who were experimenting with this new genre. Most of these contemporaries were women, who although they were generally of aristocratic extraction and fully integrated into the "high society" of late-seventeenth-century France, wrote their tales on the margins of the literary establishment.[12] In fact, it has been argued that after Louis XIV took power in 1651, the virtual undoing of the political and military power that noblewomen wielded in the first part of the century resulted in the rise of female authorship, and the creation by women of a new role for themselves as cultural arbiters and of a new, imaginary space—that of the novel.[13] By the end of the century, fairy tales, often intercalated in novels, had begun to occupy significant niches of this space. The history of the rise of the fairy tale in France was, thus, related to a series of exclusions: in particular, literary and political. This liminal space that the fairy tale occupied also had to do, of course, with the marginality of the literary fairy tale itself as a genre in this period, occupying as it still did an indefinite space between oral and popular cultures, on the one hand, and elite literary traditions, on the other. For these reasons, the fairy tale became in many ways an ideal *terra franca* of the literary world, one in which formal and thematic experimentation, as well as social criticism that would not be tolerated in more canonical genres, could be given freer rein.

In the years following 1688, which correspond to the years of the most intense tale-writing activity, Louis XIV's regime was entering a critical phase in which standards of living were lowering for all social classes and tyrannical social policies, which included a narrow and censorious view of cultural expression, were being put into place. Jack Zipes has argued that far from conceiving of their choice of the fairy tale as a purely "escapist" genre, the *conteurs*, but especially the *conteuses*, of this period used their tales as vehicles for antimonarchical polemic and ethical critique, while at the same time offering fantastic, utopian models for a transformed world in which justice, equality, and love would reign.[14] When looked at from this angle, Perrault's fame may be due to the fact that he did *not* use his tales to comment so explicitly and in such detail on the culture in which they were written and, above all, to the fact that the content of his tales was (and is) more in line with the dominant ideology of the time.

Furthermore, the precursory role of Italy in the formation of this genre has been all but ignored. It comes as no surprise, really, that three centuries after Boccaccio initiated the genre of the European novella with his *Decameron*, another Italian, Giambattista Basile, was the first in Europe to create a similarly framed collection of literary fairy tales. Up until very recently, however, the influence of a figure like Basile (and to a lesser degree, Straparola) as one of the progenitors of the modern literary fairy tale, although it has been emphasized by folklorists and Italianists, has not carried much weight in more comprehensive discussions of the development of the literary fairy tale in Europe.[15] And yet the link between Basile and the French tale-writers later in the century is truly suggestive. Not only was Basile a concrete point of reference for at least some of the later French authors,[16] but there are also significant similarities with regard to the sociopolitical situation in which he was working and to the place of his fairy-tale writing within the literary establishment. Basile too wrote in a context of political crisis: the Spanish-ruled Kingdom of Naples in which he lived and worked as court intellectual was undergoing a period of internal "refeudalization," while simultaneously being exploited as a colony by the Spanish monarchy in its desperate, all-out attempts to finance its involvement in the Thirty-Year War. These developments resulted in increasingly unbearable, not to mention unscrupulously managed, taxation and recurring scarcity of primary foodstuffs. This produced a situation of social unrest and lawlessness, which took forms such as banditry and resistance on the part of local feudal lords to monarchical directives, and would ultimately explode in the revolt of Masaniello in 1647. This state of social and political turmoil was paralleled by profound changes in the function of the court intellectual, whose role was seen less and less in the idealizing Renaissance terms of active interlocutor with those who wielded power, and increasingly as little more than an administrator, relegated to the outskirts of the cultural arena. Basile's fairy-tale project, because of the "oral" flavor of its subject matter and the "low" language in which it was written, was destined to a place at the outer limits of literary institutions and to consideration, if it was considered by elite culture at all, as an eccentric anomaly in the production of a court intellectual.[17] And Basile, like the French writers after him, makes his "tale of tales" not only a laboratory of formal experimentation but also a stage upon which polemical social dramas could be played. In short, the authors of these early tales construct a space in which to explore alternate literary languages and ideological visions and develop with relative freedom critiques of literary traditions and social institutions. These literary fairy tales, far from being segregated in the woods of a fantastic dimension, are actively engaged with contemporary, "real-world" concerns.

This volume is divided into three sections, the first two of which focus on the early Italian collections and the first wave of French production. The essays in the first section, entitled "The Rebirth of a Genre: The Creation of the Literary Fairy Tale in the Seventeenth Century," explore the genesis of the first literary tales, offsprings of a century marked by sweeping literary, social, and cultural transformations, and demonstrate that they comprised a genre that was particularly suited for expression of this ferment.

The Italian tales appeared at the bottom end of the trajectory of the novella that had begun with Boccaccio, and, moreover, at a time when humanistic literary, ethical, and epistemological models were being called into question and what is called the baroque was taking form.[18] In the literary sphere, for example, the crisis of Renaissance models of verisimilitude already in effect in sixteenth-century Italy (evidenced in the discussions regarding the epic and the marvelous, centered especially around Torquato Tasso) and the elaboration of new literary paradigms that threatened to undermine literary tradition produced, throughout the seventeenth century, a series of heated cultural debates. These were expressed in Italy in the theorizations of the poetics of the marvelous and in the *oggidì* polemic and later in France in the Quarrel of the Marvelous and the Quarrel of the Ancients and the Moderns.[19]

The first two essays in this section have as their subject Giambattista Basile's *Lo cunto de li cunti* (1634–36), the first framed collection of literary fairy tales to appear in Western Europe, and emphasize how his work should be read in the context of the developments mentioned above. Basile was born around 1575 in Naples to a middle-class family, and led a professional life that might have served as a model for a man of letters of his day. He served as a soldier and courtier at courts in Italy and abroad, was a member of several academies, and by his death in 1632 was a count. His Italian works won him substantial recognition during his lifetime, though by the end of the seventeenth century they had already faded into oblivion. But Basile had a second literary persona. The only works for which he is remembered today, indeed, are those he composed in Neapolitan dialect: above all, *Lo cunto de li cunti*.

Nancy Canepa, in her essay, " 'Quanto 'nc'è da ccà a lo luoco dove aggio da ire?': Giambattista Basile's Quest for the Literary Fairy Tale," discusses the significance of Basile's decision to rewrite the fairy tale, up to this point a predominantly oral genre, in literary form, and analyzes a number of the tales in which the outstanding metaliterary concerns of Basile's project are thematized. Since this collection heralds the entrance of the fairy tale into the "authored" canon of Western literature, the frame tale in particular has the essential function of staging the birth of this new genre, and its negotiation with various traditions. The first tale of the collection, "The Ogre," then proceeds to tell the tale of the acquisition of the "tools of the trade" of popular culture, in which the rite of passage of the tale's protagonist parallels Basile's own initiation into and transformations of the traditions of folklore and dialect literature. "The Dove" is a brilliant example of Basile's use of metaphor to rupture the surface linearity of the fairy tale and to reveal an ideological subtext in which social practices of the time are parodied and critiqued. "The Cockroach, the Mouse, and the Cricket" embodies Basile's unique model of the "fairy-tale carnivalesque." Finally, "Splendid Shine" which tells the tale of a girl who fashions a husband from almond paste and jewels, is an explicit dramatization of Basile's construction of a new fairy-tale subject. In *Lo cunto*, Canepa concludes, numerous traditions intersect to create an "open" text in which linguistic and cultural hierarchies, as well as the conventional fairy-tale hierarchies, are rearranged or made to show their weak spots. The true novelty of *Lo cunto* lies in the figural and ideological interpolations, the references to diverse social realities and narrative traditions, that crowd the tales and disturb their illusory "happy-ever-after" closure.

According to many folklore scholars, one of the distinctive traits of the folktale is its predilection for sharp oppositions: the tales' protagonists, for example, are either kings or paupers, beautiful or ugly, good or evil. In her essay, "Beauty and the Hag: Appearance and Reality in Basile's *Lo cunto de li cunti*," Antonella Ansani explores the problematic ways in which Basile, just as he adopts the formal features of the genre as a model for his innovative literary fairy tale, at the same time calls these very features into question, suggesting that the extreme oppositions of the fairy tale are not so unequivocally delimited. This ambiguity emerges clearly in Basile's treatment of the beauty and ugliness of women, a theme developed in the tales "The Myrtle," whose protagonist is a beautiful myrtle/fairy, and "The Old Woman Who Was Skinned," where two utterly ugly and grotesque women are seen in action. Although in both of these tales there is an apparent and clear contrast between beauty and ugliness, upon closer reading this distinction becomes blurred. Ansani suggests that through the celebration of the female grotesque the traditional Renaissance topos of the "naked truth" is reversed, and the world of appearances and baroque rhetoric triumphs. Basile's deconstruction of these bipolarities not only questions, then, the absoluteness of ethical and aesthetic categories, but also highlights rhetorical and epistemological shifts that were taking place in this period.

In the essay entitled "Perrault's *Contes*: An Irregular Pearl of Classical Literature," Claire Malarte-Feldman further investigates the status of the literary fairy tales as eminently baroque. The *Contes*, traditionally considered "the classical text par excellence," are not only "classical," but also contain baroque stylistic and thematic elements that have been brought to light, and in some cases emphasized, by the iconographic interpretations that they have received. In this context Malarte-Feldman draws on Foucault's discussion of perspective in baroque artistic works, on the questions he poses about the significance of the glances exchanged inside and outside of paintings, and on his elaboration of a system based on the presence and/or absence of the spectator in the space that it provides. Perrault himself stressed the baroque tendency of his fairy tales to establish distinct contrasts between the exterior and the interior, comparing what he called a "playful narrative" to an "envelope" inside which there is hidden a serious moral lesson. This tension between exterior and interior, which can be found in the language, style, and themes used by Perrault, was conveyed particularly well by Gustave Doré's illustrations of the *Contes*. Still today, illustrators of Perrault's tales propose their own baroque representations of the text, forcing us to revise some of our concepts about what comprises classical and baroque literature.

As has been noted by various scholars, the fairy tale contains within itself what might seem to be a paradoxical double stance with regard to literary tradition and society.[20] Its nostalgic longing for a social order and oral tradition no longer retrievable (if they ever were) in integral form coexists with a utopian vision of an even better future that, moreover, often also implies a subversive critique of the present. Such a stance is a suggestive allegory of the equally paradoxical attitudes of an age in which the coordinates— sociopolitical, economic, epistemological, scientific, literary—that had pre- viously sufficed for a comprehension of the world were being systematically rearranged or put into question.[21] The anxiety and insecurity regarding these shifts, on the one hand, and, on the other, the intellectual excitement that these transformations also engendered, were obliquely mirrored in these first authors of literary fairy tales. Just as they recognized the tradition in which the tales were rooted, they were equally aware of the potential that their nascent genre had for offering a new model of narrative representation, and within this, new paradigms for social and personal interaction, concerns always at the heart of the fairy tale.

This brings us to another topic implicit in the study of the fairy-tale genre: the crucial role that these tales have in highlighting the intersections between the oral and the textual, between popular and elite cultures. The sixteenth, and to a larger extent, the seventeenth centuries witnessed, across the lines of literary genres, a marked interest in and appropriation of material that had previously been relegated to a heterogeneous spectrum of popular genres such as street theater, broadsides and chapbooks, festivals (such as Carnival) and, of course, folktales.[22] Authors like Basile or d'Aulnoy certainly do acknowledge their debts to the tradition of oral telling, and this should not surprise us, when we consider that they, unlike the Grimms, did not have any literary tradition to claim as sources even had they so desired. But what strikes the reader are the extraordinarily complex ways in which the dialectic between official and unofficial culture (the second not only in the form of popular, lower-class culture but also in its many other hybrid manifestations: the dialect tradition, in the case of Basile, court and salon conversation, and so forth) plays itself out in these early tales, which use simulations of various forms of orality, the tension between the realistic and the fantastic, and the dialogue between high and low cultures and canonical and noncanonical genres as an essential part of their narrative and ideological strategies. These authors indeed employ an archaic narrative form to put into question the hegemony of "high" tradition and the society in which it was nurtured, and this acknowledgment of the original orality of fairy tale in order to put it to complex, and quite often subversive, uses, is, naturally, a radically different operation from the manipulations of the "oral" and the "folk" that would later occupy romantic writers such as the Grimms.

Considerations such as these might lead us to ask: Is there something characteristically complex, even "unfairy-tale-like," in these early tales, that made them the prime candidates for exclusion when the fairy tale was canonized and infantilized in the nineteenth century? What, precisely, were the defining traits of this re-created genre? It would seem like a contradiction in terms to speak of "unfairy-tale-like" fairy tales, but any attempt to see how faithfully the literary fairy tales of the seventeenth and eighteenth centuries conform to the formal, thematic, and stylistic definitions of the genre as they have been elaborated in this century leads straight to that conclusion. For example, although Vladimir Propp's sequence of functions is somewhat respected by an author such as Basile, many of the other authors treated in this volume do not even follow this sequence.[23] And more to the point, what Propp dismisses as mere "attributes"—names, descriptions, appearance, and other details that he finds marginal—are often, in these tales, blown up to enormous proportions and become, in fact, the repositories of the most significant cultural content. Moreover, in an author like Basile the superabundance of these "peripheral" elements is highlighted by the stylistic treatment that they receive, another of the "freer zones" about which Propp has little to say: "The storyteller is free in his choice of linguistic means. This highly rich area is not subject to the morphologist's study. The *style* of a tale is a phenomenon which must be studied separately."[24] It is, then, the structuralist focus of Propp's study and, indeed, of much of the later narratological analysis that he inspired, that ultimately bears little fruit when applied to many of the texts under question here.

Likewise, a brief glance at the descriptive categories that another eminent folklore scholar, Max Lüthi, designates for the fairy tale, are of limited usefulness in understanding the early Italian and French tales. For Lüthi, the European fairy tale is distinguished by its "one-dimensionality," or coexistence of human and supernatural characters in the same metaphysical or spiritual dimension; "depthlessness," or lack of representation of characters' psychological life, environment, or history; "abstract style," or linear, essentializing descriptive techniques that avoid rhetorical ornament, especially excessive use of metaphor; "isolation and universal interconnection," or characters' lack of sustained relationships or experiences that change them, and the consequent ability to enter into and exit from associations without any sort of lasting effects; and "sublimation and all-inclusiveness," the lack of concreteness and realism in the fairy tale, which although it does not offer in-depth analyses, at the same time produces "an effortless interplay that includes all the important themes of human existence."[25]

Part of the problem lies, of course, in the fact that the most stringent definitions of the fairy tale have concentrated on its formal and stylistic characteristics, while avoiding any discussion of context. But studies such as Propp's and Lüthi's have also tended to have the oral folktale as their main point of reference, thus ignoring the crucial distinctions between what must really be regarded as two distinct genres. Although it is outside the scope of this volume to propose a systematic phenomenology of the early literary fairy tale, the essays here all contain analyses that point in the direction of a reevaluation of what exactly characterizes the literary fairy tale, and especially of how the literary tale distinguishes itself from the oral tale.[26]

The essays in the second section of the volume, entitled "From Genre to Gender and Ideology," investigate the manner in which gender and ideological concerns play themselves out in the genre of the literary fairy tale. To some readers it might seem self-evident, indeed an obvious trait of any literary text, that fairy tales engage with the culture in which they were created. But others might ask: How can feminist reflections on gender identity or critiques of the monarchy find fruitful expression in a genre populated by fairies and ogres that inhabit enchanted woods and imaginary kingdoms? Rosemary Jackson has pointed out particularly well how this essential equivocation has persisted in readings of all varieties of fantastic texts, in which the explicit content—the unreal—is taken to be evidence of the lack of involvement with, often in the form of transcendence of, the real at all levels.[27] She has argued convincingly, on the contrary, that in these texts the "introduction of the 'unreal' is set against the category of the 'real'—a category which the fantastic interrogates by its difference."[28] Thus, in the fairy tale is also embodied this apparent paradox: despite its fantastic trappings, it has a "harshly realistic core"; its "enchantments also universalize the narrative setting, encipher concerns, beliefs, and desires in brilliant, seductive images that are themselves a form of camouflage, making it possible to utter harsh truths, to say what you dare."[29] The situation of fairy-tale action in imaginary worlds apparently distant from real-life drama, coupled with the origins of the fairy tale as an oral genre that constituted, in encrypted form, an act of wish-fulfillment on the part of oppressed groups (the peasantry), made it, as we have seen, a genre that attracted seventeenth-century writers engaged in debates about the literary and social institutions of their times. The French writers, especially women such as d'Aulnoy, perfected the art of using the fairy tale as a form in which to express polemical views about their own society and utopian projections of an alternative social order.[30]

Moreover, in the case of the fairy tale (vs. other forms of "fantastic" literature), the situation of a given work in a precise sociocultural context is further obfuscated by the tendency to regard fairy tales, even when they are literary creations of individual authors, along the same lines as oral folktales: that is, as collective, anonymous products of a tale-telling community that may span vast chronological and geographic boundaries.[31] Thus, the universalizing approaches in genre criticism that Jameson has discussed, which tend to focus on semantic (identification of the "worldview" or essence of a particular genre) and syntactic (structural) aspects of a genre without giving sufficient consideration to how mental categories are historical and not absolute in nature, find an already receptive terrain in the particular case of the fairy tale. Jameson comments that "every universalizing approach . . . will be found to . . . repress its own historicity, by strategically framing its perspective so as to omit the negative, absence, contradiction, repression, the *non-dit*, or the *impensé*."[32]

In his essay, "Marvelous Realities: Reading the *Merveilleux* in the Seventeenth-Century French Fairy Tale," Lewis Seifert investigates the place of the fairy tale within seventeenth-century aesthetic debates, and analyzes the implications of changing aesthetic categories on the ideological content of the French tales. After defining the distinctive narrative structure of the *contes de fées*, he shows how the fairy-tale marvelous produces ambivalent ideological effects in relation to the seventeenth-century aesthetic category of verisimilitude (*vraisemblance*): the *contes* both uphold and flout the dominant moral and social codes encompassed by verisimilitude. By definition, however, this marvelous does not observe the plausible laws of the empirical world nor is it reduced to an overarching moral or aesthetic system, as are other literary uses of the *merveilleux* at this time (for example, mythology or Christian epics). Seifert argues that this implausibility (*invraisemblance*) especially fosters the expression of desires and fears about the body and, by extension, gender identities. When situated in a marvelous setting, the body becomes a central object of nostalgic and utopian longing.

It should be clear at this point that the study of these early tales provides a piece of literary history that has been largely missing up until now. One of the common aims of all the essays in this volume is, in fact, to expand on the question, briefly treated above, of why this moment is so important, and how better understanding it can help us to grasp the cultural dynamics of these centuries in a more comprehensive way. The very fact that this *is* a fairly unknown phase in the development of the literary tale leads, of course, to another large question: that of canon formation. Elizabeth Harries confronts this question in her essay, "Fairy Tales about Fairy Tales: Notes on Canon

Formation," which has as its point of departure the fact that, although in the 1690s many women, and a few men, published fairy tales in France, only the tales written by men, particularly Perrault, are the ones that have become part of the canon of fairy tales published and republished until our time. She asks: How did it come about that the very origins of this genre, except for Perrault, have still remained relatively unstudied? What governed the selection of the tales by Perrault and the omission of the tales written by women? Harries argues that the process of exclusion began in 1699, in a caustic booklet by Pierre de Villiers entitled *Entretiens sur les contes de fées*, and was reinforced during the revolutionary period, when many women writers were systematically excluded from the French canon, primarily (though not always explicitly) on the grounds of their sex. In the nineteenth century, as the combination of romantic notions about the "folk," oral transmission, and national culture transformed Perrault's tales, which seemed more natural and authentic, into the canonical French contributions to the genre, the eradication of the women became even more absolute. Why, for example, do the Grimms, in the 1812 preface to their *Kinder-und Hausmärchen*, praise Perrault but condemn some of his female contemporaries? The Grimms' criteria for "valid" fairy tales, mirrored in the presentation of their own heavily rewritten tales as unadulterated transcriptions of oral tales that had come straight out of the peasant's mouth, are, in fact, largely at odds with those espoused by the earlier women writers.[33] Harries concludes that the romantic judgments by which the *contes* by women writers were measured and found wanting still affect our thinking about fairy tales today, and argues for a revision of the fairy-tale canon.

A good part of the credit for the development of ideological criticism of the literary fairy tale over the past several decades should be given to the fairy-tale scholar Jack Zipes, who in works such as *Breaking the Magic Spell: Radical Theories of Folk and Fairy Tales* (1979) and *Fairy Tales and the Art of Subversion* (1983) has created a sturdy foundation for a social history of the genre. Zipes has affirmed that "the individual tale was indeed a symbolic act intended to transform a specific oral folktale (and sometimes a well-known literary tale) and designed to rearrange the motifs, characters, themes, functions and configurations in such a way that they would address the concerns of the educated and ruling classes of late feudal and early capitalist societies," and argues for consideration of "fairy-tale discourse as dynamic part of the historical civilizing process, with each symbolic act viewed as an intervention in socialization in the public sphere."[34] The essay by Zipes included here, entitled "Of Cats and Men: Framing the Civilizing Discourse of the Fairy Tale," is a natural continuation of this research. Zipes demonstrates that the literary fairy tale as genre established a male framework for a discourse about mores, manners, sexuality, and ethics, and that this discourse is still influential in the twentieth century, even in fairy-tale films. By focusing on the different versions of "Puss in Boots" by Giovan Francesco Straparola, Giambattista Basile, Charles Perrault, and Walt Disney, he shows how the role of the cat as either female or male protagonist, depending on the tale, is crucial to understanding the meanings of the different tales, and through a study of the ideological perspectives of the authors traces the development over time of this meaning and the intimate relationship between the various versions of this tale. Zipes concludes that although we must be cautious in forming assumptions about the development of the fairy tale as genre based on a comparative study of just one tale such as "Puss in Boots," his essay is intended to serve as a case study and to open up a discussion about the manner in which literary forms are related to ideological concerns.

Recent scholars of the literary fairy tale have come to recognize that one of the most ideologically charged aspects of tales is to be found in their representations of gender. As Zipes maintains, tales written by men contribute to the creation of a hegemonic civilizing process. But many of the tales written by women in late-seventeenth-century France tell a different story. In "Reflections on the Monarchy in d'Aulnoy's *Belle-Belle ou le cheva-lier Fortuné*" Adrienne Zuerner explores the feminocentric representation of female desire and sexuality that characterizes many of Marie-Catherine d'Aulnoy's fairy tales and the fierce political critique that this questioning of gender identities implies. In particular, *Belle-Belle ou le chevalier Fortuné* (1698), a tale that features female cross-dressing, constitutes one compelling instance of this author's challenge to gender orthodoxy. By foregrounding the textual construction of gender, Zuerner demonstrates that *Belle-Belle* assesses the limits of the category "Woman," and deconstructs the unmarked gender, "Man." Moreover, this fairy tale critically portrays the seventeenth century's ideal masculine subject, the king. *Belle-Belle* dramatizes a symbolic dismemberment of the king's "double body" and, by exploiting the erotic ambiguities of cross-dressing, focuses on the ways in which the complex network of interdependences that binds king and courtiers renders the former vulnerable and blurs the distinction between the monarch as a private individual and as the incarnation of the state. In *Belle-Belle*, d'Aulnoy weaves into the basic narrative framework of her tale a penetrating and merciless portrait of the monarchy during the last years of the reign of Louis XIV. In so doing, this tale prefigures the parodic and licentious fairy tales of the eighteenth century.

Although many of the essays in this volume have as their subject the fantastically rich corpus of fairy tales written in the years around 1700, the fairy tale remained an immensely popular genre throughout the eighteenth century, especially in France. After the first, more experimental wave of the "salon fairy tales," which, as we have seen, were written primarily by women and were used as vehicles for social critique and utopian musings, the oriental fairy tale took center stage (1704–20). Antoine Galland's version of *The Thousand and One Nights* (1704–17) was arguably the single most important stimulus to the many translations, real and false, of Arabic works in this period, and many writers of tales created pastiches of oriental and French folkloric motifs. In the third and final phase of the vogue in France, writers of fairy tales, which at this point comprised an accepted literary genre, generally took one of two directions. They either "conventionalized" the fairy tale, erasing much of the subversive content of the earlier tales and in doing so preparing the way for its institutionalization as one of the stock genres of children's literature, or they wrote comic versions of fairy tales. The institutionalization of the genre reached its culminating point at the end of the century with the publication of the forty-one-volume collection *Cabinet des fées* (1785–89), which included tales from the various "waves."[35]

The essays of the third section, entitled "Eighteenth-Century Parodies and Transformations of the Fairy Tale," have as their subject parodic fairy tales, and the ways fairy tales or even isolated motifs were integrated into or intersected with very different genres later in the century. In her essay, entitled "Fractured Fairy Tales: Parodies for the Salon and Foire," Mary Louise Ennis offers a reassessment of the parodic fairy tales of 1705–22, and traces the passage from ludic imitation to satiric transformations of subjects and style. Often oriental and almost always scabrous, these tales spawned an enormously popular genre whose authors included Crébillon *fils*, Caylus, and Voisenon, as well as, later in the century, Diderot, Voltaire, and Rousseau. In particular, Ennis examines the earliest recorded parodies, written for the refined *salons* by Antoine Hamilton (*Le Bélier, l'Histoire de Fleur d'Epine*) and for the coarser fair theaters by Alain-René Lesage (*Arlequin, roi des Ogres ou les Bottes de sept lieus*). Hamilton's stories, set within a narrative frame pastiche inspired by *The Thousand and One Nights,* participated in heated contemporary discussions on the didactic uses of parody, and with their overintercalated structure, improbable chronology, illogical plot development, overblown hyperbole, and absurd anachronisms, playfully underscored the weaknesses of the fairy tale and oriental tale. Hamilton's later parody recorded the influence of the carnivalesque humor of the Foire, which was also found in Lesage's play. Whimsically alluding to Perrault and Hamilton, *Arlequin,* with its world-upside-down theme of "Ogres are people, too," is a trenchant comment on the efforts of France to colonize the New World. Ennis thus concludes that all of these works contain encoded literary and religious debates, and that in them the marvelous is used to denigrate contemporary society and morals.

In Italy, Basile's monumental work was not followed by a flurry of tale-writing activity similar to that in France. Although numerous editions of *Lo cunto* were published throughout the second half of the seventeenth century, and although Basile's influence on the French authors of tales and on the whole subsequent history of the genre is undebatable, his remained a relatively isolated effort in the context of Italian literary history. This was perhaps due to the fact that Basile wrote in a language—his own, very baroque reworking of Neapolitan dialect—that was not universally accessible, or even more so to the fragmented political condition of Italy at this time. In the 1600s France was already a nation with a monarch and a centralized government, and the grounds for a general discourse on the "civilizing process," which presupposed a sense of a nation with common cultural and moral concerns, were fertile. Italy, on the other hand, was still far from these sorts of elaborations.[36] This is not to say, however, that Basile's example faded into complete oblivion in the 1700s. On the contrary, an eighteenth-century Italian author such as Carlo Gozzi demonstrated a vivid awareness of Basile's heritage and, above all, of the "metaliterary" potential of the fairy tale that had been exploited by both Basile and the French writers, and elaborated a new type of hybrid work—theatrical fairy tales.

The essay by Ted Emery, "The Reactionary Imagination: Ideology and the Form of the Fairy Tale in Gozzi's *Il re cervo* [The King Stag]," stresses the hybrid nature of Carlo Gozzi's *Fiabe teatrali* [Fairy Tales for the Theater], which are uneasy mixtures of quite disparate elements, and proposes an ideological reading of this formal indeterminacy. As Emery points out, serious, noble characters speaking verse share the stage with commedia dell'arte masks who improvise in dialect prose; fairy-tale plots are interrupted by references to the contemporary reality of eighteenth-century Venice; spectacular special effects and theatricality for its own sake clash with the author's frequent polemical diatribes and sometimes overt didactic intentions. Why this energetic heterogeneity? Current scholarship has answered this query by relying on a notion of ideology as explicit content: a specific program of beliefs or messages present (or not) in a given text. Emery draws on more current theories of ideology to demonstrate, through his analysis of one of the *Fiabe*, *Il re cervo*, that the *fiabe* are nowhere as ideological as in their seemingly free play of fairy-tale fantasy, which is used by Gozzi to demonize social mobility, revealing his own inability to perceive value as a matter of "exchange." But the problem of value as exchange, never explicitly recognized in the *Fiabe*, is nevertheless present in figured form in the frequent physical metamorphoses of men and women into beasts and inanimate objects. The function of the fairy-tale material in *Il re cervo* is thus, Emery concludes, to allow an imaginary resolution of an ideological problem that the author cannot resolve at the level of the real.

Cynthia Craig's essay, entitled " 'Lecteur, ne vous allarmez pas' [Reader, be not afraid]: Giacomo Casanova and Reading the Fantastic," offers another example of integration of fairy-tale material into other literary genres, in this case the novel and the autobiography. Craig examines three examples of the *merveilleux* found in Casanova's texts: an episode in the autobiography *Histoire de ma vie*, which is constructed like a miniature *conte de fées;* a list of fabulous, often magical "Mondes ou îles" found in his unpublished papers in the Prague archives; and the five-volume novel, the *Icosameron*, which details an imaginary utopian voyage to the center of the earth. These three texts, taken together, demonstrate a significant but not commonly known aspect of Casanova's writing: the use of traditional fairy-tale elements in a wide range of narrative strategies as part of a self-conscious commentary upon genre and modes of reading. As Craig points out, the fairy tale was likely to interest Casanova because of its potential for expressing the motifs that dominate all of his literary works: exile, exclusion, the exotic, and the decentering of the prevailing culture. Fairy-tale motifs thus continued to further their expressive potential under Casanova's pen.

In the final essay of the volume, "Little Red Riding Hood as Fairy Tale, *Fait-divers,* and Children's Literature: The Invention of a Traditional Heritage," Catherine Velay-Vallantin investigates the intersections between fairy tales and a very different sort of genre: that of the *fait-divers* or news item, usually of the criminal sort. The central part of this study is dedicated to the analysis of the textual accounts that contributed to the elaboration of the legend of the "Beast of Gévaudan" in eighteenth-century France. Velay-Vallantin then shows both how later versions of "Little Red Riding Hood," which had become a classic tale after Perrault's rendition, were contaminated by this legend, and how the legend itself was influenced by earlier versions of the tale. A full understanding of the ways in which this tale was rewritten at the end of the nineteenth century to fit the requisites of children's literature, Velay-Vallantin maintains, depends on the editorial and symbolic associations between the actual fairy tale and the *fait-divers* and ensuing legends. She concludes that the meanings of both the fairy tale and the *fait-divers* must be investigated in terms of the differences between text and context, discourse and ritual, and social practice and writing.

This last essay already extends into a century in which the fairy tale acquired vastly different forms and functions from those that it had had in the earlier centuries, a period that would require another introduction for itself alone.[37] But what we would like to emphasize, in conclusion, is that after the construction of the genre of children's literature in the eighteenth and especially nineteenth centuries and the appropriation of the fairy tale as one of its mainstays, the rebirth of the adult tale today, alluded to at the beginning of this introduction, only attests to the fact that the fairy tale is a narrative form that lends itself extraordinarily well to being regenerated and updated to speak to the concerns of readers of any era. In the last century in particular the fairy tale, which ever since its first oral forms has presented a utopian vision of a world where good triumphs over evil, has been adopted to express a wide spectrum of ethical positions that, naturally, use as points of departure radically diverging concepts of just what "good" and "evil" are. Perhaps the most widely known versions of fairy tales in the twentieth century and certainly the most commercially successful have been the adaptations produced by the Disney Studios. But although contemporary "rewritings" of this sort, which tend to reinforce prevailing stereotypes or to parody attempts to put them into question (such as Garner's book), perhaps attract the most public attention, there has also been a wealth of alternative experimentations with the genre. Writers engaged with, for example, feminist, pacifist, and antimaterialist concerns have been drawn to the fairy tale. In particular, over the past few decades there has been a veritable explosion of fairy-tale writing,[38] which has led one scholar of the genre, Marina Warner, to suggest eloquently that at this point in history fairy tales, which offer themselves as "potential conduits of another way of seeing the world, of telling an alternative story," may address more aptly than any other genre the existential dramas confronting us today:

> Fairy tales are indeed still criticized—and with reason—for the easy lies, the crass materialism, the false hopes they hold out, but in the last decade of the century, in conditions of radical change on the one hand, and stagnation on the other, with ever increasing fragmentation and widening polarities, with national borders disappearing in some places and returning with a bloody vengeance in others, as a millenarian feeling of ecological catastrophe gains momentum, and the need to belong grows ever more rampant as it becomes more frustrated, there has been a strongly marked shift towards fantasy as a mode of understanding, as an ingredient in survival, as a lever against the worst aspects of the status quo and the direction it is taking.[39]

As will be clear after reading the essays in this volume, there is nothing new in the recognition of the historicizing potential of the fairy tale, seemingly a fantastic genre removed from real-world concerns, nor in the acknowledgment of the value that the imaginary worlds that they create hold for comprehending and taking action in our own world. The very first authored tales of Western Europe, written in the sixteenth to eighteenth centuries in Italy and France, were consciously appropriated by professional men and women of letters from the oral tradition and transformed into the new genre of the literary fairy tale. Far from being "entertainment for little ones" (as the tongue-in-cheek subtitle of Basile's *Lo cunto de li cunti* declares), they were sophisticated creations of literati who engaged in an implicit dialogue with the "high" literary culture of their time and the traditions that shaped

it. These first tales are, then, the most elegant and convincing examples of
the fact that the universality of the literary fairy tale consists precisely in its
remarkable capacity for being reworked by individual authors into stories of
their own times.

Notes

1. James Finn Garner, *Politically Correct Bedtime Stories* (New York: Macmillan,
   1994); Alison Lurie, ed., *The Oxford Book of Modern Fairy Tales* (New York:
   Oxford University Press, 1993); Jack Zipes, ed., *The Outspoken Princess and the
   Gentle Knight* (New York: Bantam, 1994).

2. In France and Italy, there has been somewhat less neglect of the seventeenth-
   and eighteenth-century tales, though the realization of the importance of these
   authors has emerged only over the last century, and especially over the last several
   decades. France has always recognized Perrault as the father of the French literary
   fairy tale, but his many female contemporaries who also wrote fairy tales are still
   far from being awarded the critical recognition that they deserve, and, with few
   exceptions, have by no means entered into the canon of "classic" fairy tales (one
   of the most famous exceptions is Mme Leprince de Beaumont's mid-eighteenth-
   century version of "Beauty and the Beast"). The forty-one-volume *Cabinet de fées*,
   a compendium of tales written in the hundred years preceding its publication in
   1785–89, signaled the institutionalization of the genre in France, but it has been
   only recently that full-length scholarly works have been dedicated to the French
   fairy-tale "vogue." See, for example, Mary Elizabeth Storer, *Un Épisode littéraire de
   la fin du XVIIe siècle: La Mode des contes de fées (1685–1700)* (1928; rpt., Geneva:
   Slatkine Reprints, 1972); Jacques Barchilon, *Le Conte merveilleux français de 1690
   à 1790* (Paris: Champion, 1975); and Raymonde Robert, *Le Conte de fées littéraire
   en France de la fin du XVIIe à la fin du XVIIIe siècle* (Nancy: Presses Universitaires
   de Nancy, 1982). In the field of Anglo-American scholarship, see esp. Lewis C.
   Seifert, *Fairy Tales, Sexuality, and Gender in France, 1690–1715: Nostalgic Utopias*
   (Cambridge: Cambridge University Press, 1996), but also Marina Warner, *From
   the Beast to the Blonde: On Fairy Tales and Their Tellers* (New York: Farrar, Straus
   and Giroux, 1995). The most important fairy-tale collection of Italy, Basile's
   Neapolitan *Lo cunto*, was translated into Italian in 1925 by Benedetto Croce,
   and has over the past twenty years been the object of a number of penetrating
   essays (though only one or two monographs). But it is still a work that is fairly
   unfamiliar to the general public. Indeed, even if at least two new translations in
   Italian have appeared in the last ten years, this greater accessibility of Basile's
   text has not seemed to affect the choices made in Italian anthologies of fairy
   tales (for children), which although they occasionally contain a watered-down
   tale or two from Basile, for the most part draw from the collections of Perrault,
   the Grimms, and Calvino's 1958 *Fiabe italiane* (in which Basile's tales were often
   used as points of departure for Calvino's own original elaborations). The only
   full-length scholarly work in part dedicated to Basile that has been published

in this country is James M. McGlathery's *Fairy Tale Romance: The Grimms, Basile, and Perrault* (Urbana and Chicago: University of Illinois Press, 1991). McGlathery's book has the merit of considering these three figures as eminently literary authors who consciously reworked the oral tradition that gave origin to their tales, although his explicitly ahistorical approach does little to illuminate the complex cultural contexts in which these collections were created.

3. Warner, *From the Beast*, 148.

4. See, for example, Vladimir Propp, *Morphology of the Folktale*, 2nd ed., trans. Laurence Scott, rev. and ed. Louis A. Wagner (Austin: University of Texas Press, 1968); Max Lüthi, *The European Folktale: Form and Nature*, trans. John D. Niles (Bloomington: Indiana University Press, 1986) and *The Fairytale as Art Form and Portrait of Man*, trans. Jon Erickson (Bloomington: Indiana University Press, 1984); Stith Thompson, *The Folktale* (New York: Holt, Rinehart and Winston, 1946); Bruno Bettelheim, *The Uses of Enchantment* (1975; rpt., New York: Vintage, 1989); Marie-Louise von Franz, *Individuation in Fairy Tales* (Dallas: Spring Publications, 1984).

5. Jack Zipes, ed., *Beauties, Beasts and Enchantment: Classic French Fairy Tales* (1989; rpt., New York: Meridian, 1991), 1–2.

6. For these and further details on the evolution of the literary fairy tale, see Jack Zipes, ed., *Spells of Enchantment: The Wondrous Fairy Tales of Western Culture* (New York: Penguin, 1991), xi–xxx.

7. The principal collections of this period were Giovan Francesco Straparola's *Le piacevoli notti* (of which, however, only thirteen of the seventy-four stories can be rightly classified as fairy tales), Basile's *Lo cunto*, and Pompeo Sarnelli's *Posilicheata* (1684). Fairy-tale motifs, however, were present in many late medieval and Renaissance novella collections, such as Ser Giovanni Fiorentino's *Il Pecorone* (c. 1380), Giovanni Sercambi's early-fifteenth-century *Novelliere*, Cieco da Ferrara's *Mambriano* (1509), and Girolamo Morlini's early-sixteenth-century *Novellae*. For a survey of fairy-tale motifs in Italian literature, see Mario Petrini, *La fiaba di magia nella letteratura italiana* (Udine: Del Bianco, 1983).

8. It is pertinent to regard the fairy tale in terms of the Renaissance debate about the purpose of literature, which, for example, in discussion of the novella centered around the two terms of *utile* and *dulce*, or whether tales should be told for their utility or as recreation. For a discussion of Renaissance theories of the novella, see ch. 1 of Robert J. Clements and Joseph Gibaldi, *Anatomy of the Novella: The European Tale Collections from Boccaccio and Chaucer to Cervantes* (New York: New York University Press, 1977). When considering the fairy tale instead of the novella, the terms of the question work themselves out in very different ways. Whereas the novella, a genre that usually evokes what could be everyday occurrences, suggests the possibility that these occurrences be taken as models for real-life behavior, the relevance of the fantastic worlds of the fairy tale to our own worlds is less explicit. Thus, it was easier for fairy-tale writers of this period (before the fairy tale had become conventionalized as a didactic children's genre) to disguise the "usefulness" of the fairy tale for conveying, for example, social critique, than it would have been had they chosen a more realistic genre such as the novella or the novel.

9. Zipes, *Spells of Enchantment*, xviii–xix.
10. See Seifert's *Nostalgic Utopias* for an excellent analysis of this phase of fairy-tale production in France.
11. See Zipes, *Beauties, Beasts and Enchantment*, 17–19. For more extensive biographical information on Perrault, see Jacques Barchilon and Peter Flinders, *Charles Perrault* (Boston: Twayne, 1981).
12. See Zipes, *Beauties, Beasts and Enchantments*, 7.
13. See, for example, Joan DeJean, *Tender Geographies: Women and the Origins of the Novel in France* (New York: Columbia University Press, 1991).
14. Zipes, *Beauties, Beasts and Enchantments*, 5–6.
15. Max Lüthi, one of the most ambitious scholars with respect to the project of considering the evolution of the genre, sees Basile as somewhat of an anomaly, making only marginal references to him in his work, and many other more recent scholars follow in his footsteps.
16. Warner gives evidence that L'Héritier, for example, was familiar with Basile's *Cunto* (*From the Beast*, 172). Regarding a possible influence of Basile on Perrault she is less certain (322). But see also Denise Escarpit, *Histoire d'un conte: Le Chat Botté en France et en Angleterre*, vol. 1 (Paris: Didier, 1985), 88–120. As Jack Zipes notes in his essay in this volume, Escarpit maintains that the French authors, in particular Perrault, were probably familiar with the earlier Italians.
17. Michele Rak has hypothesized (although no documents concerning the actual fruition or "performance" of the text exist) that the audience of *Lo cunto* may have consisted of the members of the provincial courts around Naples where Basile served, and that the tales were read aloud as part of after-dinner fun and games (Giambattista Basile, *Lo cunto de li cunti*, ed. and trans. Michele Rak [Milan: Garzanti, 1986], 1057).
18. There are problems inherent in any attempt at rigid periodization, of course, but the cultural shifts that Europe underwent as it moved from the sixteenth century into the seventeenth have been discussed by scholars in all disciplines. See, for example, José Antonio Maravall, *Culture of the Baroque: Analysis of a Historical Structure*, trans. Terry Cochran (Minneapolis: University of Minnesota Press, 1986) on general developments in culture and ideology; Gilles Deleuze, *The Fold: Leibniz and the Baroque*, trans. and foreword Tom Conley (Minneapolis: University of Minnesota Press, 1993), and Michel Foucault, *The Order of Things: An Archeology of the Human Sciences*, trans. A. M. Sheridan Smith (1971; rpt., New York: Vintage, 1973) on philosophy and epistemology; Erwin Panofsky, *Three Essays on Style* (Cambridge: MIT Press, 1995), and Joy Kenseth, ed., *The Age of the Marvelous* (Hanover, N.H.: Hood Museum of Art, 1991) on the figurative arts; Alexandre Koyré, *From the Closed World to the Infinite Universe* (Baltimore: Johns Hopkins Press, 1957), and Marjorie Nicolson, *The Breaking of the Circle* (New York: Columbia University Press, 1960) on science; and Frank Warnke, *Versions of Baroque: European Literature in the Seventeenth Century* (New Haven: Yale University Press, 1972), Jean Rousset, *La littérature de l'age baroque en France: Circé et le paon* (Paris: J. Corti, 1953), Ezio Raimondi, *Letteratura barocca: studi sul*

Seicento italiano (Florence: Olschki, 1961), and Aldo Scaglione, ed., *The Image of the Baroque* (New York: P. Lang, 1995) on literature.

19. For the state of these discussions in Italy, see Carlo Calcaterra, *Il Parnaso in rivolta. Barocco e Antibarocco nella poesia italiana* (Bologna: Il Mulino, 1961), esp. chs. 4 ("Gli hoggidiani") and 5 ("L'antibarocco"). For the later debates in France, see, for example, Aron Kibédi-Varga, ed., *Les Poétiques du classicisme* (Paris: Aux Amateurs de Livres, 1990), esp. the introduction, and for the place of fairy tales in these debates, Seifert, *Nostalgic Utopias*.

20. See, for example, the introductions to Warner's *From the Beast* and Seifert's *Nostalgic Utopias*.

21. Some examples of these developments were absolutism and the rise of nation-states, the formation of early capitalist economies, the shifts from the representational to the referential, Galileo and the "New Science," the birth of new literary genres, and the revisions of traditional genres.

22. For the sixteenth century, the example of Rabelais towers above all others. Popular culture might here be defined in the words of Peter Burke: as "an unofficial culture, the culture of the non-elite, the 'subordinate classes' as Gramsci called them" (Prologue 1, *Popular Culture in Early Modern Europe* [New York: New York University Press, 1978]). For a general account of the encounters between popular and elite culture in early modern Europe, see Burke (above). For literary studies on the same theme, see Mikhail Bakhtin's classic *Rabelais and His World*, trans. Hélène Iswolsky (Bloomington: Indiana University Press, 1984); Marc Soriano, *Les Contes de Perrault: culture savante et traditions populaires* (Paris: Gallimard, 1968); and Piero Camporesi, *La maschera di Bertoldo* (Milan: Garzanti, 1993).

23. Propp's groundbreaking 1928 study, *Morphology of the Folktale*, set forth a series of thirty-one "functions" or elements of action that constitute the fairy tale (though not all are present in every individual tale): "*Function is understood as an act of a character, defined from the point of view of its significance for the course of the action*" (*Morphology of the Folktale*, 21). With regard to the sequence of functions, Propp specifies: "Morphologically, a tale (skázka) may be termed any development proceeding from villainy (A) or a lack (a), through intermediary functions [which almost invariably include encounters with magical helpers and antagonists] to marriage (W*), or to other functions employed as a dénouement" (92). The general thematic progression of the fairy tale is, then, from a lack or a problem (a state of disorder or disequilibrium) to a resolution of the same (state of equilibrium). These functions are distributed, according to Propp's schema, among seven dramatis personae—villain, donor, helper, princess and her father, dispatcher, hero, and false hero (80)—to whom in turn correspond "spheres of action," which include specific groups of functions (79). Propp's structural analysis has been criticized as being, on the one hand, too all-inclusive, since in its most general contours, it could define many narrative forms that are not fairy tales. On the other hand, it has been considered too limiting, for although most fairy tales do indeed follow the lack-to-resolution progression, this is not the case for all forms that we nonetheless consider fairy tales.

24. Ibid., 113.

25. Lüthi, *European Folktale*, 73. Most of the authors discussed in this volume are, with the exception of Perrault, absent from Lüthi's *European Folktale*, which in the few pages it devotes to the distinction between oral and literary tales, contains this affirmation: "Wilhelm Grimm's stylistic recasting was largely responsible for the creation of the literary folktale" (110).

26. Even recent critical anthologies such as the otherwise valuable Ruth B. Bottigheimer, ed., *Fairy Tales and Society: Illusion, Allusion, and Paradigm* (Philadelphia: University of Pennsylvania Press, 1986) do not use the oral/literary divide in significantly innovative ways.

27. "Literature of the fantastic has been claimed as 'transcending' reality, 'escaping' the human condition and constructing alternate, 'secondary' worlds" (Rosemary Jackson, *Fantasy: The Literature of Subversion* [London and New York: Methuen, 1981], 2).

28. Ibid., 4. Although Jackson later distinguishes between the fantastic literature of such nineteenth-century writers as Poe and Kafka, and romance and marvelous literature, she considers them all part of a fantastic "mode" (in the Jamesonian sense) to which the general reflections cited refer.

29. Warner, *From the Beast*, xxi. Warner elaborates: "The disregard for logic, all those fairytale non-sequiturs and improbable reversals, rarely encompasses the emotional conflicts themselves: hatred, jealousy, kindness, cherishing retain an intense integrity throughout. The double vision of the tales, on the one hand charting perennial drives and terrors, both conscious and unconscious, and on the other mapping actual, volatile experience, gives the genre its fascination and power to satisfy. At the same time, uncovering the context of the tales, their relation to society and history, can yield more of a happy resolution than the story itself delivers with its challenge to fate: 'They lived happily ever after' consoles us, but gives scanty help compared to 'Listen, this is how it was before, but things could change—and they might.' "

30. Warner comments, with regard to the French women writers: "Fairy tale constituted in itself a genre of protest; at the level of content it could describe wrongs and imagine vindications and freedom; from the point of view of form, it was presented as modern, homegrown, comic fabulism, ironically suited to express the thoughts of an inferior group" (*From the Beast*, 163). A number of studies, especially recent ones, have focused on the relationship of fairy tales to realities both distant and contemporary to them. A later work by Propp, *The Historical Roots of the Wonder Tale* (1946) occupies itself not with the form of the fairy tale, but with its content, which according to Propp has historical referents in the initiation and funeral rites of archaic societies (*Le radici storiche dei racconti di magia*, 2nd ed., trans. Salvatore Arcella, intro. Cecilia Gatto Trocchi [Rome: Newton Compton Editori, 1982]; no English translation exists). Another scholar who has stringently illuminated the fairy tale's ties to historical reality, but in this case both past and present, is Lutz Röhrich. In his 1979 work *Folktales and Reality*, he recognizes that "the folktale as a genre is generally defined in contradistinction to experience, reality, and religious belief," and contests this common view by maintaining that "folklore genres represent perceived, experienced, and imagined reality" (*Folktales*

and Reality, trans. Peter Tokofsky [Bloomington: Indiana University Press, 1991], 1 and ix [Dan Ben-Amos, foreword]).

31. Fredric Jameson sums up in concise fashion the views put forth by Jakobson and Bogatryev on the relation of individual creation and style to folktales, and notes how this influences the perceptions of all forms of this genre, oral or literary: "No doubt everything in the fairy tale originates with the individual . . . but this necessary fact of invention in the first place is somehow the least essential characteristic of folk literature. For the tale does not really become a fairy tale, given the oral diffusion of this literature, with its obvious dependence on word of mouth circulation, until the moment when it has been accepted by the listeners who retain it and pass it on. Thus the crucial moment for the fairy tale is not that of the *parole*, that of its invention and creation (as in middle-class art), but that of the *langue*; and we may say that no matter how individualistic may be its origin, it is always anonymous or collective in essence: in Jakobsonian terminology, the individuality of the fairy tale is a redundant feature, its anonymity a distinctive one." (*The Prison-House of Language* [Princeton: Princeton University Press, 1972], 29). But see also Catherine Velay-Vallantin's *L'Histoire des contes* (Paris: Fayard, 1992), in particular 25–39, for a discussion of how these types of distinctions between the oral and written traditions are in many respects artificial.

32. Jameson, *The Political Unconscious: Narrative as a Socially Symbolic Act* (Ithaca: Cornell University Press, 1981), 109–10.

33. For a brief account of the Grimms' ideological manipulations of their material, see Jack Zipes's introduction to *The Complete Fairy Tales of the Brothers Grimm* (New York: Bantam, 1987), as well as the chapter on the Grimms in his *Fairy Tales and the Art of Subversion* (1983; rpt., New York: Routledge, 1991). Two insightful full-length studies of the Grimms' tales that treat these issues are Maria Tatar, *The Hard Facts of the Grimms' Fairy Tales* (Princeton: Princeton University Press, 1987), and Ruth B. Bottigheimer, *Grimms' Bad Girls and Bold Boys* (New Haven: Yale University Press, 1987). Even a twentieth-century collector/rewriter like Italo Calvino (often considered a sort of Italian equivalent of the Grimms), who states up front that he is changing, sometimes in major ways, the tales, does not seem to perceive the full implications of this sort of cultural appropriation.

34. Zipes, *Fairy Tales and the Art of Subversion*, 6 and 11.

35. This outline of the phases of development of the French fairy tale is drawn from Zipes, *Beauties, Beasts and Enchantment*, 1–12. For a more complete survey of the various "vogues," see Barchilon, *Le conte*, and Robert, *Le conte*.

36. Similar discussions would take place in Italy only shortly before its unification in 1860.

37. For these developments, which reached culmination in the work of the Grimms, see, for example, Maria Tatar, *Off with Their Heads! Fairy Tales and the Culture of Childhood* (Princeton: Princeton University Press, 1992); Ruth Bottigheimer, *Grimms' Bad Girls and Bold Boys*; and Jack Zipes, *Fairy Tales and the Art of Subversion*.

38. To name only a few, for the list would be quite long, Angela Carter, Anne Sexton, Salman Rushdie, Margaret Atwood.
39. Warner, *From the Beast*, 415.

Bibliography

Bakhtin, Mikhail. *Rabelais and His World*. Trans. Hélène Iswolsky. Bloomington: Indiana University Press, 1984.

Barchilon, Jacques, *Le Conte merveilleux français de 1690 à 1790*. Paris: Champion, 1975.

Barchilon, Jacques, and Peter Flinders. *Charles Perrault*. Boston: Twayne, 1981.

Bottigheimer, Ruth B., ed. *Fairy Tales and Society: Illusion, Allusion, and Paradigm*. Philadelphia: University of Pennsylvania Press, 1986.

———. *Grimms' Bad Girls and Bold Boys*. New Haven: Yale University Press, 1987.

Burke, Peter. *Popular Culture in Early Modern Europe*. New York: New York University Press, 1978.

Clements, Robert J., and Joseph Gibaldi. *Anatomy of the Novella: The European Tale Collections from Boccaccio and Chaucer to Cervantes*. New York: New York University Press, 1977.

DeJean, Joan. *Tender Geographies: Women and the Origins of the Novel in France*. New York: Columbia University Press, 1991.

Escarpit, Denise. *Histoire d'un conte: Le Chat Botté en France et en Angleterre*. 2 vols. Paris: Didier, 1985.

Garner, James Finn. *Politically Correct Bedtime Stories*. New York: Macmillan, 1994.

Jackson, Rosemary. *Fantasy: The Literature of Subversion*. London and New York: Methuen, 1981.

Jameson, Fredric. *The Prison-House of Language*. Princeton: Princeton University Press, 1972.

———. *The Political Unconscious: Narrative as a Socially Symbolic Act*. Ithaca: Cornell University Press, 1981.

Lurie, Alison, ed. *The Oxford Book of Modern Fairy Tales*. New York: Oxford University Press, 1993.

Lüthi, Max. *The European Folktale: Form and Nature*. Trans. John D. Niles. Bloomington: Indiana University Press, 1986.

———. *The Fairytale as Art Form and Portrait of Man*. Trans. Jon Erickson. Bloomington: Indiana University Press, 1984.

McGlathery, James M. *Fairy Tale Romance: The Grimms, Basile, and Perrault*. Urbana and Chicago: University of Illinois Press, 1991.

Petrini, Mario. *La fiaba di magia nella letteratura italiana*. Udine: Del Bianco, 1983.

Propp, Vladimir. *Morphology of the Folktale*. 2nd ed. Trans. Laurence Scott. Rev. and ed. Louis A. Wagner. Austin: University of Texas Press, 1968.

———. *Le radici storiche dei racconti di magia*. 2nd ed. Trans. Salvatore Arcella. Rome: Newton Compton Editori, 1982.

Rak, Michele, ed. and trans. *Lo cunto de li cunti* by Giambattista Basile. Milan: Garzanti, 1986.

Robert, Raymonde. *Le Conte de fées littéraire en France de la fin du XVIIe à la fin du XVIIIe siècle*. Nancy: Presses Universitaires de Nancy, 1982.

Röhrich, Lutz. *Folktales and Reality*. Trans. Peter Tokofsky. Bloomington: Indiana University Press, 1991.

Seifert, Lewis C. *Fairy Tales, Sexuality, and Gender in France, 1690–1715: Nostalgic Utopias*. Cambridge: Cambridge University Press, 1996.

Storer, Mary Elizabeth. *Un Episode littéraire de la fin du XVIIe siècle: La Mode des contes de fées (1685–1700)*. 1928. Reprint, Geneva: Slatkine Reprints, 1972.

Tatar, Maria. *The Hard Facts of the Grimms' Fairy Tales*. Princeton: Princeton University Press, 1987.

————. *Off with Their Heads! Fairy Tales and the Culture of Childhood*. Princeton: Princeton University Press, 1992.

Velay-Vallantin, Catherine. *L'Histoire des contes*. Paris: Fayard, 1992.

Warner, Marina. *From the Beast to the Blonde: On Fairy Tales and Their Tellers*. New York: Farrar, Straus and Giroux, 1995.

Zipes, Jack, ed. *Beauties, Beasts and Enchantment: Classic French Fairy Tales*. 1989. Reprint, New York: Meridian, 1991.

————, ed. *The Complete Fairy Tales of the Brothers Grimm*. 2 vols. New York: Bantam, 1987.

————. *Fairy Tales and the Art of Subversion*. 1983. Reprint, New York: Routledge, 1991.

————, ed. *Spells of Enchantment: The Wondrous Fairy Tales of Western Culture*. New York: Penguin, 1991.

————, ed. *The Outspoken Princess and the Gentle Knight*. New York: Bantam, 1994.

The Rebirth of a Genre:
The Creation of the Literary Fairy Tale
in the Seventeenth Century

PART
I

"Quanto 'nc'è da ccà a lo luoco dove
aggio da ire?":
Giambattista Basile's Quest
for the Literary Fairy Tale

Nancy L. Canepa

 GIAMBATTISTA BASILE'S *Lo cunto de li cunti*, published posthumously in 1634–36, constituted a grand culmination of the interest in popular culture and folk traditions that permeated the Cinquecento. In Italy, isolated fairy tales had appeared in many earlier novella collections, most notably in Giovan Francesco Straparola's *Le piacevoli notti*, published in 1550–53, and popular material shaped, thematically and structurally, many of the texts belonging to what critic Nino Borsellino calls the sixteenth-century "anticlassicist" tradition, which included Aretino, Ruzante, Berni, and especially Folengo.[1] In the seventeenth century, specifically fairy-tale elements made their ways into all literary genres, often merging with legends and other types of popular narrative in an eclectic move that is typical of this century.[2]

Lo cunto de li cunti, or, as it is sometimes called, *Il Pentamerone*, is composed of forty-nine fairy tales contained by a frame story, the fiftieth tale, itself also a fairy tale. It is the first such framed collection of fairy tales in Western Europe, and "can lay claim to being the foundation stone of the modern literary fairy tale."[3] Written in the Neapolitan dialect, the tales were intended to be read or recited as part of the "courtly conversations" that were an integral part of elite pastimes in Basile's day.[4] *Lo cunto* contains some of the best known of fairy-tale types (Sleeping Beauty, Puss in Boots, Cinderella, and many others), and has been a central point of reference for subsequent fairy-tale writers in Europe as well as a treasure chest for folklorists.

Why, of all the forms of popular culture, did Basile choose to rewrite the fairy tale? First of all, and most obviously, the rewriting of the fairy tale as a literary genre satisfied the thirst, expressed in the baroque poetics of the marvelous, for the new, the fantastic, the unexpected, the prodigious, and the desire for discovering new worlds, new inspirations, and new forms of poetic expression. Central to this poetics was also the power of language, in its metaphorical capacity, to evoke an attitude of sophisticated wonder and initiate into the realm of the marvelous.[5] The seventeenth century was distinguished in many disciplines by the search for new methods and instruments for comprehending and interpreting the human and extrahuman universe (Galileo and the "New Science," the rise of the novel, the flowering of mysticism, and so forth), and Basile's reelaboration of popular, oral culture—in the form of the fairy tale—into an eminently literary product may be inscribed in this search. The self-conscious construction, on the part of Seicento authors, of the persona of the heroic explorer of untrod domains was made concrete in Basile's quest for rediscovery and modernization of a narrative form that had up to this point been almost exclusively oral and of a language—Neapolitan—whose full literary potential would only now be exploited. This was also, however, an age wrought by socioeconomic turmoil, an age whose cultural and historical transformations could engender an anguished sense of the unstable, ever-shifting nature of things, which in turn inspired a pessimistic waning of confidence in the human capacity to fathom reality and to act with the benefit of that knowledge. Alongside—and often, indeed, inextricably linked to it—the excited awareness of living in a time of flux was also an attraction to the idea of a world "ruled by uniform, general laws, a world that God maintains in its perennial order."[6] The fairy tale simultaneously embodies these anxieties and responds to them. Its typical heroes and heroines are cut off from the binds of time, space, and causality, and although they often seem almost to undergo a fate controlled by magical forces (as opposed to constructing their own destinies, as did the typical protagonists of the Renaissance novellas), they ultimately emerge triumphant. The fairy tale tells the secular story of a search for "wholeness"; the hero or heroine's initiatory quests always lead to a reassuring final resolution of their initial lack.

Basile fully participated in the culture that was engaged with these literary considerations; the trajectory of his professional life might have served as a model for a man of letters of his day.[7] He was born around 1575, in or near Naples, to a middle-class family that included a number of courtiers and artists (his sister Adriana was one of the most acclaimed operatic *virtuose* in Italy). The Naples of Basile's time was, in Europe, second in population only to Paris, and has been called "one of the most important laboratories of the baroque."[8] Basile spent his life in military and intellectual service at courts in and around Naples, in Mantua, and in Crete, was active in several academies, served administrative roles in the government of the Neapolitan provinces, and by the end of his life had, at least nominally—he received the title of count—ascended to the neofeudal aristocracy of the Kingdom. His literary production consisted principally of works in Italian that ranged from sacred and mythological poems to piscatorial and pastoral dramas to odes and madrigals to philological commentaries on the work of Cinquecento lyric poets such as Bembo and Della Casa. Many of these works, which were written in the style of the illustrious Neapolitan poet Giambattista Marino, were composed for theatrical pageants or for court entertainment, and stylistically and thematically incorporated an eclectic range of materials drawn from various traditions, including the "semiliterate" dialect tradition that had developed through the fifteenth and sixteenth centuries.[9] They were well enough received during his lifetime but have been virtually unread since the end of the seventeenth century. What has survived over the centuries and, in fact, attracted ever more scholarly interest is Basile's "other" literary corpus in Neapolitan, radically different in its popular content and playful style from his more orthodox Italian works. Besides Lo cunto, Basile's dialect production consists of Le Muse napolitane, satiric eclogues depicting popular culture in Naples, and a series of Lettere.

Benedetto Croce's assessment of Basile as an unconscious ironizer of the baroque and of Lo cunto as "il più bello [libro italiano barocco], appunto, perché il barocco vi esegue una sua danza allegra e vi appare per dissolversi" [the greatest literary work of the Italian baroque, for the very reason that in it the baroque executes a gay dance and is on the verge of disintegration] does little to illuminate the complexity of Basile's literary project.[10] More recently, Lo cunto has been read as a jocosely erudite catalog of folkloric materials and metaphoric pyrotechnics inspired by aristocratic curiosity, or as "una splendida e cinica evasione dalle difficoltà e dalle contraddizioni in cui si dibatteva la cultura aristocratica della Napoli spagnola" [a splendid evasion of the difficulties and contradictions in which the aristocratic culture of Spanish Naples was immersed].[11] These approaches, however useful they may be when considering certain aspects of Lo cunto, seem ultimately, however, to reduce Basile's work to either an eccentric incarnation of the poetics of the marvelous or a cynical reaction against the courtly culture in which he lived and that he actually intended as the audience for Lo cunto. Instead, I would argue, with Michele Rak, that "il Cunto è un'operazione sui modelli, sulla raccolta dei materiali popolari, sull'ideazione di una logica" [the Cunto is an operation involving literary models, the gathering of popular materials, and the creation of a new logic], making it one of the most complex and artistically suggestive works of the Italian baroque.[12] Basile does not offer easy answers to the problem of how an archaic, oral narrative form can, or should, be reproposed in literary form; in *Lo cunto* high and low cultures intersect to create an "open," heteroglossic text in which linguistic and cultural hierarchies, as well as the conventional fairy tale hierarchies, if they are not abolished, are rearranged or made to show their weak spots.[13] Narrative and ideological closures are always tenuous in *Lo cunto*: Basile makes no pretense of substituting one cultural voice—popular, "anticlassicist," or high—for another, while at the same time he recognizes, and dramatizes, within his text, the risks inherent in any operation of "cultural negotiation and exchange."[14] Rak acutely comments: "La bellezza e la qualità letteraria del *Cunto* sta nell'incrocio comico e sofisticato dei materiali di due culture diverse, ricche di conoscenze e entrambe alterate e parodiate dal loro contatto nella logica di questo nuovo modello narrativo" [The beauty and literary quality of *Lo cunto* lies in the comic and sophisticated intersection of the materials of two different cultures, each extremely rich and each changed and parodied by their contact with this new narrative model].[15] And this "translation" of the materials of the oral fairy tale into a literary form that self-consciously alters the contours of the genre characterizes Basile's work as a strikingly modern text.[16]

Moreover, there is in *Lo cunto* a pervasive dialectic between the state of equilibrium and resolution of contradictions toward which the fairy tale conventionally moves and the underlying threats to this equilibrium that insinuate their way into the text by means of what Propp would call the attributes of the tale: the characters' "external appearance and nomenclature, particularities of introduction into the narrative, and dwelling place," and all other information incidental to the main "functions" of the story.[17] The true novelty of *Lo cunto* is not so much in the "morphology" of the tales, which generally follow Propp's scheme of the oral folktale, but in the figural and ideological interpolations, the references to diverse social realities and narrative traditions, that crowd the *cunti* and disturb their illusory "happy-ever-after" linearity.[18]

Basile's choice of a literary language—Neapolitan dialect—offers further evidence of his situation at a cultural crossroads. The beginning of the seventeenth century witnessed a veritable blossoming of experimentations with dialect in many areas of Italy, but especially in Naples, where literature in dialect reached a level of sophistication unprecedented in Naples itself and lacking in many other regions.[19] Dialect was to some degree an ideal vehicle of expression for the baroque poetics of the marvelous, in which metaphors, topoi, and languages conventionally marginal to literary canons acquired aesthetic value by virtue of their very novelty. Furthermore, the elaboration of a "new" literary language, local and anti-Tuscan, constituted an original position in the battle of the ancients and the moderns that provoked much debate in this period.[20] The use of dialect implied a questioning of the "illustrious" literary tradition by offering proof of abilities previously attributed to the ancients or to Tuscan (Italian) authors. It was no coincidence, in fact, that the three figures most responsible for the evolution of Neapolitan as a literary language at this time—Basile, Giulio Cesare Cortese, and the enigmatic Felippe de Scafato Sgruttendio—each proposed in his dialect corpus a rewriting, often in subversive, carnivalesque form, of a traditional genre.[21] Basile's literary project was, however, notably more ambitious than that of his Neapolitan colleagues. Like them, he recognized that the time was ripe for moving dialect literature out of the ghetto of buffoonery and "low" ribaldry and awarding it a more respected place in literary tradition. But unlike his colleagues, he used this awareness, together with an intimate acquaintance with the modalities of baroque poetics, to transform a genre that had lacked referents in the canonical tradition into a thoroughly new literary genre. These fairy tales, moreover, were intended for a hybrid audience composed of members of the middle class and aspiring aristocrats. At the same time, though, the tales constituted an all-encompassing parody of the social status quo, by making kings and princesses speak in the language that had previously (above all in the theatrical tradition) belonged to peasants, vagabonds, fools, and other butts of laughter.[22] Finally, the use of dialect, in some sense a "secret language" due to the limited number of people who could actually understand it, coupled with the choice of a genre that apparently lacked real-world referents, permitted greater liberty to treat topics that might have been riskier to address in the realm of "official" literature.[23]

In this essay I argue that many of Basile's *cunti* tell not only stories of princesses, ogres, and fools, but also the metaliterary story, in its many phases and aspects, of the new genre of the literary fairy tale. The frame tale dramatizes the move from the "court" of canonical literary tradition to the "forest" of the fairy tale and then back again to another court within the frame tale itself, in which a fairy-tale prince initiates the tale-telling of *Lo cunto* and in which is allegorized Basile's own hybrid telling project. The first tale of this project, "Lo cunto dell'uerco" [The Ogre (1.1)], is a tale of initiation that mirrors in compelling ways Basile's own initiatory quest for a new literary genre and a language in which to express it. The tale "La palomma" [The Dove (2.7)] exemplifies one of Basile's preferred techniques for rewriting popular material and making it speak to contemporary literary and social concerns. Radical use of metaphor not only distinguishes Basile as one of the most original practicers of the baroque poetics of the marvelous but is also used in such a tale to call into question the linear happy-ever-after closure of the fairy tale and to insinuate references to sociohistorical reality into its seemingly fantastic world. "Lo scarafone, lo sorece e lo grillo" [The Cockroach, the Mouse, and the Cricket (3.5)] presents Basile's model of the "fairy-tale carnivalesque" in its most striking form, and "Pinto Smauto" [Splendid Shine (5.3)], which tells of a Pygmalionesque creation of an ideal spouse, is an apt metaphor for the new fairy tale to which Basile gives life.

Since Basile's collection heralds the entrance of the fairy tale into the "authored" canon of Western literature, the frame tale has the function of staging the birth of this new genre, and its negotiation with various traditions. (The collection's title, in fact—which can be translated as "The Telling of the Tales" or "The Tale of (the) Tales," points to the centrality of the frame as a hermeneutic key to the entire collection.) The frame story is a fairy tale itself, in the tradition of Eastern collections (like *The Thousand and One Nights*), thus departing from the frame of the novelistic tradition, exemplified in the *Decameron*, of a "simulazione di realtà rispetto alla finzione-finzione dei racconti inquadrati" [a simulation of reality with respect to the double fiction of the framed tales].[24] This move already constitutes a polemical stance toward the "tradition" of established literary genres. Basile neither mediates—and contains—the textual fiction by giving it a realistic frame, nor positions his work as a parody of an exemplary model (strategies common to both the anticlassicist and dialect traditions), thus subordinating it to some degree to these models. Instead, he opts for a self-referential frame that highlights the difference of his choice.[25] Thus, although Basile presents *in nucis* a number of the themes that will be taken up in the *giornate* of *Lo cunto* and, in particular, dramatizes the birth of this new literary form, the frame does not have the *explicitly* periphrastic or didactic—the metatextual—function that it has in most novella collections from Boccaccio on. Instead of "interrogating its birth" as archaic genre rooted in oral folkloric narratives, it assumes this as a common cultural given, and shifts its focus to a documentation, from within the confines of the genre itself, of its metamorphosis into the genre of the *literary* fairy tale.[26]

The frame story begins with reference to a proverb, as do many of the *cunti*:

Fu proverbeio de chille stascioniato, de la maglia antica, che chi cerca chello che non deve trova chello che non vole e chiara cosa è che la scigna pe cauzare stivale restaie 'ncappata pe lo pede, come soccesse a na schiava pezzente, che non avenno portato maie scarpe a li piede voze portare corona 'n capo.

[A seasoned proverb, minted long ago, says that they who search for what they should not, find what they would not, and it's inevitable that an ape who tried to put on a boot got caught by its foot, just like what happened to a ragged slave girl, who, never having worn shoes on her feet, wanted to wear a crown on her head.][27]

42

The use of a proverb to open *Lo cunto* would seem to foreground the authority that sedimented popular tradition (here, in the form of proverbial wisdom) will have in this text. It also makes explicit reference to an important thematic element of the frame tale, the fact that the slave Lucia will deceitfully cheat princess Zoza of her future husband, and in its appeal to a justice meted out on the basis of differences of class and race (Lucia is destined to get caught because she is not fit, socially, for the role of princess), evokes a rigidly hierarchical view of society in which one's place is a static given. But the subtext of this proverb, as Croce tells us in his notes, is the practice, common among hunters, of taking off and putting on boots in the presence of an ape, and then filling the boots with glue, so that when the ape attempts to imitate the hunter's act, it remains trapped in the boots.[28] With this information in mind, a very different reading emerges: what causes the ape's downfall is its slavish imitation of the human model; the proverb cautions against unquestionably "aping" a model, and thus dramatizes the necessity of *not* assuming popular tradition as an absolute authority. This short but significant example of the multiple, and often contrasting, layers of significance that permeate *Lo cunto* is both a statement of artistic intent (Basile, in his relation to the popular culture that supplies him with the primary material for his work, will not merely imitate) and an exhortation to read the text in an equally creative fashion.[29]

The frame unfolds as follows: the king of Valle Pelosa [Hairy Valley] is in a desperate state over his daughter Zoza, whom no one or nothing can seem to make laugh. After many unsuccessful projects, he has a fountain of oil erected outside the royal palace, which he hopes might, by the involuntary antics that it causes, induce Zoza to lose her seriousness. He orders

> che se facesse na gran fontana d'ueglio 'nante la porta de lo palazzo, co designo che, schizzanno a lo passare de la gente, che facevano comm'a formiche lo vacaviene pe chella strata, pe non se sodognere li vestite averriano fatto zumpe de grille, sbauze de crapeio e corzete de leparo sciulianno e, morrannose chisto e chillo, potesse soccedere cosa pe la quale se scoppasse a ridere.(10)

> [that a great fountain of oil be erected before the gate of the palace, with the scheme that as it sprayed the passersby, who came and went like ants along that street, so as not to lubricate their clothes they would hop about like crickets, jump like goats and run like hares, slipping and bumping into each other, and in this way something might happen to excite his daughter to a burst of laughter.]

The desired "incident" does, in fact, occur. An old woman stops at the fountain and begins to sop up the oil with a sponge and wring it into a jar.

While she is busy at her task, a "devil of a court page" throws a rock at her jar, shatters it, and in response to her long string of lewd imprecations continues to tease her until the old woman, exasperated, lifts up her skirts: "perdenno la vusciola de la fremma e scapolanno da la stalla de la pacienza, auzato la tela de l'apparato fece vedere la scena voscareccia, dove potea dire Sirvio 'Ite svegliano gli occhi col corno'" (12) [Losing her phlegmatic compass bearings and charging from the stable of patience, she raised the stage curtain and revealed a woodsy scene about which Silvio might have said: "Go and open eyes with your horn"]. Zoza, up until now still gloomy, cannot control her laughter at this spectacle and the old woman, infuriated, says to her: "'Va', che non puozze vedere mai sporchia de marito, si non piglie lo prencepe de Campo Retunno'" (12) ["Begone, and may you never pluck even a blossom of a husband unless you take the prince of Campo Retunno"]. This prince, Tadeo, is currently under a sleeping-spell at a fountain outside another kingdom, and only she who fills a large urn full of her tears in the space of three days will be able to awaken him and claim him as her spouse. Uncertain how to take the old woman's words, Zoza ascertains that this threat is substantial (and not merely a continuation of the previous name-calling). She asks the woman "se l'aveva 'ngiuriata o iastemmata" (12) [if she had insulted her or laid a curse on her], if this is a mere insult or, instead, a spell that will take her into the fairy-tale world definitively. She then departs on the mission that will, by the end of the initial episode of the frame story, lead to the birth of the Lo cunto as a means to pursue fulfillment of the old woman's prophecy.

Before Zoza reaches Tadeo's fountain, she encounters three fairies, who give her three magic objects, a walnut, a chestnut, and a hazelnut. At the fountain, she is within inches of filling the urn when she falls asleep. Lucia, a black slave who had been spying on her, seizes the urn and cries the last few tears needed to fill it. Tadeo wakes up and takes Lucia back to his kingdom to marry her. Zoza follows them there and sets herself up in a house that faces the royal palace, where she exhibits on her windowsill, one by one, the three gifts. The walnut produces a tiny man who sings divinely, the chestnut twelve golden chicks, and the hazelnut a miniature gold-spinning doll, and Lucia, by now pregnant and slave to her cravings, demands to have them. Her whims are quickly satisfied, since she threatens to pound her stomach and kill the unborn child otherwise. Zoza begs the last object, the doll, to instill in Lucia an irrepressible longing to hear fairy tales, which it does. The best ten tale-tellers of the city are summoned, and Tadeo and members of his court take their places around a fountain in the palace garden, where the cunti are told for five days. On each day after the first, Tadeo's "court" plays games until it is time to eat, and after eating the telling begins. At the end of the first through four days' tales, two of Tadeo's servants recite eclogues, which, far from being the pastoral compositions to which their name refers, are pessimistic satires in dialogue form on the vices of the times, particularly those rampant in the courts. On the final day Zoza is asked to substitute an ill teller and recounts her own vicissitudes up to that point as the last tale (which is also the conclusion to the frame story). Lucia's intrigue is exposed and she is killed, and Zoza finally marries Tadeo.

Already in this opening sequence there is a density of textual references to non-fairy-tale traditions. From its first moments the frame is clearly a version of the widespread fairy-tale motif of the "princess who would not laugh" even though, until the point when the old woman casts a full-fledged curse on Zoza, it could pass as a realistic sequence. In the king's first attempts to make his daughter laugh he makes use of figures that commonly appeared in the street theater or carnival spectacles of Basile's day (but which were also commonly appropriated for court performances):

> chille che camminano 'ncoppa a le mazze, mo chille che passano dinto a lo chirchio, mo li mattacine, ma Mastro Roggiero, mo chille che fanno iuoche de mano, mo le Forze d'Ercole, mo lo cane che adanza, mo Vracone che sauta, mo l'aseno che beve a lo bicchiero, mo Lucia canazza e mo na cosa e mo n'autra. (10)

> [men who walk on stilts, hoop-jumpers, acrobats, Master Ruggiero, jugglers, strongmen, the dancing dog, Vracone the jumping monkey, the ass who drinks from a glass, bitchy Lucia's dance and this and that other.][30]

In his appropriation of these popular "acts," the king employs a cultural strategy akin to the one that Fredric Jameson has described, in which "folk music and peasant dance find themselves transmuted into the forms of aristocratic or court festivity . . . and popular narrative . . . is ceaselessly drawn on to restore vitality to an enfeebled and asphyxiating 'high' culture." But the utter ineffectiveness of this attempt to vitalize, in a very literal sense, the king's courtly world, suggests a reaction on Basile's part to the sort of "cultural universalization" in which popular culture is abstracted from its original context and transformed into nothing more than an amusing and "folkloristic" pastime.[31]

None of these appeals to the masters of contemporary popular spectacle work, however; Zoza remains as melancholic as ever. The king's next move involves a much more ambitious spectacle in which the appropriation of popular subjects is even more direct, involving not actors, but unknowing townspeople who happen to wander onto his stage. He constructs a fountain of oil and hopes that one of the acrobatic but impromptu "street numbers" that it causes will succeed in making Zoza laugh.

In many traditional versions of the "princess who would not laugh" motif, slippery obstacles are the source of the desired laughter. For example, Propp cites one variant in which after the king promises to marry his daughter to the man who makes her laugh, the hero, in the company of animal helpers, falls into mud or a puddle in view of the palace. The animals then clean him off and help him up, and at the sight of this the princess laughs.[32] The king of Valle Pelosa enacts a very baroque transformation of this motif, in which the "natural" body of water becomes an elaborate oil-spewing fountain, a reference to the trick or decorative fountains that were so often a part of courtly spectacles of the time, and that did indeed spew oil, though more commonly wine. Moreover, seventeenth-century Naples was in the throes of significant social and demographic change, and festive spectacles such as the one Basile makes reference to here served the "political" purpose of circulating information on the evolution of power relationships among the socially heterogeneous group in attendance. This information could be of use to the ruler organizing the spectacle, but also to the participants. As Rak notes, "la festa era il grande spettacolo collettivo in cui queste identità diverse si mostravano" [the festival was the great collective spectacle in which these diverse identities put themselves on display].[33] But besides providing a marvelous show, this fountain above all stages a dazzling display of the king's power. With its provocative flaunting of abundance, in particular in a historical period fraught by famines and plague, the king's prop is a "fountain of rhetoric" for an absolutism that governs even recreational moments.[34] It proves successful in its persuasion when the old woman falls into the trap set for her. This spectacle, then, signals a break in the group communication that such occasions *could* engender. Instead, it becomes an occasion for the staging of the king's all-encompassing control, rendered particularly outrageous in the sole justification that it has of making his daughter laugh.

But on a different level, does the king's scheme backfire? On the one hand, what ultimately makes Zoza laugh is not an involuntary *lazzo* but a protest against being used in this way. On the other hand, this rebellion on the part of a low-class figure might not be a crack in the usual structure of such a spectacle, but instead might make for a more spirited performance. Yet what follows is of fundamental importance. In a radical jump from festive but controlled court spectacle to audacious subversion of the same, the old woman hoists up her skirt, and so also the curtain of the stage where *Lo cunto* will be played. This countering of the king's theatrical display with her own bushy show marks the moment in which the story-generating power passes from the king to the old woman, and then to Zoza, who is set off on her journey in search of Prince Tadeo. Furthermore, the "woodsy scene" under the woman's skirts recalls not only the name of the kingdom where all of this is taking place—Valle Pelosa—and, more generally, the quintessential fairy-tale backdrop, the forest, but is also an ironical reference to a literary genre—the pastoral—that in this period evolved principally as a courtly genre. We have already seen that Basile inserts a line from one of the most well-known pastoral works of the time, Guarini's *Il pastor fido*, in this scene— "Ite svegliano gli occhi col corno." (We might also remember the subtitle of Tasso's *Aminta*, "favola boscareccia," Marino's *Egloghe boscherecce*, and so forth.)[35] The pastoral ideal of rustic peace in a dimension cut off from the ravages of history was, in fact, a strong compensatory myth during this period of socioeconomic malaise. But this "ossessione boschiva" [obsession with the woods] that ran through seventeenth-century culture also had a flip side in the decidedly antipastoral tradition of the *satira del villano,* in which the real inhabitants of the countryside—the peasants who were under the siege of food shortages, epidemics, and feudal tyranny—were depicted as beastly, dim-witted semihumans.[36] With the transformation of both the pastoral *silva* and the degraded *villa* into the fairy tale *bosco,* we have yet another example of Basile's polemic with tradition, in the form of an implicit critique of the pastoral's aristocratic romanticization of rural life and the *satira's* demonization of the same. Finally, on an autobiographical level this initial scene of the frame tale recalls Basile's own role as organizer of court entertainments, and the moment in which the spectacle starts to veer off in an entirely unorthodox manner may also be seen as a "public" announcement that his own literary endeavors are taking a new direction.

This scene, in its fourfold articulation of the old woman collecting oil, lifting her skirts when provoked, Zoza laughing, and the woman responding with the curse, marks the point at which *Lo cunto* unequivocally enters the realm of the fairy tale. In the first segment of the scene the old woman gathers the oil in order to put it to a constructive use: economy and good sense reign. In the second segment, when the woman's patience is stretched to its limit, the industrious—and silent—*popolana* transforms into a grotesque hag who defies all laws of linguistic and bodily propriety. Oil is a conventional symbol of seriousness and wisdom[37] and, by extension, a figure for Zoza's initial melancholy and the courtly culture in which it was bred. When the vessel in which it has been so carefully collected is shattered, the dispersion of the oil signals the shift to another domain, one in which the old woman speaks and reveals her body.[38] Her transgression of the courtly ideology that has shaped the scene up to this point brings with it not only an exposure of the "underside" of the courtly rhetoric of the palace from which the rock was hurled, but a recovery of one of the voices of popular culture.[39] She addresses the page:

> "Ah, zaccaro, frasca, merduso, piscialietto, sautariello de zim- maro, pettola a culo, chiappo de 'mpiso, mulo canzirro! ente, ca puro li pulece hanno la tosse! va', che te venga cionchia, che

mammata ne senta la mala nova, che non ce vide lo primmo
de maggio! va', che te sia data lanzata catalana o che te sia
data stoccata co na funa, che non se perda lo sango, che te
vengano mille malanne, co l'avanzo e presa e viento a la vela,
che se ne perda la semmenta, guzzo, guitto, figlio de 'ngabellata,
mariuolo!" (12)

["Ah, you worthless thing, you dope, piece of shit, bedpisser,
leaping goat, diaper-ass, hangman's knot, bastard mule! So even
fleas have a cough! Go and may paralysis seize you! May your
mother receive bad news of you! May you not see the first of May!
May you be thrust by a Catalan lance, or may you be strangled by
a rope, so that no blood is wasted! May a thousand ills come to
you with haste and speed and wind in their sails! May your seed
be lost, rascal, beggar, son of a taxed woman, rogue!"]

The princess's laughter is provoked by a popular or "carnivalesque"
scene from which, however, she is still able to maintain a safe distance;
the woman's acts continue to be framed as an amusing interlude in a court
spectacle.[40] It is only upon second thought, after the woman curses her, that
Zoza realizes that the gesture is to be interpreted not in the context of festive
forms, and that the figure of the old woman does not belong entirely in
the carnivalesque tradition (which had, by the seventeenth century, become
emptied of much of its regenerative force), but that she inhabits a different
realm—that of the fairy tale—in which these inversions recover their creative
power.[41] As the power dialectic between Zoza and the woman evolves from
that between princess and subject, to that between princess and transgressive
subject, and finally to that between enchanted and enchantress, the three
moments of oil-gathering, obscene gesture, and curse also coincide with three
symbolic stances, on the part of Basile, toward literary tradition: faithful
respect of it, inversion of it, and, using as springboard this subversion, exiting
from it altogether. And these positions in turn coincide with the three
concrete literary personae of Basile, author of conventional Tuscan works,
author of dialect works—Le Muse napoletane and the Lettere—informed by
the Renaissance "anticlassicist" tradition and the contemporary popular genre
of dialect literature, and author of Lo cunto.

Laughter, in fairy tales and more in general, in myths and rituals, often
signals a moment of symbolic death, and rebirth, a crucial phase of the
initiation process; it is "endowed not only with the power to accompany
life but also the power to call it forth."[42] Through laughter the world is
experienced anew, and through it, old, decaying forms (be they immature
sexuality, or decrepit institutions, or a literary tradition on the brink of

exhaustion) are demolished and new life regenerates from their ruins.[43] Moreover, ritual use of obscenities can also be a decisive moment in a regenerative cycle. We might recall, in this regard, the maiden Iambe who when she exposes herself to the solemn Demeter makes her laugh, thereby triggering the return of spring to earth, or alternately, the obscene female demon Baubo, who performs a similar function.[44] Choosing this motif to frame a text that is a rebirth in literary form of the fairy tale is particularly apt; Zoza's laughter coincides with the diminished power of the courtly culture that her father represents, and her—as well as our—definitive entrance into the realm of the fairy tale. Folkloric laughter can also foretell pregnancy, and this more explicit theme of generativity is, of course, present in the frame tale. It is in satisfaction of Lucia's pregnant longings that the tales are told, though when Lucia dies, still pregnant, at the end of the frame tale, it becomes clear that what is to be born is not Lucia's child but the collection of tales itself.

Zoza's regenerative laughter takes place at a fountain, the *fonte,* or source, of a new direction in her life and a new literary genre. This is also a reworking of the traditional fairy-tale motif of the princess who creates springs wherever she goes, and in fact, as we shall see, the two other pivotal scenes of the frame, in which Zoza performs her crying-task at Tadeo's tomb and in which the tale-telling begins, also take place at fountains.[45] After the old woman's curse she feels herself "tirata co no straolo da chella passione che ceca lo iodizio e 'ncanta lo descurzo dell'ommo" [pulled as if by a capstan by that passion that blinds men's judgment and enchants their discourse], by the "ammore sopierchio a cosa non conosciuta" (14) [overwhelming love for something unknown]; and her passionate voyage into unknown territories mirrors Basile's own quest for new literary territories. Just as she must overcome the obstacle of Lucia, who by imitation and deception tries to substitute her, Basile, in order to achieve success in his creation of a new literary genre, must get beyond a literary project based on mere emulation (an apt definition of his own works in Italian).[46]

If in this first scene we note a progression from courtly models to inversion of them to a move into a completely "other" dimension, the rest of the frame is occupied with a new series of mediations. The second fountain of the frame is located in an orthodoxically fairy-tale realm—in a forest, outside Tadeo's kingdom—and hosts the scene of exchanged identities in which the slave Lucia usurps Zoza's place as future wife of Tadeo. But the third, and last fountain, the locus of the actual narration, is in the garden of Tadeo's palace, and is thus described:

> S'abbiaro palillo palillo a no giardino de lo palazzo stisso, dove
> li rame fronnute erano così 'ntricate, che no le poteva spartire

lo Sole co la perteca de li ragge e, sedutese sotto no paveglione commegliato de na pergola d'uva, 'miezo a lo quale scorreva no gran fontana mastro de scola de li cortesciani che le 'mezzava ogne iuorno de mormorare, commenzaie Tadeo così a parlare: "Non è chiù cosa goliosa a lo munno, magne femmene meie, quanto lo sentire li fatti d'autro, né senza ragione veduta chillo gran felosofo mese l'utema felicità dell'ommo in sentire cunte piacevole, pocca ausolianno cose de gusto se spapurano l'affanne, se da sfratto a li penziere fastidiuse e s'allonga la vita, pe lo quale desederio vide l'artisciane lassare le funnache, li mercante li trafiche, li dotture le cause, li potecare le facenne; e vanno canne aperte pe le varvarie e pe li rotielle de li chiacchiarune sentenno nove fauze, avise 'mentate e gazzette 'n aiero." (22)

[They made their way with measured step to a garden of the same palace, where the leafy branches were so entangled that the sun wasn't able to separate them with his rod; and when they had taken their seats under a pavilion topped by a pergola of vines in the middle of which flowed a large fountain, a fountain which daily instructed courtiers in the art of murmuring, Tadeo began to speak in this manner: "There is nothing in the world that more whets the appetite, my good women, than to hear about the doings of others, nor without obvious reason did that great philosopher set the supreme happiness of man in hearing pleasant tales; because when you lend an ear to tasty items, cares evaporate, irksome thoughts are dispelled, and life is prolonged. And so for this desire you see artisans leave their workshops, merchants their commerce, lawyers their cases, shopkeepers their businesses, and go open-mouthed to barbershops and mingle with the gossips to hear the chatter of false news, invented scandal-sheets and airy gazettes."]

This third fountain is a figure of ambivalence: originally described as a burbling model for Tadeo's courtiers in their gossipy murmuring and arts of dissimulation, it is the central prop of the stage on which the flood of *cunti* will flow. The immediate function of these *cunti* is to feed Lucia's pregnant cravings, but, as the seasoned fairy-tale reader knows, they will ultimately serve to unmask the dissimulation and lies by means of which she has taken Zoza's place, and therefore restore truth and justice. Moreover, in Tadeo's speech, another, extratextual purpose for the telling, ostensibly at odds with the *utile* of the tales' function within *Lo cunto*'s frame, is offered: they are a pleasurable relief from everyday cares, aimed principally at a middle-class public (and here we have, perhaps, a reference to the text's real audience). The site of this last fountain is a middle ground, where court, anticourt, and fairy-tale rhetorics and worldviews coexist, and as such, sets the stage for the heteroglossia that will be a constant of *Lo cunto*.

Finally, with the ten "most expert and gossipy" townswomen, who are selected for their tale-telling abilities, the carnivalesque makes its return, as is evident from the grotesque epithets used to describe them: "Zeza sciof-fata, Cecca storta, Meneca vozzolosa, Tolla nasuta, Popa scartellata, Antonella vavosa, Ciulla mossuta, Paola sgargiata, Ciommetella zellosa e Iacova squacquarata" (22) [lame Zeza, twisted Cecca, goitered Meneca, big-nosed Tolla, hunchback Popa, drooling Antonella, snout-faced Ciulla, cross-eyed Paola, mangy Ciommetella, and diarrhetic Iacova]. As Marina Warner has observed, "by the seventeenth century the outward form of the garrulous crone was established as an allegory of disobedience, opinion, anger, outspokenness, and general lack of compliance with male desires and behests," and Basile's employment of old hags as tellers implies a similarly transgressive attitude toward the social and literary status quo.[47] (The Renaissance "anticlassicist" tradition had, of course, already abundantly used the grotesque woman to figure their rebellion against canonical tradition.)

Moreover, the playful overturning of the conventions of the novella is especially evident here. In particular, these ten lower-class crones who will tell the tales are an explicit and grotesque negative of Boccaccio's elegant upper-class *brigata* (composed mostly of women) who gather to tell the tales of the *Decameron*. As Ada Testaferri has noted, significant differences between Basile's and Boccaccio's tellers, in addition to the obvious ones of social class and physical characteristics, lie in the fact that Boccaccio's tellers initiate their retreat to the country, and themselves decide to start telling tales, whereas Basile's hags are chosen by Prince Tadeo to perform for him and his court. If the function of the group or "microsociety" introduced in the frame is frequently, in the novella tradition, to offer a model for social interaction,[48] then Boccaccio's "democratically" organized *brigata* contrasts sharply with Basile's "monarchically" structured court. But as is often the case in *Lo cunto*, reality offers a multiplicity of faces: Tadeo, although he governs the telling, really only "institutionalizes" the situation that Zoza has created. And although he frequently intervenes in the preambles with an injunction to the next teller to get on with her story, he never imposes directives (or censure) regarding the actual subject matter of the tales, which is entirely at the choosing of the individual tellers. In the world of fairy tales, where proper names and common nouns often converge, the truest indicator of Tadeo's nature is in his name itself (etymologically, "stupid"). He is a good-natured but rather ineffectual simpleton (after all, he is asleep during the central action of the frame tale, and once he wakes up is generally portrayed in the guise of a henpecked husband) who "rules" the unwieldy world of *Lo cunto* only in the most superficial way.[49]

After the choice of the tellers, the frame tale is suspended, and the telling of the forty-nine tales that make up the body of *Lo cunto* begins. At the beginning of the last day, it is announced that one of the tale-tellers—the one who has in the preceding days told the last tale of each day—is sick, and Zoza herself is asked to substitute for her. The group has four hours to fill before they eat and start the tales, however, and Tadeo orders Cola Iacovo, one of the servants who has previously recited an eclogue, to think of a game to pass the time. Cola gives a speech that echoes Tadeo's at the end of the opening segment of the frame tale:

> "Però non foro trovate li trattenemiente e le veglie pe no piacere dessutele, ma pe no guadagno gostuso perzì, pocca non sulo se vene a passare lo tiempo co sta manera de iuoche, ma se scetano e fanno prunte li 'nciegne a saperese resorvere e a responnere a chello che se demanna, comm'a punto soccede a lo iuoco de li iuoche c'aggio pensato de fare." (878)

> ["Pleasures without some element of usefulness, my ladies, have always been insipid. For this reason amusements and evening gatherings were not invented for a pleasure without advantages, but for tasty profit, for such games serve not only to pass the time, but also stimulate the mind, making it quick in resolving problems and answering questions, just like what happens in the game of games that I have thought of."]

The "game of games" that the group will play is intended not only as a sweet pastime but also as a way to get a hermeneutic grip on the world. To Tadeo's *dulce* is united a *utile*. The success of a player in this game consists of "decoding" the name of a game through the refusal to play it because it is linked to a devious social practice (many of the same ones that are critiqued in the eclogues), after which Tadeo clarifies more explicitly the link between the game and the vice. Tadeo's role in the game is that of an interpreter who sums up the connections that the tellers make, thus mirroring the role he has in the telling of the *cunti*: he merely uses his power to legitimate the lesson learned.[50] So, for example, when Cola proposes the game of "trionfiello" [small triumph] to Zeza, she counters with: " 'Non ce voglio ioquare, perché non so' mariola!' 'Bravo!', disse Tadeo, 'ca chi arroba ed assassina chillo trionfa!' " (880) ["I don't want to play, because I'm not a thief." "Well done!" said Tadeo, "because those who rob and kill are those who triumph!"]. This activity suggests the necessity of reading social or ideological content into what might seem to be even the most frivolous or ludic of pastimes. But since the "game of games" is a clear parallel to the whole tale-telling enterprise of the "tale of tales," it also suggests a reading of the *cunti* in this key. In fact, since the same degraded aspects of society to which the game refers have been amply criticized in the course of *Lo cunto*, and since the game-players are the tale-tellers, the *cunti* have prepared the tellers for their brilliant performance in the game.

It should be underlined that the principal "move" of this game lies in the refusal to play the proposed game. That is, the primary (or "frame") game (the *game* of games) involves a negation of the secondary, embedded games (the game of *games*), and in this sense is a negative version of the "tale of tales" in which the primary tale (the frame) *generates* the *cunti* that follow it. The individual games are refused because they are associated with thieves, courtiers, cuckolds, flatterers, prostitutes, police informers, court gossips, and pedants, a cast of characters that has already appeared repeatedly in the eclogues. But in the eclogues the target of Basile's criticism is not so much the fact that there are such human types, as the fact that in the society he describes the noble facades erected to mask deficient foundations are so often accepted without question. Or, in Basile's own words, that appearances rarely correspond to reality:

> Siente fi'm ponta,
> chiano, ca me spalifeco chiù meglio.
> Quanto a la 'ncornatura e a primma fronte
> pare cosa de priezzo,
> tutto 'nganna la vista,
> tutto ceca la gente,
> tutto è schitto apparenzia.
> Non ire summo summo,
> non ire scorza scorza,
> ma spercia e trase drinto,
> ca chi non pesca 'n funno
> è no bello catammaro a sto munno! (224–26)

> [Hear to the end,
> So can I make my meaning clear.
> All things that in appearance at first sight
> Seem most to be of worth, are a deceit,
> Blinding the sight with nought but outward show.
> You should not cease to penetrate within,
> Cut through the bark, fish to the lowest depths,
> Or you will be accounted for a fool.][51]

The ability of the narrators/players to read the negative connotations behind the apparently innocuous names of the various games proposed (such as "trionfiello" [small triumph], "quatto mentuni" [four corners of the street], and "ve dongo la mano" [I'll give you my hand]), not only proves that they are adept readers of social reality. In their staged refusal of the games they also embrace an ethos of unmasking that is an implicit critique of courtly society and its emphasis on *sprezzatura* and dissimulation: a refusal of its games. Moreover, it is significant that this occurs in a work that presents itself, as a text, as an alternative to court conversation and, within the thematic developments of the text, as a new ethical model for courtly interaction between those who wield power and courtiers like Basile, with its stories of the morally virtuous, unveiling of truth, downfall of the envious, and so forth.

But finally it is Zoza's turn, and she, unlike the others, fails at the game. She is asked to play the game of "sbracare" (taking off: literally, one's pants), and answers ambiguously: " 'Chisso è iuoco de peccerelle' " ["This is a child's game"].[52] Is this her "counterstatement" or answer within the game's frame? Or is this her reaction to all of this gaming, the entire "game of games," from a point of view outside of the game's frame (that is, within her own frame, that of the *cornice*): it is childish? Which frame is she in, her own frame story or the telling situation that her frame story generated? If her answer is simply wrong, she isn't able to read the connections between games and social reality that the others are. But if she is criticizing the gaming in general, she ruptures the transparency of passage between the ludic and the social that the others are so expert at. Considering what occurs by the end of this day, the second interpretation would seem the most valid: the problem with this game, Zoza would imply, is that it doesn't go far enough. It is cynical social critique that deconstructs but fails to offer any other alternative. A game of games, just as a tale of tales, must have a more vital, restorative function. But perhaps Zoza's answer is both wrong *and* (or *because* it is wrong) a refusal to take part in the general gaming, a strategically constructed wrong answer that will lead her to her desired goal, the telling of her own story and the revindication of her lost rights. She is, we should remember, the grand architect, within the frame tale, of the whole *Cunto*. It is not that she objects to "pulling her pants down" (that is, revealing her real story). Indeed, the reference to the pivotal scene at the beginning of the frame story, where a similar gesture radically changes the course of the events that follows, is clear. It is that she objects to doing it in the circumscribed context of this gaming. The punishment imposed on her by Lucia for answering incorrectly, the singing of a *villanella*, turns, in fact, into a veiled poetic warning to Lucia that the moment of revelation is soon to come. Here, too, we can note the structural links between the telling and the gaming. Just as, within the frame of the tales of *Lo cunto*, the last tale (the forty-ninth, which is a thinly veiled version of Zoza's own frame story) reveals the "truth" that is necessary to bring the telling to an end and serve justice, within the frame of the frame tale the last game will also lead to Zoza's "real" account of her story.

Zoza enacts her philosophy of telling when at the end of this day she finally tells her own story. In the opening speech that she gives before her tale she stresses the truth value of the tale that she will tell, at the same time warning that truth is "mamma dell'odio" [the mother of hatred] and the opposite of the courtly practices of "fegnere 'menziune" [constructing lies] and "tessere favole" [weaving tales], and that "la verità non è recevuta a la presenzia de li principe" (1016–18) [truth is not received in the presence of princes]. After Zoza's own story, Tadeo's "court" is in tears and Tadeo himself is described as "levatose la mascara e ietanno la varda 'n terra" (1018) [having removed his mask and thrown off his harness]. The flurry of unmasking triggered by Zoza's tale extends, of course, to Lucia, the frame's figure of deception, who, still pregnant, is killed. The extratextual audience, however, never actually hears the (re)telling of Zoza's story, but only, and secondhand, its barest outline:

> commenzanno apunto da la naturale malanconia soia, 'nfelice agurio de chello che doveva passare, portannose da la connola la 'mara radeca de tutte le male sciagure, che co la chiave de no riso sforzato la sforzaro a tante lagreme; secotaie dapo' la iastemma de la vecchia, lo pellegrinaggio suio co tante angosce, l'arrivata a la fontana, lo chiagnere a vita tagliata, lo suonno tradetore causa de la roina soia. (1018)

> [She told from beginning to end all her woes, beginning with her own melancholic nature, which had been the unhappy augury of what would happen to her, since she had carried with her from the cradle the bitter root of all her cruel misfortunes, which with the key of a forced laugh had forced her to shed so many tears. She then went on to tell of the old woman's curse, of her anguished pilgrimage, her arrival at the fountain, her crying as if she were a cut vine, the sleep which betrayed her and caused her ruin.]

The new, truth-bearing form of telling that is celebrated in this scene, a telling that redresses all injustices done and provides closure in the best "happily-ever-after" fashion is, however, conspicuously absent from the tales that *are* told in Lo cunto, as are its solemn tone and tear-jerking effect on the listeners. Although a nostalgia, or utopian longing, for closure may be implicit in Basile's very choice of the fairy tale as a genre, Lo cunto is an "open" text that neither definitively establishes the absolute truth or justice of a single ending nor eradicates contradictions within and among tales, but instead foregrounds these very incongruities. What Basile proposes as an alternative to courtly lying, it becomes clear at this point, is not a sphere of transparent language and action, but one of more transparent, or perhaps ethical, rhetorical intentions, in which lying is substituted by telling and dissimulation by fiction.[53]

Tale 1.1, "L'uerco" [The Ogre], is "one of the most widely spread tales in the whole collection," and in its main plot is quite similar to #36 of the Grimms' collection ("The Magic Table, the Golden Donkey, and the Club in the Sack") or #127 of Calvino's.[54] As the very first tale of *Lo cunto* it assumes the status of the first step in Basile's own initiation into the fairy tale, and can, in fact, be read as a tale of the acquisition of the "tools of the trade" of popular culture. The story proceeds as follows: the simpleton Antuono (a stock proper name for the fool) is exiled by his exasperated mother and meets up with an ogre. He lives in the wilds with the ogre for a time, but when he gets homesick the ogre sends him back to his town with a jewel-defecating donkey. Antuono stops at an inn on the way back and gives away the secret of the donkey's ability to the innkeeper, who steals it from him and replaces it with a common donkey. When Antuono arrives home and gives his command to the donkey, it dirties the better part of his sisters' dowry of linens that his mother had pulled out for the occasion. His mother kicks him out again. The same thing happens a second time, but with a tablecloth that fills itself up with food. The third time Antuono is given a club that attacks on command, and he uses it on the innkeeper to regain the other two magic objects, after which he returns home, marries off his six sisters, and lives happily ever after with his mother.

Antuono departs from Maragliano, a real town in, ironically, the Terra di Lavoro ("The Land of Labor") area of Campania (where Basile himself died). His "apprenticeship" is with a likable midget ogre, "brutto de facce e bello de core" (40) [ugly-faced and kind-hearted] as well as sensitive and rhetorically astute, who lives at the foot of a mountain in the wilds. When he first meets up with him, Antuono gives a fine demonstration of his own lack of rhetorical skills and simplemindedness, as evidenced by his incapacity to ask the right questions. He greets the ogre: "'A dio messere, che se fa? comme staie? vuoie niente? quanto 'nc'è da ccà a lo luoco dove aggio da ire?'" ["Good day, sir, what's up? How are you? You want anything? How far is it from here to the place where I have to go?"]. The ogre replies: "'Vuoi stare a patrone?'" ["Do you want to work for me?"]. Antuono: "'Quanto vuoie lo mese?'" ["How much do you want a month?"]. The ogre: "'Attienne a servire 'noratamente, ca sarrimmo de convegna, e farraie lo buono iuorno'" (34) ["Just make sure you tend to my needs decently: we'll get along fine and you'll see good times"]. They bind this relationship ("sto parentato," closer to a kinship), and Antuono moves in with the ogre. It is pertinent to contrast Basile's tale with a better-known version of the tale, the Grimms', in which the three sons serve real apprenticeships with various tradesmen. Antuono, on the other hand, is totally cut off from the world of labor and responsible citizenry; in fact, he does as little that is useful for the ogre as he had done for his mother at home. (It is, furthermore, significant that in many other tales of *Lo cunto*, too, protagonists strike up relationships with ogres that are defined as familiar in nature. The fact that real fathers are substituted by woodsy ogres suggests an insufficiency on the part of figures of authority—fathers—and a need to search for "paternal" guidance outside the realms of "civilization" and literary tradition, and should be considered in the context of the general experimentation with canons and redefinitions of "authority" that characterizes baroque culture.)

If Antuono does not mature into a socially integrable subject in the course of the tale, he does, under the ogre's mentorship, acquire a certain rhetorical maturity, an awareness of the workings of language and increased linguistic control of the situations in which he finds himself. On his first two returns home, Antuono displays no initiative whatsoever in managing the fairy-tale objects that the ogre presents him with and, above all, in mastering the magical formulas that unleash their secrets. He is capable, at most, of parroting the formulas indiscriminately. This obviously has disastrous consequences, since he tells the innkeeper not to use those very words and thus becomes an accomplice to his own loss of the objects. When he goes back to the ogre after losing the second object, the tablecloth, the ogre makes quite explicit, through a string of insults that link physical to linguistic incontinence, that Antuono's failures are a result of his lack of rhetorical control:

> "No saccio chi me tene che no te sborzo na lanterna, cannarone vesseniello, vocca pedetara, canna fraceta, culo de gallina, *ta-ta-naro*, trommetta de la Vicaria, che d'ogne cosa iette lo banno, che vuommeche quant'hai 'n cuorpo e no puoie reiere le cicere! si tu stive zitto a la taverna no te soccedeva chello che t'è socciesso, ma pe farete la lengua comm'a taccariello de molino haie macenato la felicetà che t'era venuta da ste mano." (42)

> ["I don't know what keeps me from tearing out one of your eyes, fart-throat, gas-mouth, filthy gullet, hen's ass, tattler, court trumpeter: you make a public announcement of every private matter, you vomit whatever is in your body and you can't even keep in chickpeas! If you had shut up at the inn, all this would not have happened to you, but since you used your tongue like the sail of a windmill, you've ground the happiness that this hand had given to you!"]

And this time, Antuono, rising to the occasion as he accepts the third magic object, the club, finally dialogues shrewdly with the ogre: " 'Va c'aggio puosto la mola de lo sinno e saccio quanta para fanno tre buoie! no so' chiù peccerillo, ca chi vo' gabbare Antuono se vo' vasare lo guveto!' " (42) ["You'll see, I've cut my wisdom teeth and I know how many pairs make three oxen! I'm not a little boy anymore and whoever wants to cheat Antuono must kiss his own elbow first!"]. On his third trip home, although the ogre has given him both parts of the command for the club—"Up, club!" and "Down, club!"—this time Antuono shows some, however minimal, astuteness when he gives away only half of the formula to the innkeeper.

What Antuono has achieved when he uses the third object correctly, and by doing so gets back the first two, is the passage from a passive acceptance of the popular utopian myths of unlimited and unearned wealth and food uncoupled with the rhetorical power to use them, to an aggressive retrieval and actualization of their powers.[55] Antuono thus finally learns, with the club, that its command "no fù parola chesta, ma arte de 'ncanto" (44) [was not a word, but the art of enchantment], and with this, learns to produce words that do not only describe enchantment but are a form of enchantment themselves. This rite of passage does not bring him the adulthood in the form of social validation that is so frequently the fairy tale's endpoint, but it does lead to his appropriation of the power to manipulate his magic objects, and reality, through an effective use of language.[56] The command of this ability, learned from the ogre, in this tale a figure of the master-artist of popular tradition, leads to the return home to his mother: his motherland, Naples, and his mother tongue, Neapolitan. And it parallels Basile's own initiation into and transformations of the traditions of folklore, popular culture, and dialect literature after a period of cultural apprenticeship spent experimenting with the instruments of these traditions.

In tale 2.7, "La palomma" [The Dove], we are given a brilliant example of Basile's use of metaphor not only to rupture the surface linearity of the fairy tale but also to link the fantastic world of the fairy tale to contemporary sociohistorical concerns and, in general, to intimate that in these *cunti* there is far more than meets the eye. The fact itself that metaphor plays such an important part in the figurative strategies employed in this text is already a substantial departure from conventional fairy-tale usage, for, as it has been defined by scholars, the European tale is characterized by linear narrative and representational techniques.[57] Aristotle, the central point of reference for Baroque theorists of metaphor, states: "A good metaphor implies an intuitive perception of the similarity of the dissimilar,"[58] and Basile's dynamic use of metaphor indeed reveals a cosmos where the usual extreme oppositions of the fairy tale (good and evil, beautiful and ugly, rich and poor, and so on) are no longer so tenable. (On the thematic level we may also note throughout *Lo cunto* indications of this breakdown in the usually strict fairy-tale categories in, for example, the abundance of kings and princes who live on the other side of a wall from ogres or paupers.) The fairy tale portrays thematically the magic of physical and social transformation, and therefore has at least the potential—often undeveloped but fully exploited in the case of Basile—for foregrounding the figural magic of metaphor. In the world of *Lo cunto* objects, people and language are involved in a vortex of metamorphic movement in which reality ultimately assumes the aspect of a continuum in which everything can and inevitably does become its other.[59] By the nature of the metaphors that he uses, then, Basile calls into question, on the figural plane, the conventional closure of the fairy tale, which he more often than not respects on a thematic plane.[60] Moreover, this dramatization of the rift between what is told and how it is told is part of a general attention to the tensions between appearance and reality and to the questions of illusion and masking that characterize many works of this period, questions that Basile himself addresses in more explicit fashion over and over again in the eclogues that divide the days of *Lo cunto*.

"La palomma" opens with a realistic portrayal of an impoverished old woman, again situated in a concrete geographical place (eight miles outside of Naples):

> era tanto sbriscia de diente quanto carreca d'anne, cossì auta de scartiello comme vascia de fortuna: aveva ciento crespe a la faccie, ma era totalemente screspata, che si be' aveva la capo carreca d'argiento non se trovava uno de ciento vinte a carrino pe sorzetarese lo spireto. (372)

> [she was as free of teeth as she was burdened with years; the hump on her back was as high as her luck was low; her face was wrinkled in a hundred places but her pocket in not a one, and although her head was weighed down with silver, she wasn't able to find a single coin to bring her spirits up.]

Nardo Aniello, son of a king, happens to pass by the old woman's house and, as part of a bet with his servants, knocks a pan containing her meager meal of beans off the windowsill. The old woman, in a sequence very similar to that of the frame, casts upon him the curse that he fall in love with an ogress's daughter and be tortured by her mother. Hours later, when the prince meets this woman, who also happens to be a fairy, his first impressions are referred in terms that are typical of Basile's extravagant metaphor:

> Lo prencepe, che se vedde comparere 'nante sto scrittorio de le cose chiù preziose de la Natura, sto banco de li chiù ricche deposete de lo cielo, st'arzenale de le chiù spotestate forze

d'Ammore, non sapeva che l'era socciesso e da chella facce tonna de cristallo trapassanno li ragge dell'uocchie all'esca de lo core suio, allommaie tutto de manera che deventaie na carcara, dove se cocevano le prete de li designe pe fravecare la casa de le speranze. (376)

[the prince, who saw in front of him this writing-table which held Nature's most precious possessions, this bank of the heavens' richest deposits, this arsenal of Love's most furious forces, didn't understand what had happened to him, and the rays of her eyes, passing through that round crystal face until they reached the bait of his heart, lit him up to such a degree that he became a furnace that baked the stones of the plans for construction of the house of his hopes.]

Basile calls on the love tropes of the Petrarchan tradition (and its later incarnation in Marino and the poets who emulated him) for this abstract figuration of a lady. But if we look at the actual metaphors he uses, it becomes evident that Basile emulates this tradition only to turn it on its head. The terms of Nardo's declaration, in fact, are drawn from the middle-class language of court scribes, bankers, and soldiers. Even when he seems to ascend to the more metaphysical realms of a *dolce stil novo*-derived theory of itinerant rays that have the power to carry love from the eye of the beloved to the heart of the lover, he wraps things up with a metaphor taken from the science of construction. After the prince's and Filadoro's eyes meet—"li sguardi erano trommette de la Vicaria, che spobrecavano lo secreto dell'arma" [their gazes were trumpets of the tribunal, which made public the secrets of their souls]— the prince, "spilato lo connutto de la voce" [unclogging the sewer-pipe of his voice], tries again to find the appropriate words of love. He says to her: " 'Da quale prato è sguigliato sto shiore de bellezza? da quale cielo è chioppeta sta rosata de grazia? da quale menera è venuto sto tesoro de bellezzetudene cose?' " (376) ["In which meadow has this flower of beauty blossomed? From which sky has rained this dew of grace? From which mine has come this treasure of beauteous things?"]. And although he starts out more encouragingly this time, with metaphors that evoke a pastoral dimension uncontaminated by the world of exchange, he ends up again quantifying beauty with a reference to mining. This shifting between or conflation of registers—high and low (or middle, as is the case here), Petrarchan and carnivalesque—is characteristic of Basile's style. Especially significant in the passages cited above is the way that such a technique is used to deconstruct the concept of courtly love. The presence of the language of commerce and contracts in Nardo's declaration of a "love at first sight" suggests that even in love, he is guided by a merchant's mentality that tends to quantify the most ineffable of attributes, such as beauty.

Nardo's most intense emotional moments in the course of the tale, in fact, occur when he is in danger of seeing his socioeconomic status threatened. As he is kissing Filadoro's hand, her mother the ogress appears (whose description is a classic of negative *effictio* that recalls the anti-Petrarchan literary portraits of, for example, Berni) and, after dragging Nardo back to her house, gives him a series of impossibly large tasks to do. Nardo's reaction is not entirely what we would expect. He says to Filadoro:

> "No me spiace l'essere sciso da lo cavallo all'aseno, né l'avere cagnato lo palazzo riale co sto cafuorchio, li banchette vannute co no tuozzo de pane, lo cortiggio de serveture co servire a staglio, lo scettro co na zappa, lo fare atterrire l'asserzete co vedereme atterruto da na brutta caiorda, perché tutte le desgrazie meie stimarria a ventura co starece presente e schiuderete co st'uocchie. Ma chello che me spercia lo core è che aggio da zappare e sputareme ciento vote le mano, dove sdegnava de sputareme na petinia e, *cot peio*, aggio da fare tanto che non 'nce vastarria tutto no iuorno no paro de vuoie, e si non scompo stasera lo fattefesta sarraggio cannariato da mammata e io non tanto averraggio tormiento de scrastareme da sto nigro cuorpo quanto de scantoniareme da ssa bella persona." (380)

> ["I don't mind having descended from a horse to an ass, nor having exchanged my royal palace for this hole, sumptuous banquets for a crust of bread, my train of servants for manual service, my scepter for a hoe, seeing armies terrified for being terrified by a nasty skunk, for I deem all of my misfortunes fortunate if I am near you and can worship you with my eyes. But what pierces my heart is that I have to dig and spit in my hands a hundred times, whereas before I wouldn't even spit on a pimple and, what's worse, I have more to do than two oxen could get done in a day, and if I don't finish the task by tonight I'll be eaten by your mother, and my torment in detaching myself from this miserable body will not be as great as having to separate myself from your beautiful person."]

Each of the two sections of Nardo's speech concludes that what sustains him even in such a terrible situation, and what he will most miss if he were to die, is his love for Filadoro. But in fact he spends the majority of his words not so much despairing over the magnitude of the tasks, as is the usual reaction to this situation in fairy tales, as complaining of the humiliation of his "new" social position. He almost seems to add the evocation of the strength of his love for Filadoro as an afterthought; it is not love that propels this tale but the prince's desire to reacquire the power he lost upon first entering the woods.

Nardo does display the attributes of the lovesick—he cries, grows pale, and so forth—but the true cause of this state is horror at the prospect of hard work.

Filadoro finally digs a hole in her garden that connects to a tunnel running to Naples, and escapes with Nardo. However, once they get within sight of the city, Nardo, ever more caught up with ceremony and social convention than with Filadoro herself, instructs her: "'Bene mio, non convene lo farete venire a lo palazzo mio a pede e vestuta de sta manera. Però aspetta a sta taverna ca torno subeto co cavalle, carroze, gente e vestite ed autre fruscole'" (384) ["My beloved, it is not appropriate for you to come to my palace on foot and dressed like that. So wait in this inn, and I will soon return with horses, carriages, servants, clothes and other nice things"]. In the meantime, the ogress, having discovered their absence, establishes that with the first kiss he receives, Nardo will forget Filadoro. When Nardo gets back to his palace, his mother kisses him, he forgets Filadoro, who at this point seems relegated to the sphere of youthful flings in the forest, and most willingly agrees to marry a noblewoman from Flanders. Filadoro hears of the wedding, appears at the banquet in the form of a dove that flies out of a meat pie, and admonishes Nardo for having abandoned her:

> "Haie magnato cellevriello de gatta, o prencepe, che te sì scordato 'n ditto 'n fatto l'affrezione de Filadoro? cossì te so' sciute de mammoria li servizie recevute, o scanoscente? cossì paghe li beneficie che t'ha fatto, o sgrato? . . . è chesta la gran mercè che daie a chella sfortunata figliola de lo sbisciolato ammore che t'ha mostrato? . . . o negra chella femmena che troppo se 'mprena de parole d'uommene, che portano sempre co le parole la sgratetudene, co li beneficie la sconoscenza e co li debete lo scordiamiento! . . . và, non te curare, facce de nega-debeto!" (388)

> ["Have you eaten cat's brain, prince, and forgotten in word and deed Filadoro's affection? This is how the services received have left your memory, oh thankless one? Is this how you pay the favors that she did you, ingrate? . . . Is this the compensation that you give to the unlucky girl for her ardent love? . . . Oh, the wretched woman who lets herself be impregnated by the words of men, who always accompany words with ingratitude, favors with thanklessness, and debts with oblivion! . . . Go ahead, don't worry about it, deadbeat-face!"]

This is language that Nardo can understand: the language of debts and compensation, services rendered, the language of exchange. Being the businessman that he is, "se venne ad allecordare l'obrecanza c'aveva stipolata 'n facce soia a la curia d'Ammore, subeto la facette auzare e sedere a canto ad isso, contanno a la mamma l'obreco granne c'aveva a sta bella giovane" (390) [he began to remember the obligations that he had stipulated with her in the tribunal of Love and immediately had her get up and sit next to him, telling his mother of the great debt that he owed this fair young woman]. And perhaps he has second thoughts about his Flemish noblewoman: she brings good blood and material riches to the marriage, but Filadoro brings her magical powers, which have a far greater potential. Filadoro is substituted as his wife, and it would seem that the "deal" has been made to the satisfaction of all involved, until a "horrible mask" interrupts the second wedding banquet. It is the ghost of the old woman of the beginning of the tale, who died of hunger after Nardo's cruel joke and is now back to try another curse on him: "'pe memoria de lo danno che me faciste, te puozze trovare sempre 'nante li fasule che me iettaste e se faccia vero lo proverbio *chi semmena fasule le nasceno corna*'" (392) ["in remembrance of the damage you did me, may the beans of mine that you threw away always appear in front of you and may the proverb *he who sows beans sprouts horns* come true"].[61] The prince shows no remorse for his act, but does pale at the double specters, invoked by the curse, of a life of hard work and a renegation of the deal that he has just closed with Filadoro. The old woman, who initially served as gatekeeper to the fairy-tale realm (like the old woman in the frame), is, however, ineffective in Nardo's Naples, where one has power only if one has something to exchange. She is no match for the ogress's daughter-turned-princess, who annuls the curse.

What might look like a tale about Nardo's initiation into the plea-sures, and moral responsibilities, of love thus comes, when we investigate its figural trappings, to assume the contours of a very different sort of tale. This "submerged" tale tells of the maturation of a bourgeois business-sense in a Neapolitan prince and a provincial fairy that leads to a matrimonial "deal" from which each stands to profit: the prince because it gives him the "magical" instruments necessary to counter the threats of figures such as the old woman, and the fairy because it awards her the social validation that comes with a title of nobility. This union, indeed, suggests allegorical interpretation on two levels. As political allegory, the marriage represents the attempt on the part of an urban administrator, represented by the prince, to find allies among the most "attractive" members of the *massari* (rich peasant) class. (That Filadoro and her mother have a relatively prosperous life is suggested by Nardo's desperate realization that the agricultural tasks that the ogress orders him to do are of such a magnitude that he will never be able to perform them without magical intervention.) Such alliances would have been made to circumvent the formation of other potential alliances (for example, among the *massari* themselves or between the *massari* and simple peasants) that could threaten the political status quo.[62] On the literary level, the marriage between Nardo and the fairy may be read as an allegory of one aspect of Basile's project of amalgamating diverse traditions: the "union" of high and low cultures that he inaugurates in *Lo cunto* at times necessarily involves a sublimation (or exorcism) of the most disturbingly realistic details of each (in this case, the encounter between Nardo and the old woman) into the realm of magic.

The next tale to be considered is a model of Basile's "fairy-tale carnivalesque." Tale 3.5, "Lo scarafone, lo sorece e lo grillo" [The Cockroach, the Mouse, and the Cricket], depends for its structure, in fact, on the series of symbolic inversions and binarisms that characterize grotesque realism as defined by Bakhtin. We learn in the first lines of the tale that Nardiello is the son of a very rich peasant, yet another reference to this emerging socioeconomic class (they live on the Vomero, a hill above Naples that was home, at the time, to country houses and villas). Nardiello, a good-for-nothing simpleton, has consumed half of his father's savings in taverns, bordellos, and gambling-houses, where he is generally "kneaded like a pizza." Miccone, his father, in order to get him away from what he sees as the root of the problem, sends him off with a hundred ducats to buy some steer, instructing him:

> "allontanate dalle accasiune, ca te scraste da lo vizio: remota la causa, desse chillo, se remmove l'effetto. Eccote perzò sti ciento docate: và a la fera de Salierno e accattane tante ienche, ca 'n capo de tre o quatto anne farrimmo tante vuoie; fatte li vuoie, 'nce mettarrimmo a fare lo campo; fatto lo campo, 'nce darrimmo a fare mercanzia de grano e si 'nce 'matte na bona carestia mesurarrimmo li scute a tommola e quanno mai autro te compro no titolo sopra na terra de quarche ammico e sarrai tu puro tritolato comm'a tante autre. Perzò attienne, figlio mio, ca ogne [cosa] capo ha, chi no accomenza non secoteia." (538)

> ["If you keep yourself far from the occasion, you'll keep yourself far from the vice; if you get rid of the cause, said that fellow, you get rid of the effect. So here are one hundred ducats: go to the Salerno fair and buy a lot of steer, so that in three or four years we'll have a lot of oxen; once we've got the oxen, we'll work the fields; once we've worked the fields, we'll start dealing in wheat, and if we meet up with a good famine we'll weigh our coins by the bushel and if nothing else, I'll buy the title on some friend's land and you'll have a title like so many others. So be careful, my son, everything has a head; he who doesn't begin, doesn't continue."]

In this first episode a number of oppositions are apparent. Miccone is intent on accumulating wealth and moving up the social hierarchy (by buying a title of nobility), without worrying too much about how he does it; if a disaster such as a famine furthers his aims, all the better. Nardiello, on the other hand, spends his energies dispersing this wealth. Miccone has a rational, if cynical, way of structuring his existence ("everything has a head"); Nardiello is governed by his physical needs. Nardiello's frequenting of those three commonplaces of the comic-burlesque tradition, the tavern, the bordello, and the gambling-house (we should remember Cecco Angiolieri's sonnets on the same subject), in fact, constitutes an inversion of the order and containment that governs his father's world.

On the way to the fair Nardiello meets a fairy who shows him a guitar-playing cockroach. Nardiello buys it, returns home, is reprimanded by his father, but is sent twice again to the fair. The second time he buys a dancing mouse, and the third time a singing cricket. All three of these animals also enter into the tale's scheme of inversions, for they are transformed from domestic creatures, which, at least in the case of the first two, are usually associated with destruction or undoing, to artists, cultural constructors.

Nardiello is sent away by his father with a sound beating, and ends up in Lombardy at the court of a "great nobleman," Cenzone, whose daughter Milla has not laughed for seven years and who has offered to give her in marriage to the man who makes her laugh. Nardiello succeeds where no one else has with the help of his three animals, and the king, although he considers Nardiello "the dregs of humanity," agrees to give him three days to consummate the marriage. If he is unsuccessful, he will be thrown to the lions. Nardiello, an expert consumer, declares that in three days he will not only consummate the marriage, but also consume the daughter and the whole house. The king slips him a sleeping pill each night, and after the third night Nardiello is thrown to the lions. In the face of imminent death he frees the cockroach, the mouse, and the cricket, but they vow to help him to escape the lions and regain Milla.

In the meantime Milla has been married to "a great German nobleman" and is spending her first night with him, though not in very passionate style, as he has eaten and drunk too much and falls asleep immediately. The cockroach enters into action at this point:

> se ne sagliette chiano chiano pe lo pede de la travacca e remorchi-atose sotto coperta se 'nficcaie lesto lesto a lo tafanario de lo zito, servennolo de soppositario 'n forma tale che le spilaie de manera lo cuorpo, che potte dicere co lo Petrarca: *d'amor trasse inde un liquido sottile*. La zita, che 'ntese lo squacquarare de lo vesenterio, *l'aura, l'odore, il refrigerio e l'ombra*, scetaie lo marito. (546)

> [it crawled quietly up the foot of the bed and when it had worked its way under the covers, nimbly slipped into the bridegroom's

ass, working in him like a suppository and uncorking his body in such a way that one might have said, with Petrarca: "love drew from him a subtle liquid." The bride, who heard the rumbling of this dysentery, "the breeze and the fragrence and the coolness and the shade," woke her husband up.]

The second night, although the German prepares an elaborate diaper to protect himself from another such outpouring, the mouse and the cockroach collaborate:

arrivato sopra la facce de lo luoco, commenzaie a rosecare li panne e a farele no pertuso a leviello dell'autro, pe dove trasenno lo scarafone le fece n'autra cura medecinale de manera che fece no maro de liquido topazio e l'arabi fumme 'nfettarono lo palazzo. (546)

[when the mouse had arrived in sight of its goal, it started to gnaw the cloth and to make a hole that corresponded to that other one. The cockroach went in, and administered some more of his medicine, so that a sea of topaz liquid flowed forth and the Arabian fumes infected the palace.]

On the third night, the exasperated German declares to his worried relatives, this time using the authority of Virgil:

"Non dubitare . . . ca stanotte, si dovesse crepare, voglio stare sempre all'erta, non lassonnome vencere da lo suonno ed otra a chesto pensarrimmo che remmedio potimmo fare ad appilare lo connutto maistro, azzò non me se dica *tre volte cadde ed a la terza giacque!*" (548)

["Have no doubt . . . because tonight, even if I have to die, I intend to stay awake, and not let sleep win me over. Besides, we'll think of some way to stop up the main pipe, so that no one may say to me: 'three times he fell and the third time, lay still!' "][63]

He has a special wooden plug made, gets into bed and lies there motionlessly, "pe trovarese lesto ad ogne recercata de stommaco" (548) [so that he could be ready for any movement that his intestines might make]. But the cricket sings him to sleep and the mouse rubs mustard under his nose until he "commenzaie a sternutare accossì forte che sbottaie lo tappo co tanta furia che, trovannose votato de spalle a la zita, le schiaffaie 'm pietto accossì furiuso che l'appe ad accidere" (550) [started to sneeze so hard that the plug flew out so violently that, since he had his back to the bride, it hit her in the chest with such force that it almost killed her]. The king realizes the injustice he has done Nardiello, who, after he is turned into a "handsome young man" by his animals, is finally able to consummate his new life.

The princess's laughter coincides in this tale, too, with a rebirth, the rebirth of Nardiello as a "winning" protagonist, but especially, the rebirth of the carnivalesque tradition in fairy-tale form. The animals had originally delighted Milla because of the contrast between what she expected of them as common animals and their exquisite artistry. In their second job as magic helpers they revert back to their "natural" role as deconstructors, though this time not of domestic order but of the containment and order of the hierarchies that structure the world of the German nobleman. The bedroom scenes are dominated by images of the German's grotesque body: a body turned inside out by the uncontrollable diarrhetic flow that the animals cause, a body voided of its substance and progressively degraded, despite the desperate attempts at closure, until the inversion culminates in the symbolic transformation of this great nobleman into an ass and his expulsion from the kingdom (before the third night his relatives tell him the cautionary tale of a man whose first two farts were diagnosed by doctors as "sanitatibus" and "ventositatibus," but the third as "asinitatibus"). And the undoing of the German's social and corporeal identity is accompanied by a similar inversion of the literary tradition that embraces the Platonic, or courtly, conception of love that is made to show its underside in this episode: it is Petrarch himself who glosses the "accident."[64]

The "maturation" of Nardiello consists of his progression from being a negative agent of indiscriminate dispersion of his father's wealth to the "institutionalization" of this dispersion by means of magic helpers who effect the dissipation of the German's bodily wealth and, symbolically, the wealth of the "high" tradition. Moreover, these inversions of social realities and cultural forms, sustained by the carnivalesque "magic" that the animals enact, provide the impetus not only for the transformation of Nardiello into a prince but also the foundations for a literary model that retrieves an archaic narrative form and, in the process, carnivalizes the "high" tradition.

Whereas a tale like 3.5 presents a brilliant example of a grotesque body that figures the deconstruction of canonical tradition, in 5.3, "Pinto Smauto" [Splendid Shine], we find a very different sort of body: a precious, edible, and very baroque body that is Basile's most explicit dramatization of his project of constructing of a new fairy-tale subject. Betta, the daughter of a merchant who is very eager to see her married, shows no interest in men. But one day, when her father goes to a fair, she asks him to bring back

> "no miezo cantaro de zuccaro de Palermo e miezo de ammennole
> ambrosine, co quatto o sei fiasche d'acqua d'adore e no poco de

musco e d'ambra, portannome perzì na quarantina de perne, dui
zaffire, no poco de granatelle e rubini, co no poco d'oro filato e
sopra tutto na mattara e na rasora d'argiento." (910–12)

["half a quintal of Palermo sugar and half of ambrosian almonds,
with four or six flasks of rose water and a little bit of musk and
amber, and also bring me about forty pearls, two sapphires, a few
garnets and rubies and some spun gold and, above all, a modeling
bowl and a silver scalpel."]

From these "primary materials" she molds a husband:

"se 'nchiuse dintro na cammara e commenzaie a fare na gran
quantità de pasta d'ammennole e zuccaro, 'mescata co acqua rosa
e sprofummo e commenzaie a fare no bellissimo giovene, a lo
quale fece li capille de fila d'oro, l'uocchie de zaffire, li diente de
perne, le lavra de robine e le dette tanta grazia che no le mancava
se no la parola." (912)

[she shut herself in a room and started to knead together a large
quantity of almond paste and sugar, mixed with rose water and
perfume, and started to model a splendid young man, for whom
she made hair from the spun gold, eyes from the sapphires, teeth
from the pearls, lips from the rubies, and she gave him so much
grace that the only thing missing was speech.]

Encouraged by her remembrance of "a certain king of Cyprus" who had made
his statue live, she prays to the goddess of love until he comes alive.[65]

Pinto Smauto is an example of a metaphor made literal. This is a
common enough occurrence in fairy tales and, in general, in folklore, where
commonplaces can, through magic, come to life and regain their original vitality. Stefano Calabrese has commented on how this technique, in
Basile's age, is part of a more general aesthetic trend: "Il fiabesco del Basile
si mostra allora come il farsi 'cosa' di quel linguaggio figurale, secondo
una conversione della retorica all'emblematica che in quegli stessi anni
dà vigore alla moda delle 'imprese' " [Basile's fairy-tale techniques involve
an "objectification" of figural language, following a conversion of rhetoric
into the study of emblems that in those same years fed the vogue of "devices"]. Calabrese also cites the great Seicento theoretician of metaphor,
Emanuele Tesauro (Il cannocchiale aristotelico, 1654), and observes how his
words seem to apply precisely to fairy tales such as Basile's (Tesauro is
describing argutezza, or wit): "per miracolo di lei, le cose mutole parlano,
le insensate vivono, le morte risorgono, le tombe, i marmi, le statue da
questa incantatrice degli animi ricevendo voce, spirito, movimento, cogli

uomini ingegnosi ingegnosamente discorrono. . . ." [miraculously, because of it, mute objects speak, inanimate ones come to life, dead ones are resurrected; tombs, marbles, and statues receive voice, spirit, and movement from this enchanter of souls, and converse wittily with witty men. . . .][66] Indeed, we should note that *ingegnoso* is used in the above passage to refer not to intelligence, but to wit, in the specifically Seicento sense of ability to manipulate language in the most unexpected of ways, principally through metaphor.

When seen in this light, Betta's *ingegno* consists, on the most explicit of levels, of her ability to couple delectable foods and precious gems with the idea of a living, breathing person, and to make the one live in the other.[67] This sort of metaphorical construction of an object of desire had long been, of course, one of the central conceits of the Petrarchan lyric portrait, in which each attribute of the beloved lady was likened to a precious substance; descriptions similar to that of Pinto can be found in any of dozens of Renaissance sonnets. Where Betta's project diverges, however, is in the fact that her reified object of desire does not even pretend to have any real referent, and that, of course, it exists simultaneously as metaphorical construction and actual physical being. Thus, Pinto becomes a literalized metaphor for old, tired metaphor (as the Petrarchan repertoire was by Basile's time) revivified and given magical vigor. And Betta's creation of a perfect mate (and fairy-tale hero) from both precious and common materials is not so different from Basile's own quest for the re-formation of the fairy tale. In an act of literary alchemy, he too models a variety of "raw" materials gathered at the fair of literary history, which include both the "low" dialect and carnivalesque as well as the more precious "high" Petrarchan-Marinist traditions, into a unique, and thoroughly "consumable," end product.[68]

Lo cunto thus emerges, on the one hand, as a model of baroque textuality, participating fully in this period's radical innovations in literary themes and languages and rich cultural debates on the intersection of official and nonofficial traditions. Basile's work is the most significant Italian example of the baroque technique of conflating canonical and noncanonical genres into an extremely original synthesis that, adhering in the most extensive sense to the central tenets of the poetics of the marvelous, ironically, and delightfully, subverts the literary and ideological expectations of its readers and listeners. Yet through its simultaneous inscription of the fairy tale into the "high" literary canon and, by doing so, popularization of the canon itself, it also opens up questions about the viability of any notion of a dominant, unitary culture and the literary and social authorities that sustain it. As such *Lo cunto* remains a towering monument of seventeenth-century Italian culture, and one of the most complex tributes to the power of the fairy tale not only to entertain but also to interpret the world.

Notes

1. Nino Borsellino, *Gli anticlassicisti del Cinquecento* (Bari: Laterza, 1975). The "anticlassicist" side of Renaissance culture has alternately been referred to as the "anti-Renaissance" (Eugenio Battisti, *L'antirinascimento* [Milan: Garzanti, 1989]); the jocose, burlesque or comic-realist tradition; the anticanonical school; or the popular-festive or carnivalesque (Mikhail Bakhtin, *Rabelais and His World*, trans. Hélène Iswolsky [Bloomington: Indiana University Press, 1984]), although each of these terms has its own particular shades of meaning. See Bakhtin's *Rabelais and His World*, esp. ch. 1, for further discussion of the cross-fertilization between "official" and "non-official" cultural forms. The reasons for the explosion of interest in "popular culture" at this time are, of course, complex and cannot be treated comprehensively here. Nevertheless, one of the more suggestive hypotheses is that of Giuseppe Cocchiara, who opens his volume *The History of Folklore in Europe* with this thesis: "In Europe the discovery of America nourished a new humanism, one that added the study of the folk and of more remote civilizations to the study of the classical world." Thus, the geographical discoveries in remote corners of the globe also engendered more local ethnographic discoveries of vernacular cultures and languages, in the forms of popular proverbs, narratives, songs, games, and so forth: in a sense, the discovery, on the part of Europe, "of itself as a historical and cultural entity" (Giuseppe Cocchiara, *The History of Folklore in Europe*, trans. John N. McDaniel [Philadelphia: Institute for the Study of Human Issues, 1981 (1952)] 13 and xxii). But it has been noted by other critics how this humanistic fascination with the "popular" did not go hand in hand with a "continued vitality of popular culture" itself. On the contrary: the cataloging of popular forms coincided with, and was a symptom of, the objectification of these forms into material for "learned study, literary representation and pastoral reform" (Stephen J. Greenblatt, *Learning to Curse: Essays in Early Modern Culture* [New York and London: Routledge, 1990], 68). With specific regard to Rabelais, Greenblatt states: "Indeed, some of Rabelais's power derives from the evanescence of the festive tradition, or more accurately, from the sense of a literary, social, and religious world hardening in its commitment to order, discipline and decorum" (68). See also Peter Burke's remarks on the "reform of popular culture" in process in the sixteenth and seventeenth centuries throughout Europe (*Popular Culture in Early Modern Europe* [New York: New York University Press, 1978], in particular, chs. 8 and 9).

2. Mario Petrini, *La fiaba di magia nella letteratura italiana* (Udine: Del Bianco, 1983), 20.

3. Marina Warner, *From the Beast to the Blonde: On Fairy Tales and Their Tellers* (New York: Farrar, Straus and Giroux, 1995), 148. Although fairy tales had been included in earlier novella collections, such as Straparola's *Le piacevoli notti*, never before had there appeared an entire collection of fairy tales framed by another fairy tale. See the first pages of the essay by Jack Zipes in this volume for further information on Straparola's *Notti*. For an insightful analysis of the *Notti*, see the two essays on Straparola ("Sui materiali in opera nella *Piacevoli notti* di Giovan Francesco Straparola" and "La narrativa di Giovan Francesco Straparola: società

e struttura del personaggio fiabesco") in Giancarlo Mazzacurati, *Società e strutture narrative dal Trecento al Cinquecento* (Naples: Liguori, 1971), and Giorgio Bàrberi Squarotti, "Problemi di tecnica narrativa cinquecentesca: lo Straparola," *Sigma* 2, no. 6 (1965): 84–108.

4. For more on the audience of *Lo cunto*, see Michele Rak, "Il racconto fiabesco," in Giambattista Basile, *Lo cunto de li cunti*, ed. Michele Rak (Milan: Garzanti, 1986), 1055–1111.

5. A number of critics have remarked on the appropriateness of the fairy tale as a baroque genre. See, for example, Alberto Asor Rosa: "Il mondo complicato e nello stesso tempo ingenuo, infantile, della fiaba veniva incontro a quel senso così diffuso della meraviglia, anch'esso raffinato e puerile, colto e superficiale, che contraddistingue gli sviluppi della letteratura italiana fra la crisi del Rinascimento e la fioritura del barocco" [The complicated and at the same time innocent and childlike world of the fairy tale encountered that pervasive sense of the marvelous, also refined and childlike, learned and superficial, that distinguishes Italian literature between the crisis of the Renaissance and the flowering of the baroque]. "Giambattista Basile," *Dizionario biografico degli italiani* (Rome: Istituto della Enciclopedia Italiana, 1971) 7:80. This and all other translations from secondary sources are my own.

6. José Antonio Maravall, *Culture of the Baroque: Analysis of a Historical Structure*, trans. Terry Cochran (Minneapolis: University of Minnesota Press, 1986), 182.

7. For more extensive biographical information, see Vittorio Imbriani, "Il Gran Basile. Studio biografico e bibliografico," *Giornale napoletano di Filosofia e Lettere, Scienze morali e politiche*, 1 (1875): 23–55, and 2 (1875): 194–219, 335–66, and 413–59; Benedetto Croce, *Saggi sulla letteratura italiana del Seicento* (Bari: Laterza, 1911), 3–24, and Salvatore S. Nigro, "Dalla lingua al dialetto. La letteratura popolaresca," *I poeti giocosi dell'età barocca*, by Alberto Asor Rosa and Salvatore S. Nigro (Bari: Laterza, 1979), 106–7.

8. Michele Rak, *Napoli gentile. La letteratura in "lingua napoletana" nella cultura barocca (1596–1632)* (Bologna: Il Mulino, 1994), 41.

9. Rak summarizes: "Era l'ambiente—a metà cortigiano e teatrale—per cui Basile, i suoi fratelli e sorelle e nipoti preparavano le loro canzoni non troppo culte e non troppo popolari, saccheggiando tutti i patrimoni alla ricerca del solo effetto utile per un cortigiano: il consenso e il divertimento dei suoi ascoltatori" [It was the environment—in part that of the courts, in part that of the theater—in which Basile, his brothers, sisters, nieces and nephews prepared their works, which were neither too learned nor too popular, and for which they sacked all available heritages in their search for the only effects important for a courtier: consensus and the amusement of the audience]. *Napoli gentile*, 55.

10. Benedetto Croce, ed. and trans., *Il Pentamerone*, by Giambattista Basile. 2vols. (Bari: Laterza, 1982), xl.

11. Amedeo Quondam, *La parola nel labirinto. Società e scrittura del Manierismo a Napoli* (Bari: Laterza, 1975), 114; Giulio Ferroni, *Storia della letteratura italiana. Dal Cinquecento al Settecento* (Turin: Einaudi, 1981), 280.

12. Rak, *Napoli gentile*, 317.

13. See Umberto Eco's remarks on the "open form" of the baroque in chapter 1 ("The Poetics of the Open Work") of his *The Role of the Reader* (Bloomington: Indiana University Press, 1984). With regard to the "plastic mass" in the baroque work of art, he notes that it "never allows a privileged, definitive, frontal view; rather, it induces the spectator to shift his position continuously in order to see the work in constantly new aspects." He continues: "man opts out of the canon of authorized responses and finds that he is faced . . . by a world in a fluid state which requires corresponding creativity on his part" (52). For the concept of heteroglossia see Mikhail Bakhtin, *The Dialogic Imagination*, ed. Michael Holquist. Trans. Caryl Emerson and Michael Holquist (Austin: University of Texas Press, 1981).

14. Greenblatt defines "cultural negotiation and exchange" as "the points at which one cultural practice intersects with another, borrowing its forms and intensities or attempting to ward off unwelcome appropriations or moving texts and artifacts from one place to another" (*Learning to Curse*, 169).

15. Rak, *Napoli gentile*, 312.

16. Rak notes how "la cultura della modernità è stata prodotta anche da quest'idea dominante: che tutti i testi siano leggibili in altre lingue, ogni volta perdendo qualcosa della cultura che li ha preparati ma certamente guadagnando qualcosa d'altro in un'altra cultura" [the culture of modernity was produced by this dominant idea: that all texts are legible in other languages, and that each time they are "translated" they lose something of the culture that created them but they also certainly acquire something else from the contact with another culture]. *Napoli gentile*, 37.

17. Vladimir Propp, *Morphology of the Folktale*, 2nd ed., trans. Laurence Scott, rev. and ed. Louis A. Wagner. (Austin: University of Texas Press, 1968), 88.

18. This characteristic of Basile's text has been frequently noted. Vittorio Imbriani first commented on what he saw as the reconciliation of "personalità spiccata e impersonalità popolare" [distinct personality and popular impersonality] in *Lo cunto* ("Il gran Basile," 448), and Bruno Porcelli has more recently considered similar issues ("Il senso del molteplice nel *Pentamerone*," in *Novellieri italiani. Dal Sacchetti al Basile* [Ravenna: Longo, 1969], 195).

19. Neapolitan had been used for *villanelle* and other popular forms of the fifteenth and sixteenth centuries, but only in the seventeenth century did it acquire full-fledged literary status. As Benedetto Croce notes: "Il Basile, come il Cortese, non scrivevano un dialetto già letterariamente formato e definito, ma un dialetto che essi andavano creando come lingua letteraria, nella sua grammatica e nella sua ortografia" [Basile, like Cortese, did not write in a dialect that was already formed and well-defined in literary terms, but in a dialect that they themselves were in the process of creating as a literary language, in its grammar and spelling]. Introduction, *Lo cunto de li cunti*, by Giambattista Basile (Naples: Biblioteca Napoletana di Storia e Letteratura, 1891), clxxxii. Rak makes a similar observation: "Sino al decennio 1590–1610 la lingua napoletana costituì raramente una componente pregiata della cultura locale" [Until the decade 1590–1610 the Neapolitan language was rarely considered an esteemed component of local culture]. *Napoli gentile*, 88.

20. Quondam, *La parola*, 305.

21. Basile, at the tail end of the medieval and Renaissance novella tradition, while employing some of its conventions exits from it to elaborate the literary fairy tale; Cortese turns many of the conventions of the epic on their head in his popular mock-epics that have as protagonists urban servants and lowlifes; Sgruttendio's *canzoniere*, which celebrates the gritty, lower-class "lady" Cecca, is a bawdy reversal of the Petrarchan mode. A significant reference to the self-conscious canonization of Neapolitan literature can be found in the fourth canto of Cortese's *Viaggio di Parnaso* (1621).

22. Rak, *Napoli gentile*, 197 and 312.

23. See Rak, *Napoli gentile*, 41. See also Michele Rak, "La tradizione letteraria popolare-dialettale napoletana tra la conquista spagnola e le rivoluzioni del 1647–48" (in *Storia di Napoli*, vol. 7 [Naples, 1974], esp. 422–23), for a discussion of the esthetic and ideological judgments implicit in the choice of dialect in this period. Mario Petrini discusses Basile's use of dialect "per scrollarsi di dosso le incrostazioni stilistiche che il genere 'novella' si portava dietro" [to shake off the stylistic incrustations that the novella genre was burdened with]. *La fiaba di magia*, 62.

24. Stefano Calabrese, "La favola del linguaggio: il 'come se' del Pentamerone" (*Lingua e stile XVI* [Jan.–Mar. 1981]: 18–19).

25. Calabrese, "La favola," 20. See also Rak for a discussion of the divergences between Basile and other dialect authors of his time, especially Giulio Cesare Cortese ("La tradizione," 484).

26. Calabrese ("La favola," 21) comments on this absence of a "metaliterary" frame in *Lo cunto*: "Fra l'altro—sembra dirci Basile—quello fiabesco è un 'genere' così standardizzato che un *frame* nel senso proprio del termine non è indispensabile: il celebre 'C'era una volta' ('Dice ch'era 'na volta'), il cui uso si istituzionalizza proprio col Basile, equivale di per sé all'*as though* della cornice" [Among other things, Basile seems to be saying to us, the fairy tale is such a standardized genre that a conventional frame is not indispensable: the famous "Once upon a time," whose use is institutionalized with Basile, is the equivalent in itself of the "as though" of the frame].

27. Basile, *Lo cunto de li cunti*, ed. Michele Rak, 10. All subsequent quotations are from this edition (page numbers given in parentheses), and all translations are mine.

28. Croce, *Il Pentamerone*, 539.

29. For a discussion of the move from Renaissance *imitatio* to baroque *inventio* see, for example, Ezio Raimondi, *Letteratura barocca* (Florence: Olschki, 1982), lxvii.

30. Rak notes how this sequence is a "sintetico elenco delle pratiche teatrali e festive del teatro basso ricordate nella tradizione in napoletano" [synthetic list of the theatrical and festive practices of popular theater that are frequently evoked in the Neapolitan tradition]. *Napoli gentile*, 99.

31. Fredric Jameson, *The Political Unconscious: Narrative as a Socially Symbolic Act* (Ithaca: Cornell University Press, 1981), 86.

32. Vladimir Propp, "The Ritual Uses of Laughter," in *Theory and History of Folklore*,

ed. and intro. Anatoly Liberman. Trans. Ariadna Y. Martin and Richard P. Martin (Minneapolis: Minnesota University Press, 1984), 131.

33. *Napoli gentile*, 365. Rak also comments on how, owing to this central role of festivities, they became central *loci* of the "collective imagination" (366): "Le feste vanno considerate il regolatore della comunicazione sociale nell'area. . . . erano confronti rituali, battaglie segniche e non sanguinose tra i gruppi all'interno della città. Il sistema delle feste stabilizzava i luoghi obbligati dell'immaginario" [Festivals should be considered as regulators of social communication in this area. . . . they were ritual confrontations, bloodless battles of signs between the various groups who lived in the city. The system of the festivals rendered stable the obligatory sites of the collective imagination].

34. For information on political and economic developments in the Kingdom of these years see Benedetto Croce, *Storia del Regno di Napoli* (1925; reprint, Bari: Laterza, 1984), and, especially, Rosario Villari, *La rivolta antispagnola a Napoli* (Bari: Laterza, 1967). For another brief but suggestive analysis of this scene see Paolo Valesio, *Ascoltare il silenzio* (Bologna: Il Mulino, 1986), 322–25. Valesio makes the observation, similar to those that I have proposed, that: "Questo spargimento di olio si pone come duplice trasgressione, violando com'esso fa un'etica predominantemente sociale e un'etica tutto economica" (323) ["This outpouring of oil is posed as a double transgression, since it violates a predominantly social ethic as well as another ethic which is purely economical]. But Valesio ultimately sees the flowing of oil as "l'emblema della retorica scatenata—forse, della retorica impazzita. Esso viene a simboleggiare, insomma, il discorso umano in quanto esso ha raggiunto la sua pienezza, il discorso che rischia di traboccare, in dispersione e dissolvimento" (324) [the emblem of unleashed rhetoric—perhaps, of rhetoric gone crazy. It comes to symbolize, in short, human discourse at its fullest, discourse that risks overflowing into dispersion and dissolution].

35. One of the masters of the Italian (and European) pastoral tradition was Neapolitan himself—Jacopo Sannazaro. His late-fifteenth-century *Arcadia* was an important point of reference for both elite literary culture and the Neapolitan dialect writers.

36. Gino Benzoni, *Gli affanni della cultura. Intellettuali e potere nell'Italia della Controriforma e barocca* (Milan: Feltrinelli, 1978), 136. At this time there was also an explosion of writings that portrayed the poorest categories of the urban lower classes—prostitutes, beggars, the homeless—in a merciless light.

37. Bakhtin, *Rabelais*, 285 and 71.

38. This is an interesting, and ironic, variation on the bad luck that spilling oil proverbially, then as now, brings. In this case, though, what changes after the oil spills is not luck, but the course of the narration.

39. See Bakhtin's discussion of the "classical body" and the "grotesque body" as emblems of two distinct traditions (*Rabelais*, 49 and 154).

40. Rak comments, with regard to the role of laughter in the realm of the "low style" of dialect literature: "Faceva ridere tutto quello che la letteratura culta non nominava perché contraddiceva le buone maniere" [Everything that learned literature did not name because it went against good manners became a source of laughter]. *Napoli gentile*, 13–14.

41. Bakhtin discusses at length these two conceptions of laughter: one in which it is relegated to "low" literary genres and "light amusement," and the other in which it is a complex expression of a folk culture whose roots extend far back in time and share traits with rituals, etc., of preliterate societies. And he sees this very period, the seventeenth century, as the point in which the rich laughter of folk culture loses its universality and is exiled from "high" literature. (*Rabelais*, 66–67.)

42. Propp, "Ritual Uses," 131. See also Bakhtin, *Rabelais*, esp. ch. 1.

43. Bakhtin, *Rabelais*, 66–67.

44. See Propp, "Ritual Uses," 139, and Warner, *From the Beast*, 150, who notes the similarities between Basile's scene and these classical precedents.

45. See Propp, "Ritual Uses," 143–44.

46. There is a clear reference, in the figure of Lucia, to the *luciata*, a contemporary "microgenre" of street theater that centers around "Lucia's dance," already mentioned in the list of popular amusements used at the start of the frame tale to attempt to coax Zoza to laugh. Rak discusses a typical *luciata* of 1628, which had as its protagonists black slaves (among whom the principal is Lucia) as well as commedia dell'arte masks. Lucia dances provocatively, is joined in her "dirty dancing" by another slave, who when the dance ends announces that he has possessed Lucia. The spectacle ends as the newborn baby is brought onto the stage, and the wild dancing resumes (*Napoli gentile*, 129–31). In the frame Lucia, then, we see yet another representative figure of Neapolitan popular culture who has "escaped" from her tradition to take on a very different role, and yet another allusion to Basile's project of reworking the contours of this culture to fit into the new genre that he is constructing.

47. Warner, *From the Beast*, 43. Warner cites earlier examples of tales told by gossipy women with burlesque names, specifically the 1475 collection *Les Evangiles des quenouilles* [The Gospel of Distaves], one of the first secular collections attributed to women authors (36–37).

48. Marziano Guglielminetti, *Sulla novella italiana. Genesi e generi* (Lecce: Milella, 1990), 31 (Guglielminetti cites Giorgio Bárberi Squarotti).

49. For more on Basile's tellers, see Ada Testaferri, "Baroque Women in Medieval Roles: The Narrative Voices in Basile's *Pentamerone*," *Rivista di Studi Italiani* 8, nos. 1–2 (June–Dec. 1990): 39–45.

50. Games were a common form of social recreation among the upper classes in courtly circles, and were frequently evoked in novella frames. The most famous Renaissance description of this sort of gaming is found in Baldassare Castiglione's *Libro del Cortegiano* (published in 1528), but see also Stefano Guazzo's *La civil conversazione* (1574), and esp. book 4, where a group of ten people play "il gioco della solitudine," which has striking structural similarities with Basile's *iuoco de li iuoche* (Stefano Guazzo, *La civil conversazione*, ed. Amedeo Quondam, 2 vols. [Modena: Franco Cosimo Panini Editore, 1993]). See also the proceedings of a 1991 conference held in Pienza, Italy, on medieval and Renaissance games, published as *Passare il tempo. La letteratura del gioco e dell'intrattenimento dal XII al XVI secolo* (Rome: Salerno Editrice, 1993). French authors later in the century also had a predilection for linking fairy tales to games: in many cases, in fact, fairy

tales grew out of salon games and storytelling. Lewis Seifert specifies that "the seventeenth-century [French] fairy tales are often embedded in frame-narratives as a jeu d'esprit, a salon game in which one player improvises according to certain rules while the others guess at the meaning of the riddle-like piece" (*Fairy Tales, Sexuality, and Gender in France, 1690–1715: Nostalgic Utopias* [Cambridge: Cambridge University Press, 1996], 76.

51. From Norman Penzer's English translation of *Lo cunto* (*The Pentameron of Giambattista Basile,* 2 vols. [London: John Lane and the Bodley Head, 1932], 110).

52. This reference to taking off pants recalls the crone at the beginning of the frame tale. It could be said that the woman's subversive gesture has been by this point co-opted by the motley court and made part of their socially acceptable gaming, while Zoza, in a sense, reacts against this move.

53. See Calabrese, "La favola," 24.

54. Penzer, *Pentamerone,* 24.

55. The donkey that defecates gold is, of course, a standard folkloric topos. Another representation of such a donkey, which supports the interpretation of Antuono's magic objects as figures of the popular, "unofficial" traditions that Basile retrieves, can be found in G. C. Cortese's *Viaggio di Parnaso* (1621). In the first canto the poet-traveler comes across a donkey who, instead of gold, lets go four dialect poems by Cortese himself. See Rak, *Napoli gentile,* 174.

56. Rak notes how in Basile's tales "la trasformazione si realizza tra l'intervento di un potere violento e capriccioso—impersonato dagli orchi e dalle fate—, le imprevedibili concatenazioni del Caso e gli strumenti magici dei letterati. A turno sono questi tre elementi che producono la metamorfosi e il miglioramento sociale" [transformations are effected by interventions of violent and capricious powers—impersonated by ogres and fairies—, unpredictable concatenations of Fate and the magical instruments of the learned. These three elements take turns in producing metamorphosis and betterment of social status]. *Napoli gentile,* 303.

57. Max Lüthi, *The Fairytale as Art Form and Portrait of Man,* trans. Jon Erickson. (Bloomington: Indiana University Press, 1984), 40–41. Lüthi also comments on the rarity of extravagant metaphor in fairy tales: "Metaphors condense, create a complex whole; the comparison separates, sets up two poles. It is simpler than the metaphor, more artless; it corresponds to the tendency in the fairy tale toward juxtaposition (parataxis, sequencing of episodes, good beside bad, etc.) while the metaphor creates a merger" (110–11). I do not intend to discuss metaphor and simile within the context of baroque poetics; suffice it to say that the former was vastly preferred to the latter. See, for example, Frank Warnke, *Versions of Baroque: European Literature in the Seventeenth Century* (New Haven: Yale University Press, 1972), 22: "Baroque literature displays an obsessive concern with the contradictory nature of experience. In poetry, for example, simile largely gives way to metaphor." See also Giuseppe Conte, *La metafora barocca* (Milan: Mursia, 1972).

58. Aristotle, Poetics 1458b, cited in "Metaphor," *Princeton Encyclopedia of Poetry and Poetics,* enlarged ed., ed. Alex Preminger et al. (Princeton: Princeton University Press, 1974), 491.

59. "Gli oggetti si mettono a girare, come le parole. Il relativismo e il pluralismo prospettico, tipici della visione del mondo barocco, intervengono a improntare le pagine più animate del *Pentamerone*" [Objects begin to move, as do words. Relativism and the pluralism of perspectives, typical of the baroque worldview, leave their mark on the most animated pages of the *Pentamerone*]. Giovanni Getto, *Barocco in prosa e in poesia* (Milan: Rizzoli, 1969), 386. See also Italo Calvino, who observes that "l'operazione di Basile è pienamente riuscita là dove tra fabulazione ed espressione verbale si forma una specie di osmosi, per esempio quando il convulso antropomorfismo del mondo inanimato sconfina dal piano della metafora a quello dei fatti narrati" [Basile's operation meets with complete success in those cases in which storytelling and verbal expression have a sort of osmotic relationship, for example when the convulsive anthropomorphism of the inanimate world leaves the metaphoric plane and enters the plane of the narrated events], and cites as an example the episode near the beginning of "La cerva fatata," in which, while a handmaid is shut up in a room preparing a sea-dragon's heart that will serve to impregnate the infertile queen, she herself, and all of the furniture in the room, become pregnant and after several days give birth (*Sulla fiaba* [Turin: Einaudi, 1988], 140).

60. Claudio Varese notes that in *Lo cunto* "nasce . . . una forma di equivoco non esclusivamente scherzoso e lubrico, ma in una certa misura morale. La metafora assume una funzione di indagine e insieme di giudizio" [is born . . . a form of equivocation that is not exclusively playful and bawdy, but to a certain degree also moral. Metaphor functions to investigate, as well as to judge]. Cited in Calabrese, "La favola," 27.

61. "Avere le corna" [to have horns] means, in Italian as in Neapolitan, to be cuckolded.

62. The seventeenth century was, in the Kingdom of Naples, a time of growing strain on the social fabric, owing to heavy taxation, scarcity of primary foodstuffs, and a general lawlessness resulting from power conflicts between the Spanish "colonial" government and the local aristocracy. This situation led to rebellion by some sectors of the lower classes (for example, in the form of banditry or organized movements such as the 1647 "revolt of Masaniello"), increased marginalization of certain social groups (destitute peasants—like the old woman of this tale—beggars, and so forth), and increasingly repressive measures on the part of both monarchical and local government. For an excellent survey of the fragile power relations in the seventeenth-century Kingdom of Naples, see Villari, *La rivolta*. For other literary representations of social marginality, see Piero Camporesi, *La maschera di Bertoldo*, 2nd rev. ed. (Milan: Garzanti, 1993). See also Croce's remarks, in *Storia del regno*, 111–13, on the decay of the nobility and the rise of a certain middle class, especially lawyers and speculators, in the Kingdom of Naples of this time, as well as on the "inflation" of noble titles.

63. The passages from Petrarch are from the *Rerum vulgarium fragmenta* (*Rime Sparse*), 185 and 327. Rak notes that the *Rerum* was "uno dei modelli per la tradizione della lirica italiana" [one of the models for the Italian lyric tradition]. *Lo cunto*, 274 n. 57. The verse from the *Aeneid* ("tre volte cadde . . .") is found at the end

of book 4, and is cited in the 1581 translation of Annibale Caro (Rak, *Lo cunto,* 555 ns. 15, 16, and 18).

64. Rak comments on how canonical classical and Tuscan authors were often used by writers in Neapolitan as low comic relief, but also as part of a general critique of literary and social institutions: "I frammenti aulici vengono usati per argomenti ir- regolari come l'evacuazione o la sensualità, con un effetto di parodia dell'ideologia letteraria e delle sue forme di celebrazione del potere politico e religioso" [erudite fragments are used for "incorrect" topics such as defecation or sensuality, with the effect that the reigning literary ideology and its forms of celebration of political and religious powers are parodied]. Another technique used at this time for addressing the ideology of literary production was the translation of classic authors into Neapolitan (*Napoli gentile,* 135–36). See Camporesi for discussion of other Italian attempts to "turn upside down" official culture. The classic study on this subject remains, of course, Bakhtin's *Rabelais and His World.*

65. The reference is, of course, to Pygmalion, and this is a curious example, and not the only one of its sort in *Lo cunto,* of how for Basile's characters the fact that they inhabit a fairy tale where the most marvelous transformations are possible does not always suffice to resolve their dilemmas. In such cases, the legitimizing authority of another tradition (in this case, classical mythology) needs to be evoked in order for the tale to progress.

66. Calabrese, "Dalla favola," 18–19.

67. In the preamble to this tale, the importance of having *ingegno* is presented as the main theme of the tale: "se vede pe lo chiù persona che n'ha trascurso saglire dov'è lo bene, ma pe carestia de 'nciegno vrociolarene a bascio" (910; emphasis mine) [we often see people who lack reason climb up to good, but then, for lack of wits ('*nciegno*) tumble down again].

68. Cortese, in his *Viaggio di Parnaso,* describes Neapolitan itself in similarly "de- licious" terms: "Le parole de Napole 'mpastate / non songo, frate mio, d'oro pommiento / ma de zuccaro e mele" ("The words of Naples are kneaded, my brother, not of false gold but of sugar and honey" (1.22; cited in Rak, *Napoli gentile,* 185).

Bibliography

Asor Rosa, Alberto. "Giambattista Basile." In *Dizionario biografico degli italiani.* Rome: Istituto della Enciclopedia Italiana, 1971. 7:80.

Bakhtin, Mikhail. *Rabelais and His World.* Trans. Hélène Iswolsky. Bloomington: Indiana University Press, 1984.

——. *The Dialogic Imagination.* Ed. Michael Holquist. Trans. Caryl Emerson and Michael Holquist. Austin: University of Texas Press, 1981.

Bárberi Squarotti, Giorgio. "Problemi di tecnica narrativa cinquecentesca: lo Stra- parola." *Sigma* 2, no. 6 (1965): 84–108.

Basile, Giambattista. *Lo cunto de li cunti.* Ed. Michele Rak. Milan: Garzanti, 1986.

——. *The Pentameron of Giambattista Basile.* 2 vols. Trans. and ed. Norman Penzer. London: John Lane and the Bodley Head, 1932.

Battisti, Eugenio. *L'antirinascimento*. Milan: Garzanti, 1989.

Benzoni, Gino. *Gli affanni della cultura. Intellettuali e potere nell'Italia della Controriforma e barocca*. Milan: Feltrinelli, 1978.

Borsellino, Nino. *Gli anticlassicisti del Cinquecento*. Bari: Laterza, 1975.

Burke, Peter. *Popular Culture in Early Modern Europe*. New York: New York University Press, 1978.

Calabrese, Stefano. "La favola del linguaggio: il 'come se' del Pentamerone." *Lingua e stile* 16 (Jan.–Mar. 1981): 13–34.

Calvino, Italo. *Sulla fiaba*. Turin: Einaudi, 1988.

Camporesi, Piero. *La maschera di Bertoldo*. 2nd rev. ed. Milan: Garzanti, 1993.

Cocchiara, Giuseppe. *The History of Folklore in Europe*. Trans. John N. McDaniel. Philadelphia: Institute for the Study of Human Issues, 1981 (1952).

Conte, Giuseppe. *La metafora barocca*. Milan: Mursia, 1972.

Croce, Benedetto, ed. *Lo cunto de li cunti*, by Giambattista Basile. Naples: Biblioteca Napoletana di Storia e Letteratura, 1891.

———, ed. and trans. *Il Pentamerone*, by Giambattista Basile. 2 vols. Bari: Laterza, 1982.

———. *Saggi sulla letteratura italiana del Seicento*. Bari: Laterza, 1911.

———. *Storia del Regno di Napoli*. 1925. Reprint, Bari: Laterza, 1984.

Eco, Umberto. *The Role of the Reader*. Bloomington: Indiana University Press, 1984.

Ferroni, Giulio. *Storia della letteratura italiana. Dal Cinquecento al Settecento*. Turin: Einaudi, 1981.

Getto, Giovanni. *Barocco in prosa e in poesia*. Milan: Rizzoli, 1969.

Greenblatt, Stephen J. *Learning to Curse: Essays in Early Modern Culture*. New York and London: Routledge, 1990.

Guazzo, Stefano. *La civil conversazione*. Ed. Amedeo Quondam. 2 vols. Modena: Franco Cosimo Panini Editore, 1993.

Guglielminetti, Marziano. *Sulla novella italiana. Genesi e generi*. Lecce: Milella, 1990.

Imbriani, Vittorio. "Il Gran Basile. Studio biografico e bibliografico." *Giornale napoletano di Filosofia e Lettere, Scienze morali e politiche* 1 (1875): 23–55, and 2 (1875): 194–219, 335–66, and 413–59.

Jackson, Rosemary. *Fantasy: The Literature of Subversion*. London and New York: Methuen, 1981.

Jameson, Fredric. *The Political Unconscious: Narrative as a Socially Symbolic Act*. Ithaca: Cornell University Press, 1981.

Lüthi, Max. *The European Folktale: Form and Nature*. Trans. John D. Niles. Bloomington: Indiana University Press, 1986.

———. *The Fairytale as Art Form and Portrait of Man*. Trans. Jon Erickson. Bloomington: Indiana University Press, 1984.

Maravall, José Antonio. *Culture of the Baroque: Analysis of a Historical Structure*. Trans. Terry Cochran. Minneapolis: University of Minnesota Press, 1986.

Mazzacurati, Giancarlo. *Società e strutture narrative dal Trecento al Cinquecento*. Naples: Liguori, 1971.

Nigro, Salvatore S. "Dalla lingua al dialetto. La letteratura popolaresca." In *I poeti giocosi dell'età barocca* by Alberto Asor Rosa and Salvatore S. Nigro. Bari: Laterza, 1979.

Passare il tempo. La letteratura del gioco e dell'intrattenimento dal XII al XVI secolo. Rome: Salerno Editrice, 1993.

Petrini, Mario. *La fiaba di magia nella letteratura italiana.* Udine: Del Bianco, 1983.

Porcelli, Bruno. "Il senso del molteplice nel *Pentamerone.*" In *Novellieri italiani. Dal Sacchetti al Basile.* Ravenna: Longo, 1969.

Princeton Encyclopedia of Poetry and Poetics. Ed. Alex Preminger et al. Princeton: Princeton University Press, 1974.

Propp, Vladimir. *Morphology of the Folktale.* 2nd ed. Trans. Laurence Scott, rev. and ed. Louis A. Wagner. Austin: University of Texas Press, 1968.

―――. "The Ritual Uses of Laughter." In *Theory and History of Folklore.* Ed. and intro. Anatoly Liberman. Trans. Ariadna Y. Martin and Richard P. Martin. Minneapolis: Minnesota University Press, 1984.

Quondam, Amedeo. *La parola nel labirinto. Società e scrittura del Manierismo a Napoli.* Bari: Laterza, 1975.

Raimondi, Ezio. *Letteratura barocca.* Florence: Olschki, 1982.

Rak, Michele. "La tradizione letteraria popolare-dialettale napoletana tra la conquista spagnola e le rivoluzioni del 1647–48." *Storia di Napoli.* Vol. 7. Naples, 1974.

―――. *Napoli gentile. La letteratura in "lingua napoletana" nella cultura barocca (1596–1632).* Bologna: Il Mulino, 1994.

Seifert, Lewis C. *Fairy Tales, Sexuality and Gender in France, 1690–1715: Nostalgic Utopias.* Cambridge: Cambridge University Press, 1996.

Testaferri, Ada. "Baroque Women in Medieval Roles: The Narrative Voices in Basile's *Pentamerone.*" *Rivista di Studi Italiani* 8, nos. 1–2 (June–Dec. 1990): 39–45.

Valesio, Paolo. *Ascoltare il silenzio.* Bologna: Il Mulino, 1986.

Villari, Rosario. *La rivolta antispagnola a Napoli.* Bari: Laterza, 1967.

Warner, Marina. *From the Beast to the Blonde: On Fairy Tales and Their Tellers.* New York: Farrar, Straus and Giroux, 1995.

Warnke, Frank. *Versions of Baroque: European Literature in the Seventeenth Century.* New Haven: Yale University Press, 1972.

CHAPTER 2

Beauty and the Hag:
Appearance and Reality in Basile's
Lo cunto de li cunti

Antonella Ansani

 ACCORDING TO many folklore scholars, one of the distinctive traits of the folktale is its predilection for sharp conflicts: the tales' protagonists, for example, are either kings or paupers, beautiful or ugly, good or evil.[1] Among these oppositions, the dichotomy between appearance and reality is the theme that "stands in first place in the fairy tale."[2] It should not come as a surprise, then, to find this opposition at the core of Giambattista Basile's *Lo cunto de li cunti* [The Tale of Tales; 1634–36], the first European collection of literary fairy tales, for the conflict between appearance and reality is not only characteristic of the fairy tale, but is also one of the dominant antitheses taken up in seventeenth-century literature.[3] In this essay I will show that Basile, while adopting the themes and formal features of the genre as a model for his innovative literary fairy tales, at the same time calls these very features into question, suggesting that the extreme oppositions of the fairy tale are not so unequivocally delimited. As critics have recognized,[4] the opposition between appearance and reality is extensively thematized in the four eclogues that conclude the first four days of narration, particularly in the first, "La coppella" [The Crucible], which develops the idea of the discrepancy existing between essence and pretense, of the difference between people's true nature and the mask that conceals it:

> Quanto a la 'ncornatura e a primma fronte
> pare cosa de priezzo,

tutto 'nganna la vista,
tutto ceca la gente,
tutto è schitto apparenzia.
Non ire summo summo,
non ire scorza scorza,
ma spercia e trase drinto,
ca chi non pesca 'n funno
è no bello catammaro a sto munno!
adopra sta coppella, ca fai prova
se lo negozio è vero o fegneticcio,
s'è cepolla sguigliata o s'è pasticcio.[5]

[All things that in appearance at first sight
Seem most to be of worth, are a deceit
Blinding the sight with nought but outward show.
You should not cease to penetrate within,
Cut through the bark, fish to the lowest depths,
Or you will be accounted for a fool.
But use this crucible and you shall prove
If the thing in hand be pure or tainted,
If the face be natural or painted.][6]

In this first eclogue, Basile cynically portrays all contemporary social types: noblemen, courtiers, merchants, soldiers, lovers, astrologers, and scholars; and he unmasks the bleak reality of their conditions. Women are not spared either; Basile also directs his satire against their artificial physical appearance:

Si vide pe fortuna a na fenestra
una, che pare a te che sia na fata,
ha li capille iunne,
che pareno a bedere
catenelle de casocavalluccio;
lo fronte comme a schiecco,
ogn'uocchio che te parla e mire 'n frutto
doie lavra comme a felle de presutto;
no piezzo de schiantone,
auta e desposta comme a confalone
e tu non tanto 'nce haie 'mpizzato l'uocchie,
che muore ashevoluto,
che spanteche speruto!
catammaro, catarchio,
saccela coppellare,

ca chello che te pare
na bellezza de sfuorgio
trovarraie ch'è no destro 'mpetenato,
no muro 'ntonacato,
mascara ferrarese,
ca la zita have spase li trappite:
le trezze so' a posticcio,
le ciglia songo tente a la tiella,
la facce rossa a chiù de na scotella
de magra, cauce vergene e bernice,
ca s'alliscia, se 'nchiacca,
se strellicca, se 'nchiastra e se 'mpallacca!
tutta cuonce ed agniente,
tutta pezze, arvarelle,
purvere e carrafelle,
che pare, quanno fa tanto apparato,
che boglia medecare no 'nchiagato!
quanta defiette e quanta
copreno le camorre e sottanielle!
otra ca si se leva li chianielli,
co tante chiastre e tante cioffe e tante,
vedarraie fatto naimo no giagante. (254–56)

[If you should chance to raise your eyes
There at the window, one who seems to be
A fairy having hair of purest gold
Like chains of caciocavalluccio hung,
Her forehead seems of highly polished glass,
Her eyes both look and speak, and then her lips
Are like some tasty morsel. She's indeed
A sturdy plant, as upright and as tall
As any gonfalone you may see.
The moment you have cast your eyes on her,
Burning with passion, you will faint away
With longing to possess her as your own.
Oh, what a fool, an idiot you become.
Quickly now, put her in the crucible.
For she who seems so wonderful to you,
Of such amazing beauty, you will find
Is nothing but a polished privy stool,
A whitewashed wall, a mask from Ferrara,
A bride who will display her house all draped,

With clothes and carpets! All her hair is false,
Her eyebrows tinted from a sooty pan,
Her cheeks more red than a vermilion bowl,
With purest chalk, and with enamel too
She smooths her wrinkles, and then on a base
Of pearly hue she daubs and paints her face—
Cosmetics, ointments, colour-sticks and dyes,
Powders and little phials, so it seems
With all this apparatus that she tries
To heal the anguish of a wounded man.
What numbers of defects are hidden there
Under the petticoats and skirts, and now
If you remove the pattens from her feet
With all the thickness that make them up,
Then will the giantess become a dwarf. (122–23)]

This passage certainly supports Ruffo Chlodowski's observation that Basile's eclogues possess ideological poignancy, and are the key for grasping the intimate ideological and thematic unity of the *Cunto*. For him "La coppella," as well as the other eclogues, represent Basile's clear condemnation of appearance and falsehood, and his celebration of reality and truth.[7] Things, however, are not so straightforward in the *Cunto*, and the analysis that follows will demonstrate how Chlodowski's reading ultimately ends up being too literal.

Many elements indicate that in the *Cunto* the boundaries separating appearance and reality are ambiguously defined. Modeled on Giovanni Boccaccio's *Decameron*, the *Cunto*, narrated during five days (hence the other name by which it is known, *Pentamerone*), consists of forty-nine tales, which are framed by a fiftieth story, itself a fairy tale. Very succinctly, the frame tale runs as follows. Princess Zoza, daughter of the king of Valle Pelosa, has never been seen to laugh. In a last attempt to dispel her melancholy, her father has a fountain of oil built in front of his palace, so that people passing by will skid and fall, and will, he hopes, make her laugh. An old woman arrives and begins to fill a jar with the precious fluid. When a court page throws a stone and breaks the jar, a spirited verbal exchange ensues between the two. Eventually at a loss for words, the old woman in frustration lifts up her skirt and displays the "scena voscareccia" [woodland scene]. At this spectacle Zoza finally laughs, but her mirth enrages the old woman, who lays a curse on her: she will never have a husband unless she marries Tadeo, Prince of Campo Retunno, who under a spell is lying asleep at a fountain in another land. Zoza leaves on her quest for Tadeo, is endowed with magic gifts by three fairies, and finally arrives at the fountain where, in order to free Tadeo from the spell, she will have to fill a pitcher with her tears within three days. She has almost completed her task when, overcome by fatigue, she falls asleep. Lucia, a black slave who has been secretly watching her, takes her place, quickly fills the pitcher with her own tears, and thus secures Tadeo as a husband. Zoza follows them to their kingdom, where with the help of the three magic objects she inculcates in Lucia an uncontrollable desire to hear fairy tales. The ten best narrators in town are thus bidden to come to the palace; here they tell their tales to members of Tadeo's court who have gathered around a fountain in the garden. On the fifth day one of the tellers becomes ill, and Zoza, requested to take her place, narrates her personal tribulations in the last tale. Lucia is thus unmasked and consequently killed, and Zoza finally becomes Tadeo's wife.

The very structure of the frame tale undoubtedly points to the inde-terminate and specular relation between the real and the illusory. Differently from the model proposed by Boccaccio, where the frame story marks a movement from city to garden, from history to literature, the frame tale in the *Cunto* covers a circular route, from court to court, from fountain to fountain, from literature to literature, in a world where all separations and distinctions are blurred.[8]

This ambiguous relation between the real and the illusory is also con-veyed by the overwhelming presence of theatrical elements in the frame tale. Here, all of the king's attempts to make Zoza laugh are theatrical in nature: first, he assembles all different types of street theater performers: acrobats, singers, jugglers, gymnasts, dancers, and trained animals. Subsequently, the construction of the fountain of oil is meant to produce yet another theatrical performance:

> co designo che, sghizzanno a lo passare de la gente, che facevano comm'a formiche lo vacaviene pe chella strata, pe non se sodeg-nere li vestite averriano fatto zumpe de grille, sbauze de crapeio e corzete de leparo sciulianno e, morrannose chisto e chillo, potesse soccedere cosa pe la quale se scoppasse a ridere. (10)

> [He thought that the people passing like ants up and down the street, in order to avoid soiling their clothes with the jets of oil, would skip like grasshoppers, leap like goats and run like hares, slipping and stumbling, and that in this way something might happen to amuse his daughter and make her laugh. (4)]

By transforming the entire kingdom of Valle Pelosa into a living theater, the king's act literalizes the great baroque metaphor of "the world as a stage."

Tadeo's kingdom (and thus the reign of fairy tales), like the king of Valle Pelosa's land, is also represented as a vast theater.[9] Zoza's entrance into that kingdom begins through a stage, when she laughs at the old woman who, "auzato la tela de l'apparato fece vedere la scena voscareccia, dove potea dire Silvio 'Ite svegliano gli occhi col corno' " (12) [lifted up the curtain of the stage and displayed a woodland scene that might have inspired Silvio to say: "Go, awaken the eyes with the horn" (5)]. The old woman's eloquent gesture of raising up her skirt and showing her genitals is conveyed through very explicit theatrical references: the lifting of the stage curtain on the one hand, and on the other a quotation from Guarini's *Il pastor fido,* one of the most celebrated pastoral plays of the Renaissance. Again, we see that the baroque metaphor of "the world as a stage" is at the core of the *Cunto.* As José Antonio Maravall clearly illustrates, this metaphor conveys the baroque perception that the condition of the world is "similar to the stage representation, . . . that the boundaries between actor and spectator, between the daily world and the world of illusion come to be very fluid."[10]

Last, but not least, the most powerful manifestation of the lack of a clear delimitation between appearance and reality is Basile's phantasmagorical use of metaphor. As Giovanni Getto has maintained, in the *Cunto* there is a definite connection between the theme of appearance, of the mask behind which the true nature of things is concealed, and the theme of the perpetual transformative, metaphorical condition of reality.[11] This brief analysis offers just an indication of how many different elements contribute to the construction and formulation of the complex relation between reality and appearance in the *Cunto.* In addition, the following investigation of how the opposition between the illusory and the real unfolds in two tales of the *Cunto,* will both confirm the centrality of this theme and disclose its metaliterary significance in Basile's work.

The two tales, "La mortella," [The Myrtle (1.2)] and "La vecchia scortecata" [The Old Woman Who Was Skinned (1.10)], just like the passage from "La coppella" quoted above, deal with the beauty of women, albeit very differently and with a complexity absent in the eclogue.

In the story "La mortella," a woman's desperate desire to conceive is finally fulfilled; at the end of nine months of pregnancy, however, the woman gives birth not to a child but to a beautiful branch of myrtle. The king's son, seeing the plant on the windowsill, takes an instant fancy to it, and convinces the woman to let him take it home, where he puts it in his own bedroom, lovingly watering and caring for it himself. One night in the darkness, while everybody is asleep, the branch changes into a beautiful girl who lies in bed with the prince. For several nights the prince sleeps with the girl; he is so curious to see what this unknown velvety creature looks like that on the seventh night, when the girl is asleep, he calls a valet to light the candles, and in the light he sees the most beautiful girl one could possibly imagine. They sport night after night, but one day, when the prince is forced to leave, he asks the girl to return to the myrtle, which he entrusts to the care of a faithful servant. A bell, which is attached to the myrtle, will inform the plant of the prince's return. Feeling neglected, seven wanton women kept by the prince take advantage of his absence and break into his room to look for the cause of his sudden indifference toward them. When they ring the bell, the girl appears and is immediately torn to pieces by the jealous women, who divide the spoils of her body. The servant, arriving on the scene and finding this devastation, assembles any skin, bones, and blood he can find and replants them. When the prince returns and is in despair because the girl does not answer his calls, the fairy, who in the meanwhile has begun to grow again out of the planted remains, feels sorry for the prince and all of a sudden leaps out of the flowerpot and comes back to him. They marry, and the women who had attempted to slay the fairy are buried alive.

Like in the story of Cupid and Psyche, and many others belonging to the same type, the central moment of "La mortella" is constituted by the nocturnal visitation of a lover who, incarnated in a beautiful human body at night, is something else (a plant, a monster) during the day.[12] Implied in this double nature is the typical fairy-tale dichotomy between beauty and ugliness, good and evil, reality and appearance, where beauty, which is good and real, triumphs, while ugliness, which is evil and false, gets destroyed. In "La mortella" this opposition would seem somewhat softened by the fact that the fairy is beautiful both as woman and as plant. The myrtle/fairy is in fact presented in all its splendor; as a plant, she is repeatedly described as *bella*—lovely—and capable of enchanting the king's son. As a woman, her first embrace with the prince, as Italo Calvino remarks, is characterized by a rare "struggente trepidazione sensuale" [consuming sensual trepidation] and the description of their encounter is "uno dei più delicate passi del Basile" [one of Basile's most delicate passages.][13]

> Ma quando se sentette accostare lo chiaieto e tastianno se addon-
> aie dell'opera liscia e dove penzava de parpezzare puche d'estrece
> trovaie na cosella chiù mellese e morbeta de lana varvaresca, chiù
> pastosa e cenera de coda de martora, chiù delecata e tenera de
> penne de cardillo, se lanzaie da miezo a miezo e, stimannola na
> fata (comme era 'n effetto) se afferraie comme purpo e, ioquanno
> *a la passara muta*, facettero *a preta 'n sino*.
>   Ma, —'nnanze che lo sole scesse comme a protamiedeco a fare
> la visita de li shiure che stanno malate e languede—se sosette
> lo recapeto e sbignaie, lassanno lo prencepe chino de docezze,
> prieno de curiosità, carreco de maraveglia. (54–56)

[When he felt the person near him, and stretching out his hand felt something soft, and where he expected to find porcupine's quills discovered something softer and finer than Barbary wool, more downy and silky than a marten's tail, more yielding and tender than a bull-finch's feathers, he hastened to embrace her, thinking she must be a fairy (as indeed she was), and clinging to her like an octopus he began to play at "dumb sparrow" and "stone in the apron." However, before the Sun, like the head-physician, had been on the rounds to visit the flowers that night had rendered pale and languid, his companion rose and slipped away, leaving the Prince full of tenderness, teeming with curiosity, and aglow with wonder. (26–27)]

Once the prince finally sees her, his description of her beauty becomes even more eloquent:

"Ora va' te 'nforna, dea Cocetrigno! chiavate na funa 'ncanna, o Elena! tornatenne o Criosa, e Shiorella, ca le bellezze vostre so' zavanelle a paragone de sta bellezza a doi sole, bellezza comprita, 'nteregna, stascionata, massiccia, chiantuta! grazie de sisco, de Seviglia, de truono, de mascese, de 'mportolanzia, dove no 'nce truove piecco, no 'nce ashie zeta!" (56)

["Now be off and bake yourself, Cyprian goddess, go hang yourself, Helen, go home, Fiorella, your beauty pales before this beauty that is absolute, complete, solid, firm-planted, this marvelous grace, the grace of Seville, rare, enchanting, splendid, in whom I can find no blemish, no fault to correct!" (27)]

Notwithstanding this insistence on the fairy's beautiful appearance, her perfection is underhandedly put into question at the very beginning of the tale; here we are told that when she was born as a myrtle, her mother "co no gusto granne, pastenatola a na testa lavorata co tante belle mascarune" (54) [with great joy planted it in a flower-pot, ornamented with many fine looking *mascarune* (26)].[14] Grammatically, the word *mascherone* is an augmentative of *maschera*, mask; besides signifying a big mask, it also indicates an artistic representation of a face, enlarged or deformed in a grotesque way, or a face unnaturally covered with heavy makeup. Consequently, if the fairy is metaphorically described as a wonder, metonymically she is portrayed as a grotesque creature. Through this initial detail, the opposition between beauty and ugliness, between reality and appearance, which had been obscured by the radiant, univocal representation of the fairy's beauty, reemerges, albeit obliquely. It is precisely this indirectness that leaves the reader uncertain about the "true" nature of this enchantress. In addition, the theatrical connotation tied to the word *mascherone*, together with the idea of cover that a mask conveys, reinforces the indefiniteness of the opposition between reality and appearance at the core of this tale.

The ambiguity pertaining to the fairy surfaces again later on in the text. On the night the prince sees her for the first time, the sight of her splendor inspires him to sing her praises in a two-page tour de force—of which I have given a brief example above—quoted by Croce as "conform[e] alle regole e ai modelli dei trattati di rettorica fiorita" [true to the rules and models offered in treatises on flowery rhetoric].[15] When the prince finally concludes his panegyric,

> la bella fata rossa comme a vampa de fuoco respose: "Non tante laude, signore prencepe: io te so' vaiassa e pe servire ssa faccia de re iettarria perzì lo necessario e stimo a gran fortuna che da rammo de mortella pastenato a na testa de creta sia deventato frascone de lauro 'mpizzato a l'ostaria de no core de carne e de no core dove è tanta grannezza e tanta vertute." (58)

> [the lovely fairy, growing red as a burning flame replied, "Cease from your praise, my Lord Prince; I am your slave, and to serve your kingly countenance I would willingly empty the chamber pot, for I hold it a great good fortune that from a myrtle branch planted in a clay flower-pot I have become a laurel bough hung over the tavern of a heart of flesh, of a heart where dwells such greatness and virtue." (28)]

The fairy's words are very revealing. First of all, the chamber pot is a false note within the context of this tale that, differently from many others in the *Cunto*, generally avoids scatological references; and it sounds even more inappropriate within the specific context of the prince's discourse of love. It has the effect of underlining once again the grotesque qualities of this otherwise beautiful creature, those qualities that had already been introduced through the presence of *mascheroni* on the flowerpot. Second, and most important, the myrtle, which has just changed into a human being, declares her happiness in having become a laurel bough, thus ostensibly denying herself any human form. What does this curious claim mean?

Momentarily leaving the problem of the grotesque aside, I would like to concentrate on the meanings traditionally associated with the myrtle and the laurel, the understanding of which will help us in the interpretation of this tale. The myrtle, of course, is the plant sacred to Venus, and this amorous aspect of the fairy befits the thematic development of the story. Concerning the birth of the branch of myrtle, we are told that the mother "[la] cacciae da li Campi Elise de lo ventre (54)" [brought [it] forth from the Elysian Fields of her womb (26)]. This assertion may be read as a general allusion to the world of the dead, and thus as a metaphor for the mother's sterility; however, through the textual reference to Virgil, who places the souls of dead lovers in a wood of myrtles (*Aeneid* 6.441), this plant is associated with love and death, but also with poetry, eloquence, and rhetoric. The laurel itself, tree of Apollo, god of poetry, perhaps even more than the myrtle symbolizes poetry, a connection powerfully developed by Petrarch in his *Rime sparse;* and both are metaphors for writing.[16]

We can now affirm that the fairy, being both a myrtle and a laurel, comes to represent the magic force of eloquence that bursts forth in the prince's speech, and consequently, in the *Cunto*. In addition, as we have already pointed out, she is defined as grotesque, and through this quality she is associated with the other grotesque figures that in the *Cunto* embody the rhetoric of the new genre of the fairy tale: first of all the old woman, who by lifting up her skirt sends Zoza on her (literary) quest, but also the ten narrators whose voices convey the tales. If in the first tale of the *Cunto*, the protagonist Antuono's apprenticeship represents Basile's own entry into the world of fairy tales,[17] in the second tale we find that the prince, here a figure of the artist, is already mastering the genre's rhetoric, figured by the myrtle, which declares itself his slave, willing to do anything for his sake.

The metaliterary significance of the female grotesque in the *Cunto* comes back with a vengeance in the tenth and last tale of the first day, entitled "La vecchia scortecata" [The Old Woman Who Was Skinned]. Two sisters, "lo reassunto de le desgrazie, lo protacuollo de li scurce, lo libro maggiore de la bruttezza" (198) [the summary of all misfortunes, the record of all monstrosities and the register of all ugliness (94)], move into a basement below the king of Rocca Forte's dwelling. Because they grumble and complain about the slightest noise the king makes, he infers from this extreme susceptibility that "sotto ad isso fosse la quintascienza de le cose cenede, lo primmo taglio de le carnumme mellese e l'accoppatura de le tennerumme" (200) [under him lived the sum of all graces, the first cut of the finest flesh and the flower of all delicacy (95)] and is thus seized by the desire to see them. Eventually the two hags, enticed by the king's promises, agree that in eight days they will allow him to look at just one of their fingers. In preparation for the event, the two women begin to suck their fingers, with the agreement that the one with the smoothest finger will show it to the king. The honor goes to the oldest of the two, and when at the sight of the finger the king implores her to grant him her favors, she complies, but she asks to be allowed to go to his bed by night and without lights. Upon the granting of this request, she prepares for the night. In the dark she goes into the king's bed; when he touches her, he begins to have some suspicions, but nonetheless embraces her. As soon as the woman falls asleep, though, he lights a lamp, and realizes that she is not at all the beauty he had envisioned, but an old hag. In a frenzy, he has her thrown out the window, and the old lady, falling on a fig tree, remains suspended from one of its branches. Seven fairies happen to walk by, and at the sight of the hag hanging from the tree, they are overcome by a fit of laughter, for which they reward the woman by making her "giovane, bella, ricca, nobele, vertolosa, voluta bene e bona asciortata" (210) [young, beautiful, rich, noble, accomplished, beloved and fortunate (99)]. The king marries her, and the old sister is invited to the wedding. When she sees how young and beautiful her sister has become, she insists on knowing her secret, and when her sister tells her that she had herself skinned, she goes to a barber's shop and, insisting on being skinned, ends up dying.

This tale is interesting for various reasons. First of all, it shares many elements with "La mortella." If we compare the two stories, we see that both are introduced by an invective against women. In "La mortella" wanton women are targeted for the ruin and destruction they bring on other people, while in this last tale the attack is directed against women's cursed vice of wanting to appear beautiful. Both stories contain a bedroom scene, where the men receive the women in their beds in the dark, and finally see them while they sleep in the light of a candle, or a lamp. Both stories end with a marriage and with the demise of jealous and envious women. It is quite clear, however, that "La vecchia scortecata" and "La mortella" are not simply two variants of the same tale, for the former represents a specular reversal of the latter. Through this reversal, two contrasting effects are simultaneously obtained: on the one hand the existence of a definite opposition between beauty and ugliness is emphasized; on the other, the oblique surfacing of the grotesque in "La mortella" and the parallel substitution of the grotesque with absolute beauty in "La vecchia scortecata" result in the blurring of that very opposition.

The most striking inversion occurs in the love scene, which, as we have already seen, in "La mortella" is one of the most delicate moments in the *Cunto*, while what happens in the king of Rocca Forte's bedroom is, I believe, one of the most gruesome love scenes in Italian literature:

> Ma, venuta la Notte . . . la vecchia, tiratose tutte le rechieppe de la perzona e fattone no rechippo dereto le spalle legato stritto stritto co no capo de spao, se ne venne a la scura, portata pe mano da no cammariero drinto la cammara de lo re, dove, levatose le zandraglie, se schiaffaie drinto a lo lietto.
>
> Lo re, . . . commo la 'ntese venire e corcare, . . . se lanzaie comm'a cane corso drinto a lo lietto: e fu ventura de la vecchia che portasse lo re tanto sproffummo, azzò non sentesse lo shiauro de la vocca soia, l'afeto de le tetelleche e la mofeta de chella brutta cosa.

Ma non fu così priesto corcato, che, venuto a li taste, s'accorze a lo parpezzare de lo chiaieto dereto, adonannose de le caionze secche e de le vessiche mosce ch'erano dereto la poteca de la negra vecchia e, restanno tutto de no piezzo, non voze per tanno dicere niente, pe se sacredere meglio de lo fatto e, sfarzanno la cosa, dette funno a no Mantracchio, mentre se credeva stare a la costa de Posileco e navecaie co na permonara, penzannose de ire 'n curzo co na galera shiorentina.

Ma non cossì priesto venne a la vecchia lo primmo suonno, che lo re, cacciato da no scrittorio d'ebano e d'argiento na vorza de cammuscio co no focile drinto, allommaie na locernella, e, fatto perquisizione drinto a le lenzola, trovato n'Arpia pe Ninfa, na Furia pe na Grazia, na Gorgona pe na Cocetrigna, venne 'n tanta furia che voze tagliare la gomena c'aveva dato capo a sta nave. (206–8)

[When Night began to fall, . . . the old woman smoothed out her wrinkles and gathered them all into a knot behind, which she tied up tight with some packthread. A page led her by the hand through the darkness and showed her into the King's bedroom, there she threw off her rags and got into bed. . . . As soon as [the King] heard her get into bed, he ran to her like an unleashed hound. It was lucky for the old hag that he was too strongly perfumed to smell the fetor of her mouth, the stench of her armpits and the stink of that ugly thing. But as soon as he was beside her and could touch her he felt with his hands the knot behind her shoulders, her wrinkled skin and the flaccid bladders that hung from the warehouse of that unlucky old hag. He became petrified, but he spoke no word, however, before making sure of the matter, and plucking up his courage, plunged into Mandracchio when he had thought to find himself on the Posilipean beach; he set sail in a hulk when he had thought to be racing in a Florentine galley. As soon as the old woman had dropped off into her first sleep, the King drew a little chamois bag from an ebony and silver coffer and taking out a tinder, lit the lamp. He looked under the sheets, and when instead of a nymph he found a harpy, instead of one of the Graces a Fury, instead of Venus a Gorgon, he flew into such a rage that he wanted to cut the cable that held the vessel. (98)]

This scene, however, does not represent the only reversal; another can be observed in the very structure of the two tales. "La mortella" clearly develops, from the very beginning, like a fairy tale: magical elements appear without delay in this story, starting with the motif of the enchanted birth of the myrtle. On the other hand, "La vecchia scortecata" is strictly speaking not a fairy tale at all, at least not until the end, where an unfairy-tale-like unhappy conclusion is avoided only by the sudden, almost unexpected, intervention of the seven fairies. The most interesting and revealing reversal, however, concerns the characters of the rivals in the two stories. In "La mortella" the seven wanton women are essential to the plot development: without them there would be no villainy, according to Propp *the* indispensable function of the fairy tale. The sister in "La vecchia scortecata," however, does not have any narrative purpose; she is completely pleonastic, and the story could fully unfold even without her presence. So why is this character so important that the story is named after her?

Before we can answer this question, we must examine in more detail the representation of the grotesque woman in this tale. Writing about Tifi Odasi's hideous description of an apothecary's wife in his *Macaronea*, Barbara Spackman argues that such grotesque

> is not an isolated occurrence, nor does it appear only in the satirical "literature of the underside"; it belongs to the genealogy of the topos of the enchantress-turned-hag, a topos that opposes the beautiful enchantress (woman as lie) to the ugly, toothless old hag hidden beneath her artifice (woman as truth). . . . Indeed, this particular female grotesque stands as the hermeneutic figure par excellence, for it would reveal truth beneath falsehood, plain speech beneath cosmetic rhetoric, essence beneath appearance.[18]

Examples of these grotesque women in Italian literature can be found in Dante's "femmina balba" (*Purgatorio* 19.7–9, 16–21), Ariosto's Alcina (*Orlando Furioso*, 7.73.1–74.4), Machiavelli's "lavandaia" in his letter to Luigi Guicciardini,[19] and, as we have seen, in Basile's "La coppella" as well. The description of the women in "La vecchia scortecata" follows these literary models very closely; it does so, however, with a twist: in Basile's tale, in fact, rather than encountering an enchantress-turned-hag, we find the representation of a hag-turned-enchantress. At the same time, Basile also swerves from the fairy-tale paradigm, where beauty is always represented as the true status of the hero/heroine, which is restored after it has been lost only temporarily. The "unfairy- tale-like" narrative progress of this tale clearly affirms that the true condition of the protagonist is old age and ugliness, while her beauty, rather than her ugliness, is the result of a powerful enchantment.

By reversing both the literary and the fairy-tale topoi, Basile seems to celebrate falsehood over truth, cosmetic rhetoric over plain speech, appearance over essence. This interpretation is ultimately supported by the presence of the sister and of her burning desire to become beautiful, an obsession that brings her to her ruin. Traditionally, the critique of women's yearning to appear beautiful has always been connected to their desire to adorn their bodies, and to their practice of *putting on* makeup and beautiful clothes, as if to cover, hide, and conceal their true appearance.[20] In an analogous way, attacks against rhetoric have equated it to an external garment, to the makeup that, as a mask, covers and thus ruins a beautiful face.[21] According to this antirhetorical rhetoric, the danger and seductiveness of rhetoric lies in the garment, not in the naked body.[22]

In "La vecchia scortecata" Basile, again, assimilates and at the same time reverses the conventional topos: the sister's desire to be beautiful, in fact, induces her not to cover up her body but to uncover it completely, to the extent of taking off her very skin, an action that will kill her. The presence of the sister in this tale acquires a clear significance: with her death the traditional and valued principle of the "naked truth" that she represents dies as well, while the world of appearances and of baroque rhetoric (represented by her "beautiful" sister) triumphs.

Basile's deconstruction of the contrasts typical of fairy tales not only questions the absoluteness of ethical and aesthetic categories (good vs. evil, beauty vs. ugliness, and so on) but also highlights rhetorical and epistemological shifts that were taking place in this period. With the creation of these grotesque figures, wherein beauty and ugliness conflate and coexist in a vortex of metaphors, Basile offers us a seductive example of the taste for exuberance and extremes that characterizes the aesthetic of his time. Even more, by personifying rhetoric in these grotesque figures, he also proposes one of the most suggestive representations of the "new" baroque rhetoric.

Notes

1. For an examination of this characteristic in fairy tales, see Max Lüthi, *The European Folktale: Form and Nature*, trans. John D. Niles (Bloomington: Indiana University Press, 1986), 34–35.

2. For a discussion on the theme of appearance and reality in fairy tales, see Max Lüthi, *The Fairytale as Art Form and Portrait of Man*, trans. Jon Erickson (Bloomington: Indiana University Press, 1984), 29–32 and 125–129.

3. See Ezio Raimondi, *Il mondo della metafora. Il Seicento letterario italiano* (Bologna: C.U.S.L. a r.l., 1987), 62: "*L'antitesi all'origine*, la ritroveremo poi modulata in tanti modi man mano che avanzeremo nei testi del '600, *è il conflitto di fondo tra l'essere e l'apparire*, tra la sostanza e l'immagine, l'oggetto e lo specchio" [*The original antithesis*, which we will find in a variety of modulations as we advance through seventeenth-century texts, *is the fundamental conflict between being and appearance*, between substance and image, object and mirror (emphasis in the original)].

4. See for example Ruffo Chlodowski, "Il mondo della fiaba e il *Pentamerone* di Giambattista Basile. Dai sistemi narrativi del Rinascimento al sistema narrativo del barocco nazionale italiano," *Cultura meridionale e letteratura italiana: i modelli narrativi dell'età moderna*, Atti dell' XI Congresso dell' Associazione Internazionale per gli Studi di Lingua e Letteratura Italiana (Naples: Loffredo, 1985): 191–252, and Giovanni Getto, "La fiaba di Giambattista Basile," in *Barocco in prosa e in poesia* (Milan: Rizzoli, 1969), 381–400.

5. Giambattista Basile, *Lo cunto de li cunti*, ed. Michele Rak (Milan: Garzanti, 1986), 224–26. All subsequent quotations are from this edition.

6. Norman Penzer, ed. and trans., *The Pentamerone of Giambattista Basile*, 2 vols. (London: John Lane and the Bodley Head, 1932), 1:110. All subsequent translation of Basile's *Cunto* are from this edition.

7. "Nel *Pentamerone* gli uomini che nascondono la loro vera faccia sotto la maschera dell'ipocrisia sono biasimati con espressioni abbastanza forti. Il Basile si metteva maschere per togliere le maschere dal mondo che lo circondava. L'unica cosa che non può mai venire a noia all'uomo è la conoscenza della realtà" [In the *Pentamerone* people who hide their true faces under the mask of hypocrisy are rebuked quite severely. Basile put on masks in order to unmask the world surrounding him. The one thing that never causes man tedium is the investigation of reality (Chlodowski, "Il mondo della fiaba," 243)].

8. On the absence of a "true" frame story in the *Cunto*, see Stefano Calabrese, "La favola del linguaggio: il 'come se' del *Pentamerone*," *Lingua e Stile* 16 (1981): 18–20, as well as Nancy Canepa's essay included in this volume.

9. See Nancy L. Canepa, "From Court to Forest: The Literary Itineraries of Giambattista Basile," *Italica* 71 (1994): 291–310, where she accurately observes that in this scene "the fountain of courtly spectacle becomes the locus of the *fonte* of a new literary genre, the fairy tale" (301). See also her chapter in this collection, where she also refers to the richness of theatrical references in the *Cunto*.

10. José Antonio Maravall, *Culture of the Baroque: Analysis of a Historical Structure*, trans. Terry Cochran (Minneapolis: University of Minnesota Press, 1986), 198.

11. "Ma quando dalle egloghe si passa alle fiabe, il tema dell'apparenza, della tintura, della maschera, dietro cui si nasconde il volto delle cose, e quindi il tema della trasformazione delle cose, della loro perpetua condizione metaforica e metamorfica, assume un eccezionale rilievo. Attraverso la metafora la natura perde il suo aspetto fermo e consueto. . . . Tutto il reale entra per così dire in metafora. E la visione metaforica del mondo risulta dominante. Ma la metafora tende a passare dalla condizione di fatto puramente espressivo a quella di un fenomeno fisico, esistenziale. Il reale perciò entra in metamorfosi. Si sciolgono le leggi che regolano l'esistenza, i confini delle cose cadono" [But when we move from the Eclogues to the fairy tales, the themes of appearance, dyeing, masks behind which is hidden the face of things—and therefore the theme of the transformation of things, of their perpetual metaphoric and metamorphic condition—assumes exceptional importance. Through metaphor nature loses its fixed and usual appearance. . . . All of reality enters, as it were, into metaphor. And the metaphoric vision of the world dominates. But the metaphor tends to pass from a purely expressive condi-

tion to a condition in which it becomes a physical and existential phenomenon. Thus, all reality enters into metamorphosis. The laws that regulate existence come undone, the boundaries between things fall (Getto, *Barocco*, 389–90)]. On Basile's use of metaphor, see also Nancy Canepa's analysis of "La palomma" in her essay published in this collection.

12. One of the many metaphors used to describe the fairy is "lo coccopinto de Venere" (56) which, as indicated in Croce's comment, is a periphrasis for Cupid. See Benedetto Croce, introduction to *Il Pentamerone, ossia La Fiaba delle fiabe*, by Giambattista Basile, 2 vols. (Bari: Laterza, 1982), 27.

13. Italo Calvino, "La mappa della metafore," in *Il Pentamerone, ossia La fiaba delle fiabe*, by Giambattista Basile (Bari: Editori Laterza, 1982), viii.

14. Penzer's translates the word *mascarune* into "sculptured figure," but the rendition is inadequate, as it overshadows the important connotations of the original word.

15. See Croce, introduction to *Il Pentamerone*, xxxviii.

16. See Albert Ascoli, *Ariosto's Bitter Harmony: Crisis and Evasion in the Italian Renaissance* (Princeton: Princeton University Press, 1987), 157–61, where he discusses the rich poetic symbolism of the myrtle and the laurel in the context of Ariosto's episode of Astolfo. In particular, Ascoli affirms that "the representation of a natural scene, and particularly of the tree, is actually a collage of artistic precedents. . . . The landscape is inhabited by the usual pastoral paradox of intense naturalness linked to the most precious artifice, a juxtaposition which is never quite as harmonious as it seems, and in fact gives rise to the slippage between appearance and reality, art and nature, which is a perennial motif of the Renaissance" (159).

17. For an interpretation of this tale as "the first step in Basile's own initiation into the fairy tale, . . . as a tale of the acquisition of the 'tools of the trade' of popular culture," see Nancy Canepa's essay included in this collection.

18. Barbara Spackman, "*Inter musam et ursam moritur:* Folengo and the Gaping 'Other' Mouth," in *Refiguring Woman: Perspective on Gender and the Italian Renaissance*, ed. Marilyn Migiel and Juliana Schiesari (Ithaca: Cornell University Press, 1991), 22.

19. "Spectabili viro L. Guicciardini in Mantova tanquam fratri carissimo," *Lettere*, ed. Giusepppe Lesca (Firenze: Rinascimento del Libro, 1929), 26–27.

20. Incidentally, but perhaps not coincidentally, Boccaccio tackles this theme in the tenth story of the first day of the *Decameron*, which, just like "La vecchia scortecata," begins with an invective against women's desire to appear beautiful.

21. A forceful example of this kind of critique of rhetoric can be found in Giovanni Pico della Mirandola's famous letter to Ermolao Barbaro of 1485, where the seductiveness of rhetoric is compared to the truthfulness of philosophy. The following apology of philosophy discloses all the defects of rhetoric: "Ob eam causam nudam se praebet philosophia undique conspicuam, tota sub oculos, sub iudicium venire gestit, scit se habere unde tota undique placeat. Quantum de ea veles, tantum de forma veles, tantum de laude minuas; sinceram and impermixtam se haberi vult; quicquid admisceas, infeceris, adulteraveris, aliam feceris" [Therefore philosophy offers itself stark naked, visible from all sides;

it is eager to come under investigation; it knows that it has the wherewithal to give pleasure in its totality and from every direction. However much of it you might cover, so much would you cover of its beauty, so much would you diminish its praise; it wants to keep whole [sincere] and pure; whatever you mix into it would corrupt it, contaminate it, make it other than it is]. "Ioannes Picus Mirandulanus Hermolao Barbaro suo s.," *Prosatori latini del Quattrocento*, ed. Eugenio Garin (Milan–Naples: Riccardo Ricciardi Editore, 1952), 816–18 (my translation).

22. See Paolo Valesio, *Ascoltare il silenzio. La retorica come teoria* (Bologna: Il Mulino, 1986), 335–37.

Bibliography

Ascoli, Albert. *Ariosto's Bitter Harmony: Crisis and Evasion in the Italian Renaissance.* Princeton: Princeton University Press, 1987.

Basile, Giambattista. *Lo cunto de li cunti.* Ed. Michele Rak. Milan: Garzanti, 1986.

Calabrese, Stefano. "La favola del linguaggio: il 'come se' del *Pentamerone.* " *Lingua e Stile* 16 (1981): 13–34.

Calvino, Italo. "La mappa della metafore." Preface to *Il Pentamerone, ossia La fiaba delle fiabe*, by Giambattista Basile. Bari: Laterza, 1982.

Canepa, Nancy L. "From Court to Forest: The Literary Itineraries of Giambattista Basile." *Italica* 71 (1994): 291–310.

Chlodowski, Ruffo. "Il mondo della fiaba e il *Pentamerone* di Giambattista Basile. Dai sistemi narrativi del Rinascimento al sistema narrativo del barocco nazionale italiano." In *Cultura meridionale e letteratura italiana: i modelli narrativi dell'età moderna*, Atti dell' XI Congresso dell' Associazione Internazionale per gli Studi di Lingua e Letteratura Italiana. Naples: Loffredo, 1985.

Croce, Benedetto. Introduction to *Il Pentamerone, ossia La Fiaba delle fiabe*, by Giambattista Basile. 2 vols. Bari: Laterza, 1982.

Getto, Giovanni. "La fiaba di Giambattista Basile." In *Barocco in prosa e in poesia.* Milan: Rizzoli, 1969.

Guicciardinio, Luigi. *Lettere.* Ed. Giuseppppe Lesca. Florence: Rinascimento del Libro, 1929.

Lüthi, Max. *The European Folktale: Form and Nature.* Trans. John D. Niles. Bloomington: Indiana University Press, 1986.

———. *The Fairytale as Art Form and Portrait of Man.* Trans. Jon Erickson. Bloomington: Indiana University Press, 1984.

Maravall, José Antonio. *Culture of the Baroque: Analysis of a Historical Structure.* Trans. Terry Cochran. Minneapolis: University of Minnesota Press, 1986.

Penzer, Norman, ed. and trans. *The Pentamerone of Giambattista Basile.* 2 vols. London: John Lane and the Bodley Head, 1932.

Pico della Mirandola, Giovanni. "Ioannes Picus Mirandulanus Hermolao Barbaro suo s." In *Prosatori latini del Quattrocento.* Ed. Eugenio Garin. Milan–Naples: Riccardo Ricciardi Editore, 1952.

Raimondi, Ezio. *Il mondo della metafora. Il Seicento letterario italiano*. Bologna: C.U.S.L. a.r.l., 1987.

Spackman, Barbara. "*Inter musam et ursam moritur:* Folengo and the Gaping 'Other' Mouth." *Refiguring Woman: Perspective on Gender and the Italian Renaissance*. Ed. Marilyn Migiel and Juliana Schiesari. Ithaca: Cornell University Press, 1991.

Valesio, Paolo. *Ascoltare il silenzio. La retorica come teoria*. Bologna: Il Mulino, 1986.

CHAPTER 3

Perrault's *Contes*: An Irregular Pearl of Classical Literature

Claire-Lise Malarte-Feldman

cet envahissement de l'imaginaire du siècle de Louis XIV par des angelots hérités tout droit de la Contre-Réforme. . . . y aurait-il une relation
privilégiée entre l'enfance et l'art baroque, ce dernier devançant le classicisme comme la jeunesse devance la maturité?

[this invasion of the imagination during the Century of Louis XIV by
cherubs directly inherited from the Counter-Reformation. . . . might
there be a privileged relationship between childhood and baroque art,
the latter preceding classicism as youth precedes maturity?]

JEAN PERROT, *ART BAROQUE, ART D'ENFANCE*

 BETTER KNOWN as *Les Contes de Perrault*, the *Histoires
ou contes du temps passé avec des moralités* [Stories of Past
Times, with Morals] is one of the most closely analyzed
and diversely labeled texts in French literature. In the last
thirty years, Charles Perrault's works have been dissected
by specialists in a broad range of fields and microscopically
examined by an eclectic group of critics in hundreds of articles and dozens of
books. Perrault is a highly interesting seventeenth-century persona because
the wide variety of his writings unveils the two sides of a fascinating personality: one public, one private. Today's readers get to see both the external
facade of the official Perrault and the inner self of a much more private man.
This psychic duality brings to mind the contrast between the exterior and the
interior that Gilles Deleuze considers an essential characteristic of baroque
architecture, which he defines as a "severing of the facade from the inside,
of the interior from the exterior, and the autonomy of the interior from the
independence of the exterior."[1]

Colbert's right arm on cultural matters at the court of Louis XIV, Perrault occupied a position of power and influence when absolutism was at its height. As "Contrôleur des Bâtiments du Roi" [Inspector of Royal Buildings] for nearly twenty years, he was directly involved in the supervision of building sites, acquiring thus a firsthand, comprehensive knowledge of architecture. He was directly in charge of promoting the Sun King's glory, composing mottoes for medals and inscriptions for monuments. Moreover, his responsibilities as a French Academician entailed, among other things, working at the codification and the promotion of the belles lettres. His numerous accomplishments in artistic and scientific matters were of significant importance at the time, and a large part of his life was dedicated to aesthetic issues. As an official author, Perrault wrote an abundant—rather mediocre, one must add—amount of literature, the ultimate goal of which was to proclaim to the world that the century of Louis le Grand was superior to Greek and Roman antiquity.

Having shed the trappings of a long political life, by contrast, Perrault as a private man left a trail of touching and sincere works, some of them unfinished. His *Pensées chrétiennes* reveals the sensibility and depth of a religious and philosophical mind. His *Mémoires de ma vie* is the fascinating testimony of an aging man who looks back upon his life and enables us, more than three hundred years later, to look behind the scenes of the century of Louis le Grand. But Perrault's most important legacy is clearly the *Contes*, which, according to Jacques Barchilon, "are among the most meaningful [stories] ever written and link Perrault's name to the mythology, folklore and psychology of modern man."[2]

Given his multifaceted personality, it has been greatly debated whether Perrault was a true *moderne* (in the perspective of the Quarrel between the Ancients and the Moderns), a rationalist, a moralist, a misogynist, a folklorist, a sadist, a romantic ahead of his time—even a feminist! In the same fashion, all kinds of epithets have been assigned to the style of Perrault's *Contes*: classical, burlesque, romanesque, worldly, perverse, *précieux*, to name just a few. The *Contes* have, moreover, been approached from a plurality of critical perspectives: literary-historical, psychoanalytical, folkloristic, and semiotic, among others.[3] Whatever the attribute one chooses to associate with this author's name and work, Perrault remains an outstanding figure among the many writers of a period considered as the epitome of French classicism. A man turned toward progress and modernity, Perrault is the archetypal "honnête homme" [gentleman], a man for whom "le bon goût" [good taste] and "la morale" [morals] were the guiding virtues of his classical ideal, virtues that were acclaimed in all of his major works, which sang the praise of the absolute monarch. It is ironic that today he has remained famous because of a small collection of fairy tales, a marginal literary genre in his time and, in his own eyes, a minor opus, written in the twilight of his career and his life.

It is to that opus, however, Perrault's *Contes*, that I would now like to turn in an effort to comment on seventeenth-century aesthetics and to scrutinize Perrault's text in a new light.

The *Contes*, traditionally considered a classical text par excellence, is not only classical, as has been so often demonstrated, but also baroque in terms of certain stylistic and thematic elements that may escape one's attention at first and of which Perrault himself was not even aware. In the domain of the arts—architecture, painting, sculpture, music, and also literature—classicism is often considered poles apart from the baroque. According to Claude-Gilbert Dubois,

> Le classicisme recherche l'unité, le milieu, le centre: c'est l'art de rester dans ces points médians qu'on appelle "sagesse", "bon goût", "bon sens", discrétion", "honnêteté". C'est par excellence un art de la convergence. En ce sens, la période 1600–1660 est aux sources du classicisme; elle prépare, dans l'effort et à travers de périodiques remises en question des résultats acquis, la monarchie unitaire et le culte de la nature et d'un art où règne l'unité organisatrice dans la monstruositd'un esprit lucide.
>
> Le baroque, malgré les apparences, reste un art centrifuge: il recherche l'énorme, l'excès—dans la monstruosité ou l'héroïsme, le sublime ou le grotesque, peu importe. Il tend à pousser l'esprit jusqu'à l'extrême limite de ses recherches et de ses possibilités. Jamais au centre, toujours aux extrêmes, tel est son lieu favori: peu importent les directions, morales ou immorales, libertines ou mystiques, raffinées ou vulgaires; ne retenons de lui que cette horreur du milieu. Il s'éparpille comme l'eau, il se multiplie, s'élance, rebondit, se déverse en cascades, se divise en ruisselets.[4]

> [Classicism seeks unity, the middle, the center: it is the art of remaining within these median points called "wisdom," "good taste," "common sense," "discretion," "decency." It is the art of convergence par excellence. In that sense, the period 1600–1660 was at the root of classicism, preparing the way, after much effort and through the recurring questioning of its acquired results, for absolute monarchy and the glorification of nature and of an art ruled by the organizing unity of a lucid mind.
>
> The baroque, in spite of appearances, remains a centrifugal art: it seeks enormity and excess; whether this is in monstrosity or heroism, in the sublime or the grotesque, it does not matter. Its tendency is to push the mind to the extreme limit of its pursuits

and possibilities. Never in the middle, always at the extremes, such is its favorite locus. No matter which directions it chooses—moral or immoral, libertine or mystical, refined or vulgar—what is remembered is only its horror for the middle. It scatters like water, it multiplies, it leaps forward, it bounces, it pours into cascades, divides into rivulets.]

This is not to say that Dubois sees the two genres as opposites that would be exclusive of each other. On the contrary, he noted recently in his book *Le Baroque en Europe et en France:*

> La distinction entre des tendances dites "classiques" et des tendances qui constituent le baroquisme formel s'expriment [*sic*] progressivement par une série d'excroissances, comme la préciosité ou le burlesque, le concettisme et le cultisme qui sont autant de maniérisations sur le tronc commun, et des retranchements, des mises en ordre, qui s'expriment à travers le purisme malherbien, le puritanisme anglais ou hollandais, le jansénisme à la française, la mise au pas de la langue par la bienséance et l'académisme, la méthode cartésienne, qui sont autant de freins "classiques". Mais classicisme et baroquisme n'ont jamais été en opposition, comme le montre une analyse globale de la société, des moeurs et de l'art au temps de Louis XIV. Si un classicisme, d'origine singulièrement française, a réussi à percer, en s'appuyant sur les tendances générales à la rationalité et au juste milieu qui caractérisent la bourgeoisie technicienne et mercantile qui prend en mains la conduite de l'économie à partir du XVIIIe siècle, et à diffuser son influence à travers l'Europe, celle-ci [*sic*] se combine à des caractères issus d'un baroquisme non marqué par le classicisme français.[5]

[The distinction between so-called "classical" and formal baroque tendencies expresses itself progressively through a series of outgrowths, such as the *préciosité* or the burlesque, concettism or cultism. These are all forms of mannerism which stem from a common root, and which, after adjustments and reorganizations express themselves in the purism of Malherbe, in English or Dutch Puritanism, in French Jansenism, in the codification of language by the Academy and its rules of decorum, in the Cartesian method, all of which are all "classical" control mechanisms. But classicism and baroque have never been in conflict, which is proven by a global analysis of the society, morals and art in the time of Louis XIV. If a specifically French form of classicism can be perceived, its general tendencies are rationality and the search for a happy mean, which are characteristics of the technical and mercantile bourgeoisie that starting in the eighteenth century took control of the economy and spread its influence through Europe. This specific form of classicism is combined with characteristics coming from a baroque which is not influenced by French classicism.]

And indeed, if the lyricism and sensuality of De Viau's or Saint-Amand's poetry are undeniable examples of a baroque literature that stands at the opposite extreme of the rigorously controlled composition of the verses of a Boileau or a La Fontaine, the borders between genres are not often as clearly defined, even where the canons of seventeenth-century literature are concerned. Most of Corneille's theater, some of Molière's characters—Don Juan in particular—and even, as Dubois insists, Racine's *Phèdre* "have a horror for the middle."[6] Some of the most classical works of this period do play with illusions and appearance, sharply contrasting darkness with brightness; in brief, they often show a flaw in the smoothness of their pure facade.

It is thus my hope to stay away from the common notion that classical means the reverse of baroque and to present Perrault's *Contes* in a more nuanced way, arguing that both genres can coexist and even complement each other within this complex work. The apparently crystal-clear limpidity of the text itself, a limpidity that has always been attributed to the pure classical tradition, may mislead more than one reader of Perrault. And although its undeniably classical characteristics are a warranty of its eternal youth, beneath its apparent simplicity is hidden a rather intricate network of influences, one of the strongest being its origins in an anonymous fund of popular and multicultural narratives. Perrault's enterprise, after all, consisted in adapting to the taste of worldly circles a collection of popular folktales that he raised to the rank of French literary masterpieces. His literary sources, nonetheless, come from the Italian Renaissance and baroque tradition. Perrault borrowed freely from the *Piacevoli notti* by the Venetian novelist Straparola and sought inspiration for his own fairy tales in *Lo cunto de li cunti* or *Pentamerone* by the Neapolitan Giambattista Basile.[7] Herein lies one of the many paradoxes of Perrault's *Contes*: what we call today a "classique de la littérature" originated in the various folklores of France and Italy. From then on and over the course of three centuries, the *Contes* ceaselessly evolved, underlining the malleable nature of the fabric of which they are made: mobile, unstable, irregular, transformable, unfinished—characteristic traits of the baroque, "ennemi de toute forme stable, et hostile à l'oeuvre achevée" [enemy of any form of stability, hostile to any completed work] according to Rousset in *La Littérature de l'âge baroque en France*.[8]

The *Contes* went so much against the grain of the kind of literature that Perrault wrote abundantly during his long official career that he tried to convince his readers that their real author was his son, Pierre Darmancour. In an unusual act of self-derision on the part of a literary author, he scattered his text with ironic comments on the marvelous elements in his own tales.[9] In his preface to the *Contes*, Perrault had already attempted to justify himself by saying that his "bagatelles n'étaient pas de pures bagatelles, qu'elles renfermaient une morale utile" [his trifles of stories were not only purely that, they contained a useful moral lesson], an assertion that calls to mind what Gilles Deleuze has to say about contrasting relations between inside and outside that are characteristic of baroque architecture. In fact, Perrault himself stressed the baroque aspect of his fairy tales in establishing a sharp contrast between the exterior and interior, comparing what he calls a "récit enjoué" [a playful narrative] to an "enveloppe" [envelope] inside which is hidden the serious moral lesson he wants to teach. In the same preface, Perrault reminds us repeatedly that he takes pride in his collection of fairy tales, because nothing in them can offend "le bon goût" and the "bienséance," which were the classical imperatives of the time; moreover, inside the entertaining narratives are hidden strict principles of "moralité" [morals] and "bonnes moeurs" [accepted standards of behavior], which would please his seventeenth-century readers. This vocabulary is reminiscent of what Dubois calls the "median points" that define classicism. But despite Perrault's moralistic claims, what has survived today of this work is essentially the exterior of his *Contes*, their excess, the fantastic characters, and the grotesque elements: all that is, according to Dubois, "never in the middle."

Rousset has convincingly demonstrated that baroque aesthetics in literary prose have traditionally been defined with respect to baroque aesthetics in the realm of visual art. He notes that in a baroque building the facade becomes the essential component of the whole structure, as if the building existed only for what is visible from the outside, adding that in some cases the facade even exists just for itself, having nothing to hide inside. With the decor playing a primordial role, it seems natural that baroquism and theater have shared a longtime complicity. The sumptuous theatrical events at Versailles represent a point of convergence between these two realms. Complex stage machinery, extravagant costumes, the inclusion of special effects, and the music of the hundreds of fountains scattered throughout the park helped turn theater into a complete spectacle that put all the emphasis on appearance. We are not so far here from the fashion that consisted of polished conversationalists telling each other fairy tales in the literary salons of the late seventeenth century. The tale itself was not as important as the staging of its narration. In both cases, the art of representation is what counted; the "facade" would thrust itself forward at the risk of having nothing to hide inside. What we remember today of Perrault's *Contes* is not their "moralités" but the seven-league boots and the glass slippers, not their "bon sens" but the Marquis de Carabas and the Fée Carabosse.

It thus comes as no surprise that baroque art, as Jean Perrot, the homonym of our famous author, has shown, was used to illustrate Perrault's tales for children.[10] Perrot developed the idea that the baroque art used to illustrate children's books was particularly well adapted to the child's imagination, and he applied this insight to the study of other authors read by children in his *Art baroque, art d'enfance*. Moreover, the discreet but nevertheless perceptible baroque elements scattered throughout the *Contes* have been brought to light, and in some cases emphasized, by the iconography of Perrault's fairy tales. A number of illustrators have proposed their own representations of the text, reinforcing a point that was brilliantly made by Michel Foucault in the introductory chapter of *Les Mots et les choses* [translated as *The Order of Things*]. In his in-depth analysis of one of the most important baroque paintings of the seventeenth century, *Las Meninas* (1656) by Velázquez (figure 3.1), a "styliste de l'apparence" [a stylist of appearances] in Dubois's words,[11] Foucault raises issues of perspective in artistic works, asking questions about the significance of the glances exchanged between the characters inside the painting and the models standing outside the frame, posing for the painter, Velázquez, in the process of representing on his canvas the royal family of Spain. This *mise en abîme* is a clever play with several levels of perspective, leading Foucault to see in Velázquez's work the ultimate "representation . . . of Classical representation"[12] and to elaborate a whole system based on the presence and/or absence of the spectator in the space of the artistic work, a system based on the tension between what is external and what is internal to the frame.

These opposite forces that rule baroque aesthetics in the visual arts also underlie the language, the style, and some of the themes used by Perrault and are perfectly illustrated (in the literal sense of the term) by the iconography of the *Contes*. The artists who have been inspired by Perrault's fairy tales have, in some extremely telling instances, been attracted by precisely those elements of Perrault's text that lend themselves to a baroque spillover of images. In *The Fold*, Deleuze observes as another baroque characteristic that "matters tend to spill over in space."[13] Indeed, by way of its illustrations, Perrault's text literally jumps out of its frame. Gustave Doré is probably the first famous illustrator of Perrault who comes to mind. He dedicated to the *Contes* a whole series of compositions that were published for the first time by Pierre-Jules Hetzel in 1861.[14] His powerful drawings have made an indelible impression, at least in France, on the collective memory of generations of children who have felt at once attracted and repulsed by the baroque evocations and the grotesque elements in drawings that convey a combination of terror, malice,

FIGURE 3.1. Velázquez, *Las Meninas.*

and mischief. Still today, a certain number of talented illustrators of Perrault's tales propose their own baroque representations of the text.

In the first edition of the dictionary of the Académie Française in 1694, the definition of the word *baroque* reads as follows: "Se dit seulement des perles qui sont d'une rondeur fort imparfaite. Un collier de perles baroques" [Can only be said about pearls which are not perfectly round. A necklace of baroque pearls].[15] In the edition of 1740, we find this interesting addition: "Se dit aussi au figuré pour irrégulier, bizarre, inégal. Un esprit baroque, une expression baroque, une figure baroque" [Can also be used in the figurative sense for irregular, bizarre, unequal. A baroque mind, a baroque expression, a baroque figure]. The fashion of literary fairy tales in the latter part of the seventeenth century and the early years of the eighteenth century can be considered as a sort of oddity in the larger framework of the *Siècle classique* and the *Siècle des Lumières*. It can thus be argued that the *Contes*, along with the large number of fairy tales that were written at that time, stand out as "irregular" in the sense that they do not follow the norm, "bizarre" inasmuch as they go against the grain of the literary canons of the time, which puts the *Contes* on an "unequal" footing with respect to both classical and Enlightenment literature.[16]

To use the terminology of the French Academy dictionary, one can attribute the baroque coloration of the *Contes* to their "bizarre" character. It is significant that Perrault himself used that same word to refer to Italian architecture, underlining his inability to find any form of unity in its creations. Commenting on the blueprints proposed for the Louvre by the famous baroque architect Bernini, he noted in book 2 of his *Mémoires de ma vie*: "ces dessins étaient tous fort *bizarres* et n'avaient aucun goût de la belle et sage architecture" [all these drawings were quite bizarre, they did not show any taste for beauty and sober architecture].[17] Perrault's own inclination was toward the sober, noble, and dignified "colonnade" designed by his brother Claude. Perrault's taste in architecture was restricted to classical shapes, which in his opinion were better suited to glorify the Century of Louis XIV because they conferred the necessary amount of dignity and pomp. As we know, Claude Perrault's proposal for the expansion and embellishment of the Louvre was finally adopted by the king. The whole episode of Bernini's visit to France at the invitation of Louis XIV to work on the Louvre is a metaphor for the mixed feelings of the French toward the baroque: Bernini's entrance into Paris was triumphant; he was treated with all the honors usually reserved for the highest personalities. The bust he made of the king was unanimously applauded for its movement, fluidity, and life, and Louis XIV, for fear Bernini might spoil it, asked him not to touch it ever again. Bernini kept working on it, though, for another couple of months, never entirely happy with his work and, in a characteristically baroque fashion, never able to consider it completely finished.

Despite strong feelings against baroque architecture in the second half of the seventeenth century, however, the existence of a baroque influence in France is impossible to deny. In fact, several links can be established, bridging the gap between the baroque and classicism, architecture and literature. Victor Tapié observes the existence of a baroque foundation underlying French classicism and the clear contradictions it brought about in both architecture and literature. Too often the baroque and classical traditions have been considered mutually exclusive of each other, whereas both of them can and often do coexist. At the Palace of Versailles, for example, "the classical style predominated, but this was not to the exclusion of all Baroque characteristics."[18] The perfect order of the gardens, the splendid symmetry of the buildings, the regularity and sobriety of the facade illustrate classicism at its perfection. But what, then, do we say about the musical waters of the hundreds of fountains in the gardens, the stunning succession of mirrors in the famous Hall of Mirrors lavishly decorated by Le Brun, and the dazzling effect of Le Vau's marble Ambassadors' Staircase dominated by Bernini's bust of Louis XIV? These are striking examples of the coexistence of the two architectural styles, of the contrast evoked by Heinrich Wölfflin, if one only reverses the order of the terms: "It is precisely the contrast between the exacerbated language of the facade and the serene peace of the inside that constitutes one of the most powerful effects that Baroque art exerts upon us."[19] Commenting on the dual nature of Versailles, Dubois concludes: "les deux styles se confortent comme si l'un était le refoulé de l'autre, et agissait de manière convergente avec son contraire devenu de ce fait son complice. Le 'baroque' est le 'langage oublié' du classique, et réciproquement: chacun construit on apparence ou sa manière en prenant l'autre pour étai" [both styles reinforce each other as if one were the other's repressed expression, interacting in a convergent manner with its opposite, thus made an accomplice. The baroque is the "forgotten language" of classicism and vice versa: each one builds its appearance or its style by supporting itself on the other].[20] Clearly, the serenity of the facade of Versailles hides quite a few instances of baroque extravagance inside the palace.

In similar fashion, it can be said that the apparent classicism of Perrault's fairy tales hides a number of baroque traits, and the Contes have their own Hall of Mirrors. After all, Bluebeard's magnificent house counts, among other luxuries, "des miroirs, où l'on se voyait depuis les pieds jusqu'à la tête, et dont les bordures, les unes de glace, les autres d'argent et de vermeil doré, étaient les plus belles et les plus magnifiques qu'on eût jamais vues" [mirrors in which they could see themselves from head to foot. Some mirrors had frames of glass, and some of gold gilt, more beautiful and more magnificent than they [the neighbors and friends of the young bride] had ever seen].[21] The split already noted in the personality of Perrault himself is reflected, then, in his own literary work. Most certainly, Perrault would not have appreciated such an observation; he might also have resented some of the illustrations of his fairy tales. Nevertheless, the baroque goes beyond the text and its illustrations, spilling over into the collective unconscious of contemporary readers who can appreciate its multiple versions and subversions.

Rousset established four essential characteristics of the baroque literary work: instability, mobility, metamorphosis, and emphasis on the décor.[22] The Contes display a good number of these traits. Perrault excelled in painting brief but strikingly evocative backgrounds in which to set the plots of his fairy tales. For example, Cinderella's mean sisters enjoy the comfort of "chambres parquetées, où elles avaient des lits des plus à la mode, et des miroirs où elles se voyaient depuis les pieds jusqu'à la tête" (157) [rooms with parquet floors and the most fashionable beds and mirrors in which they could regard themselves from head to toe (25)]. At Sleeping Beauty's baptism, each fairy godmother is given "un couvert magnifique, avec un étui d'or massif, où il y avait une cuiller, une fourchette, et un couteau de fin or, garni de diamants et de rubis" (97) [a magnificent plate with a massive gold case containing a spoon, fork and knife of fine gold, studded with diamonds and rubies (44)], and once under the spell of the jealous wicked fairy, Sleeping Beauty will rest for a hundred years on "un lit en broderie d'or et d'argent" (99) [a bed of gold and silver embroidery (45)]. Bluebeard's wealth does not consist only of mirrors, rare and costly novelties during the seventeenth century. He also owns "de belles maisons à la ville et à la campagne, de la vaisselle d'or et d'argent, des meubles en broderie, et des carrosses tout dorés" (123) [fine town and country houses, gold and silver plates, embroidered furniture, and gilded coaches (31)]. And when he trusts his wife with the fatal keys, he specifies: "Voilà les clefs des deux grands garde-meubles, voilà celles de la vaisselle d'or et d'argent qui ne sert pas tous les jours, voilà celles de mes coffres-forts, où est mon or et mon argent, celles des cassettes où sont mes pierreries" (124) [These are the keys to the chests in which the gold and silver plates for special occasions are kept. These are the keys to the strongboxes in which I keep my money. These keys open the caskets that contain my jewels (31–32)]. This abundance of detail reminds us of Gilbert Rouger's comment on the priceless objets d'art and paintings that Charles Perrault himself accumulated during his life: "on croirait visiter le logis de la Barbe bleue" (ix) [as if one were visiting Bluebeard's dwelling]. It also illustrates Tapié's remark about the preference in France for small objects in the baroque style—furniture, cabinets, vases, or mirrors—rather than for entire buildings.

Doré's illustration of one of the rooms in Bluebeard's mansion provides a measure of the kind of impression that Perrault's evocations left on his readers' minds (figure 3.2). It features heavy contorted candelabra, chubby cherubs holding an enormous book on the lectern, a strange skull-shaped medallion on the imposing medieval armor in the background. The generous folds of the curtains, the spillover of the long heavy tablecloth, and the movements of the women's embroidered gowns provide ample illustration of a comment on baroque costumes made by Deleuze, who considers the fold as one of the distinctive signs of baroque aesthetics: "Baroque underlines matter: either the frame disappears totally, or else it remains, but, despite the rough sketch, it does not suffice to contain the mass that spills over and passes up above."[23] The whole composition insists on the richness of the textures and underlines the overall sumptuousness of the scenery. By contrast, Doré's representation of Tom Thumb's parents, their faces lit by the dim glow of a fire that we can imagine burning in the fireplace, insists on their utter destitution (figure 3.3). This composition reminds us unmistakably of Le Nain's *The Peasant's Meal* (figure 3.4), about which Tapié noted that "one should not look for the origins of Baroque art among the masses, but *The Peasant's Meal*, by Louis Le Nain, shows a type of sensitivity which awoke a lasting response among them."[24]

FIGURE 3.2. Gustave Doré, *Bluebeard*. Baroque interior. From Charles Perrault's *Les Contes de Perrault* (1861; Paris: Hachette Grandes Œuvres, 1978.)

FIGURE 3.3. Gustave Doré, *Tom Thumb*. Peasants in Le Nain. From Charles Perrault's *Les Contes de Perrault* (1861; Paris: Hachette Grandes Œuvres, 1978.)

FIGURE 3.4. Louis Le Nain, *The Peasant's Meal*. Country interior.

The metamorphosis referred to by Rousset can take a variety of forms, including disguise, trompe-l'oeil, duality, and mirror effects. These are terms that are all right at home in the universe of the fairy tale, where fairies have the power to make pearls—both regular and irregular—flow from one's mouth as a reward for good deeds, where any transformation belongs to the realm of possibilities. In fact, one could say that the most common characteristic shared by the heroes of Perrault's tales is their capacity to transform themselves: an ogre has the power to turn himself into a lion or a mouse, a wolf impersonates a grandmother, a pumpkin can turn into a gilded coach, Puss in Boots's master pretends to be the Marquis of Carabas, Cinderella rises from the ashes to turn into the most beautiful princess at the ball, Riquet's ugliness is obliterated by the power of love, and inside the repulsive skin of a donkey hides a young woman of refined taste and great beauty.

I have already stressed the flexible and transformable nature of the *Contes* and shown that mobility and instability abound both within Perrault's *Contes* and within the fairy tale as a genre. Most of the illustrators of Perrault have been highly sensitive to the unstable nature of this author's work. In his introductory chapter to his famous work *Les Contes de Perrault. Culture savante et traditions populaires*, Marc Soriano reflects on the difficulty of his task in front of such a complex literary work: on the one hand the *Contes* count among the most famous and widely read texts ever written in French, but after careful consideration, what the critic has to work with is a text without text, without author, and without audience.²⁵ It comes as no surprise that so many differing versions of the "Contes de Perrault" are erroneously attributed to the French Academician. While none of these characteristics, taken singly, can be adduced as positive proof of the baroque nature of a given text, their combined presence can surely be seen as a sign that we are dealing in Perrault with both classicism and something other than classicism.

"Peau d'Ane" [Donkey-Skin], mentioned above, deserves our attention for a moment because it provides such a good illustration of what Dubois considers in the literary realm as an "outgrowth" of the "formal baroque," *préciosité*. Written in verses in 1694, four years before the *Histoires et contes du temps passé avec des moralités*, "Donkey-Skin" is more notable for its *précieux* style than for its characteristics as a fairy tale,²⁶ a fact that raises the question much debated by Rousset of *précieux* language and its relationship with the baroque. One cannot help but note the similarity between the baroque dwelling of Donkey-Skin's fairy godmother, who lives "dans une grotte à l'écart / De nacre et de corail richement étoffée" (61) [in a grotto of coral and pearls (68)], and one of the most baroque achievements in the Gardens of Versailles, Tétis's grotto. The descriptions of Donkey-Skin's three dresses provide excellent examples of the bombastic style of the literary baroque, a style characterized by the overuse of metaphors and allegories, ostentation, emphasis, and the like. About the first dress, it is said that "Le plus beau bleu de l'Empyrée / N'est pas, lorsqu'il est ceint de gros nuages d'or, / D'une couleur plus azurée" (62) [the most beautiful blue of the firmament. There was not a color more like the sky, and it was encircled by large clouds of gold (68–69)]. The second dress, in the color of the moon, shines even more brightly: "Dans les cieux où la nuit a déployé ses voiles / La lune est moins pompeuse en sa robe d'argent / Lors même qu'au milieu de son cours diligent / Sa plus vive clarté fait pâlir les étoiles" (62) [Up in the night sky the luster of the moon's illumination makes the stars appear pale, mere scullions in her court. Despite this, the glistening moon was less radiant than this dress of silver (69)]. Finally the work involved in the making of the third dress, in the color of the sun, is so invaluable, "Si beau, si vif, si radieux, / Que le blond amant de Clymène, / Lorsque sur la voûte des Cieux / Dans son char d'or il se promène, / D'un plus brillant éclat n'éblouit pas les yeux" (63) [so beautiful and radiant that the blond lover of Clytemnestra, when he drove his chariot of gold on the arch of heaven, would have been dazzled by its brilliant rays (69)].

These examples confirm Rousset's observation that baroque and *préciosité* may sometimes overlap. But despite a few common points, in particular their shared taste for artifice and disguise, Rousset establishes unequivocally a great number of differences between the two styles, without making any mystery about his preference. *Préciosité*, born in the worldly salons of the early seventeenth century, remains a social and literary phenomenon, and, contrary to the baroque, its ambit of influence does not encompass the visual arts. In Rousset's terms, "le Précieux est l'amenuisement du baroque" [*Précieux* is the dwindling of the baroque];[27] *préciosité*, a weakened and inferior variant of the baroque, was limited to a form of entertaining literature. Fairy tales as a literary genre were a social game, an act of literary prowess that consisted of diverting a myth, a legend, or a folktale and playing with it until it became a perfect little specimen of literary art. Fairy tales were truly a society game in literature. They belonged to a realm where conversation was an art pushed to its perfection. Rousset's words about the ultimate pleasure of conversation, "c'est un art d'allusions et de mots de passe, de variation sur un thème reçu" [it is an art of allusions and passwords, an art of variation on a well-worn theme],[28] apply most fittingly to the art of the fairy tale in the salons of late-seventeenth-century aristocratic society. In his introduction to *Beauties, Beasts and Enchantment: Classic French Fairy Tales*, Jack Zipes observes that "all the writers revised their tales to develop a *précieux tone*, a unique style, that was not only supposed to be gallant, natural and witty, but inventive, astonishing, and modern. Their tales are highly provocative, extraordinary, bizarre, and implausible."[29] In this comment we should note in particular the last sentence, where Zipes's terms themselves suggest the presence of something baroque in the fairy tales as a marginal literary genre.

If the style of "Donkey-Skin" clearly displays more similarities with the *précieux* movement than with the baroque, the theme of disguise that dominates the tale is nonetheless unmistakably baroque. Not only does what Rousset calls metamorphosis apply, but the tale also reposes on the contrast between exterior and interior that we have found to typify baroque art. Inside the skin of the donkey is hidden a true jewel: "Pour vous rendre méconnaissable, / La dépouille de l'âne est un masque admirable. / Cachez-vous bien dans cette peau, / On ne croira jamais, tant elle est effroyable, / Qu'elle renferme rien de beau" (64) [We'll use the donkey's skin to make you unrecognizable. It's such a perfect disguise and so horrible that once you conceal yourself inside, nobody will ever believe that it adorns anyone so beautiful as you (70)]. Perrault further develops this theme when he adds a little later: "Que sous sa crasse et ses haillons / Elle gardait encor le coeur d'une Princesse" (76) [she realized that she still had the heart of a princess beneath her dirt and rags (71)].

Donkey-Skin's magnificent dresses, moreover, are too large to fit inside her miserable dwelling; to be fully displayed, they would have to flow over to the outside, pulling her to the exterior of her house. In other words, Donkey-Skin's split personality finds its spatial corollary in a movement that draws her from within to without: out of her garret, out of her disguise, "out of her skin," so to speak. The vividly baroque nature of the comment "Avec ce chagrin seul que leur traînante queue / Sur le plancher trop court ne pouvait s'étaler" (66) [Her only regret was that she did not have enough room to spread out the trains of the dresses on the floor (71)] may very well have impressed Flaubert, who loved Perrault's *Contes*. He was particularly enthusiastic about "Donkey-Skin," and one may wonder whether the image of Donkey-Skin's trains spilling over may not have been on his mind when he wrote about Julien's mother in *La Légende of Saint Julien l'Hospitalier* that "les cornes de son hennin frôlaient le linteau des portes; la queue de sa robe de drap traînait de trois pas derrière elle" [the points of her tall *hennin* brushed against the lintel of the doorways, the train of her fine woolen gown swept three paces behind her].[30]

It is unclear whether Doré's illustration of Donkey-Skin's flamboyant wedding celebrations applies to the original version in verse or to the prose version that was published in the *Cabinet des Fées* in 1795 (figure 3.5). In any case, it captures all the marvelous elements in the text, including "poules de Barbarie, / Râles, pintades, cormorans, / Oisons musqués, canes petières/ Et mille autres oiseaux de bizarres manières" (66) [All sorts of strange fowls were kept there: chickens from Barbary, rails, guinea fowls, cormorants, musical birds, quacking ducks, and a thousand other kinds (71)], as well as the procession of the kings from the East who arrived "montés sur de grands éléphants" (74) [mounted on huge elephants (74)]. In this particular instance Doré illustrates an aspect of the baroque that Rousset calls the "prolifération du décor aux dépens de la structure" [proliferation of decor at the expense of structure].[31] Sensitive to the few background indications given by Perrault, the illustrator focused his attention on the most spectacular moment of the tale, its climax. The artist conjures up the baroque ostentation of the arrival of the royal guests to celebrate the tale's happy ending in a lavish display of nuptial festivities.

Images of death and other morbid evocations, another fascination of the baroque, can also be found throughout Perrault's tales, and most of them lead to terrifying and everlasting visions, such as the evocation of Bluebeard's secret cabinet, where his wife "commença à voir que le plancher était tout couvert de sang caillé, et que dans ce sang se miraient les corps de plusieurs femmes mortes et attachées le long des murs (c'était toutes les femmes que la Barbe bleue avait épousées et qu'il avait égorgées l'une après l'autre)" (125) [began to perceive that the floor was covered with clotted blood of the dead bodies of several women suspended from the walls. These were the former wives of Bluebeard, who had cut their throats one after the other (32)]. We can only ask, as Perrot does in a comment on this passage of "Bluebeard," whether one could think of "une image plus étrange et plus

FIGURE 3.5. Gustave Doré, *Donkey-Skin*. Wedding celebration. From Charles Perrault's *Les Contes de Perrault* (1861; Paris: Hachette Grandes Œuvres, 1978.)

inquiétante dans sa beauté macabre" [a stranger, more disturbing image in its gruesome beauty].[32] Rousset has analyzed the important role played in the baroque by what he calls a "théâtre de la cruauté" [theater of cruelty]. He comments that "ce monde de l'illusion et du trompe-l'oeil laisse une bonne place à la mort et au cadavre" [this world of illusion and trompe-l'oeil makes ample room for death and corpses].[33] Doré's illustration of the dramatic final scene of "Bluebeard" combines several characteristics of the artist's vigorous style (figure 3.6). While in the background Bluebeard's unconscious wife is abandoned in a rigid position, the focal point of the composition consists of the violent scene of her two brothers stabbing Bluebeard in the back. The life of the whole illustration is so intense that it seems as if the mythical figure of the griffin that stands on top of the wall has been forced temporarily to open its eyes and cast a critical glance on the events taking place at its feet. The convolutions of the snake coiled around the sword in the foreground participate, too, in the movement of the whole picture.

Sometimes in Perrault's fairy-tale world, sleep strangely resembles death. For instance, when the prince arrives at Sleeping Beauty's castle, he finds himself in an eerie world where

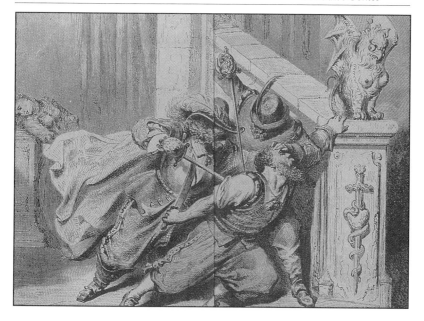

Figure 3.6. Gustave Doré, *Bluebeard*. The brothers kill Blubeard. From Charles Perrault's *Les Contes de Perrault* (1861; Paris: Hachette Grandes Œuvres, 1978.)

tout ce qu'il vit d'abord était capable de le glacer de crainte: c'était un silence affreux, l'image de la mort s'y présentait partout, et ce n'était que des corps étendus d'hommes et d'animaux, qui paraissaient morts. . . . Il traverse plusieurs chambres pleines de gentilshommes et de dames, dormant tous, les uns debout, les autres assis. (101–2)

[everything he saw froze his blood with terror. A frightful silence reigned. Death seemed to be everywhere. Nothing could be seen but the bodies of men and animals stretched out and apparently lifeless. . . . He traversed several apartments filled with ladies and gentlemen all asleep; some standing, others seated. (47)]

Doré's illustration of this episode emphasizes the sharp contrast between the prince, who stands alone in a circle of light—his vibrancy translated by the movements of the folds of his cape and of the feather on top of his hat—and the bodies of men and animals sound asleep in grotesque positions that surround him (figure 3.7). The whole composition is set against an ominous mineral and vegetal background in which the sculpted stones of an old Gothic-Renaissance building (strangely anticipatory of some of the wildest

FIGURE 3.7. Gustave Doré, *Sleeping Beauty*. The sleeping castle. From Charles Perrault's *Les Contes de Perrault* (1861; Paris: Hachette Grandes Œuvres, 1978.)

creations of a Viollet-le-Duc, for example) are, it seems, being slowly eaten up by monstrous serpents of ivy and other climbing plants.

Traditional characters in the fairy-tale landscape, ogres are present in a variety of scenes that combine morbidity with cruelty and terror. It is interesting to juxtapose two illustrations of ogres by Doré. The first one, in "Tom Thumb," fixes our gaze on the large knife that will be instrumental in the death of the ogre's own daughters (figure 3.8). This knife separates the composition into two equal triangles, the upper one being occupied by a huge menacing-looking figure whose bulging eyes, frowning forehead, and generally demented expression immediately mesmerize the viewer. In the lower triangle, we can see only five of the seven daughters. They seem to be sleeping, unless they have already been killed by their father; thus the illustration blurs again the limits between sleep and death. In their self-abandonment they show a definite aptitude to take after their father, since bones, wings with feathers, and carcasses are tucked in the folds of their bedsheets. The leftovers of this rather unrecognizable but most definitely carnivorous meal would indicate the same inclination for fresh meat that Perrault's text evokes in telling us that the little girls "promettaient beaucoup, car elles mordaient déjà les petits enfants pour en sucer le sang" (193) [showed

118

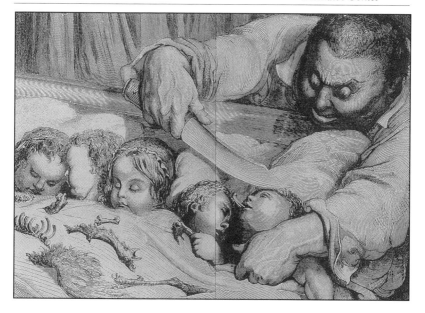

FIGURE 3.8. Gustave Doré, *Tom Thumb*. The ogre and his daughters. From Charles Perrault's *Les Contes de Perrault* (1861; Paris: Hachette Grandes Œuvres, 1978.)

great promise, for they had already begun to bite little children to suck their blood (40)].

The second illustration of the ogre is in "Puss in Boots." His face reminds us of the ogre in "Tom Thumb" with the same forehead and mean-looking eyes (figure 3.9). Nevertheless, Perrault's text specifies that "l'ogre le [le chat] reçut aussi civilement que le peut un ogre" (140) [the ogre received him [the cat] as civilly as an ogre can (23)], and Doré's twisted sense of humor captured the essence of Perrault's ambiguous message. Indeed, what kind of a host is this ogre enthroned on a seat of the most baroque making, crowned with the ugly and menacing head of a long-necked and piercing-eyed griffin? What forms does the civility of such a creature take? What do his guests eat at his table? A feast of calf and mutton brains? And what about those plump miniature dead babies lying languidly on a bed of greenery? The carcass of a dead animal indicates the ogre's impatience to start this banquet, whereas the paw that Puss in Boots holds under his chin may illustrate the cat's bewilderment, as well as our own, in the face of a display in which the morbid, the grotesque, and the terrifying make up the better part of the composition. The most marvelous case of metamorphosis can be found in this fairy tale, which will come to its happy conclusion when the cat tricks the ogre in a game of daring,

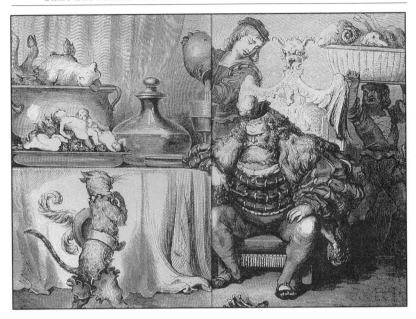

FIGURE 3.9. Gustave Doré, *Puss in Boots*. The cat received civilly by the ogre. From Charles Perrault's *Les Contes de Perrault* (1861; Paris: Hachette Grandes Œuvres, 1978.)

turning the latter into a mouse that he quickly gobbles up, thus eliminating the last obstacle to his procurement of his master's fortune.[34]

"Riquet with the Tuft" is the least "marvelous" of all the *Contes*, but it may also have the most baroque theme, inasmuch as its whole structure rests on the contrast between inside and outside. Riquet's physical appearance is off-putting, though his mind is so sharp that people around him quickly forget his ugliness and fall under his charm. Ironically, he falls in love with a beautiful princess, who is also the stupidest creature in the world. He promises her intelligence and wit in return for marrying him. She is so silly that she agrees, not fully understanding the consequences of her promise, and she becomes smart. Eventually, she loves Riquet enough to overlook his ugliness. The truly marvelous element of the tale thus resides in the power of love to transform the beloved in the lover's eyes: he who is ugly on the outside is now loved for the beauty he possesses inside. Once again dominated by the baroque theme of metamorphosis, this tale focuses on a split at the crux of both characters—ugly/smart and beautiful/dumb—who become one again in an ideal combination of beautiful/smart. Doré's single illustration of this tale was able to capture its only fantastic element: Perrault's brief evocation of an

FIGURE 3.10. Gustave Doré, *Riquet with the Tuft*. Underground world. From Charles Perrault's *Les Contes de Perrault* (1861; Paris: Hachette Grandes Œuvres, 1978.)

underground world (figure 3.10). Although the scene in question is a brief one, it creates a vivid image, exerting great power on the reader's imagination. Literally standing on the edge of the earth, Riquet shows the princess the intense activity of a mysterious kitchen lying at their feet in which reigns an army "de cuisiniers, de marmitons et de toutes sortes d'officiers nécessaires pour faire un festion magnifique" (177) [cooks, scullions, and all sorts of servants necessary for the preparation of a magnificent banquet (55)]. Doré's clever representation of the two worlds, above and below, presided over by a gigantic tree that displays not only its foliage but also its roots, stresses the duality of both characters' personalities in a fittingly baroque interpretation of Perrault's text.

Doré's illustrations of Perrault's *Contes* clearly bring up some of the questions that Foucault has raised in his reading of Velázquez's painting, questions that engage with the crucial baroque topos of the inside and outside with particular regard to the spectator's viewpoint. Doré's famous representation of "Little Red Riding Hood" illustrates this point: a disproportionately imposing wolf is turning his back to us and looking down into the eyes of a submissive/seductive little girl (figure 3.11). In this exchange, more eloquent than a thousand words, in which the bodies of the two antagonists seem to be irresistibly attracted to each other, we, the spectators, are excluded and reduced to the position of voyeurs.[35] This illustration finds a surprising translation into a contemporary setting in Sarah Moon's photographic interpretation of "Little Red Riding Hood." The gaze of the wolf becomes the threatening beam of the headlights of a black car that freezes the movement of a little schoolgirl crossing a deserted street. The vague silhouette of a German shepherd (also called "chien-loup" in French) can be seen in the upper-left corner of the photograph. Wrapped in the folds of her cape, the young girl runs toward the car. The car-wolf has become a metaphorical figure, the threat that he incarnates entirely internalized, leaving the viewer, alone with the little girl, in the ray of light.[36] One last contemporary illustration by another "styliste de l'apparence," Jean Claverie, should enable us to come full circle to Velázquez's famous canvas (figure 3.12). This illustration for "Little Red Riding Hood" can be seen as the reversed mirror-image of the seventeenth-century painting. Where in the latter glances were exchanged in and out of the frame, in the former Perrot notes that "tous les regards convergent vers le prodige, médusés ou ravis, oubliant le spectateur" [all eyes converge on the child prodigy, dumbfounded or delighted, forgetful of the audience].[37] The child is the object of the undivided attention of all the characters on Velázquez's canvas, every gaze converges toward her, her mirror image is clearly represented on the painting that is being made. Three centuries later, Claverie, in his turn, proposes a new variation on the theme of the "representation of the representation." In a typically baroque fashion,

FIGURE 3.11. Gustave Doré, *Little Red Riding Hood.* The gaze. From Charles Perrault's *Les Contes de Perrault* (1861; Paris: Hachette Grandes Œuvres, 1978.)

FIGURE 3.12. Jean Claverie, *Riquet with the Tuft*. The representation of representation. From *Love and Be Wise* (based on Riquet à la Houppe by Charles Perrault). Text by Anne Carter, illustrations by Jean Claverie. (London: Walker Books, 1988). Reproduced by permission of Walker Books, Ltd., London.

all of these compositions force us to adopt a perspective and make us move either inside or outside the frame. The baroque elements contained in the tales continue to condition the reception of these tales as well as to influence their illustration. Illustrators are, after all, first of all readers and interpreters of texts.

Jean Rousset insisted that if the hour of the baroque has elapsed, the notion of baroque is still useful as a "hypothèse de travail" [working hypothesis][38] because it corresponds to the expression of an archetypal attitude, a deeply rooted manifestation of the human soul, and not only to the aesthetic trends of a specific historical period. Although one can take issue with Rousset, I would agree that baroque art (as an aesthetic category), even today finds expression through many artistic voices even if it has escaped its strict seventeenth-century criteria. In many ways, this is what has happened with the *Contes,* which have evolved with time and adapted to the new tastes of a different audience. Be it in a building by Le Corbusier, a sculpture by Salvador Dali, or a book by Maurice Sendak, we continue to behold the breathtaking perspectives, the excessive movement, and the spillover of life so characteristic of the baroque.

In any case, the frequent incursions of the baroque into Perrault's *Contes* and their iconography force us to revise some of our concepts about classical literature. Once read in the light of an aesthetics of duality and reflection, and in the context of an intricate interplay of trompe-l'oeil and disguise, this collection of literary fairy tales from the late seventeenth century takes on quite a different relief. This text "without text and without author," to use Marc Soriano's terms, incarnates the baroque love of fluidity and movement, despite Perrault's unsuccessful attempt to "fix" the unstable elements of his tales in place. The fairy tales' magic realm of illusion and metamorphosis never did fit the recognized classical canons of the literature of the time. Marginal as a genre, "bizarre" by nature, the *Contes* survived the wear and tear of time, a testimony to the atemporality and open-endedness of baroque art that is aptly illustrated by the multifaceted nature of the scholarly reception of Perrault. It may seem somewhat ironic that a man whose highly public professional career was devoted to the architectural celebration of France's most absolute monarchy is best remembered now for an intimist genre of writing that French culture has set aside for children. For those of us looking out from within like Velázquez, this may be the most baroque detail of all.[39]

Notes

1. Gilles Deleuze, *The Fold: Leibniz and the Baroque*, trans. and foreword Tom Conley (Minneapolis: University of Minnesota Press, 1993), 28.
2. Jacques Barchilon and Peter Flinders, *Charles Perrault* (Boston: Twayne, 1981), 30.
3. For a complete critical approach to Perrault and his works, see Claire-Lise Malarte, *Perrault à travers la critique depuis 1960: Bibliographie annotée* (Paris, Seattle, and Tubingen: Papers on French Seventeenth-Century Literature, 1989).
4. Claude-Gilbert Dubois, *Le Baroque. Profondeurs de l'apparence* (Paris: Larousse, 1973), 82. Unless otherwise noted, translation of this and all subsequent quotations are my own.
5. Claude-Gilbert Dubois, *Le Baroque en Europe et en France* (Paris: Puf, 1995), 102–3.
6. Ibid., 23–28.
7. See the introduction by Gilbert Rouger to his edition of Perrault's *Contes* (Paris: Garnier Frères, 1967), xxxii–xxxiii.
8. Jean Rousset, *La Littérature de l'âge baroque en France* (Paris: José Corti, 1954), 231.
9. Several good articles have been written on the question of the rationalism and the marvelous in Perrault's fairy tales; among them we shall note Jacques Barchilon's "Aspects de la fiction et de la vraisemblance à travers romans et contes merveilleux," *P.F.S.C.L.* 8 (1977–78): 13–24, and Felix Freudman's "Realism and Magic in Perrault's Fairy Tales," *L'Esprit Créateur* 3 (1963): 116–22.
10. Jean Perrot has referred, for example, to "le baroquisme contagieux d'un classique paradoxal" in an article published in *Europe*.

11. Dubois, *Le Baroque en Europe et en France*, 147.
12. Michel Foucault, *The Order of Things: An Archeology of the Human Sciences*, trans. A. M. Sheridan Smith (1971; rpt., New York: Vintage, 1973), 16.
13. Deleuze, *Fold*, 123.
14. Gustave Doré (1833–1883), who also illustrated Rabelais, Balzac, and Dante with the same characteristic ardor, was certainly instrumental in consecrating the transition of the *Contes* from their original status as literary fairy tales for adults to their current status as children's literature.
15. This definition allows Dubois to comment in *Le Baroque. Profondeurs de l'apparence*, 20, that "la perle baroque associe en elle l'éclat et l'impureté. De même le baroque se crée une identité à partir de défauts transformés en éloquentes affirmations de nature" [the baroque pearl combines within itself luster and imperfection. In the same fashion, the baroque forges out an identity from defects transformed into eloquent affirmations of nature], stressing again the opposite tensions that underlie the baroque.
16. One should note at this point that if the *Contes* has now become one of the most famous texts of all times, it is because of its radical shift in audience and the drastic modifications that it has undergone. Indeed, the more one reads Perrault's fairy tales, the more easily one becomes persuaded that only adults could have enjoyed them, and, to a certain extent, still can. If they became a favorite children's book many years after they were first published, it was only with a little help from the publishers of children's literature, who made the necessary textual alterations to offer a young audience a more palatable collection of fairy tales. On this point, see Claire-Lise Malarte, "La Fortune des Contes de Perrault au vingtième siècle," *P.F.S.C.L.* 11, no. 21 (1984): 633–41. Also, one should note that the addition of illustrations to each tale has again greatly contributed to multiple reinterpretations of Perrault's text.
17. Quoted in Rousset, *La Littérature*, 179.
18. Victor-L. Tapié, *The Age of Grandeur: Baroque Art and Architecture*, trans. A. Ross Williamson (New York: Grove Press, 1960), 143.
19. Quoted in Deleuze, *Fold*, 28–29.
20. Dubois, *Le Baroque en Europe et en France*, 19.
21. Perrault, *Contes*, 124. Translation by Jack Zipes in *Beauties, Beasts and Enchantment: Classic French Fairy Tales* (New York: New American Library, 1989), 32. All subsequent citations from Perrault's text in French and English will be from these editions and indicated parenthetically in the text.
22. Rousset, *La Littérature*, 181–82.
23. Deleuze, *Fold*, 123.
24. Tapié, *Age of Grandeur*, 86.
25. Marc Soriano, *Les Contes de Perrault. Culture savante et traditions populaires* (Paris: Gallimard, 1977), 13.
26. For a comprehensive study of *préciosité* in its relationship with fairy tales, see Jacques Barchilon, "*Précieux* Elements in the Fairy Tale of the Seventeenth Century," *L'Esprit créateur* 3 (1963): 99–107.
27. Rousset, *La Littérature*, 241.

28. Ibid., 242.
29. Zipes, *Beauties, Beasts and Enchantment*, 7.
30. Gustave Flaubert, *Trois Contes* (Paris: Garnier-Flammarion, 1965), 87. Flaubert, *Three Tales*, trans. A. J. Krailsheimer (Oxford: Oxford University Press, 1991), 42. Perrault's verses find a striking echo in Flaubert's stunning image. The influence of Perrault's *Contes* on Flaubert's prose has already been noticed by Juliette Frolich, in "Charles Bovary et *La belle au bois dormant*," *Revue Romane* 12, no. 2 (1977): 202–9.
31. Rousset, *La Littérature*, 181–82.
32. Jean Perrot, *Art baroque, art d'enfance* (Nancy: Presses Universitaires de Nancy, 1991), 27. In this work, Perrot dedicates a whole passage to Doré's illustrations of Perrault's *Contes*, entitled "Les angelots morts de Gustave Doré et le Petit Poucet," 33–35.
33. Rousset, *La Littérature*, 81.
34. For a semiotic analysis of the animal trickster, see Claire-Lise Malarte, "The Structural Components of *Le chat botté*," *Folklore* 96, no. 1 (1985): 104–11.
35. For a thorough analysis of thirty-one different versions of "Little Red Riding Hood," Perrault's included, see Jack Zipes, *The Trials and Tribulations of Little Red Riding Hood*. 2nd ed. (New York and London: Routledge, 1993).
36. Perrault, *Le Petit Chaperon rouge,* illustrated by Sarah Moon. (Paris: Grasset-Monsieur Char, 1983), n.p. Unfortunately I was not given permission to reproduce this photograph. For the study of a number of contemporary illustrations of "Little Red Riding Hood," see Claire-Lise Malarte, "Le Petit Chaperon rouge: jeu d'images," in *Jeux Graphiques dans l'album pour la jeunesse*. (Paris: Université Paris-Nord, 1991): 235–45.
37. Perrot, *Art baroque*, 43.
38. Jean Rousset, *L'Intérieur et l'extérieur* (Paris: José Corti, 1968), 248.
39. I am greatly indebted to the Dean's Office of the College of Liberal Arts and the Vice President's Office for Research and Public Service at the University of New Hampshire for their financial support, and to my friend Joan Howard for her invaluable editorial comments.

Bibliography

Barchilon, Jacques. "*Précieux* Elements in the Fairy Tale of the Seventeenth Century." *L'Esprit créateur* 3 (1963): 99–107.
———. "Aspects de la fiction et de la vraisemblance à travers romans et contes merveilleux." *P.F.S.C.L.* 8 (1977–78): 13–24.
Barchilon, Jacques, and Peter Flinders. *Charles Perrault*. Boston: Twayne, 1981.
Carter, Anne. *Love and Be Wise*. Illustrated by Jean Claverie. London: Walker Books, 1988.
Deleuze, Gilles. *The Fold: Leibniz and the Baroque*. Trans. and foreword by Tom Conley. Minneapolis: University of Minnesota Press, 1993.
Dubois, Claude-Gilbert. *Le Baroque. Profondeurs de l'apparence*. Paris: Larousse, 1973.
———. *Le Baroque en Europe et en France*. Paris: Puf, 1995.

Flaubert, Gustave. *Trois Contes*. Paris: Garnier-Flammarion, 1965.

———. *Three Tales*. Translated by A. J. Krailsheimer. Oxford: Oxford University Press, 1991.

Foucault, Michel. *The Order of Things: An Archeology of the Human Science*, trans. A. M. Sheridan Smith. 1971. Reprint, New York: Vintage, 1973.

Freudman, Felix. "Realism and Magic in Perrault's Fairy Tales." *L'Esprit Créateur* 3 (1963): 116–22.

Frolich, Juliette. "Charles Bovary et *La belle au bois dormant*." *Revue Romane* 12, no. 2 (1977): 202–9.

Malarte, Claire-Lise. *Perrault à travers la critique depuis 1960: Bibliographie annotée.* Paris, Seattle, and Tubingen: Papers on French Seventeenth-Century Literature, 1989.

———. "La Fortune des Contes de Perrault au vingtième siècle." *P.F.S.C.L.* 11, no. 21 (1984): 633–41.

———. "The Structural Components of *Le chat botté*." *Folklore* 96, no. 1 (1985): 104–11.

———. "Le Petit Chaperon rouge: jeu d'images." *Jeux Graphiques dans l'album pour la jeunesse*. Paris: Université Paris-Nord, 1991.

Perrault, Charles. *Contes*. Ed. Gilbert Rouger. Paris: Garnier Frères, 1967.

———. *Les Contes de Perrault*. Gravures de la première édition Hetzel illustrée. Dessins de Gustave Doré. Préface par PJ Stahl. 1861. Paris: Hachette Grandes Œuvres, 1978.

———. *Le Petit Chaperon rouge*. Illustrated by Sarah Moon. Paris: Grasset-Monsieur Chat, 1983.

Perrot, Jean. *Art baroque, art d'enfance*. Nancy: Presses Universitaires de Nancy, 1991.

———. "Le Baroquisme contagieux d'un classique paradoxal." *Europe* 739–40 (1990): 142–55.

Rousset, Jean. *La Littérature de l'âge baroque en France. Circé et le paon*. Paris: José Corti, 1954.

———. *L'Intérieur et l'extérieur*. Paris: José Corti, 1968.

Soriano, Marc. *Les Contes de Perrault. Culture savante et traditions populaires*. 1968. Reprint, Paris: Gallimard, 1977.

Tapié, Victor-L. *The Age of Grandeur: Baroque Art and Architecture*. Trans. A. Ross Williamson. New York: Grove Press, 1960.

Zipes, Jack. *Beauties, Beasts and Enchantment: Classic French Fairy Tales*. New York: New American Library, 1989.

———. *The Trials and Tribulations of Little Red Riding Hood*. 2nd ed. New York and London: Routledge, 1993.

From Genre to
Gender and Ideology

PART
II

CHAPTER 4

Marvelous Realities:
Reading the *Merveilleux* in the
Seventeenth-Century French Fairy Tale

Lewis C. Seifert

ONE OF the most prominent features of folk- and fairy tales is their use of marvelous (supernatural) characters and settings. Perhaps nowhere is this more obvious than in the colloquial use of the term *fairy tale* to denote an excessively unrealistic situation or idea. By no means a feature of all folk- and fairy tales, the marvelous recurs with great frequency in literary fairy tales (as opposed to folktales). Yet, no matter how prominent, the marvelous has elicited surprisingly little critical scrutiny. Although sophisticated narratological and psychoanalytic models have been proposed for the fantastic,[1] its related textual effect, the marvelous, has yet to receive the type of theoretical attention necessary to grasp its role in the ideological workings of the literary fairy tale. I would argue that the marvelous elucidates, among other things, why the genre has appealed to adults and why particular supernatural motifs or characters recur at certain moments and in specific national traditions. As the expression and imaginary satisfaction of desire, the marvelous offers a retreat from the constraints of the real or the present and a fantasmatic resolution of ideological contradictions. The marvelous creates an alternate plane onto which the real can be transposed and reimagined. To do so, however, the marvelous must be adapted to the cultural contexts in which it is evoked and, particularly, to its prevailing cultural discourses of the "real." In this essay, I will consider the place of the fairy-tale marvelous (or *merveilleux*) in the literary and cultural contexts of late-seventeenth-century France. The *contes de fées* that appeared between 1690 and 1715 are emblematic examples that reveal the central and strategic place of the marvelous in the production and reception of the literary fairy tale.[2]

In all of the seventeenth-century *contes de fées*, as in most of the folk- and fairy tales that employ it, the marvelous is perhaps best described as a context that suspends the rules and constraints of reality. Along these lines, Tzvetan Todorov has provided a useful definition of the marvelous by contrasting it with fantastic literature. Whereas the latter hesitates between a natural (that is, empirical, scientific) and a supernatural (that is, inexplicable, transcendent) explanation of narrative events, marvelous literature assumes that only a supernatural explanation, or, rather, that *no* explanation is possible.[3] Of course, Todorov's definition in no way precludes the existence of "realistic" traits alongside marvelous ones. In folk- and fairy tales, kings and queens coexist with ogres and fairies. And yet, the melding of so-called realistic and marvelous features within these genres is part of the contradictory dynamics that François Flahault has theorized is the structural basis for folkloric narratives.[4] On the one hand, the marvelous is an estrangement of empirically defined reality since it is either an exaggeration of the real or an assertion of the impossible. On the other hand, folk- and fairy tales attenuate this impulse toward estrangement and transgression. Not only does the repetitive use of a limited number of supernatural features make them predictable (if not acceptable), but most important, the marvelous also reproduces and reaffirms familiar social structures and values. In what follows, I will argue that this tension within the marvelous is crucial to our understanding of the seventeenth-century *contes de fées*. The *merveilleux* is capable of reproducing familiar realities, but also of revealing their incoherences and suggesting, in however schematic a way, a different future. I will argue further that the ambivalent tendency of the marvelous to reiterate *and* to revamp the "real" is apparent first and foremost in representations of the body. Making itself felt in pleasures and in suffering, the marvelous foregrounds the body as the privileged site from which the "real" is to be known.

Marvelous (Im)plausibility

In her important work on the seventeenth- and eighteenth-century French literary fairy tale, Raymonde Robert proposes a definition that accounts for both the specificity of her corpus and the narrative structure of the *merveilleux* within it. Elaborating on Propp's observation that "villainy or . . . lack are the only . . . obligatory elements [of all tales],"[5] by which he means that their plot structure is predicated on the need or misfortune of the protagonist(s) at the hands of the antagonist(s), Robert outlines three basic elements that constitute the *écriture féerique* (fairy- tale writing) of her corpus:

> 1) *Explicit guarantees that the villainy or lack will be liquidated;* formulated in diverse but redundant ways, they establish the certainty of the failure of aggression even before the intervention of the aggressors.
>
> 2) *The highlighting of the heroic couple's exemplary destiny* by a particularly economical system that attributes moral or physical characteristics according to the opposed categories of heroes and adjutants on the one hand and anti-heroes and antagonistic characters on the other.
>
> 3) *The establishment of an exclusive fairy-tale order* ("ordre féerique exclusif") by which the micro-universe of the marvelous tale ("conte merveilleux") is constituted as an absolute and sufficient reference.[6]

Consider Charles Perrault's well-known version of "Cendrillon" (Cinderella) as a brief illustration of this definition. According to Robert, the first criterion of fairy-tale writing—explicit guarantees that the misdeed will be redressed— is most often carried out by a character endowed with supernatural powers.[7] In Perrault's tale, it is the heroine's fairy godmother who fulfills this role. Later, of course, the magical glass slipper resolves any remaining doubt about the outcome of this story. More significant still, Cinderella testifies to these guarantees herself by displaying a measure of self-assurance. When she is given the opportunity to try on the slipper, "Cendrillon . . . qui reconnut sa pantoufle, dit en riant: 'Que je voie si elle ne me serait pas bonne!'" [Cinderella, who . . . recognized the slipper, said with a smile, "Let me see if it will fit me!"].[8] In this moment, she shares with the narrator and the readers an omniscience denied the other characters and, thus, affirms the resolution of the misdeed or act of villainy. If we slightly modify Robert's second criterion to include the exemplary destiny of single protagonists as well as heroic couples, then it is possible to see how an absolute moral dichotomy is invoked at the very beginning of the tale and reiterated throughout. On the one hand is Cinderella's stepmother, "la plus hautaine et la plus fière qu'on eût jamais vue" [the haughtiest and proudest woman in the world] and her two daughters "qui lui ressemblaient en toutes choses" [who resembled her in every way] and, on the other, the heroine, who was "d'une douceur et d'une bonté sans exemple" [of a gentleness and goodness without parallel (171)]. Further, her physical appearance is no less exemplary than her moral stature. The tale points out early on that, in spite of her raglike clothes, she is "cent fois plus belle que ses soeurs" [one hundred times more beautiful than her sisters (172)]. It is clear that Cinderella is on the side of supreme good and beauty, and that she is the perfect match for the prince. Finally, the third criterion, the establishment of a self-sufficient fairy-tale universe, requires a dichotomous value system such as the one that opposes Cinderella to her stepmother and stepsisters. According to Robert, the *contes de fées* deploy particular structural elements so as to legitimize or motivate the Manichean binarism of good and evil.[9] And in this tale, there are at least three parts to this internal legitimation. Most obvious perhaps are the two versed *moralités* (morals) that conclude the tale. Extracting a lesson from Cinderella's good example, they legitimize (at least ostensibly) the moral context presented in the narrative. Second is what might be termed the heroine's moral genealogy since, as the tale indicates, Cinderella inherits her sweetness and goodness from her deceased mother, "qui était la meilleure personne du monde" [who had been the best person in the world (171)]. Third is the extent of her goodness: in the end, she forgives her stepsisters, brings them to the palace, and marries them to "deux grands Seigneurs de la Cour" [two great noblemen of the court (177)]. And, finally, there is the marriage closure itself, which serves as the ultimate sanction for Cinderella's virtue and beauty. Legitimating indications such as these are widely used in the *contes de fées* (and indeed in many literary fairy tales) to indicate the closure and self-sufficiency of their narrative universe.

The three characteristics of Robert's *l'écriture féerique* are particularly useful for delineating not only the relative specificity of this corpus, but also the nature of the marvelous. Going beyond *thematic* features, this tripartite definition of the *conte de fées* accounts for the *narrative* or *structural* function of the marvelous. Moreover, by recognizing the crucial role of the heroic couple, this definition reveals if only implicitly the importance of sexuality and gender in this corpus. Finally, drawing attention to the mechanisms by which the fairy tales legitimize their "micro-universe," Robert's third criterion allows us to consider how these texts construct ideological systems.

There are, however, two general limitations to this model. First, Robert explicitly excludes from her definition those tales that are either "cautionary" (for example, Perrault's "Le Petit Chaperon rouge") or "tragic" (d'Aulnoy's "L'Isle de la félicité") since in both the misdeed is not redressed but left intact at the end. Although such tales are in the minority, they are nonetheless significant limit-cases of the use of the marvelous and, as such, deserve to be considered. Second, and more problematic, this definition does not explain the extent to which the *contes de fées* contribute to an estrangement of accepted notions of reality; that is, it does not provide a way of analyzing how these fairy tales can critique or subvert ideological systems and how they can serve a utopian function. Instead, it emphasizes the internal coherence of the "magical order" and the restoration of order—the liquidation of villainy or lack—in the fairy tale's overarching narrative structure. While Robert is absolutely correct, in my view, to underscore the preeminence and redundancy of these two features, her definition does not allow for the contradictory dynamics that are so central to all folk- and fairy tales and, specifically, to the marvelous.

To understand the ambivalent effects of the *merveilleux*, we must first consider its relationship to the aesthetic principle of *vraisemblance*.[10] Although often translated as "verisimilitude" or "plausibility," this term had very precise meanings in the context of seventeenth-century France. *Vraisemblance* was the result of the *ut pictura poesis* representational system that dominated artistic practice and theory in early modern Europe. According to this system, imitation was above all artful (if not artifice) in that it employed analogy or allegory rather than direct reference. Since the relation between art and nature was mediated by use of specific codes, such as mythology, the result was not truth, but verisimilitude.[11] Accordingly, as Aron Kibédi-Varga has astutely observed, *vraisemblance* could have at least three meanings.[12] First, *vraisemblance* was called to uphold the moral objective of art by rejecting the chaos of history in favor of an ideal world in which right always triumphs over wrong. Second, *vraisemblance* served the social order as "tout ce qui est conforme à l'opinion publique" [all that conforms to public opinion], that is, the codification of what is taken for good or common sense.[13] Third, *vraisemblance* could also have ontological ramifications since it implied perfecting real individual species in accordance with a true original. "Extending what is true, bringing it to perfection, these were the goals assigned to *vraisemblance*."[14]

It is fairly obvious that these definitions of plausibility or verisimilitude do not automatically preclude marvelous literature. In other words, the *contes de fées* can indeed be *vraisemblable*. If we recall Robert's three-part definition, only the first criterion, which relies on the intervention of supernatural forces, contradicts *vraisemblance* since it goes against an empirical understanding of reality upheld by "public opinion" or "common sense." The two remaining criteria allow for moral, social, and ontological verisimilitude. Moral *vraisemblance* is affirmed through the highlighting of the heroic couple's destiny (the second criterion), which involves a polarization of characters according to moral and physical traits (for example, good vs. bad, industry vs. laziness, beauty vs. ugliness, and so on). The fact that the physical traits valorized are hyperbolically superlative confirms ontological verisimilitude. Finally, what these traits consist of and how they manifest themselves—be it by birth, education, marriage, or something else—is the domain of the narrative's exclusive fairy-tale order (the third criterion), justified by implicit and explicit social maxims.

Vraisemblance, whether or not it pertains to marvelous literature, is fundamentally ideological. It is determined by dominant public opinion and, thus, serves the interests of the most powerful by construing to their own advantage what is perceived as truth. Not surprisingly, the history of this critical notion in seventeenth-century France is that of an overtly political construct by which the absolutist state exerted control over cultural production. Perhaps the most notorious example of this control occurred with the *querelle du Cid* (1637), which was largely fought around what was and was not considered to be *vraisemblable* in Corneille's play. This debate also marked the decisive moment when the concept of verisimilitude came to designate obligation, rather than mere plausibility as an abstract referential notion. As Thomas DiPiero has concluded, "the fact that the Académie Française labeled *invraisemblables* sequences in *Le Cid* that are perfectly plausible from a material point of view drives home the point that the literary text was charged with reproducing not extratextual reality in the referential sense . . . but an ideology."[15] *Vraisemblance* played no less important a role in the development of prose fiction in this period. Since the novel and other narrative prose genres lacked a clear antecedent in classical literature, not to mention a theoretical justification, their moral utility appeared dubious at best to many critics.[16] *Vraisemblance* was to become the first theoretical concept used to defend prose fiction against accusations of moral depravity by assigning it a fully political function. Most notable in this regard were the heroic novels (*romans*) of the 1640s and 1650s, in which verisimilitude upheld the essential legitimacy of the hereditary nobility and its central place in the conservation and transmission of culture.

By the 1690s and the appearance of the first vogue of fairy tales, the dominance of both *vraisemblance* and *ut pictura poesis* as models of artistic imitation was showing signs of considerable stress. The gradual rejection of these ideals is often attributed to the rise to prominence of the *bourgeoisie*, who were increasingly unable to identify with an aesthetic that served the interests of an elite aristocracy.[17] Although the reliance on *vraisemblance* and *ut pictura poesis*, as defined above, did not completely wane until the fall of the Ancien Régime, the second half of the seventeenth century witnessed dramatic shifts away from these aesthetic principles. In prose fiction, to cite but one example, many of the *nouvelles* that flourished presented themselves as demystifications of aristocratic and especially court privilege by revealing what was purported to be the secret lives of prominent historical figures. "The *nouvelle* betrayed an undeniably democratizing tendency in its break with the traditions of the *roman*. . . . If noble readers of the *roman* felt privileged to identify with fictional characters so exclusive as to be locked into a world of their own, readers of the *nouvelle* were called upon to identify with characters whose different stations in life merely dramatized their common humanity."[18] Of course, the changes in the novel correspond to a broader epistemological change that affected all aspects of cultural production. For, the very meaning of what was considered to be "truth" as a general perceptual category was undergoing profound changes in this period. Gradually, truth proclaimed itself objective and renounced the rhetorical trappings of *ut pictura poesis*. *Vraisemblance* was giving way to the *vrai*.

Appearing in the midst of these changes, the *contes de fées* are themselves implicated in the *malaise* about the place and function of *vraisemblance* in literary representation. How this *malaise* manifested itself in the first vogue of fairy tales and, more specifically, the ambivalent impact of the marvelous on verisimilitude can be elucidated by reference to the *Querelle du merveilleux* [Quarrel of the Marvelous] that arose within theoretical discussions about epic poetry during the seventeenth century. At first glance, the *contes de fées* would seem to have little if anything to do with the *Querelle du merveilleux*. Involving one of the most prestigious literary forms as well as theoretical questions about the very nature of literary representation, this debate seems far removed from a fleeting *mondain* vogue for stylized versions of folk narratives. In spite of the obvious differences, however, the two opposing positions in the quarrel shed light on what is at stake in the fairy-tale marvelous and the extent to which it is compatible with notions of *vraisemblance*.

The Quarrel of the Marvelous (which actually consisted of several manifestoes and not one intense debate) opposed two main points of view concerning the use of the *merveilleux* in epic poetry. On one side were the proponents of the Christian marvelous (*le merveilleux chrétien*) who sought to revive and promote the use of supernatural characters and events from biblical and hagiographic sources (including God, Satan, angels, demons, saints, and sorcerers) while, generally but not always, condemning the use of gods and other figures from Greek and Roman mythology as incompatible with Christian belief.[19] Some of the most vocal advocates for this position were themselves authors of epic poems that glorified either biblical figures or personages from French history, including Chapelain (*La Pucelle*, 1655), Desmarets de Saint-Sorlin (*Clovis, ou la France chrétienne*, 1657; *Marie-Madeleine*, 1669), Le Moyne (*Saint Louis*, 1658), and Perrault (*Saint Paulin, évêque de Nole*, 1686; *Adam*, 1697). On the other side were the defenders of the so-called pagan marvelous (*le merveilleux païen*) who either tolerated both the mythological and Christian traditions (Rapin, Segrais) or promoted the exclusive use of mythological gods and characters in the epic (Le Bossu, Boileau).

Central to this quarrel were two very different considerations of what constituted a plausible *merveilleux*. Whereas the theoreticians of the Christian marvelous posited religious belief as the necessary condition for *vraisemblance*, those who defended the pagan marvelous saw in the use of mythological figures the aesthetic beauty that lent essential coherence to the text. More precisely, advocates of the Christian *merveilleux*, and particularly Perrault, argued that the plausibility of the marvelous was relative to the culture in which it was produced. Thus, the deities of Greek and Roman mythology, they argued, were not necessary features of the epic, which could accommodate supernatural powers of Christian traditions.[20] Opposing this point of view were those critics, most notably Boileau, who asserted the universal value of *la fable* (mythology) not only for the epic but for literary production as a whole. Yet, contrary to their opponents', this line of argument justified the mythological marvelous less as the representation of supernatural events than as the allegorical transposition of natural and human traits.[21] Most important, as Boileau warned, was the recognition that without this symbolic code and the aesthetic beauty it afforded there would be no poetry.[22] For the epic poets and other defenders of the *merveilleux chrétien*, then, the marvelous was culturally variable and, consequently, an article of faith concerning Christian and nationalistic dogma. The *vraisemblance* of the marvelous was first and foremost a matter of religious and political truth. For the champions of the *merveilleux païen*, by contrast, the marvelous, although compatible with the "truth" of moral verisimilitude, was by its very abstraction a universal trait of poetic beauty rather than a system that required belief. The *merveilleux* was *vraisemblable* primarily because it was aesthetically pleasing.

In several respects, the marvelous employed by the *contes de fées* resembles that proposed by theoreticians of the *merveilleux chrétien*. Like the Christian epics, the vogue of fairy tales is a recognition and exploitation of a culturally specific type of marvelous that arises from indigenous French traditions (as opposed to the purported universality of the mythological *merveilleux*).[23] The association of folkloric marvelous with the lowest classes was an important strategic maneuver that afforded a self-affirmation for *mondain* writers and readers, as well as a defense of the "modernist" cause in the *Querelle des Anciens et des Modernes*.[24] Furthermore, both fairy-tale and Christian epic forms of the marvelous depict literal (rather than allegorical) supernatural characters and events. And in both cases, this emphatic use of the *merveilleux* strains and often transgresses the generally accepted bounds of *vraisemblance*. Even the most ardent supporters of Christian epic poetry were wary about "excessive" use of the supernatural on the grounds that it led to falsifying biblical and Christian history or, even worse, making Christian figures conform to mythological models. Of course, the *contes de fées* were hardly in danger of flouting the verisimilitude of religious *doxa*. Nonetheless, critics of the first vogue often expressed disdain for the blatant *invraisemblance* that they readily associated with the *contes merveilleux* told to children.[25]

In the final analysis, however, the use of the marvelous in the *contes de fées* differs from that in both the mythological and the Christian epic. In these latter forms, the *merveilleux* ultimately conforms to verisimilitude. The mythological marvelous can claim to be plausible on moral and aesthetic grounds because its supernatural characters are either widely used conventions or abstract allegories. And even if the Christian epic attempts to uphold moral *vraisemblance* by means of supernatural effects deemed *invraisemblables* from a strictly empirical point of view, it nonetheless makes implausibility a matter of belief in the divine order, and consequently *vraisemblable*. By contrast, the *contes de fées* do not reduce the marvelous to allegorical systems of aesthetic, moral, or religious plausibility. Although they do have recourse to a moralizing pretext with the use of interspersed maxims and/or appended final morals, these serve to motivate the representation of individual characters or traits that are thereby plausible, and not the marvelous setting as a whole, which remains *invraisemblable*. Even further, the fairy tales make deliberate use of the marvelous and are, thus, deliberately implausible. This self-conscious and playful use of both the supernatural setting and the moralizing pretext distances any real belief in fairy magic, but also contributes to the readability of the text.

The difference of the marvelous in fairy tales and the more prestigious epic reveals the ambivalent function of the first vogue within the late-seventeenth-century crisis of *vraisemblance*. On the one hand, the *contes de fées* shore up and remotivate the embattled notion of *vraisemblance*. This is not unlike the reconciliation of the marvelous and plausibility by theoreticians of the epic, which, according to Kibédi-Varga, enabled these latter to counteract the reduction of verisimilitude to the truth of dominant public opinion, expressed as "clarity, the natural, but also banality and monotony."[26] In this sense, the fairy-tale vogue espouses outdated aesthetic and ideological positions. On the other hand, the seventeenth-century *contes de fées* defy norms of *vraisemblance* in their use of an unmotivated marvelous. So doing, they participate in the ongoing critique of verisimilitude (in the sense of a restrictive set of ideologies) in late-seventeenth-century literary practice.

Texts and Bodies

The textual features of the marvelous both produce and attenuate an estrangement of accepted reality, especially in its literary guise of *vraisemblance*. These contradictory dynamics are apparent in the two distinct traditions of the marvelous on which this corpus draws—the national/folkloric and the "pagan" or mythological.[27] Although elements of the national/folkloric traditions (including tale types, motifs, and characters) clearly dominate the *contes de fées*, reminiscences of the mythological marvelous (including gods, such as Jupiter and Cupid, and lesser figures, such as Zephyr, who perform supernatural deeds) are also present. Few other literary or artistic forms employ marvelous elements from more than one tradition to the extent that do the fairy tales.[28] More important, the contrast between the "high" repertory of mythological figures and the "low" inventory of folkloric types becomes one between aesthetically plausible and implausible traditions. The diegetic and rhetorical uses of Greek and Roman mythology appear as part of a widely acknowledged code whose supernatural content is fully *vraisemblable* for the elite readers of the first vogue.[29] The same is not true, however, for the national/folkloric traditions since they represent a culture that is largely alien or at least marginal in relation to the period's canonical literary intertexts. Fairies and other supernatural figures of national origin do appear in poetry, opera, and plays during the seventeenth century, most notably in *pièces à machines* (especially those of the Théâtre Italien before Louis XIV ordered it closed in 1697).[30] In such genres, as in the fairy tales, the national/folkloric *merveilleux* never attains the prestige or aesthetic *vraisemblance* of mythology. However, unlike the other genres, the *contes de fées* intensify the implausibility of the national/folkloric tradition by using it to form a context that transcends a "realistic" setting.

Although the marvelous can take the form of characters, objects, or physical elements, supernatural powers are usually attributed to an agent, principally fairies, but also ogres, giants, gnomes, sorcerers, anthropomorphic animals, and mythological figures. In those few tales without an agent, an object with "marvelous" qualities (such as the magic key in Perrault's "La Barbe bleue" [Bluebeard]) creates the requisite misfortune or lack and/or liquidates it. The agents of the marvelous in the *contes de fées* can serve any of four basic functions as either "helpers" or "opponents" to the hero/heroine:[31] 1) to predict his/her future; 2) to serve as advisors to the hero/heroine; 3) to impose a hindrance or obstacle that prevents the hero/heroine from reaching the goal of his/her quest; 4) personally to help him/her overcome the obstacle. This last function can be performed in two ways, by giving a "gift" (magical object or powers) to the hero/heroine and/or by intervening directly on his/her behalf. Throughout the 114 *contes de fées*, the specific roles played by the agents vary widely. In some tales, such as Perrault's "La Belle au bois dormant" [Sleeping Beauty], fairies appear only briefly at the beginning of the story to endow the princess with gifts that determine her future. In others, such as d'Aulnoy's "Le Nain jaune" [The Yellow Dwarf], all four of the above functions are fulfilled and hardly a moment passes without recourse to marvelous characters—the yellow dwarf himself, a good siren, twenty-four nymphs guarding a steel tower, a mysterious voice—as well as a magical (and *almost* invincible) sword. Of course, marvelous agents and the four narrative roles they play not only defy reality and *vraisemblance*, they are also the most powerful means by which these norms can be reaffirmed. The moral dichotomy that divides "helpers" from "opponents" is itself a consequence of such norms, but these agents also actively impose a familiar social order within the narrative. Helpers, for instance, often return kingdoms to their "rightful" rulers or arrange the marriage of the hero and heroine, to name but two of the most common fairy-tale closures.

Just as there is a wide variety of marvelous agents, so too are there numerous types of marvelous actions and events. Magical modes of travel (for instance, Petit Poucet's seven-league boots), gifts enhancing physical traits (the senses, intelligence, strength) and manipulation of space (for example, magical construction or destruction of castles) are but a few of the many manifestations of the marvelous. Of all these, however, metamorphosis is among the most prominent. Not only are main characters transformed into other beings or given the power to transform others, but the marvelous agents often use their powers to change their own appearance. In the majority of cases, metamorphosis is used as an obstacle—the misfortune or lack—central to the tale's narrative structure, as when a hero or heroine is transformed into another being as part of an evil spell (d'Aulnoy's "Serpentin vert" [Green Serpent] or "La Biche au bois" [The Doe in the Woods]) or when an opponent transforms him- or herself into a monstrous figure to overpower the hero/heroine (Le Noble's "L'Apprenti magicien" [The Magician's Apprentice]).[32] Yet, metamorphosis can also be used to overcome the obstacle, as when the hero and heroine in d'Aulnoy's "L'Oranger et l'abeille" [The Orange Tree and the Bee] use a wand to disguise themselves three times in order to elude their captors. Common to all of these uses of metamorphosis is a positing of the marvelous as an abnormal state that leads to or results in (what is presented as) normalcy. For instance, when the hero and heroine in "L'Oranger et l'abeille" transform themselves into an orange tree and a bee, respectively, they lose the magic wand and are unable to regain their human form. Their adventures in this guise represent an integral part of their quest, leading finally to their marriage. When metamorphosis is imposed on the hero/heroine as an obstacle or a means of overcoming it, the altered physical state serves an initiatory function since it prepares him/her to assume a preordained place in the reestablished order of the tale's conclusion. These two most common uses of metamorphosis are, then, dramatic illustrations of the fairy tales' ambivalent treatment of *vraisemblance*. The abnormal masks the normal, but the abnormal also paves the way for the normal. *Vraisemblance* is inseparable from *invraisemblance*.

Metamorphosis is perhaps only the most obvious manifestation of the marvelous to highlight the importance of the body in the *contes de fées* and all fantasy literature. Indeed, the marvelous foregrounds the body as a site of desires and fears, as a site from which to perceive how the "real" is manipulated by the literary fairy tale. Accordingly, fantasy and particularly the seventeenth-century French fairy tales display a singular fascination with the body as a "natural" essence that imparts meaning and truth. But, paradoxically, by positing the body as the inherent site of identity, these genres reveal the extent to which identity is itself a necessary differentiation from otherness in its physical form. In other words, they show the body to be a socially constructed unit of significance lacking an inherent essence. As such, representations of the body become a fundamental means by which moral, social, and ontological *vraisemblance* are both upheld and transgressed. What constitutes the acceptable and the unacceptable body is part and parcel of the same dominant social consensus that determines what is and is not plausible.

Since fairy-tale narratives are structured around a central misfortune or lack, it is not surprising that the bodies of heroes and heroines are often subjected to violence. In fact, the supernatural deeds performed by opponents (evil fairies, ogres, magicians, and so forth) are usually intended to make the protagonist(s) suffer. Although the seventeenth-century *contes de fées* are generally considered to contain less violence than many other literary fairy tales,[33] violence and the physical suffering it induces are portrayed nonetheless in this corpus, most notably in tales by d'Aulnoy, La Force, L'Héritier, and Perrault.[34] Except in the case of cautionary or tragic tales, suffering is always overcome, and usually by supernatural means that are the obverse of violence and suffering, namely bodily comfort and pleasure. Hence, their representation might be thought to expel the fear they inspire, the fear of the body's vulnerability. Through their representation, such fears are banished and replaced by the assurance of marvelous pleasures.

This process of representation and expulsion is part of a broader mechanism of fantasy literature that Rosemary Jackson has linked to desire:

> In expressing desire, fantasy can operate in two ways (according to the different meanings of "express"): it can *tell of*, manifest or show desire (expression in the sense of portrayal, representation, manifestation, linguistic utterance, mention, description), or it can *expel* desire, when this desire is a disturbing element which threatens cultural order and continuity (expression in the sense of pressing out, squeezing, expulsion, getting rid of something by force). In many cases, fantastic literature fulfills both functions at once, for desire can be "expelled" through having been "told of" and thus vicariously experienced by author and reader.[35]

There are at least two reasons that Jackson's model of desire in fantasy literature is useful for understanding the representations of the body in the *contes de fées*. First, the expulsion of culturally disruptive desires by their representation can be extended to the way the depiction of (good and evil) supernatural powers abate fears about the body. As both a source and an object of desire, the body of "normal" human proportions can only be understood or reaffirmed as such when it has been subjected to or put into contact with superhuman forces. Second, this model posits that the desires represented and/or expelled in fantasy literature have a connection with readers and writers as wish-fulfillment or what Jackson terms vicarious experience. Representations of the body in the marvelous context of the fairy tale are, thus, imbued with desires as well as fears. However, in its emphasis on the *expulsion* of desires, this model does not account for the ambivalent effects of the marvelous on representations. Far from simply reaffirming normal (or plausible) conceptions of the body (as Jackson's model would imply), the *contes de fées* are also capable of revising if not contesting these conceptions. A specific example will help to illustrate the complex ramifications of these representations in the vogue.

Marie-Rose Caumont de La Force's tale "Plus Belle que Fée" [More Beautiful than a Fairy], named for the heroine, expels the fear of physical suffering and replaces it with the pleasures of the marvelous. Plus Belle que Fée is ordered to carry out three seemingly fatal tasks by the evil fairy Nabote; but each time, her magical admirer Phraates intervenes to accomplish the task for her and to offer her innumerable pleasures—magnificent feasts, beautiful apartments, pastoral retreats—not to mention a magic wand to liberate the Reine du pays des fées, who in turn defeats Nabote. Not only are each of Nabote's plans to inflict suffering and death on Plus Belle que Fée immediately cut short, but the "marvelous" pleasures given to the heroine make her simultaneously human and superhuman. Her very name echoes the ambiguous state of her body, for she is, as the text repeatedly emphasizes, a human, born to ordinary mortals; yet her beauty surpasses even that of the most beautiful fairies. But the story does not end here. Plus Belle que Fée is guaranteed eternal life and beauty when she acquires some *eau de vie immortelle* [water of immortal life] and *fard de jeunesse* [youth cream]. With the assurance of an unchanging body, her superhuman humanity becomes, finally and quite simply, superhuman.

Throughout the *contes de fées*, the body is represented in its metonymic relations to various sorts of pleasure. For Plus Belle que Fée, immortality is desirable because it ensures continued pleasures like those her magical lover provides throughout her imprisonment. In La Force's tale and in many others (especially by the *conteuses*), the protagonist's pleasures are described in spatial terms, thus further linking him/her to the marvelous context of the tale. Instead of concentrating on the heroine's own reactions, the narrative transposes these onto the superlative objects in space, which are described in detail. Consider, for instance, the following passage in which Plus Belle que Fée and her companion Désirs enter a room provided for them by Phraates:

143

Il y avait à un des bouts de cette charmante chambre, une table couverte de tout ce qui pouvait contenter la délicatesse du goût, et deux fontaines de liqueurs qui coulaient dans des bassins de porphyre. Les jeunes princesses s'assirent dans deux chaises d'ivoire, enrichies d'émeraudes; elles mangèrent avec appétit, et quand elles eurent soupé, la table disparut, et il s'éleva à la place où elle était un bain délicieux, où elles se mirent toutes deux. A six pas de là on voyait une superbe toilette, et de grandes mannes d'or trat, toutes pleines de linge d'une propreté à donner envie de s'en servir. Un lit d'une forme singulière, et d'une richesse extraordinaire, terminait cette merveilleuse chambre, qui était bordée d'orangers dans des caisses d'or garnies de rubis, et des colonnes de cornaline soutenaient tout autour la voûte somptueuse de cette chambre: elles n'étaient séparées que par de grandes glaces de cristal, qui prenaient depuis le bas jusques en haut. Quelques consoles de matières rares portaient des vases de pierreries pleins de toutes sortes de fleurs.

[At one end of this charming room were a table covered with everything that could satisfy the most delicate taste and two fountains of liqueurs that flowed into porphyry basins. The young princesses sat down on two ivory chairs that were inlaid with emeralds. They ate heartily. When they had finished, the table vanished, and in its place there appeared a delightful bath, which they both stepped into. Just six paces away stood a magnificent washstand and large golden wicker baskets completely filled with linen so clean it made one want to use it. A bed of singular shape and extraordinary richness finished off this marvelous room, which was surrounded by orange trees in golden boxes garnished with rubies. This room's sumptuous vault was supported all around by carnelian columns which were only separated by large crystal mirrors that stretched from the floor to the ceiling. Jewel vases filled with a variety of flowers rested upon several consoles of rare material.][36]

In hyperbolic passages such as this one, the objects described stand in a metonymic relation to the characters who observe them and for whom they are intended. The superlative nature of the objects is presumed to indicate the physical pleasure they offer, such as the description of "linen so clean it made one want to use it." The table of food, the fountains of liqueurs, the jewel-encrusted chairs, the bathtubs, linen, and mirrors are all concrete extensions of the princesses' bodies. They are pleasures that firmly anchor the two women in the marvelous context literalized in the room offered by Phraates. Sumptuous descriptions such as this one situate the body within the self-enclosed fairy-tale order created by the marvelous.

To the twentieth-century reader, such descriptions are admittedly tedious; but to the late-seventeenth-century reader, they were decidedly nostalgic. Micheline Cuénin and Chantal Morlet-Chantalat have shown that detailed narrative depictions of châteaux and spatial settings drop off sharply in prose fiction after 1660.[37] While such descriptions figure prominently in the pastoral and heroic novels of the first half of the seventeenth century and often allegorize the moral qualities of inhabitants, dwellings and other locations appear much less frequently in the *nouvelles* and *histoires* of the second half of the century. When they do, they serve primarily as *effets de réel* with direct relevance to the plot structure.[38] Hence, "Plus Belle que Fée" and other seventeenth-century *contes de fées* go against the trend toward fewer and more realistic descriptions and, at first glance, appear to return to the spatial allegorizations of the earlier *romans*. In contrast to these latter forms, the fairy tales portray not moral qualities but the material and physical pleasures intended for the hero/heroine. More than signs of class elitism or even the superlative nature of the heroic couple, however, spatial descriptions like the one in "Plus Belle que Fée" represent a nostalgic conception of the body, made possible by the manipulation of reality in the marvelous. Following Susan Stewart's observation that nostalgia is capable of "generat[ing] significant objects" that in turn "transform . . . the very boundary, or outline of the self,"[39] we can conclude that the sumptuous presentation of Plus Belle que Fée's room is a nostalgic extension and material grounding of the heroine's body that also fuels desires and fantasies.

In addition to the pleasures that replace the intended suffering from her tasks, the narrative repeatedly describes Plus Belle que Fée's astonishment at the marvels that surround her (indeed, *étonnée* [astonished] becomes the most common epithet to describe her in the text). Expressions of surprise at the supernatural are commonplace in the *contes de fées*. By contrast, such reactions are much less frequent or totally absent in most other folk- and fairy tales, where the marvelous context is taken for granted.[40] By acting out the etymological sense of "marvelous" (*mirabilia*) as amazement, the fairy-tale protagonists point to what exceeds the "normal" body of the fairy-tale order. The depiction of astonishment, then, indicates the role the marvelous plays in transporting the body beyond the realm of the human and the marvelous. It suggests that when the body is transformed by the marvelous, it is infused with utopian surplus or potential, which is first of all transcendence, however limited and illusory, from the limits—the violence, suffering, and death—of the real body.

In "Plus Belle que Fée," the utopian excess of the heroine's body is also expressed in terms of gender difference. To be sure, heroines of superlative beauty are synonymous with fairy tales, and the emphasis on female beauty is hardly utopian in and of itself. In the context of seventeenth-century salon circles, however, the name "Plus Belle que Fée" would have had particular resonance for readers, since the title "fée" was often used to compliment *hôtesses*.[41] In one sense, then, the name of La Force's heroine is a humorous conceit that recuperates from sociable conversation a title itself taken from fantasy literature (Delaporte identifies the principal source as *Amadis de Gaule*).[42] In another sense, however, this name identifies the heroine with salon women and then both literalizes and exaggerates the physical powers and pleasures designated by the metaphoric title "fée." Understood in the context of attacks against sociable society and women's role in it, Plus Belle que Fée's superlative body provides a possible compensation or even vicarious experience for readers desiring a rebirth of the heyday of the salon.[43]

Yet, the representation of Plus Belle que Fée's body is simultaneously tinged with nostalgia. This is especially apparent in her gendered relation to Phraates, her helper who, in the end, becomes her husband. Although Plus Belle que Fée does liberate the Reine du pays des fées, throughout most of the tale she assumes the role of the beloved who is served and pursued by her diligent suitor. In La Force's tale, the courtly love model, a central nostalgic topos of the vogue, is intimately connected with the utopian excess of the heroine and her body. The pleasures that Plus Belle que Fée enjoys, and the immortality she acquires, are offered to her by Phraates. The heroine's utopian potential is inseparable from—indeed dependent upon—her suitor's nostalgic role. Her body expresses both unknown and familiar desires. Her body at one and the same time exceeds and stays within the confines of patriarchal tradition.

Arguably, all manifestations of fantasy literature, from whatever historical period and artistic medium, involve a rethinking of the body as that which is unimaginable and unattainable, feared and desired. At the same time, representations of the body reveal the full extent of the powers as well as the constraints of fantasy and, more specifically, the marvelous. In both defying and reaffirming literary codes of reality, the marvelous both reconceives and reproduces, first of all, what a culture defines as the body. Thus, within the seventeenth-century fairy tales, the ambivalence of the *merveilleux* toward *vraisemblance* is also an ambivalence toward representations of the body. The marvelous always begins as an explicit subversion of plausibility, and thus of what is physically possible. But the uses to which this subversion is put vary. The implausibility of the marvelous can dissolve into plausibility of one kind or another, flout plausibility, or do both at the same time. The representations of the body can, ultimately, conform to the prevailing moral, social, and ontological codes of verisimilitude, defy them, or maintain an uneasy tension between conformity and resistance. Of course, the social construction of the body invokes both desires and fears. Thus, when imagining the body, the marvelous expresses desires and expels fears—it expresses desires in order to expel fears, but it also expresses desires in order to satisfy them. In short, it provides a wish-fulfillment of which the body is the chief subject and object. By exploring the ambiguous potential of the marvelous to "produce" bodies, and more generally the "real," we can begin to glimpse the attraction of late-seventeenth-century France for the *contes de fées*.

Notes

This essay is a modified version of chapter 1 of my Fairy Tales, Sexuality, and Gender in France, 1690–1715: Nostalgic Utopias *(Cambridge: Cambridge University Press, 1996). I am grateful to Cambridge University Press for permission to reprint this material.*

1. See, for instance, Tzvetan Todorov, *Introduction à la littérature fantastique* (Paris: Seuil, 1970), and Rosemary Jackson, *Fantasy: The Literature of Subversion* (New York: Methuen, 1981), both of which I discuss below.
2. Between 1690 and 1715, approximately 114 literary fairy tales (*contes de fées*) were published in France by 16 different authors. Literary fairy tales remained popular throughout much of the eighteenth century. See Jacques Barchilon, *Le Conte merveilleux français de 1690 à 1790: Cent ans de féerie et de poésie ignorées de l'histoire littéraire* (Paris: Honoré Champion, 1975); Raymonde Robert, *Le Conte de fées littéraire en France de la fin du XVIIe à la fin du XVIIIe siècle* (Nancy: Presses Universitares de Nancy, 1982); and Mary-Elizabeth Storer, *Un Episode littéraire de la fin du XVIIe siècle: La Mode des contes de fées (1685–1700)* (1928; Geneva: Slatkine Reprints, 1972).
3. Todorov, *Introduction à la littérature fantastique*, 46–47.
4. See Lewis C. Seifert, *Fairy Tales, Sexuality, and Gender in France, 1690–1715: Nostalgic Utopias* (Cambridge: Cambridge University Press, 1996), introduction.
5. Vladimir Propp, *Morphology of the Folktale*, 2nd ed., trans. Laurence Scott, rev. and ed. Louis A. Wagner (Austin: University of Texas Press, 1968), 102.
6. Robert, *Le Conte*, 36–37.
7. Ibid., 39.
8. Charles Perrault, *Contes*, ed. Jean-Pierre Collinet, Folio 1281 (Paris: Gallimard, 1981), 176. All subsequent quotations are from this edition, and all translations are my own.
9. Robert, *Le Conte*, 45.
10. I use the French term *vraisemblance* interchangeably with the English "verisimilitude" and "plausibility." However, I use all of these in the historically specific meaning given here.

11. On the relationship between *vraisemblance* and the *ut pictura poesis* representational system, see Erica Harth, *Ideology and Culture in Seventeenth-Century France* (Ithaca: Cornell University Press, 1983), esp. 27–29.

12. See Aron Kibédi-Varga, introduction to *Les Poétiques du classicisme*, ed. Aron Kibédi-Varga (Paris: Aux Amateurs de Livres, 1990), 38–39.

13. Ibid., 38 (quote from Rapin, *Réflections sur l'éloquence, la poétique, l'histoire et la philosophie*).

14. Ibid., 39.

15. Thomas DiPiero, *Dangerous Truths and Criminal Passions: The Evolution of the French Novel, 1569–1791* (Stanford: Stanford University Press, 1992), 86.

16. For an incisive review of these critiques, see Georges May, *Le Dilemme du roman au XVIIIe siècle: étude sur les rapports du roman et de la critique (1715–1761)* (Paris: Presses Universitaires de France, 1963), 1–46.

17. See especially Harth, *Ideology and Culture*, and DiPiero, *Dangerous Truths*.

18. Harth, *Ideology and Culture*, 190–91.

19. See especially Reinhard Krüger, *Zwischen Wunder und Wahrscheinlichkeit: Die Krise des französischen Versepos im 17. Jahrhundert* (Marburg: Hitzeroth, 1986); Ralph Coplestone Williams, *The Merveilleux in the Epic* (Paris: Honoré Champion, 1925); and Victor Delaporte, *Du Merveilleux dans la littérature française sous le règne de Louis XIV* (1891; Geneva: Slatkine Reprints, 1968), 246–79.

20. Perrault provides a resolute defense of this capacity in his *Parallèle des anciens et des modernes* (Munich: Eidos Verlag, 1964), 3:16, 18.

21. Nicolas Boileau makes this very clear in "Chant III" of his *Art poétique*, *Œuvres complètes*, ed. Françoise Escal, Bibliothèque de la Pléiade (Paris: Gallimard, 1966), 172–73.

22.   "Sans tous ces ornements le vers tombe en langueur,
La Poésie est morte, ou rampe sans vigueur;
Le Poète n'est plus qu'un Orateur timide,
Qu'un froid Historien d'une Fable insipide"

[Without all these ornaments verse languishes, / Poetry is dead or creeps along lifelessly; / The Poet is nothing more than a timid Orator, / A cold Historian of an insipid Fable (*Art poétique*, 173)].

23. In this respect, both the Christian epic and the *conte de fées* are "modernist" genres. This is further suggested by the fact that prominent theoreticians of the *merveilleux chrétien*, such as Saint-Evremond and Perrault, were equally prominent polemicists in the Quarrel of the Ancients and the Moderns. Both Bernard Magné (*La Crise de la littérature française sous Louis XIV: Humanisme et nationalisme*, 2 vols. [Paris: Champion, 1976]) and Reinhard Krüger ("Perraults Erzählungen und die Metamorphosen des *merveilleux*," *Lendemains* 14, no. 53 [1989]: 76–88) have suggested that the vogue of fairy tales represents an extension or displacement of the *Querelle du merveilleux*. To my mind, more striking and ultimately more decisive are the connections of the *contes de fées* to the *Querelle des Anciens et des Modernes*.

24. See Seifert, *Fairy Tales, Sexuality, and Gender*, chapter 3.

25. Ibid., chapter 2.

26. See Kibédi-Varga, introduction to *Les Poétiques*, 41.

27. The *contes de fées* assiduously avoid any explicit appropriation of Christian marvelous elements (saints, demons, angels, etc.). In this respect, they observe the strict separation of secular and religious material common in seventeenth-century literature.

28. Examples of other forms that rely on admixtures of various marvelous traditions include the Christian epics, in which magicians and sorcerers appear alongside saints and angels, and court ballets, some of which feature fairies with nymphs, naiads, and Greek or Roman gods (see Delaporte, *Du Merveilleux*, 246–78).

29. In a detailed and insightful article, Bernard Magné has studied the narrative occurrences of mythological references in the seventeenth-century *contes de fées*. He argues that the use of mythology alongside folkloric material legitimizes the genre's less prestigious *féerie* (fairy-tale magic) and, further, "reflects an incontestable socio-cultural reality"—the neoclassical culture that dominated the arts in this period (Bernard Magné, "Le Chocolat et l'ambroisie: le statut de la mythologie dans les contes de fées," *Cahiers de littérature du XVIIe siècle* 2 [1980]: 112). Magné also demonstrates that the *conteuses* make more frequent use of mythological allusions than do the *conteurs* and attributes this difference to a desire on the part of women writers to prove their aptitude for literary creation (129–30).

30. See Guy Spielmann, "Chassez le surnaturel, il revient au galop: machines, trucages et merveilleux à l'épreuve du classicisme," *Papers on French Seventeenth-Century Literature* 19, no. 36 (1992): 23–36.

31. I am using "helper" and "opponent" in the sense outlined by Aldirgas Julien Greimas, *Sémantique structurale* (Paris: Larousse, 1966), to describe the narrative functions that either advance (helper) or hinder (opponent) the subject's quest for an object.

32. This aspect of Le Noble's "L'Apprenti magicien" (in *Le Gage touché: Histoires galantes* [Amsterdam: n.p., 1700]) is technically an example of metempsychosis, which is also featured in Mailly's "Le Bienfaisant ou Quiribirini" (in *Les Illustres fées, contes galans, Dédié aux dames*, vol. 6 of *Nouveau Cabinet des fées*, ed. Jacques Barchilon, 18 vols. [1785–88; partial rpt., Geneva: Slatkine Reprints, 1978]).

33. The usual comparison is with the Grimms' tales on this point. See Barchilon, *Le Conte merveilleux français*, 149. On the national specificity of French folklore, see Paul Delarue, "Les Caractères propres du conte populaire français," *La Pensée* 72 (1957): 57–59, and Eugen Weber, "Fairies and Hard Facts: The Reality of Folktales," *Journal of the History of Ideas* 43, no. 1 (Jan.–Mar. 1981): 93–113.

34. See, for instance, d'Aulnoy's "Le Prince Marcassin" (in *Contes nouveaux ou les Fées à la mode*, vol. 4 of *Nouveau Cabinet des fées*), La Force's "L'Enchanteur" (in *Les Contes des contes par Mlle de ****, vol. 7 of *Nouveau Cabinet des fées*), L'Héritier's "L'Adroite Princesse" (in *Œuvres meslées* [Paris: J. Guignard, 1696]), and Perrault's "La Barbe bleue" and "La Belle au bois dormant" (in *Histoires ou contes du temps passé, avec des moralités*). On violence in folk- and fairy tales, see among others Maria Tatar, *Off with Their Heads! Fairy Tales and the Culture of Childhood* (Princeton: Princeton University Press, 1992), and Marina Warner,

From the Beast to the Blonde: On Fairy Tales and their Tellers (London: Chatto and Windus, 1994).
35. Jackson, *Fantasy*, 3–4.
36. "Plus Belle que Fée," *Contes des contes par Mademoiselle ****, 1698, *Nouveau Cabinet des fées*, 7:13.
37. Micheline Cuénin and Chantal Morlet-Chantalat, "Châteaux et romans au XVIIe siècle," *XVIIe siècle* 118–119 (1978): 101–23.
38. Ibid., 111.
39. Susan Stewart, *On Longing: Narratives of the Miniature, the Gigantic, the Souvenir, the Collection* (Durham, N.C.: Duke University Press, 1993), xi.
40. Max Lüthi, *The European Folktale: Form and Nature*, trans. John D. Niles (Philadelphia: Institute for the Study of Human Issues, 1982), 37.
41. Delaporte, *Du Merveilleux*, 45–46.
42. Ibid., 44.
43. The last two verses of the final moral emphasize the distance between Plus Belle que Fée and the real "fées" of the salons:

> Fée en ce temps se fait encore voir,
> Mais on ne voit plus de miracles. (35)

[There are still fairies these days / But there aren't miracles any more.]

Bibliography

Barchilon, Jacques. *Le Conte merveilleux français de 1690 à 1790: Cent ans de féerie et de poésie ignorées de l'histoire littéraire*. Paris: Honoré Champion, 1975.
Barchilon, Jacques, ed. *Nouveau Cabinet des fées*. 18 vols. 1785–88. Partial reprint, Geneva: Slatkine Reprints, 1978.
Boileau, Nicolas. "Chant III." *Art poétique, Œuvres complètes*. Ed. Françoise Escal, Bibliothèque de la Pléiade. Paris: Gallimard, 1966.
Cuénin, Micheline, and Chantal Morlet-Chantalat, "Châteaux et romans au XVIIe siècle," *XVIIe siècle* 118–19 (1978): 101–23.
Delaporte, Victor. *Du Merveilleux dans la littérature française sous le règne de Louis XIV*. 1891. Reprint, Geneva: Slatkine Reprints, 1968.
Delarue, Paul. "Les Caractères propres du conte populaire français." *La Pensée* 72 (1957): 57–59.
DiPiero, Thomas. *Dangerous Truths and Criminal Passions: The Evolution of the French Novel, 1569–1791*. Stanford: Stanford University Press, 1992.
Greimas, Aldirgas Julien. *Sémantique structurale*. Paris: Larousse, 1966.
Harth, Erica. *Ideology and Culture in Seventeenth–Century France*. Ithaca: Cornell University Press, 1983.
L'Héritier, Marie-Jeanne. "L'Adroite Princesse." *Œuvres meslées*. Paris: J. Guignard, 1696.
Jackson, Rosemary. *Fantasy: The Literature of Subversion*. New York: Methuen, 1981.
Kibédi-Varga, Aron. Introduction to *Les Poétiques du classicisme*. Ed. Aron Kibédi-Varga. Paris: Aux Amateurs de Livres, 1990.

Krüger, Reinhard. *Zwischen Wunder und Wahrscheinlichkeit: Die Krise des französischen Versepos im 17. Jahrhundert.* Marburg: Hitzeroth, 1986.

———. "Perraults Erzählungen und die Metamorphosen des *merveilleux.*" *Lendemains* 14, no. 53 (1989): 76–88.

La Force, Marie-Rose Caumont de. "Plus Belle que Fée," *Contes des contes par Mademoiselle ****, vol. 7 of *Nouveau Cabinet des fées.* 1785–88, Partial reprint, Geneva: Slatkine Reprints, 1978.

Lüthi, Max. *The European Folktale: Form and Nature.* Trans. John D. Niles. Philadelphia: Institute for the Study of Human Issues, 1982.

Magné, Bernard. *La Crise de la littérature française sous Louis XIV: Humanisme et nationalisme.* 2 vols. Paris: Champion, 1976.

———. "Le Chocolat et l'ambroisie: le statut de la mythologie dans les contes de fées." *Cahiers de littérature du XVIIe siècle* 2 (1980): 112.

May, Georges. *Le Dilemme du roman au XVIIIe siècle: étude sur les rapports du roman et de la critique (1715–1761).* Paris: Presses Universitaires de France, 1963.

Perrault, Charles. *Parallèle des anciens et des modernes.* Munich: Eidos Verlag, 1964.

———. *Contes.* Ed. Jean-Pierre Collinet. Folio 1281. Paris: Gallimard, 1981.

Propp, Vladimir. *Morphology of the Folktale.* 2nd ed. Trans. Laurence Scott. Rev. and ed. Louis A. Wagner. Austin: University of Texas Press, 1968.

Robert, Raymonde. *Le Conte de fées littéraire en France de la fin du XVIIe à la fin du XVIIIe siècle.* Nancy: Presses Universitares de Nancy, 1982.

Seifert, Lewis C. *Fairy Tales, Sexuality, and Gender in France, 1690–1715: Nostalgic Utopias.* Cambridge: Cambridge University Press, 1996.

Spielmann, Guy. "Chassez le surnaturel, il revient au galop: machines, trucages et merveilleux à l'épreuve du classicisme." *Papers on French Seventeenth-Century Literature* 19, no. 36 (1992): 23–36.

Stewart, Susan. *On Longing: Narratives of the Miniature, the Gigantic, the Souvenir, the Collection.* Durham, N.C.: Duke University Press, 1993.

Storer, Mary-Elizabeth. *Un Episode littéraire de la fin du XVIIe siècle: La Mode des contes de fées (1685–1700).* 1928. Reprint, Geneva: Slatkine Reprints, 1972.

Tatar, Maria. *Off with Their Heads! Fairy Tales and the Culture of Childhood.* Princeton: Princeton University Press, 1992.

Todorov, Tzvetan. *Introduction à la littérature fantastique.* Paris: Seuil, 1970.

Warner, Marina. *From the Beast to the Blonde: On Fairy Tales and their Tellers.* London: Chatto and Windus, 1994.

Weber, Eugen. "Fairies and Hard Facts: The Reality of Folktales." *Journal of the History of Ideas* 43, no. 1 (Jan.–Mar. 1981): 93–113.

Williams, Ralph Coplestone. *The Merveilleux in the Epic.* Paris: Honoré Champion, 1925.

CHAPTER 5

Fairy Tales about Fairy Tales:
Notes on Canon Formation

Elizabeth W. Harries

To what extent do we continue to read, and teach, and write about the
already read *because it has already been written about?*

NANCY MILLER, *SUBJECT TO CHANGE*

I.

 IN THE introduction to the first edition of their *Kinder-
und Hausmärchen* (1812), Jakob and Wilhelm Grimm refer
briefly to some of the fairy-tale collections that had come
before theirs, particularly the tales known as Perrault's (first
published in 1697): "Frankreich hat gewiß noch jetzt mehr
[Märchen], als was Charles Perrault mittheilte, der allein sie
noch als Kindermärchen behandelte (nicht seine schlechteren Nachahmer,
die Aulnoi, Murat); er giebt nur neun, freilich die bekanntesten, die auch
zu den schönsten gehören"[1] [France must surely have more [tales] than those
given us by Charles Perrault, who alone treated them as children's tales (not
so his inferior imitators, d'Aulnoy, Murat); he gives us only nine, certainly the
best known and also among the most beautiful]. The Grimms go on to praise
Perrault for his "naive and simple manner" and for his refusal to embellish
the tales. His fairy tales, they say, have nearly the flavor and purity of the true
folktale. The Grimms' opinions rest on a number of romantic notions about
fairy tales that we still tend to share: that they are (or should be) primarily
for children; that the best of them are accurate retellings or imitations of
oral tales; that oral tales are a kind of natural but marvelous growth from the
"folk" itself, an expression of a primitive, but therefore "authentic" national
spirit; that oral storytelling is on the wane, and its traces must be preserved

in print. They believe, in short, that their collecting is an attempt to recover something valuable and "primitive" that is being lost. They say explicitly that the authentic fairy tale cannot be invented.[2]

The Grimms' preface is an example of the romantic interest in folk culture in the decades before and after 1800. In her essay "Scandals of the Ballad," Susan Stewart says that "in order to imagine folklore, the literary community of the eighteenth century had to invent a folk, singing and dancing 'below the level' of conscious literary art."[3] The Grimms, in other words, participated in the invention of a tradition of a particular kind of oral storytelling among the "folk." Though storytelling has certainly existed for millennia, the Grimms had to imagine it in a certain way in order to ground their own collecting efforts. They had to posit a rupture or separation between literate and oral culture, between modern, self-conscious writing and older, "natural," spontaneous storytelling or ballad-singing. Their nostalgia for a vanishing or vanished culture—assumed to be simpler and more poetic than their own—still permeates most fairy-tale collecting and research. We expect the written tale to be what Stewart calls a "distressed genre," a genre that is deliberately given all the patina of age and of oral transmission. Our studies of written tales have been, at least until recently, primarily attempts to find and catalogue their oral sources. And the Grimms' anxieties—about the relationship of "high" art and popular culture and about the interplay of the written and the oral—are still our own.

My quotation from the Grimms also has an important subtext, buried within parentheses: "(not so his inferior imitators, d'Aulnoy, Murat)." Marie-Catherine le Jumel de Barneville, Baronne d'Aulnoy, and Henriette-Julie de Castelnau, Comtesse de Murat, were among the aristocratic women who began the vogue of writing fairy tales down at the end of the seventeenth century. In 1690 Marie-Catherine d'Aulnoy published a fairy tale, "L'isle de la félicité", in her novel *Histoire d'Hypolite, comte de Duglas*. This tale—a strange compendium of Greek myth and folk belief—is considered to be the first literary fairy tale written in France, the earliest in a wave of tales published throughout the 1690s and much of the earlier eighteenth century, most of them by women. The Grimms seem unable to praise Perrault without belittling these women, calling them his "imitators," though in fact they began writing tales earlier.[4] The growth of interest in a supposedly simpler "folk culture" at the end of the eighteenth century, an interest that the Grimms both followed and promoted, made it impossible for them and for many later commentators to appreciate the tales d'Aulnoy, Murat, and many other women in France wrote.

These tales, in all their glitter and artificiality, actually contest the emerging association of fairy tales with the primitive, with the "folk" and with the "oral" as they were beginning to be understood, with illiterate and anonymous female tellers of tales, and with children. And their tales, rather than existing in the supposed "timeless space" of folk culture, are consciously invented as a complex and ironic comment on the historical moment in which they were produced. The style, length, and timeliness of their narratives do not fit the ideology of the fairy tale as it has been constructed in the last three centuries. They have been effectively "written out" of the history of fairy tales, an erasure that began even before the Grimms.

In 1699, for example, the Abbé de Villiers wrote a dialogue between a Parisian and a Provincial about the vogue for fairy tales, *Entretiens sur les contes des fées et sur quelques autres ouvrages du temps, pour servir comme préservatif contre le mauvais goût* [Dialogues on Fairy Tales and Some Other Works of Our Time, to Act as an Antidote against Bad Taste]. Throughout the text, Villiers struggles to establish the boundaries of good taste—or what he thinks of as correct and established literary standards. The volume is dedicated to the members of the Académie Française, the supposed "juges naturels de tous les livres" [natural judges of all books].[5] And Villiers goes on to praise Perrault ("un celebre Academicien" [a well-known member of the Academy], one of the fraternity of learned male authors) for imitating the style and simplicity of "nurses" so cleverly in his tales: "il faut être habile pour imiter bien la simplicité de leur ignorance" [one must be clever to imitate their ignorant simplicity well].[6] Villiers insists, in fact, on the simulation of the primitive and the oral as hallmarks of the good fairy tale, while dismissing the women's tales for their length, lack of unity, and precious language. Throughout he criticizes women writers' ignorance and lack of learning, the learning that paradoxically makes it possible for Perrault to simulate the voice of the "ignorant" storyteller so well. The Parisian, often apparently a mouthpiece for Villiers himself, articulates the nascent set of beliefs that govern the evaluation of fairy-tale production: written fairy tales should replicate or recapture the style and tone of "authentic" folk narrative; they should appeal to children, though written with at least one ear cocked for the reactions of adult readers; they should have "morals" that contribute to what Maria Tatar calls the "pedagogy of fear" or a "disciplinary tactic" in the education of children.

At the same time, the Parisian continually insinuates that women writers are more interested in sales than in quality. He tells a story, for example, about a woman who, pretending to be a well-known princess, sends a coach-and-six to bring a printer to the princess's house in order to drive up the price he is willing to pay for her novel. This fable—interesting both in its treatment of class and in its feigned disdain for the profit motive—is typical of Villiers's anxiety about women's writing and money, about the literary marketplace as a site where, he claims, lazy and ignorant women readers read the productions of lazy and ignorant women writers. As the Parisian says:

la plûpart des femmes n'aiment la lecture, que parce qu'elles aiment l'oisiveté & la bagatelle; ce n'est pas seulement dans la Province, c'est aussi à Paris et à la Cour qu'on trouve parmi elles ce goût pour les Livres frivoles. Tout ce qui demande un peu d'application les fatigue et les ennuïe; elles s'amusent d'un Livre avec le même esprit dont elles s'occupent d'une mouche ou d'un ruban, êtes-vous étonné aprés cela que les Contes & les Historiettes aïent du débit (286–87).

[most women only enjoy reading because they enjoy laziness and the trivial; not only in the provinces, but also in Paris and at the court one finds among women this taste for frivolous books. Everything that requires a little effort tires and bores them; they amuse themselves with a book in the same way they play with a fly or a ribbon. So does it astonish you that tales and little stories are popular?]

For Villiers, this feminine invasion of the marketplace—as writers and as consumers—interrupts what he sees as the "natural" economy of literature and the unchanging value of its monuments, giving undeserved credit and sales ("débit") to fairy tales and other short fiction. He also complains that women and provincials are unselective in their reading habits and therefore create literary fads: "Et qui ne se persuade pas que les Livres sont une marchandise qui change de mode comme les garnitures & les habits?" [And who is not convinced that books are now a modish merchandise like accessories and gowns? (278–79)]. Books have become commodities like fashionable clothing, both governed by the fickle and superficial taste of women. Fairy tales written by women are then doubly suspect: because they do not aspire to the rigorous simplicity of Perrault's tales and because they are part of a new literary economy that threatens the stability of the old. Like Boileau in his diatribes against the novels written by women earlier in the century, Villiers carefully constructs standards that exclude women's tales.

Joan DeJean has described the way seventeenth-century novels by women were denied classic status in the course of the eighteenth and nineteenth centuries; their fairy tales were subject to many of the same processes.[7] In spite of Villiers's and others' complaints, the tales by d'Aulnoy, Murat, L'Héritier, and others had continued to be reprinted throughout the eighteenth century and formed the major part of the monumental *Cabinet des fées* published from 1785 to 1789. During and after the French Revolution, however, these tales were reprinted less and less often and were rarely, if ever, included in school anthologies or classroom texts. Perrault became *the* French fairy-tale writer.

The growth of romantic nationalism contributed at the same time to a dramatic narrowing of the fairy-tale canon. Herder's 1777 essay "Von Ähnlichkeit der Mittlern Englischen und deutschen Dichtkunst" [On the Similarity of Medieval English and German Poetry] emphasizes the crucial role of folklore in establishing a national identity: "Doch bleibt's immer und ewig, dass, wenn wir kein Volk haben, wir kein Publikum, keine Nation, keine Sprache und Dichtkunst haben, die unser sei, die in uns lebe und wirke" [But it is always true that, if we have no "folk," we have no public, no nation, no language and poetry, that are truly ours, that live and work in us].[8] Herder's essay is really an appeal to German scholars to recover old folk material in German, as Percy had (and Macpherson and Chatterton pretended to have) for the English. But this process of recovery—a process that the Grimms, as well as their friends Clemens Brentano and Achim von Arnim, were deeply involved in—was guided, as we have seen, by a fairly narrow and exclusive notion of what folk culture and particularly fairy tales (or *Märchen*) ought to look like. Tales by d'Aulnoy and Murat—often cited or parodied in German literature toward the end of the eighteenth century[9]— were no longer considered authentic or moral enough to be reproduced or even to be mentioned, except in parentheses.

In 1826, a volume by C. A. Walckenaer, *Lettres sur les contes des fées* [Letters about Fairy Tales], echoes many of Villiers's themes and anxieties as well as Herder's notions about the superiority of Northern culture. The volume is structured as a series of letters from an older male adviser to a young mother who is trying to decide on appropriate material to read to her daughter. Are fairy tales really for children? If so, which ones should she choose? (Significantly we are not given the mother's letters, but only her friend's magisterial replies.) Walckenaer returns again and again to the origins of the "contes de fées" in Northern mythology and links the "fées" to the Latin *fata* as well as sibyls and Celtic fairies.[10] Though he is concerned with tracing the links of fairy tales to traditional or mythological "wise women," he, like Villiers, explicitly condemns the versions of the tales written by women. He argues that L'Héritier's story, "L'adroite princesse" [The Clever Princess], should never have been added to editions of Perrault's *Contes*, because "les avantures qui y sont racontées sont de nature à ne devoir pas être mises sous les yeux d'enfance, et encore moins de l'âge qui suit. Perrault n'aurait pas commis cette faute" [the adventures that are told there are of a nature that should never be seen by children, and even less by those who are a little older. Perrault would never have made that error].[11] Like the Grimms, he claims that Perrault published his tales first and that the women imitated him: "Le succès des contes de Perrault produisit une foule d'imitations" [The success of Perrault's tales produced masses of imitations (35)]. And he explicitly criticizes the elaborate style of the women's tales:

Mais aucun de ces receuils n'eut un succès aussi grand et surtout aussi durable que celui des contes de Perrault; et il est facile d'en trouver la raison: aucune de ces nouvelles productions ne ressemblait aux modèles auxquels Perrault ava it eu le bon esprit de se conformer. Ces nouveaux contes n'étaient plus les *Histoires du temps passé, et de la Mère l'Oye*, répétées sans cesse par les bonnes et les nourrices, à qui leur propre instinct et leur défaut même d'éducation avaient enseigné les tournures de phrases les plus simples, les plus claires, les plus naïves, et les mieux appropriées à la faible intelligence de leurs élèves (36).

[But none of these collections had a success that was as great or as long-lived as that of Perrault's tales; and it is easy to discover the reason why: none of these new productions resembled the models that Perrault had the wit to follow. These new tales were no longer the *Stories of By-gone Days and of Mother Goose*, repeated endlessly by serving-women and nurses, whose good instincts and even lack of education had taught the turns of phrase that were the simplest, the clearest, the most naive, and the best suited to the feeble intelligence of their pupils.]

Walckenaer then goes on to quote one of Villiers's criticisms of the women's tales: "Ils les ont faits si longs, et d'un style si peu naif, que les enfants mêmes en seraient ennuyés" [They made them so long, and the style so sophisticated, that children themselves would have been bored].[12] And, like Villiers, he argues later that the *conteuses* of the 1690s simply wanted to make a name for themselves, arrive at literary celebrity by an easy route (132).

Like Villiers and the Grimms, then, Walckenaer continues the myth of the lower-class woman storyteller and her simple tales. The frontispiece of Perrault's original collection gives us, in miniature, a version of what the traditional storytelling situation is traditionally thought to be (figure 5.1). The frontispiece shows a fireside scene: three fashionably dressed children seated by a fireplace, listening to a simply dressed older woman, perhaps a nurse, shown with a spindle.[13] The fire and the candle suggest that the storytelling is taking place in the evening, as in the traditional *viellée*; the lock on the door and the cat by the fireplace underscore the intimacy and the comforting domesticity of the scene. The older title of the collection, the title that Perrault had used for an earlier manuscript edition of the *Contes* in 1695, appears as a placard affixed to the door in the background, just above the spindle that is traditionally associated with women's storytelling: *Contes de ma Mere Loye* [Stories of Mother Goose]. The writing on the placard is rather irregular and clumsy, compared to the elegance of the type used

FIGURE 5.1. Frontispiece, Charles Perrault, *Histoires ou contes du temps passé* (Paris: Chez Claude Marbin, 1697). By permission of The Houghton Library, Harvard University.

on the title page, just as the title on the placard contrasts with the more elaborate and distanced formal title: *Histoires ou Contes du temps passé, avec des Moralitez* [Stories of Times Past, with Morals]. As Catherine Velay-Vallantin has pointed out, the frontispiece suggests the fictive reading situation that Perrault and his publisher wanted to prescribe, a simulation of oral tale-telling, or what she calls "factitious orality."[14] It also suggests that this orality, the voice that Perrault is simulating, is female. It confirms the prevailing notion of the appropriate role for women in the transmission of fairy tales: as patient, nurturing conduits of oral culture or as spinners of tales.

But, as folklorists have shown, women are and were not the only, or even the primary, storytellers in most oral cultures.[15] The myth of the anonymous female teller of tales, particularly strong in the murky legend of Mother Goose, is just that: a myth—but a myth that has several important functions and corollaries. If women are the tellers of tales, storytelling remains a motherly (or grandmotherly) function, tied (to use the language of French feminist critics) to the body and nature. Stories are supposed to flow from women like milk and blood. And if women are thought of as *tellers* of tales, it follows that they are not imagined as the collectors or writers of tales. As fairy tales moved from oral tales to "book tales" (*Buchmärchen*, or tales that have been written down) to written, invented tales (*Kunstmärchen*), women were subtly relegated to the most "primitive" stage. Perrault's fron-tispiece may have been an attempt to etch his female writing competitors out of existence.

The women who wrote tales did not identify themselves with "nurses" or peasant women; in fact they tended to refer to themselves, in the salons, as sibyls or fairies. (There was some element of class-consciousness here, of course, but something much more important was also at work. If they identified themselves primarily as *tellers* of tales, it would be more difficult to see themselves as *writers* of tales.) And the frontispieces of volumes of their tales often seem to be designed to contest the ideological force of Perrault's. The frontispiece of an early edition of d'Aulnoy's tales (an edition that she probably supervised in 1698), features a woman dressed as a sibyl (one of the Greek or Roman prophetesses who were known as mysterious truth-tellers and had magic powers) (figure 5.2).[16] She is writing one of d'Aulnoy's titles, "Gracieuse et Percinet" in a large folio or book, again with children as her audience, but children dressed in rather the same way and probably of the same class as the storyteller. The storyteller is *not* represented with a spindle, but rather with the flowing robes and turbanlike headpiece usually associated with a sibyl. There's a fireplace, but the fire is out. Instead of the locked door, there is a window opening out on a summer country scene. Instead of the domestic cat, there is an exotic monkey—again perhaps a reference to one of d'Aulnoy's tales, "Babiole."

FIGURE 5.2. Frontispiece, Marie-Catherine d'Aulnoy, *Suite des contes nouveaux* (Paris: Compagnie des Libraires, 1711). Courtesy, The Bancroft Library, University of California, Berkeley.

The frontispiece of the first volume in a 1725 Amsterdam edition of d'Aulnoy's tales shows a woman speaking to an audience of fashionably dressed adults (figure 5.3). (Note that she is represented as seated above, and slightly larger than, her audience—and that the gesture she is making with her left hand is the traditional gesture that asks for silent attention.) The frontispiece of the second volume represents a woman writing (figure 5.4): we see a woman with a helmet on her head (probably Athena, the goddess of wisdom, with her owl on the right; perhaps merely a representative of the classical tradition) writing on a large tablet with a quill and apparently speaking at the same time. In the foreground there is an audience of adults, in the background a scene that might represent, in miniature, the plot of one of d'Aulnoy's tales. These frontispieces, like the frontispiece of the 1698 volume that d'Aulnoy probably supervised, both show the woman in an aristocratic milieu—and in a scene that has windows, that is open to the outside, the public sphere. Far from the homely, domestic scene that Perrault used, these frontispieces underline women's authority to speak, write, and (implicitly) publish.

II.

The women who wrote tales in the 1690s, then, consciously presented themselves—both in the frontispieces and in their stories themselves—as sophisticated writers rather than as simple peasant storytellers. In most of their frontispieces, the audience is not children but adults. And their stories tend to be, unlike Perrault's, long, complex, often full of digressive episodes and decorative detail. They in fact are often self-referential, "fairy tales about fairy tales" (one of the meanings of my ambiguous title) or *mises en abîme*. Far from the simple, direct narratives that Perrault and the Grimms preferred, they tend to make self-conscious commentaries on themselves and on the genre they're part of. In d'Aulnoy's "La chatte blanche" [The White Cat], for example, a prince lost in the woods finds a castle covered with scenes from her earlier tales. Or, in another of d'Aulnoy's tales, "Le pigeon et la colombe" [The Pigeon and the Dove], the good fairy "lisait dans les astres avec la même facilité qu'on lit à présent les contes nouveaux qui s'impriment tous les jours" [read the stars with the same ease that one now reads the many new tales that are being printed every day]. These glittering tales often become mirrors of themselves, as well as of the court of Louis XIV. They are anything but naive.

We might compare, for example, two versions of a similar scene, the first from Perrault's "Cendrillon" or "Cinderella," the second from d'Aulnoy's "Finette Cendron":

> Le lendemain les deux soeurs furent au Bal, et Cendrillon aussi,
> mais encore plus parée que la première fois. Le Fils du Roi fut

FIGURE 5.3. Frontispiece, Marie-Catherine d'Aulnoy, *Nouveax contes de fées*, vol. 1 (Amsterdam: Chez Etienee Roger, 1725). Courtesy of the Piepont Morgan Library, New York: PML 84636–7.

FIGURE 5.4. Frontispiece, Marie-Catherine d'Aulnoy, *Nouveax contes de fées*, vol. 2 (Amsterdam: Chez Etienee Roger, 1725). Courtesy of the Piepont Morgan Library, New York: PML 84636–7.

toujours auprès d'elle, et ne cessa de lui conter des douceurs; la jeune Demoisells ne s'ennuyait point, et oublia ce que sa Marraine lui avait recommandé; de sorte qu'elle entendit sonner le premier coup de minuit, lorsqu'elle ne croyait pas qu'il fût encore onze heures: elle se leva et s'enfuit aussi légèrement qu'aurait fait une biche. Le Prince la suivit, mais il ne put l'attraper; elle laissa tomber une de ces pantoufles de verre, que le Prince ramassa bien soigneusement. Cendrillon arriva chez elle bien essoufflée, sans carosse, sans laquais, et avec ses méchants habits.[17]

[The next evening the two sisters went to the ball, and so did Cinderella, dressed even more splendidly than before. The king's son never left her side and kept saying sweet things to her. The young lady enjoyed herself so much that she forgot her godmother's advice and was dumbfounded when the clock began to strike twelve, for she did not even think it was eleven. She rose, and fled lightly as a fawn. The prince followed her, but could not catch her. However, she dropped one of the glass slippers, which the prince carefully picked up. Without coach or footmen, Cinderella reached home out of breath and in shabby clothes.]

Un soir que Finette avait plus dansé qu'à l'ordinaire, et qu'ell' avait tardé assez tard à se retirer, voulant réparer le temps perdu et arriver chez elle un peu avant ses soeurs, en marchant de toute sa force, elle laissa tomber une de ses mules, que était de velours rouge, toute brodée des perles.Elle fit son possible pour la retrouver dans le chemin; mais le temps était si noir qu'elle prit une peine inutile; elle rentra au logis, un pied chaussée et l'autre nu.

   Le lendemain le prince Chéri, fils aîné du roi, allant à la chasse, trouve la mule de Finette; il la fait ramasser, la regarde, en admire la petitesse et la gentillesse, la tourne, retourne, la baise, la chérit et l'emporte avec lui. Depuis ce jour-là, il ne mangeait plus; il devenait maigre et changé, jaune comme un coing, triste, abattu. Le roi et la reine, qui l'aimaient éperdument, envoyaient de tous côtés pour avoir du bon gibier et des confitures; c'était pour lui moins que rien; il regardait tout cela sans répondre à la reine, quand elle lui parlait, L'on envoya quérir des médecins partout, même jusqu'à Paris et à Montpellier. Quand ils furent arrivés, on leur fit voir le prince, et après l'avoir considéré trois jours et trois nuits sans le perdre de vue, ils conclurent qu'il était amoureux, et qu'il mourrait si l'on n'y apportait remède.[18]

[One evening when Finette had danced more than usual and had delayed her departure to a later hour, she was so anxious to get home before her sisters that she walked too hurriedly and lost one of her slippers, made of red velvet and embroidered with pearls. She tried to find it on the road, but the night was so dark, that she searched in vain. Thus she entered the house with one foot shod and one foot not.

The next day, Prince Chéri, the king's eldest son, went out hunting and found Finette's slipper. He picked it up and examined it, admiring its diminutive size and elegance. After turning it over and over, he kissed it and carried it home with him.

From that day on he refused to eat, and his looks underwent a great change: he became yellow as a quince, thin, melancholy, and depressed. The king and queen, who were devoted to him, had the choicest game and best confiture brought in from everywhere, but they meant nothing to him. He gazed blankly at everything and did not respond when his mother spoke to him. They summoned the best physicians from all around, even as far as Paris and Montpellier. After observing him continually for three days and three nights, they concluded that he was in love and that he would die if they did not find the sole remedy for him.]

Most writers about fairy tales, from the 1690s until the present, would point out the greater economy, speed, and simplicity of the Perrault version. (The glass slipper, perhaps an invention of Perrault's, has become a crucial part of the versions of "Cinderella" we now usually tell; Perrault's version has become ours.) Another way to look at the differences, however, might be to comment on the psychological interest of d'Aulnoy's portrayal of the prince, on her telling use of contemporary detail (from the embroidered, fetishistic slipper to the doctors from Paris and Montpellier), and on her ingenious elaboration of a well-known motif. Only if we believe—with Villiers, the Grimms, and Walckenaer—that the language of the fairy tale must be simple, stripped down, and pseudonaive, would we necessarily prefer Perrault's version.

We might also look at another pair, based on similar motifs: the two tales called "Riquet à la houppe" [Riquet with the Tuft], one by Perrault (first published in his *Contes* in 1697, not included in the manuscript edition of 1695), one by Catherine Bernard (first published in 1696 in her novel *Inès de Cordoue*).[19] Though there has been a fair amount of speculation about priority, no one has been able to prove which one came first—and that, in any case, is not central to my argument.[20] In fact, it's tempting to think of them as tales

165

told the same afternoon in a salon, rival versions based on a common *donnée*—just as, in the salons, one composed poems based on the same collection of rhyming words ("bouts-rimées") or made up different interpretations for the same dreams.

The two tales seem to be answers to the same question: what happens when absolute beauty is combined with stupidity, and ugliness with high intelligence? In most fairy tales the princes and princesses are both beautiful and smart—but what if they weren't? What if the beautiful princess were abysmally stupid and the clever prince hideously deformed? What if they encountered each other? How would their meeting differ from the classic "love at first sight" that dominates most tales?

Perrault and Bernard make some of the same choices. They both present the prince as the deformed, intelligent one, the princess as the beautiful one with no brains. They both give the prince an underground kingdom and a retinue of gnomes. Both play on a central exchange: the prince gives the princess the gift of intelligence, with the power the fairies had given him at birth to make up for his deformities; the princess in return must promise to marry him. Both set the crucial meetings between them exactly a year apart, the year that the prince has given the princess to enjoy and exercise her new intelligence before their marriage. And, in both stories, the marriage takes place.

Within this common framework, however, the differences are striking. Perrault begins with his usual formula: "Il y avait une fois" [Once upon a time], establishing the fairy-tale milieu in the first few words. He starts with the birth of the prince, the horror of his mother at this "si vilain marmot" [ugly little monkey], and the compensatory gift of the fairy. Then he goes on to the birth, seven or eight years later, of twin girls in a neighboring kingdom: one beautiful but stupid, one clever but ugly. (The clever but ugly princess doesn't appear in Bernard's version, and gradually fades from Perrault's, having served primarily as a foil for her sister.)

Bernard, on the other hand, begins her tale with a sentence that might lead to a very different kind of story: "Un grand seigneur de Grenade, possédant des richesses dignes de sa naissance, avait un chagrin domestique qui empoisonnait tous les biens dont le comblait la fortune" [A great nobleman of Grenada, possessing riches worthy of his birth, had a domestic sorrow that poisoned all the gifts that fortune had bestowed on him]. The setting she creates is not immediately identifiable as a fairy-tale landscape; the mention of Grenada makes it seem that she might be beginning one of the many "nouvelles" set in Spain, popular at the time, rather than a fairy tale. She begins with the birth of one princess, named Mama (oddly enough), and the "chagrin domestique" that her stupidity and lack of grace cause. Then she moves swiftly, in a paragraph and a half, to the meeting with Riquet, the prince/monster, who, in her version, is given no previous history at all. Perrault's opening, with its symmetrical families and fairy gifts, is immediately in the realm of fantasy; Bernard's, with its quasi-realistic focus on the princess and her family, initially inhabits a different kind of narrative space.

This difference seems to narrow as the stories continue, since both recount the meeting of the prince and princess in rather similar ways. It's probably significant, though, that in Perrault's version Riquet acknowledges that his power to give the princess some wit comes from the fairies, while in Bernard's version he gives her a verse to recite, rather than stressing the magic of his gift. This verse, apparently simple and banal in the extreme, nevertheless has a subtle incantatory power:

Toi qui peut tout animer,
Amour, si pour n'être bête,
Il ne faut que savoir aimer,
Me voilà prête.

[Cupid, you who can bring everything to life, if it is only necessary to know how to love in order not to be stupid, see that I am ready.]

The princess is not simply made intelligent, as in Perrault's version; she must contribute to her own transformation by repeating these words: "A mesure que Mama prononçait ces vers, sa taille se dégageait, son air devenait plus vif, sa démarche plus libre; elle les répéta" [As Mama uttered these verses, her poise improved, her posture became more lively, her movements freer; she repeated them].

And everything that happens *after* her transformation in the two stories is almost completely different. In both versions, the transformed princess finds an admirer who is rich, handsome, and intelligent. In Perrault's version, however, the princess seems to forget him as soon as she reencounters Riquet. Perrault's princess agrees to marry Riquet without hesitation when he tells her that she has the gift to make him handsome, just as he had the gift to make her intelligent.

La Princesse n'eut pas plus tôt prononcer ces paroles, que Riquet à la houppe parut à ces yeux l'homme du monde le plus beau, le mieux fait et le plus aimable qu'elle eût jamais vu. Quelques-uns assurent que ce ne furent poit les charmes de la Fée que opéreènt, mais que l'amour seul fit cette Métamorphose. . . . Dès le lendemain les noces furent faites, ainsi que Riquet à la houppe l'avait prévu, et selon les ordres qu'il en avait donnés longtemps auparavent. (180)

[No sooner had the Princess finished uttering these words, when Riquet à la houppe appeared to her eyes as the most beautiful, well-formed and charming man that she had ever seen. Some say that it was not the fairy's charms at work here, but rather simply Love that caused this Metamorphosis. . . . The wedding took place the next day, just as Riquet à la houppe had planned it, and following the orders that he had given a long time before.]

Perrault's tale ends with this sentence; Riquet and the princess, having given each other their symmetrical gifts, presumably live happily ever after, just as Riquet has planned. The story begins and ends with Riquet, his birth, his plans, and his power.

In Bernard's version, the other suitor—here given a name, Arada— is always present in the princess's thoughts, and in fact her fear of his disdain if she should become stupid again is one of the reasons she agrees to marry Riquet. But even after her marriage—and it is significant that Bernard continues to write her story "beyond the ending"[21]—she continues to think of him and finally arranges for him to join her in Riquet's subterranean kingdom. Riquet is not transformed, and remains the clever but hideous gnome he has been since the beginning. Though the princess is temporarily able to outwit him, now being clever herself, and visits her lover Arada at night, Riquet discovers her treachery and takes his revenge by turning Arada into a gnome identical to himself. Mama is no longer able to distinguish between them and lives on unhappily in the subterranean kingdom:

> Elle se vit deux maris au lieu d'un, et ne sut jamais à qui adresser ses plaintes, de peur de prendre l'objet de sa haine pour l'objet de son amour; mais peut-être qu'elle n'y perdit guère: les amants à la longue deviennent des maris (278).

> [She lived with two husbands instead of one, and never knew whom to complain to, for fear of taking the object of her hatred for the object of her love. But perhaps she hardly lost anything at all: in the long run lovers always become husbands.]

In place of Perrault's conventional wedding and happy ending, Bernard gives us this disillusioned "moral." Marriage is not a static and blissful state, and lovers do not remain the faultless creatures they have seemed. Perrault's tale is one of mutual transformation; in Bernard's there is no such magical reciprocity.

Jack Zipes once claimed that both tales are designed to discipline women into compliant daughters and wives, showing that women's unruly desires must be tamed by constant surveillance.[22] It seems to me, however, that Bernard's tale is about the dangers for women in the usual fairy-tale marriage patterns, the patterns that Perrault both reproduces and mystifies. Perrault's tale is indeed "male-centered", as Zipes claims (23ff), beginning and ending with the history of Riquet à la houppe. But Bernard's—as her very different introduction and conclusion show—is focused on the plight of a woman whose desires do *not* transform the ugly prince into a dreamboat and whose situation is never completely under her own control. (Her illusion of autonomy in the year following her transformation is cruelly shattered after Riquet's reappearance and the forced marriage.) Though perhaps not suitable for the eyes of children, as Walckenaer complained, Bernard's tale is a comic and clear-eyed subversion of romance or what we think of as "fairy-tale" patterns. Riquet as husband becomes a tyrant who can even clone himself to enforce the princess's absolute isolation in his underground kingdom. Rather than living "happily ever after," the princess lives on in adulterous bigamy, with two indistinguishable and repulsive husbands and no one she can safely confide in. The tale, in fact, may be a fairly transparent allegory of the position of women in the marriage economy of France under Louis XIV.[23]

It's not surprising that Bernard's tale has not been widely reproduced or anthologized since the eighteenth century. Though it's approximately the same length as Perrault's, unlike many of the *conteuses'* very long tales, and though its language is often as terse and compressed as his, Bernard's pessimism and her critique of established patriarchal patterns would certainly not have endeared it to the Grimms or their successors. As fairy tales gradually became naturalized as guarantors of good behavior, bourgeois family stability and submissive female purity, tales like Bernard's became less and less acceptable.[24]

III.

Our current canon of fairy tales—those fairy tales produced and reproduced in endless collections and illustrated editions of single tales—includes very few written by women. But this is not the result of differing access to literacy determined by sex. The *conteuses*—most of them aristocrats or well-connected bourgeoises—were highly literate and sophisticated writers in a culture that found their writing deeply disturbing and suspect. Though they had "access to the means of literary production," their work was almost immediately criticized and marginalized by threatened writers like Villiers.[25] Like the female writers of romances in the seventeenth century, they were in fact gradually "excluded from the canon"—a process that we need to examine and understand.[26]

As we read and analyze these noncanonical texts, we will also have to reconsider the evaluative terms that have been part of the aura surrounding the canonical ones. Canons tend to be self-validating; that is, the qualities they possess become the qualities that we look for in our reading and praise all over again when we find them. The Grimms wanted fairy tales to be simple, "naive," economical, a reflection of their ideas about the folk, and appropriate for the social education of children; the ones they chose became canonical; and now when we read fairy tales, we want them to be like the ones the Grimms promoted. (As one of my research assistants—a sophomore—said about the stories by women, "Too many diamonds and emeralds.")

My evolving project—the reexamination of the early French fairy tales written by women, and the attempt to understand the formation of the minor "canon" of fairy tales—has implications for all canon investigations. To think about a canon often means to take a hard look at the terms we use to evaluate our texts—and that's never easy. It means as well trying to analyze and make explicit the assumptions that governed the formation of the canon in the first place. Assumptions about a "good" or "authentic" fairy tale created the canon of the genre, a canon that includes Perrault but excludes his female contemporaries. We've unconsciously accepted notions that were beginning to form as Perrault was writing in the 1690s and that were made explicit by the Brothers Grimm in the early nineteenth century. Ignoring the sophisticated "fairy tales about fairy tales" the *conteuses* wrote, we've continued to believe other "fairy tales about fairy tales."

Notes

1. Brüder Grimm, *Kinder- und Hausmärchen gesammelt durch die Brüder Grimm, 1812 und 1815*, ed. Heinz Rölleke and Ulrike Marquardt (Göttingen: Vandenhoeck and Ruprecht, 1966), 1:xvi. All translations from French and from German are mine, unless otherwise indicated in the notes.
2. Rey Chow gives a particularly lucid formulation of this recurring complex of ideas. See her book *Primitive Passions: Visuality, Sexuality, Ethnography, and Contemporary Chinese Cinema* (New York: Columbia University Press, 1995), 22–23. As she says, these ideas tend to become prominent at times of cultural crisis—as the Napoleonic era certainly was for the Grimms.
3. Susan Stewart, *Crimes of Writing: Problems in the Containment of Representation* (New York: Oxford University Press, 1991), 102–3. Eric Hobsbawm, in "Inventing Traditions," his introduction to a collection of essays called *The Invention of Tradition*, makes much the same point (ed. Eric Hobsbawm and Terence Ranger [Cambridge: Cambridge University Press, 1983], 1–14). See also Peter Burke, who writes: "In this sense the subject of this book was discovered—or was it invented?—by a group of German intellectuals at the end of the eighteenth century" (*Popular Culture in Early Modern Europe* [New York: Harper Torchbooks, 1978], 8). Raymonde Robert has interesting things to say about the construction of the image of a "folk" tale-telling situation, though she does not distinguish

between the model Perrault and the Grimms followed and the very different model the women writers constructed (see her *Le Conte de fées littéraire en France de la fin du XVIIe à la fin du XVIIIe siècle* [Nancy: Presses Universitaires de Nancy, 1982]).

4. The Grimms' opinion has been the dominant one until very recently. In 1975 Jacques Barchilon continued to call them the feminine imitators of Perrault (Jacques Barchilon, *Le conte merveilleux français de 1690 à 1790* [Paris: Champion, 1975], 63); in 1985 Volker Klotz dismissed them in a few pages as "the writing beauties at court" (*Das Europäische Kunstmärchen* [Stuttgart: Metzler, 1985], 79–87); even Jack Zipes claimed in 1983 that these women "followed" Perrault (*Fairy Tales and the Art of Subversion: The Classical Genre for Children and the Process of Civilization* [1983; rpt., New York: Routledge, 1991], 15). Only Zipes's 1991 edition of French fairy tales, *Beauties, Beasts and Enchantment: Classic French Fairy Tales* (1989; New York: Meridian, 1991), and Marina Warner's *From the Beast to the Blonde: On Fairy Tales and Their Tellers* (New York: Farrar, Straus, and Giroux, 1995) have really begun to bring these women's tales out of their long obscurity, at least in the Anglo-American world.

5. As Gabrielle Verdier notes, "les femmes font les frais de cette affirmation de solidarité masculin" [women pay the price for this affirmation of masculine solidarity]. "Figures de la conteuse dans les contes de fées feminins," *XVIIe siècle* 180 (1993): 485.

6. Abbé Pierre de Villiers, *Entretiens sur les contes de fées et sur quelques autres ouvrages du temps, pour servir comme préservatif contre le mauvais goût* (Paris: Jacques Collombat, 1699), 109. See Susan Noakes, "On the Superficiality of Women" (*The Comparative Perspective on Literature*, ed. Clayton Koelb and Susan Noakes [Ithaca: Cornell University Press, 1988], 339–55), for an overview of the persistence of this motif, from medieval tracts to the present.

7. See particularly Joan DeJean's last chapter, "The Origin of Novels: Gender, Class, and the Writing of French Literary History" and a footnote about fairy tales (255–56) in *Tender Geographies: Women and the Origins of the Novel in France* (New York: Columbia University Press, 1991). Unlike DeJean, however, I can't find much evidence that Charles Perrault was defending women *writers* in his "Apologie des femmes" (1694); rather it seems a defense of the conventionally virtuous woman and wife against accusations of frivolity and sexual inconstancy.

8. Johann Gottfried Herder, *Sämmtliche Werke*, vol. 9, ed. Bernhard Suphan (Berlin: Weidmannsche Buchhandlung, 1893), 529.

9. Wieland's *Die Abenteuer des Don Sylvio von Rosalva* [The Adventures of Don Sylvio of Rosalva (1764)] is a loving mockery of d'Aulnoy's tales, just as Cervantes's *Don Quixote* (1605–15) both parodies and celebrates the prose romance of the previous century. Goethe himself refers to d'Aulnoy's tale "La chatte blanche" in his *Werther* (1774).

10. Walckenaer seems to have been influenced by Germaine de Staël's distinctions between Mediterranean and Northern literatures in her *De la littérature* (1800). Marina Warner—rather uncritically, I think—repeats some of Walckenaer's derivations and links the "fées" to wise women of earlier times, from the Queen of Sheba to the Sibyl to St. Anne. Though the women who wrote fairy

tales tended to represent themselves as "fées" or sibyls or Greek goddesses, they did this to distinguish themselves from Mother Goose or the illiterate female teller of tales.

11. C. A. Walckenaer, *Lettres sur les contes des fées* (1826; rpt., Paris: Didot Frères, 1862), 33.

12. Villiers, *Entretiens*, 74; Walckenaer, *Lettres*, 39.

13. See Maria Tatar's discussion of various imitations of this scene in Germany and England in the nineteenth century, and the accompanying illustrations (figures 8–14), in *The Hard Facts of the Grimms' Fairy Tales* (Princeton: Princeton University Press, 1987), 106–14. She notes that the middle-class grandmother replaced the lower-class nurse in later illustrations, and that she is sometimes represented then as reading from a book. *Caveat:* the frontispiece in Marina Warner's new book is said to be the Perrault 1697 frontispiece. But it isn't; it must be from a later edition.

14. See her essay "Tales as a Mirror: Perrault in the *Bibliothèque Bleue,*" in *The Culture of Print: Power and the Uses of Print in Early Modern Europe*, ed. Roger Chartier (Princeton: Princeton University Press, 1989): 92–135 (in particular 95–97 and 128–32; the term "factitious orality" appears on 130). Louis Marin's analysis of the frontispiece, in "Les Enjeux d'un frontispice" (*L'Esprit Créateur* 27 [1987]: 49–57), also suggests the ways it plays into Perrault's literary strategies in designing his collection.

15. On this problem, see Linda Dégh, *Folktales and Society: Story-Telling in a Hungarian Peasant Community*, trans. Emily M. Schossberger (Bloomington: Indiana University Press, 1969), esp. ch. 6; and Rudolf Schenda, *Von Mund zu Ohr: Bausteine zu einer Kulturgeschichtevolkstümlichen Erzählens in Europa* (Göttingen: Vandenhoeck and Rupprecht, 1993), 152–55.

16. As Verdier explains, there are no extant versions of volumes 3 and 4 of the first edition of the *Contes nouveaux*. But the edition published by the Compagnie des Libraires in 1711 is identical to the 1698 copy of volumes 1 and 2 in the Bibliothèque nationale. It seems safe to assume that volumes 3 and 4, including the frontispiece, are also identical.

17. Charles Perrault, *Contes*, ed. Gilbert Rouger (Paris: Classiques Garnier, 1967), 162. For the English translation, and all the translations that follow, I have consulted Jack Zipes's versions in *Beauties, Beasts and Enchantment*. (Though this anthology is now out of print, a new, condensed version called *Beauty and the Beast and Other Classic French Fairy Tales*, also edited by Jack Zipes, has just been published as a Signet Classic.)

18. Madame de d'Aulnoy, *Les Contes des Fées* (Paris: Mercure de France, 1956), 250–51.

19. Both tales are easily accessible in French in the Classiques Garnier edition of Perrault's *Contes*, and in English in Jack Zipes's *Beauties, Beasts and Enchantment*. The editor of the Garnier volume, Gilbert Rouger, believes that Bernard's uncle or mentor Fontenelle may have been involved in the production of the tale; though this is not impossible, it does seem typical of the continuing effort of literary

historians to show that women in the seventeenth century did/could not write alone. (See DeJean, *Tender Geographies*, 128–29.)

20. Jeanne Roche-Mazon claims that Bernard's came first, but her argument is not really convincing ("De qui est Riquet à la houppe?" *Revue des Deux Mondes*, July 15, 1928). Marina Warner gives no reasons at all for her assumption that Perrault's is a "rebuttal" of Bernard's version (*From the Beast*, 253–55). Dates of publication are not a reliable indicator of priority, since the tales probably circulated in oral form first.

21. I borrow this phrase from Rachel Blau du Plessis's book *Writing Beyond the Ending*, though she confines her analysis to twentieth-century women's texts.

22. Zipes, *Fairy Tales and the Art of Subversion*, 34–36. His opinion seems to have changed, however; see his introduction to Bernard's tale in *Beauties*, 93–94.

23. It would be possible to argue that Bernard undercuts this interpretation by having a particularly unattractive and jealous character tell this tale in *Inès de Cordoue*. (I have in fact argued in my article "Simulating Oralities: French Fairy Tales of the 1690s" [*College Literature* 23 (June 1996): 100–115] that we ignore the frames of the *conteuses* tales at our peril.) But the counterideological force of the ending of the tale seems unmistakable.

24. See Maria Tatar's *Hard Facts*, particularly ch. 1, for a study of the changes the Grimms made in the tales in *Kinder- und Hausmärchen* between 1812 and 1857, and Jack Zipes's description of the petrification of tales into myth in the introduction to *Fairy Tale as Myth/Myth as Fairy Tale* (Lexington: University Press of Kentucky, 1994).

25. John Guillory, *Cultural Capital: The Problem of Literary Canon Formation* (Chicago: University of Chicago Press, 1993), 349. I agree with Guillory's critique of the bases of the current "canon debate"—the ways in which both sides claim that the existing canon reflects an unchanging and monolithic Western culture. But his analysis fails to explain how a "research program" like the one many feminist literary scholars have been engaged in can have any effect on the shape of syllabi or the kinds of texts that circulate in university culture and the culture at large. One of the things such "research programs" can show is precisely the repetitive processes of exclusion that obscure the origin of categories ("*the* fairy tale") we tend to take for granted. And canons do have considerable influence outside the precincts of the university—a fact that the dissemination of the fairy tale makes particularly apparent.

26. For examples of examination of the process, see DeJean, *Tender Geographies*, and Barbara Johnson's essay "Teaching Ignorance: *L'Ecole des Femmes*" in *A World of Difference* (Baltimore: Johns Hopkins University Press, 1987), particularly pp. 77–79, on the way the "precious ladies" are now remembered.

Bibliography

d'Aulnoy, Madame de. *Les Contes des Fées*. Paris: Mercure de France, 1956.
Baader, Renate. *Dames de Lettres: Autorinnen des preziösen, hocharistokratischen und "modernen" Salons (1649–1698)*. Stuttgart: Metzler, 1986.

Barchilon, Jacques. *Le conte merveilleux français de 1690 à 1790*. Paris: Champion, 1975.

Burke, Peter. *Popular Culture in Early Modern Europe*. New York: Harper Torchbooks, 1978.

Chow, Rey. *Primitive Passions: Visuality, Sexuality, Ethnography, and Contemporary Chinese Cinema*. New York: Columbia University Press, 1995.

Dégh, Linda. *Folktales and Society: Story-Telling in a Hungarian Peasant Community*. Trans. Emily M. Schossberger. Bloomington: Indiana University Press, 1969.

DeJean, Joan. *Tender Geographies: Women and the Origins of the Novel in France*. New York: Columbia University Press, 1991.

Dundes, Alan. *Interpreting Folklore*. Bloomington: Indiana University Press, 1980.

Grimm, Brüder. *Die Kinder- und Hausmärchen gesammelt durch die Brüder Grimm, 1812 und 1815*. Ed. Heinz Rölleke and Ulrike Marquardt. Göttingen: Vandenhoeck and Ruprecht, 1966.

Guillory, John. *Cultural Capital: The Problem of Literary Canon Formation*. Chicago: University of Chicago Press, 1993.

Harries, Elizabeth W. "Simulating Oralities: French Fairy Tales of the 1690s." *College Literature* 23 (June 1996): 100–115.

Herder, Johann Gottfried. *Sämmtliche Werke*. Vol. 9. Ed. Bernhard Suphan. Berlin: Weidmannsche Buchhandlung, 1893.

Hobsbawm, Eric. "Introduction: Inventing Traditions." In *The Invention of Tradition*. Ed. Eric Hobsbawm and Terence Ranger. Cambridge: Cambridge University Press, 1983.

Johnson, Barbara. *A World of Difference*. Baltimore: Johns Hopkins University Press, 1987.

Klotz, Volker. *Das Europäische Kunstmärchen*. Stuttgart: Metzler, 1985.

Marin, Louis. "Les Enjeux d'un frontispice." *L'Esprit Créateur* 27 (1987): 49–57.

Miller, Nancy. "Men's Reading, Women's Writing." In *Displacements; Women, Tradition, Literatures in French*. Ed. Joan DeJean and Nancy Miller. Baltimore: Johns Hopkins University Press, 1991.

———. *Subject to Change*. New York: Columbia University Press, 1988.

Noakes, Susan. "On the Superficiality of Women." In *The Comparative Perspective on Literature*. Ed. Clayton Koelb and Susan Noakes. Ithaca: Cornell University Press, 1988.

Perrault, Charles. *Contes*. Ed. Gilbert Rouger. Paris: Classiques Garnier, 1967.

Robert, Raymonde. *Le Conte de fées littéraire en France de la fin du XVIIe à la fin du XVIIIe siècle*. Nancy: Presses Universitaires de Nancy, 1982.

Roche-Mazon, Jeanne. "De qui est Riquet à la houppe?" *Revue des Deux Mondes*, July 15, 1928.

Schenda, Rudolf. *Von Mund zu Ohr: Bausteine zu einer Kulturgeschichtevolkstümlichen Erzählens in Europa*. Göttingen: Vandenhoeck and Rupprecht, 1993.

Stewart, Susan. *Crimes of Writing: Problems in the Containment of Representation*. New York: Oxford University Press, 1991.

Tatar, Maria. *The Hard Facts of the Grimms' Fairy Tales*. Princeton: Princeton University Press, 1987.

Velay-Vallantin, Catherine. "Tales as a Mirror: Perrault in the *Bibliothèque Bleue*." In *The Culture of Print: Power and the Uses of Print in Early Modern Europe*. Ed. Roger Chartier. Princeton: Princeton University Press, 1989.

Verdier, Gabrielle. "Figures de la conteuse dans les contes de fées feminins." *XVIIe siècle* 180 (1993): 481–99.

[Villiers, Abbé Pierre de.] *Entretiens sur les contes de fées et sur quelques autres ouvrages du temps, pour servir comme préservatif contre le mauvais goût*. Paris: Jacques Collombat, 1699.

Walckenaer, C. A. *Lettres sur les contes des fées*. 1826. Reprint, Paris: Didot Frères, 1862.

Warner, Marina. *From the Beast to the Blonde: On Fairy Tales and Their Tellers*. New York: Farrar, Straus, and Giroux, 1995.

Zipes, Jack. *Beauties, Beasts and Enchantment: Classic French Fairy Tales*. 1989. Reprint, New York: Meridian, 1991.

———. *Fairy Tales and the Art of Subversion: The Classical Genre for Children and the Process of Civilization*. 1983. Reprint, New York: Routledge, 1991.

———. *Fairy Tale as Myth/Myth as Fairy Tale*. Lexington: University Press of Kentucky, 1994.

CHAPTER 6

Of Cats and Men:
Framing the Civilizing Discourse
of the Fairy Tale

Jack Zipes

 IT IS said that a man's best friend is his dog, but those of us who read fairy tales know better. Time and again, cats have come to the aid of poor suffering young men, much more than dogs have ever done, and in two of the more famous examples, Charles Perrault's "Puss in Boots" (1697) and Madame d'Aulnoy's "The White Cat" (1697), cats have enabled disadvantaged and often maltreated youngest sons to attain wealth and power. In the case of "Puss in Boots," a miller's son becomes a rich marquis and marries the king's daughter thanks to a cat. In "The White Cat," a young nobleman is helped by a strange, gracious cat, in reality a princess, who marries him and makes him a wealthy man. Indeed, there are hundreds if not thousands of oral folktales and literary fairy tales throughout the world in which a cat either takes pity on an unfortunate young man or helps him advance in society. Why, then, do we still proclaim that man's best friend is his dog?

Is it because cats have frequently been associated with females and goddesses, and men must worship them or pay the consequences? Is it because men and women are supposedly total opposites and often fight like cats and dogs? Is it because cats are allegedly duplicitous and devious and cannot be trusted? Or is it because cats have learned that men are dumb and ungrateful and not worth maintaining as friends?

It is difficult to answer these questions because the folklore about the relations between cats and men is much too rich and too varied. One need only glance at *Nine Lives: The Folklore of Cats* (1980) by the renowned British folklorist Katharine Briggs or *The Folktale Cat* (1992) by the noted American scholar Frank de Caro to ascertain this fact, to name but two of the more fascinating books on the subject.[1] Yet, no matter how mysterious and variegated the folklore is, one aspect about cats is clear: in both the oral and the literary tradition in Europe and America, cats play a very special role in *civilizing men* and in explaining how the civilizing process operates in Western society. In fact, I want to suggest that, by studying the *literary* tradition of "Puss in Boots" from Giovan Francesco Straparola's 1550 version down through Walt Disney's silent animated film of 1923, we can learn, thanks to an assortment of gifted cats, an immense amount about the sociohistorical origins of the literary fairy tale in the West and why honorable cats perhaps have decided not to be man's best friend.

To speak about the honor of cats in literary fairy tales necessitates redeeming the honor of two neglected writers of fairy tales, namely Giovan Francesco Straparola and Giambattista Basile, and setting the record straight about the historical origins of fairy tales in the West. It also means grasping how the narrative discourse of the fairy tale as a genre was essentially framed by men who unconsciously and consciously set an agenda that has gender-specific consequences for the manner in which we expect the miraculous turn of events in a tale to occur. In short, if we study the major formative "Puss in Boots" versions of Giovan Francesco Straparola, Giambattista Basile, and Charles Perrault, we shall see that the narrative strategies of these authors, the transformations of motifs and characters, the different styles, and the implied historical symbolical meanings and overtones constitute a generic mode of discourse that establishes the frame for the manner in which we discuss, debate, and propose manners and norms in Western civilization. As Marina Warner has demonstrated in her remarkable and comprehensive study, *From the Beast to the Blonde: On Fairy Tales and Their Tellers*,[2] it is a male frame that needs to be expanded and questioned if not subverted.

But let us begin by trying to understand how this frame may have originated, and that means beginning with Giovan Francesco Straparola. Frankly speaking, we do not know much about this man. But our lack of knowledge does not mean that he deserves the neglect that he has suffered. In fact, he could even be called the "father" of the modern literary fairy tale in the West, for Straparola was the first truly gifted author to write numerous fairy tales in the vernacular and cultivate a form and function for this kind of narrative to make it an acceptable genre among the educated classes in Italy and soon after in France, Germany, and England.

Born in approximately 1480 in Caravaggio, a town in the region of Lombardy, Straparola's name itself may even be a pseudonym, for it means someone who is loquacious, and Straparola may have been given this name, or used the name in a satiric manner. Whatever the case may be, we do know that he moved to Venice and published a collection of sonnets under the title of *Opera nova da Zoan Francesco Streparola da Caravazo novamente stampata Sonetti* in 1508. Then, forty-two years later in 1550, the first part of his major work *Le Piacevoli Notti* [Pleasant Nights] appeared, and it was followed by the second part in 1553. Soon after, owing probably to a favorable reception, a second edition was printed in 1556, and by 1560 it was also translated into French. From indications in the Italian editions, it is probable that Straparola died in 1558.

Straparola was not an original writer, but he was the first to make a substantial contribution to the shaping of the literary fairy tale and to give it a prominent place in his unusual collection of tales. The frame for the *Le Piacevoli Notti*, first translated into English as *The Facetious Nights* by W. G. Waters in 1880,[3] was modeled after Boccaccio's *Decameron*. Here the narrative frame has strong political implications. The prologue reveals how Ottoviano Maria Sforza, the bishop-elect of Lodi (most likely the real Sforza, who died in 1540) was compelled to leave Milan because of political plots against him. He takes his daughter, Signora Lucretia, a widow, with him, and since her husband had died in 1523, it can be assumed that the setting for the *Nights* is approximately some time between 1523 and 1540. The bishop and his daughter flee first to Lodi, then to Venice, and finally settle on the island of Murano. They gather a small group of congenial people around them: ten gracious ladies, two matronly women, and four educated and distinguished gentlemen. Since it is the time of Carnival, Lucretia proposes that the company take turns telling stories during the two weeks before Lent, and consequently, there are thirteen nights in which stories are told, amounting to seventy-four in all.

As was generally the case in upper-class circles, a formal social ritual is followed. Each night there is a dance by the young ladies. Then Lucretia draws five names of the ladies from a vase, and those five ladies are to tell the tales that evening. But before the storytelling, one of the men must sing a song, and after the song a lady tells a tale followed by a riddle in verse. Most of the riddles are examples of the double entendre and have strong sexual connotations, especially those told by the men. The object is to discuss erotic subjects in a highly refined manner. During the course of the thirteen nights, the men are invited every now and then to replace a woman and tell a tale. In addition, Lucretia herself tells two tales.

There are very few "tragic" tales among the seventy-four, and the optimism, humor, and graceful style of the narratives may be attributed to the fact that Straparola was writing in Venice at a time when there was relative harmony in that society. To a certain extent, the fictional company on the island of Murano can be regarded as an ideal representation of how people can relate to one another and comment in pleasing and instructive ways about all types of experience. The stories created by Straparola are literary fairy tales (thirteen of the seventy-four), revised oral tales, anecdotes, erotic tales, *buffo* tales of popular Italian life, didactic tales, fables, and tales based on writers who preceded him such as Boccaccio, Franco Sacchetti, Ser Giovanni Fiorentino, Giovanni Sercambi, and others.

During the eleventh night, the lady Fiordiana begins the storytelling by relating the first known literary version of "Puss in Boots" in Europe. Yet, as we shall see, there are no boots, and the cat is really not a cat. The story reads as follows:

There was once a poor woman in Bohemia named Soriana, who had three sons named Dusolino, Tesifone, and Costantino. Right before she dies, she leaves her two oldest sons a kneading trough and a pastry board, and her youngest, Costantino, a cat. The older sons are able to earn a good living with their inheritance, but they treat Costantino cruelly and do not share anything with him. The cat, who is a fairy in disguise, takes pity on him and helps him by providing the king with rabbits and winning his good graces with many other gifts. Since the cat frequently returns to Costantino with wonderful food and drink, the two older brothers are jealous, but there is nothing they can do. The cat cleans the blotched face of Costantino with her tongue and eventually takes him to meet the king. When they near the castle, the cat tells Costantino to take off his clothes and jump into the river. Then the cat yells for help, and the king sends his men to rescue Costantino and dress him in noble garments. Of course, the king wants to know why the now good-looking young man almost drowned, and Costantino, who is baffled, must depend on the cat who tells the king that Costantino was on his way with a great treasure of jewels for the king when he was robbed and thrown into the river to drown. Impressed by the alleged wealth of Costantino, the king arranges for him to marry his daughter. After the ceremonies and festivities, Costantino is given ten mules with gold and rich garments, and he is expected to take his new wife with a group of people to his castle, which he does not have. Again, the cat comes to his rescue by riding in advance, warning cavaliers, shepherds, and herdsmen to beware of a great troop of armed men. Unless they say they serve Master Costantino, they will be in trouble. Then the cat arrives at a castle, which is weakly defended. In fact, Signor Valentino, the lord of the castle, has recently died during a journey to seek his wife. So, the cat easily convinces the guards and company of people at this castle to say they serve Costantino too. When Costantino finally arrives with his bride, he can easily establish himself as the lord of the castle. Soon after, the king of Bohemia dies, and Costantino inherits the throne. He and his wife have many children and live a long life. When they die, their children become the heirs of his kingdom.

Although this one tale cannot represent how the literary fairy tale came to be established and institutionalized in Europe, and although it cannot be considered representative of all the tales in Straparola's *Pleasant Nights*, I should like, nevertheless, to use it illustratively as a possible means for opening perspectives and questions about the origins of the literary fairy tale and the ramifications of such origination or institutionalization.

It is possible to approach this tale as a literary adaptation of an oral tale that was perhaps common in Italy and generally involved an animal that comes to the rescue of a forlorn human being, usually a man, who manages to pull himself up by the bootstraps in the end. Folklorists generally categorize this type as AT 545b "Puss in Boots." But the fact is, we do not know exactly what oral tale Straparola knew and used as the basis for his literary narrative. We can only assume that he had heard some version of the "Costantino" story, and he decided to write his own. In other words, Straparola appropriated popular lore to represent it in his own manner and comment on the mores and values of his time. If we thus regard it as a mode of representation that was intended to indicate how a young man was to behave in a certain social situation, we shall see that it has a great deal to say about Venetian society of Straparola's times.

What are the important features of the tale to bear in mind? 1) A young peasant, who is ugly and has no manners, is placed at a disadvantage in life because he is poor and his mother leaves him nothing but a cat when she dies. 2) The cat, however, turns out to be a fairy, or his good fortune. 3) The cat endows him with good looks, clothes, and manners and puts him on display. 4) Only through her intercession, through fortune and knowledge of the civilizing process, does Costantino have a chance of moving up in society from a poor peasant to king of Bohemia. 5) The cat uses threats and the show of force to help Costantino succeed. 6) Costantino's climb is based on duplicity, spectacle (display of gifts, clothes, richness), marriage of convenience, and patriarchal absolute rule. The king's word is the final word, and Costantino's words will also become absolute after he becomes king of Bohemia.

If we take these features together, we can draw some interesting parallels with Venetian and Italian society of the sixteenth century that have ramifications for the future development of the literary tradition. In many city and state republics in Italy, it was difficult but possible to rise from the lower classes and become a rich lord. Everything depended on making the right connections, luck, a good marriage, shrewdness, and the ability to wield power in an effective way. Moreover, social mobility was more accessible to men than to women, and the social institutions created in the cities were to benefit men just as the family structure was designed around the male as the seat of all power. Women were to grace and serve men, provide them with the means to establish themselves and their families.

Though "Costantino" focuses on a poor, dismal peasant boy in Bohemia, there is little doubt that the Italian readers of that time, who were very few and were from the upper classes, read the tale metaphorically as the "lucky" rise of a male who learns how to use the civilizing process to his advantage. In Straparola's version of the "Puss in Boots" type tale, the highest virtue that a man can achieve is that of becoming lord or king, no matter what it takes. There is no real rational or moral basis for Costantino's rise and success, and the only thing that he must learn is how to fool other people, wear the right clothes, pretend, and take power through force. Clearly, the strategy of the narrative, the purposeful unfolding of the author's desire, becomes a rationalization and legitimation of patriarchy, in which women play a key role. But they are dispensable in the end, just as they become dispensable in Straparola's *Nights* at the end, when Lent arrives and it is time to repent for one's sins.

Now, if Straparola established a particular literary manner in which the tales of cats and men were to be told, how did other authors consciously respond to this initial tale? Do we have proof that other writers knew of Straparola's tale and changed it to comment on their own times? Were they interested in representing power relations within the civilizing process?

Let us see.

The next literary version of the "Puss in Boots" type tale was written by Giambattista Basile. We know a great deal about him, unlike Straparola, including that he probably had read Straparola's "Costantino" and may have been familiar with other oral versions. But let us first turn to a quick synopsis of his version, entitled "Cagliuso," which appears as the fourth tale of Day Two of his *Lo cunto de li cunti*.

This tale concerns an old beggar in Naples who bequeaths his elder son Oraziello a sieve so he can earn a living and his younger son Cagliuso a female cat, because he is the baby of the family. While Oraziello goes out into the world and begins to have success, Cagliuso bemoans his fate and worries that he now has two mouths to feed. However, the cat tells him, " 'Tu te lamiente de lo sopierchio e haie chiù sciorte che sinno, ma non canusce la sciorte toia, ca io so' bona a farete ricco si me 'nce metto' " ["You are complaining too much, and you've more luck than wits! You don't know your good fortune, for I am able to make you rich if I put myself to it"].[4]

Now Cagliuso apologizes to her catship, who goes fishing and hunting and carries her catch to the king as humble presents from Lord Cagliuso. At one point the cat tells the king that Lord Cagliuso would like to place himself at the king's service and would like to visit him the next day. When the next day arrives, however, the cat tells the king that Cagliuso's servants have robbed him and left him without even a shirt to his back. In response, the king sends clothes to Cagliuso from his own wardrobe, and soon the beggar's son appears at the king's court, dressed as a lord. A banquet is prepared, but the dumb Cagliuso can think only of regaining his proper beggarly rags, and the cat must constantly tell him to keep his mouth shut. Eventually, the cat manages to have a private conversation with the king in which she praises Cagliuso's intelligence and wealth and expresses her desire to arrange a marriage of convenience. Since she knows that the king will want some proof of Cagliuso's immense wealth, the cat suggests that the king send trusty servants with her to Cagliuso's estates around Rome and Lombardy to procure information about the young man's situation. The cat runs ahead of the king's servants and threatens shepherds, keepers, and farmers that robbers are on their way, and if they do not say that everything belongs to Lord Cagliuso, they will be killed. Consequently, the king's servants hear the same message wherever they go and are convinced that Cagliuso owns a tremendous amount of property. Now the king becomes anxious to bring about a marriage between his daughter and Cagliuso and promises the cat a rich reward if she can arrange everything, which she does.

After an entire month of feasting, the cat advises Cagliuso to take his wife's dowry and buy some land in Lombardy. The beggar's son follows this advice and soon becomes a wealthy baron. He continually thanks the cat and promises her that, whenever she should die, he would have her embalmed and placed inside a golden cage. To test Cagliuso, the cat pretends to die and learns how ungrateful her master is when Cagliuso wants to take her by the paws and simply throw her out the window. All at once the cat jumps up and exclaims,

> "Và, che te sia marditto quanto t'aggio fatto, ca non mierete che te sia sputato 'n canna! bella gaiola d'oro che m'avive apparecchiata, bella sepetura che m'avive consignata! và, sierve tu, stenta, fatica, suda ped avere sto bello premio! o negrecato chi mette lo pignato a speranza d'autro! disse buono chillo felosofo: *chi aseno se corca, aseno se trova!*" (332)

> ["Get out of my sight, and may a curse be on everything I've done for you because you're not even worth spitting on! What a fine golden cage you prepared for me! What a beautiful grave you've assigned me! I go and serve you, work and sweat, only to receive this reward. Oh, woe is he who boils his pot for the hope of others! That philosopher put it well when he said, 'Whoever goes to bed an ass wakes up an ass.'"]

Though Cagliuso tries to make amends, the cat runs through the door and keeps on running while muttering the following moral to end the tale:

dio te guarda de ricco 'mpoveruto
e de pezzente quanno è resagliuto. (332)

[Oh God keep you from those rich men turned poor
And from beggars grown rich who now have more.]

As we can see, Basile's version of "Puss in Boots" is immensely different from that of Straparola's, and obviously the changes have a lot to do with the different life that Basile led and wanted to represent. Born in Naples in 1575, Basile came from a middle-class family and spent his youth in his native city. In 1600 he took a trip to Venice, where he became a soldier to earn a living and began writing poetry. By 1609, he had begun publishing his poetry, and thanks to his sister, a famous singer, he received a position at the court of Mantua in 1613. From this point on in his life, Basile held various positions as administrator or magistrate. In 1620, he returned to Naples and was appointed a captain in Lagonegro. He continued having success as a poet and became a member of various literary academies. Yet it was not his poetry that was to make him famous but his decision to write a book of fairy tales in Neapolitan prose dialect. He began writing this book, entitled *Lo cunto de li cunti* [The Tale of Tales] in the early part of the 1630s. Unfortunately, he never saw the published version, for he died from a disease that he contracted during an epidemic in 1632. His sister arranged for the publication of *Lo cunto de li cunti*, which appeared in four separate volumes between 1634 and 1636. By the fourth edition in 1674, the title of the collection of tales was changed to *Il Pentamerone*.

Like Straparola, Basile set a frame for his tales, but unlike Straparola, he used a fairy tale as his "tale of tales" to set the stage for fifty marvelous stories. In this frame tale, Zoza, the melancholy daughter of the king of Valle Pelosa, is finally made to laugh by the sight of an old woman who in the course of an argument lifts up her skirts. The old woman, indignant, curses Zoza by saying, " 'Va', che non puozze vedere mai sporchia de marito, si non piglie lo prencepe de Campo Retunno' " (12) ["Be off with you, and may you never see the bud of a husband unless it is the Prince of Camporotondo!"]. To her dismay, Zoza learns that this prince named Tadeo is under a sleeping spell and can only be wakened by a woman who fills a pitcher with her tears. After encountering three fairies who give her magic gifts, she arrives at Tadeo's tomb and weeps into the pitcher for two days. When the pitcher is almost full, she falls asleep; a slave girl takes her place, wakes and marries Tadeo, and becomes pregnant. Zoza rents a house across from Tadeo's palace and uses the magic gifts to attract his attention. The final one, a doll that spins gold, stirs an uncontrollable passion in the slave girl to hear stories during her pregnancy. Tadeo invites to his court ten women from the rabble known for their storytelling, and one tale is told by each of them for five nights. Finally, on the last day, Zoza is invited to tell the last tale, and she recounts what happened to her. Tadeo has the slave girl buried alive pregnant, and he marries Zoza.

If we were to compare just the frame tale of Straparola's *Notti* and of Basile's *Pentamerone*, it would again be apparent that there are major differences between the two. Basile is much more witty, vulgar, and complex than Straparola. He wrote in a mannered Neapolitan dialect to address a new reading public that had begun to form at the beginning of the sixteenth century and was not interested in the courtly culture of representation. This reading public was open to dialect and materials from the oral culture. According to Barbara Broggini,[5] Basile shifted the perspective of the folktale so that both the peasant and aristocratic classes are critiqued. For instance, the value system of civility is transformed in the tales to favor the standards of the rising middle classes in the process of establishing their interests throughout Italy. As a consequence, Basile parodied the peasantry and condemned the corruption of court society, arguing for self-determination and the ethics of fairness through hard work. One of the reasons Basile chose dialect and popular tales is that he could incorporate many levels of meaning in these tales and escape aristocratic censorship.

If we now return to "Cagliuso," we can see that there is definitely a shift in ideological perspective and style in comparison to Straparola's "Costantino." Whereas Straparola celebrated the good fortune of a deprived young man, who is the hero of his story and represents the continuity of patriarchal rule as the new king of Bohemia, Basile focuses on the female cat as "tragicomic" heroine, who serves a stupid and ungrateful peasant and a greedy and gullible king. Caught in the middle, the cat can literally be taken for a middle-class protagonist, who speaks for a middle-class morality (not to mention the role of women). In some ways, the cat's situation resembles that of Basile, who was expected to administer the popular class while serving the whims of the aristocracy. The cat's power is not "magic" as in the case of the fairy cat in Straparola's tale but resides in her shrewdness, cunning, and industriousness. She knows that the court is interested in nothing but show (clothes) and wealth, and she also knows that it is important to have the right manners and speech if one is to succeed in society. She takes pride in her work, her ability to arrange contracts and to maintain loyalty, and she expects only due justice and compensation in the end. When she realizes that Cagliuso will behave in the manner that most rich lords do, she parts company with him for good.

Basile's tale, though humorous, contains a devastating critique of the feudal system of that time and represents a moral code that was not yet fully instituted within the civilizing process in Europe. Throughout the tale, the cat is completely loyal to her master, works hard, and demonstrates that wits are more important than fortune. Indeed, the cat saves her own life and sees through the facade of the servant-master relationship because she is smart and knows how to use the feudal system to her advantage. The difficulty is that she cannot achieve the security that she would like to have—something that Basile apparently desired.

This is not the case with Charles Perrault's cat, the famous Puss in Boots, the first literary cat to wear boots. Indeed, the security and destiny of this master cat may be attributed to the fact that the high bourgeoisie at Louis the XIV's court was more secure and respected, as was Perrault himself. Though it was the aristocracy that established most of the rules and behavioral codes in the civilizing process in the *ancien regime*, the norms and values of *civilité* and their modalities would have been impossible to maintain without the cooperation of the middle classes.

Perrault himself was an important administrator, member of the Académie Française, a noteworthy poet, and a cultural critic who challenged Nicolas Boileau's theories in the controversial Quarrels of the Ancients and the Moderns. Perrault regarded himself as a modernist, who wanted to break away from the neoclassicist rules dependent on Greco-Roman models, and he published his famous *Histoires ou contes du temps passé* [Stories or Tales of Past Times] in 1697 in part to prove that France had its own unique traditions that could be cultivated in innovative ways. In fact, the fairy tale had gradually become en vogue during the 1690s, and Perrault was only one among many other writers in the literary salons to begin promoting this genre. The prominent writers were mainly women. Mme d'Aulnoy, Mlle L'Héritier, Mlle de La Force, Mme Lubert, and Mlle Bertrand all published important collections of tales to establish the genre as a literary institution, but we remember mainly Perrault because, as I want to suggest, the frame for our reception of the tales was set by male writers, who have more or less marked the way we are to interpret and analyze them. Certainly, they have inscribed their concerns and desires within them so that they play a role in determining our readings of the tales.

Let us take Perrault's "The Master Cat or Puss in Boots." As Denise Escarpit has demonstrated in her immense study, *Histoire d'un conte: Le Chat Botté en France et en Angleterre* (1985), there is a strong probability that Perrault knew the literary versions of Straparola and Basile,[6] and he most likely knew some of the oral versions that had become common in France. Whatever the case may be, Perrault was not satisfied with them and, by writing his own version, he entered into a dialogue with them and sought to articulate his position regarding the position of the cat, his hero, as a mediator between a miller's son and king. Here again it is important to review the essential components of the plot.

A miller dies and bequeaths his three sons a mill, an ass, and a cat. The youngest son is so dissatisfied with inheriting the cat that he wants to eat it and make a muff of his skin. To save his life, the cat responds, " 'Ne vous affligez point, mon maître, vous n'avez qu'à me donner un Sac, et me faire faire une paire de Bottes pour aller dans les broussailles, et vous verrez que vous n'êtes pas si mal partagé que vous croyez' " ["Don't trouble yourself, master. Just give me a pouch and a pair of boots to go into the bushes, and you'll see that you were not left with as bad a share as you think"].[7]

The extraordinary cat goes into the woods where he proceeds to catch rabbits, partridges, and other game, and he gives them to the king as presents from the Marquis de Carrabas. On a day that the cat knows the king will be taking a drive on the banks of a river with his daughter, he instructs his master to take off his clothes and bathe in the river. When the king comes by, the cat pretends that robbers have taken his master's clothes. Consequently, the king provides the miller's son with royal clothes, and his daughter immediately falls in love with him. The young man gets into the royal coach, while the cat runs ahead and warns peasants, who are mowing and reaping in the fields, that if they do not say that the estate belongs to the Marquis de Carrabas, they will be cut into tiny pieces like minced meat. Of course, the peasants obey, and in the meantime the cat arrives at a beautiful castle owned by an ogre. He flatters the ogre, who can change himself into anything he wants, by asking him to transform himself into a lion. Then he dares him to change himself into a rat or mouse, and when the ogre performs this feat, he is promptly eaten by the cat. When the king, his daughter, and the miller's son arrive at this beautiful castle, they are all overwhelmed by its splendor, and after the king has had five or six cups of wine, he proposes that the marquis become his son-in-law. No fool, the "marquis" accepts, and after he marries the princess, the cat becomes a great lord and never again runs after mice except for his own amusement.

Perrault's version combines elements of the Straparola and Basile tales to forge his own statement that he states in two ironic verse morals at the end of his tale:

Moralité
Quelque grand que soit l'avantage
De jouir d'un riche héritage
Venant à nous de père en fils
Aux jeunes gens pour l'ordinaire,
L'industrie et la savoir-faire
Valent mieux que des biens acquis.
Autre Moralité
Si le fils d'un Meunier, avec tant de vitesse,
Gagne le coeur d'un Princesse,

Et s'en fait regarder avec des yeux mourants,
C'est que l'habit, la mine et la jeunesse,
Pour inspirer de la tendresse,
N'en sont pas de moyens toujours indifférents. (142)

[*Moral*
Although the advantage may be great
When one inherits a grand estate
From father handed down to son,
Young men will find that industry
Combined with ingenuity,
Will lead to prosperity.
Another Moral
If the miller's son had quick success
In winning such a fair princess,
By turning on the charm,
Then regard his manners, looks, and dress
That inspired her deepest tenderness,
For they can't do one any harm. (24)]

These morals reflect two of the major themes in Perrault's tales that were also significant in the tales of Straparola and Basile. In the first instance, Perrault asserts that the best means by which one can become a rich nobleman is through brains and industry. In the second instance, he maintains that show and the proper clothes (spectacle and display) can also enable a man from the lower class to move up in society. But Perrault deals with more than just these two themes in his tale. He also demonstrates how speech and writing can be used to attain power within the civilizing process.

In his highly perceptive essay, "*Puss in Boots:* Power of Signs—Signs of Power," Louis Marin points out that

> the cat is an operator of change: he articulates a spatial continuum that differentiates space by a temporal program or better strategy. The cat as trickster figure in North American Indian myths is always wandering in the different parts of the world. But his trips in our tale cannot be separated from his tricks. I mean his use of language. This use is manifested in the tale by the fact that the cat always anticipates his master's itinerary toward the cultural (social and economic) maximum. Everything occurs as if his master's coming in a place actualizes what his cat says just before. Textually speaking, the cat is the representative of the narrative modalizations (mainly the modality of desire) and his master, the vehicle of narrative assertions (or wish fulfillments).[8]

It is not only through the manipulation of speech within the tale, however, that we find the outlines for how men can succeed in society, but it is in the very writing of the text itself by Perrault that generic prescriptions take hold, assume power, and become established models for reading and writing. If we begin first by examining the text, it becomes evident that Perrault's tale consolidates crucial elements from the Straparola and Basile versions that transform the cat into the *master cat,* whose story effaces all those before his and determines the project of all those to come. Perrault's Puss demonstrates what it takes for a middle-class administrator to succeed in French society of his time: 1) Loyalty and obedience to one's master, otherwise one will be killed; 2) the proper tools to do one's job; the cat needs a pouch to capture his prey and boots of respectability to gain entrance to the king's castle; 3) gracious speech that is also duplicitous; 4) cunning to take advantage of those who are more powerful; 5) the acquisition of land and wealth by force; 6) the readiness to kill when necessary; 7) the ability to arrange business affairs such as a marriage of convenience that will lead to permanent security.

In the process, it is important to note that women are pushed to the margins in this tale, just as they are in the world of men. They are there as display, as chattel, as bargaining items. They are speechless. The words of the cat that generate the action and mediate everything are crucial for attaining success. The cat knows how to plea, flatter, advise, threaten, dupe, and generate a proposition from the opposing side.

But we must remember that these words are the words of Perrault, manipulating, arranging, and playing with them on a page. Perrault contemplating known literary and oral versions, changing them in his mind, thinking about his own society and literary debates, seeking to endow his words with the power of conviction so that they might become exemplary.

And exemplary they did become. Almost all of the eight tales that he published in *Histoires ou contes du temps passé*—"Sleeping Beauty," "Cinderella," "Little Red Riding Hood," "Little Tom Thumb," "Blue Beard," "Riquet with the Tuft," "The Fairies," and "Puss in Boots"—have become classics in Western society. In the case of "Puss in Boots," it was disseminated through chapbooks and broadsides at the very beginning of the eighteenth century, translated into English and German by 1730, and became embedded in the oral tradition as well. Obviously, there were many different versions that continued to be told and spread, but for the most part, the literary tradition of "Puss in Boots" was now mainly that of Perrault. For all intents and purposes, the versions of Straparola and Basile were erased from Western memory. Indeed, they were no longer necessary, for Perrault's literary text became the standard-bearer of a male civilizing process at a time when French culture was dominant in Europe and setting cultural standards, and at a time when the literary fairy tale itself was being firmly established as a literary institution by Perrault and numerous other French writers.

It is interesting to note that by the time the Brothers Grimm began publishing their collection of fairy tales in 1812, they reproduced a version that was very similar to Perrault's. In fact, they decided to drop the tale from their collection because the tale was either too much within the French literary tradition or too commonly known as a literary tale to be considered a "true" folktale. Although nobody could claim true authorship or ownership to "Puss in Boots" by the nineteenth century because it had become appropriated in many different ways by both the literary and oral traditions, it is important to note that the dominant paradigm repeatedly resembled Perrault's tale. In other words, it became the classical reference point or touchstone in publishing and in oral folklore, and it did not matter whether the tale was attributed to or signed by Perrault because his signature and his social class and gender signature had become deeply woven in the tale itself through the relations between cat and master. Furthermore, the tale became one of the many more or less fixed classical tales like "Sleeping Beauty," "Cinderella," and "Little Red Riding Hood" that have determined the manner in which we socialize children and ourselves and set up "civilized" standards of behavior in the West. It is a male frame that is not entirely rigid, but it is within this enunciated symbolic code and order, whether oral or literary, that we discuss and debate norms, values, and gender roles.

Whether for children or adults, fairy tales in all forms have played and continue to play a crucial role in the socialization process and in aesthetic development. The genre of the fairy tale has developed through oral, literary, and cinematic means, and "Puss in Boots" again enables us to grasp how the frame for our absorption and appropriation of fairy tales is determined through a male denominator in the films and videos of the twentieth century. Here the case of Walt Disney is very important.

Of all the early animators, Disney was the one who truly revolutionized the fairy tale as institution through the cinema. One could almost say that he was obsessed by the fairy-tale genre, or, put another way, Disney felt drawn to fairy tales because they reflected his own struggles in life. After all, Disney came from a relatively poor family, suffered from the exploitative and stern treatment of an unaffectionate father, was spurned by his early sweetheart, and became a success owing to his tenacity, cunning, and courage and his ability to gather talented artists and managers like his brother Roy around him.

One of his early films, *Puss in Boots*, is crucial for grasping his approach to the literary fairy tale and for understanding how he used it as self-figuration that would mark the genre for years to come.[9] Disney did not especially care whether one knew the original Perrault text of "Puss in Boots" or some other popular version. It is also unclear which text he actually knew. What is clear is that Disney sought to replace all versions with his animated version and that his cartoon is astonishingly autobiographical.

The hero is a young man, a commoner, in love with the king's daughter, who fondly returns his affection. At the same time, the hero's black cat, a female, is having a romance with the royal white cat, who is the king's chauffeur. When the gigantic king discovers that the young man is wooing his daughter, he kicks him out of the palace, followed by Puss. At first, the hero does not want Puss's help, nor will he buy her the boots that she sees in a shop window. Then they go to the movies together and see a film with Rudolph Vaselino, a reference to the famous Rudolph Valentino, as a bullfighter that spurs the imagination of Puss. Consequently, she tells the hero that she now has an idea that will help him win the king's daughter, providing that he will buy her the boots. Of course, the hero will do anything to obtain the king's daughter, and so he decides to disguise himself as a masked bullfighter. In the meantime Puss explains to him that she will use a hypnotic machine behind the scenes so he can defeat the bull and win the approval of the king. When the day of the bullfight arrives, the masked hero struggles but eventually manages to defeat the bull. The king is so overwhelmed by his performance that he offers his daughter's hand in marriage, but first he wants to know who the masked champion is. When the hero reveals himself, the king is enraged, but the hero grabs the princess and leads her to the king's chauffeur. The white cat jumps in front with Puss, and they speed off with the king chasing after them in vain.

Although Puss as cunning cat is crucial in this film, Disney focuses most of his attention on the young man who wants to succeed at all costs. In contrast to the traditional fairy tale, the hero is not a peasant, nor is he dumb. Read as a "parable" of Disney's life at that moment, the hero can be seen as young Disney wanting to break into the industry of animated films (the king) with the help of Ub Iwerks (Puss), his friend and best collaborator at that time. The hero upsets the king and runs off with his prize possession, the virginal princess. Thus, the king is dispossessed, and the young man outraces him with the help of his friends.

But Disney's film is also an attack on the literary tradition of the fairy tale. He robs the literary tale of its voice and changes its form and meaning. Since the cinematic medium is a popular form of expression and accessible to the public at large, Disney actually returns the fairy tale to the majority of people. The images (scenes, frames, characters, gestures, jokes) are readily comprehensible for young and old alike from different social classes. In fact, the fairy tale is practically infantilized, just as the jokes are infantile. The plot records the deepest oedipal desire of every young boy: the son humiliates and undermines the father and runs off with his most valued object of love, the daughter/wife. By simplifying the oedipal complex semiotically in black and white drawings and making fun of it so that it had a common appeal, Disney also touched on other themes:

1) Democracy—the film is very *American* in its attitude toward royalty. The monarchy is debunked, and a commoner causes a kind of revolution.

2) Technology—it is through the new technological medium of the movies that Puss's mind is stimulated. Then she uses a hypnotic machine to defeat the bull and another fairly new invention, the automobile, to escape the king.

3) Modernity—the setting is obviously the twentieth century, and the modern minds are replacing the ancient. The revolution takes place as the king is outpaced and will be replaced by a commoner who knows how to use the latest inventions.

But who is this commoner? Was Disney making a statement on behalf of the masses? Was Disney celebrating "everyone" or "every man"? Did Disney believe in revolution and social change in the name of socialism? The answer to all these questions is simply "no."

Disney's hero is the enterprising young man, the entrepreneur, who uses technology to his advantage. He does nothing to help the people or the community. In fact, he deceives the masses and the king by creating the illusion that he is stronger than the bull. He has learned, with the help of Puss, that one can achieve glory through deception. It is through the artful use of images that one can sway audiences and gain their favor. Animation is trickery—trick films—for still images are made to seem as if they move through automatization. As long as one controls the images (and machines) one can reign supreme, just as the hero is safe as long as he is disguised. The pictures conceal the controls and machinery. They deprive the audience of viewing the production and manipulation, and in the end, audiences can no longer envision a fairy tale for themselves as they can when they read it. The pictures deprive the audience now of visualizing their own characters, roles, and desires. At the same time, Disney offsets the deprivation with the pleasure of scopophilia and inundates the viewer with delightful images, humorous figures, and erotic signs. In general, the animator, Disney, projects the enjoyable fairy tale of his life through his own images, and he realizes through animated stills his basic oedipal dream that he was to play out time and again in most of his fairy-tale films. It is the repetition of Disney's infantile quest—the core of American mythology— that enabled him to strike a chord in American viewers from the 1920s to the present, a chord that has also resounded across the ocean in Europe, for Disney continued framing the discourse of civility within a male frame in the tradition of writers like Straparola, Basile, Perrault, the Brothers Grimm, Ludwig Bechstein, and Henri Pourrat as well as illustrators like Gustav Doré.

All of these men have bonded, so to speak, or collaborated for the same reason: to use cats for their own self-figuration and to rationalize the manner in which power relations are distributed to benefit men in Western society.

Perhaps this is why cats are not man's best friend. In the literary and cinematic fairy-tale tradition of "Puss in Boots," they have been manipulated to extol male prowess and to represent the difficulties of middle-class writers and administrators to establish a secure position for themselves in societies that are dominated by display and force. The only writer who spoke for cats and against servility was Basile, but who remembers his version? Who remembers his smart cat who long ago grasped the duplicity of men who tried to frame her life? She escaped the frame, but the tradition of "Puss in Boots" reveals how the origins of this frame and its borders of enclosure are still very much with us as we approach the twenty-first century.

Notes

1. See also Patricia Dale-Green, *Cult of the Cat* (Boston: Houghton Mifflin, 1963), and Mildred Kirk, *The Everlasting Cat* (Woodstock, N.Y.: Overlook Press, 1985).

2. Marina Warner, *From the Beast to the Blonde: On Fairy Tales and Their Tellers* (London: Chatto and Windus, 1994).

3. See *The Facetious Nights of Straparola*, trans. W. G. Waters, illus. Jules Garnier and E. R. Hughes, 4 vols. (London: Society of Bibliophiles, 1881). In the fourth volume, there is an excellent "Terminal Essay" (237–74) by Waters that provides the literary and social background to Straparola's work.

4. Giambattista Basile, *Lo cunto de li cunti*, ed. Michele Rak (Milan: Garzanti, 1986), 326. For the English I have relied on Giambattista Basile, *The Pentamerone of Giambattista Basile*, trans. and ed. Norman M. Penzer, 2 vols. (London: John Lane and the Bodley Head, 1932), though frequently, here and subsequently, modifying Penzer's translation. All subsequent quotations from the original Neapolitan are from the Rak edition.

5. Barbara Broggini, *Lo cunto de li cunti von Giambattista Basile: Ein Ständepoet in streit mit der Plebs, Fortuna und der höfischen Korruption* (Frankfurt am Main: Peter Lang, 1990), 95–102.

6. See Denise Escarpit, *Histoire d'un conte: Le Chat Botté en France et en Angleterre*, vol. 1 (Paris: Didier, 1985), 88–120.

7. Charles Perrault, *Contes*, ed. Gilbert Rouger (Paris: Garnier, 1967), 137. Translation is my own, from Jack Zipes, ed., *Beauties, Beasts and Enchantment: Classic French Fairy Tales* (New York: New American Library, 1989), 21. Subsequent quotations are from these editions.

8. Louis Marin, "*Puss-in-Boots*: Power of Signs—Signs of Power," *Diacritics* 7 (June 1977): 57.

9. Walt Disney, "Puss in Boots," [1922], *161*. *Cartoon Classics #3 (1917–1925–USA)* (Sandy Hook, Conn.: Video Images, 1984).

Bibliography

Bárberi Squarotti, G. "Problemi di tecnica narrativa cinquecentesca: lo Straparola." *Sigma* 2, no. 6 (1965): 84–108.

Basile, Giambattista. *The Pentamerone of Giambattista Basile.* Trans. and ed. Norman M. Penzer. 2 vols. London: John Lane and the Bodley Head, 1932.

———. *Lo cunto de li cunti.* Ed. Michele Rak. Milan: Garzanti, 1986.

Briggs, Katharine M. *Nine Lives: The Folklore of Cats.* New York: Pantheon, 1980.

Broggini, Barbara. *Lo cunto de li cunti von Giambattista Basile: Ein Ständepoet in streit mit der Plebs, Fortuna und der höfischen Korruption.* Frankfurt am Main: Peter Lang, 1990.

Burke, Peter. *The Italian Renaissance: Culture and Society in Italy.* Rev. ed. Princeton: Princeton University Press, 1987.

Caro, Frank de, ed. *The Folktale Cat.* Illus. Kitty Harvill. Little Rock: August House, 1992.

Dale-Green, Patricia. *Cult of the Cat.* Boston: Houghton Mifflin, 1963.

Disney, Walt. "Puss in Boots" [1922]. *161. Cartoon Classics #3 (1917–1925–USA).* Sandy Hook, Conn.: Video Images, 1984.

Escarpit, Denise. *Histoire d'un conte: Le Chat Botté en France et en Angleterre.* 2 vols. Paris: Didier, 1985.

Kirk, Mildred. *The Everlasting Cat.* Woodstock, N.Y.: Overlook Press, 1985.

Larvaille, Pierre. *Perspectives et limites d'une analyse morphologique due conte, pour une révision du schéma de Propp.* Paris: Centre de recherches de langue et littérature italienne, Université Paris X-Nanterre, 1973.

Marin, Louis. "*Puss-in-Boots*: Power of Signs—Signs of Power." *Diacritics* 7 (June 1977): 54–63.

Mazzacurati, G. *Forma e ideologia.* Naples: Liguori, 1974.

———. "Sui materiali in opera nelle *Piacevoli Notti* di Giovan Francesco Straparola" and "La narrativa di Giovan Francesco Straparola: sociologia e struttura del personaggio fiabesco." *Società e strutture narrative dal Trecento al Cinquecento.* Naples: Liguori, 1971.

Motte-Gillet, Anne, ed. *Conteurs italiens de la Renaissance.* Intro. Giancarlo Mazzacurati. Trans. Georges Kempf. Paris: Gallimard, 1993.

Motte-Gillet, Anne. "Giovan Francesco Straparola: Les Facétieuses Nuits." In *Conteurs italiens de la Renaissance.* Ed. A. Motte-Gillet. Intro. Giancarlo Mazzacurati. Trans. Georges Kempf. Paris: Gallimard, 1993.

Perrault, Charles. *Contes.* Ed. Gilbert Rouger. Paris: Garnier, 1967.

Straparola, Giovan Francesco. *Le Piacevoli notti.* Ed. Pastore Stocchi. Rome-Bari: Laterza, 1975.

Warner, Marina. *From the Beast to the Blonde: On Fairy Tales and Their Tellers.* London: Chatto and Windus, 1994.

Zipes, Jack, ed. *Beauties, Beasts and Enchantment: Classic French Fairy Tales.* New York: New American Library, 1989.

CHAPTER 7

Reflections on the Monarchy in d'Aulnoy's *Belle-Belle ou le chevalier Fortuné*

Adrienne E. Zuerner

 ONE OF the principal creators of the literary fairy tale in seventeenth-century France, Mme d'Aulnoy was one of the most read and appreciated writers during her lifetime.[1] Author of an impressive corpus of fairy tales, novels, and pseudomemoirs, admired and celebrated in the salon society of her day, the countess d'Aulnoy remained popular into the eighteenth century when numerous reprints of her tales appeared.[2] Relegated to critical obscurity for almost three centuries, d'Aulnoy's work now garners scholarly attention and serious appraisal. Yet critics remain divided over the extent to which d'Aulnoy's fairy tales constitute an imaginary reconception of prevailing notions of "femininity." While some scholars minimize the import of her critique of gender roles, others argue for d'Aulnoy's feminocentric representation of female desire and sexuality.[3] Focusing primarily on inscriptions of female subjectivity, few of these critics have examined d'Aulnoy's portrayals of masculinity.[4]

Belle-Belle ou le chevalier Fortuné [Gorgeous or the Fortunate Knight; 1698] constitutes a compelling instance of d'Aulnoy's challenge to gender orthodoxy.[5] In this tale, d'Aulnoy reprises the theme of cross-dressing featured briefly in her popular first novel, *Histoire d'Hypolite, Comte de Duglas* [The Story of Hippolyte, the Count of Duglas; 1690]. Like other transvestite narratives of this period, *Belle-Belle ou le chevalier Fortuné* emphasizes the textual construction of gender and reveals how the female author's awareness of gender is reflected in fiction. Apposing the "real" and the "unreal," an

194

apposition that underlies the fantastic mode,[6] *Belle-Belle ou le chevalier Fortuné* represents a fantasy of feminine power: cross-dressed, the heroine vanquishes evil, travels, and achieves public renown precluded by the norms of female decorum. The privileged place accorded to cross-dressing situates the fairy tale within the tradition of literary transvestism revived at the beginning of the seventeenth century with Honoré d'Urfé's popular and influential pastoral novel, *L'Astrée*. But unlike d'Urfé's romance novel, in which the principal narrative of male transvestism buttresses dominant gender ideology, d'Aulnoy's fairy tale assesses the limits of the category "Woman" and, more striking, deconstructs the "unmarked" gender—"Man." Moreover, d'Aulnoy targets the seventeenth century's ideal masculine subject, the king. In *Belle-Belle ou le chevalier Fortuné*, d'Aulnoy weaves into the basic narrative framework of her tale a penetrating and unsparing portrait of the monarchy during the last years of the reign of Louis XIV.

The fairy tale traces the adventures and peripeteia of its eponymous heroine, Belle-Belle, the youngest daughter of an impoverished provincial nobleman. Upon his defeat at the hands of the emperor Matapa, the vanquished king issues a call to arms to all the knights of the realm. Unable to pay the tithe the king exacts from those families who cannot send a son, Belle-Belle's elderly and infirm father reluctantly allows his two oldest daughters to disguise as knights in order to answer the king's summons. When they are unmasked by a fairy, both daughters return home in shame. Belle-Belle, however, earns the favor of the good fairy. Aided by the fairy and seven magical men, the disguised Belle-Belle, known as Fortuné, combats a dragon and the hostile emperor, restores the king's property, saves his honor and that of her father, and in the tale's closure, marries the king after a dramatic revelation scene. Embedded in the fairy tale is a story of unrequited love and violent passion: powerfully drawn to the handsome young knight Fortuné, the spurned queen repeatedly yet unsuccessfully seeks his death and finally falsely accuses him of attempted rape. Poisoned by her lady-in-waiting, she dies in the end, thus preparing the tale's conventional moral: reward awaits the virtuous, albeit cross-dressed heroine, while punishment befalls her nemesis, the queen.

That d'Aulnoy was concerned with rescripting gender roles and plots emerges clearly from a study of the ways in which she adapted the master-tale type. In the standard catalog of French folktales, *Le Conte populaire français*, authors Paul Delarue and Marie-Louise Tenèze identify *Belle-Belle ou le chevalier Fortuné* as a variant of the master-tale type #513, *Le Bateau qui va sur terre comme sur mer* or *Les Doués* (AT "The Land and Water Ship" or "The Extraordinary Companions").[7] The French catalog further indicates that the ending of *Belle-Belle* corresponds to the Aarne and Thompson master-tale type #884A, "A Girl Disguised as a Man Is Wooed by the Queen."[8] Surprisingly, in their description of d'Aulnoy's version of the folktale, Delarue and Tenèze refer only once to the heroine's cross-dressing, and they make no mention of the mutual affection shared by the king and his intimate friend, Fortuné. But in d'Aulnoy's fairy tale both of these elements occupy a prominent place in the narrative. Additionally, d'Aulnoy modifies the androcentric plot of master-tale type #513, in which the king promises his daughter's hand to the man who can build the extraordinary ship. Rather than underscore the exchange of women between men, d'Aulnoy opens her tale with a scene of masculine lack—the despoliation of the king at the hands of a conquering emperor—thereby inaugurating the text's interrogation of masculinity.

D'Aulnoy's deployment of cross-dressing suggests her interest in "ce qu'il y a d'inné ou d'acquis dans la polarisation sexuelle" [what is innate or acquired in sexual polarization],[9] a preoccupation shared by writers throughout the seventeenth century. Some scholars have directly linked the fairy-tale genre to d'Urfé's transvestite novel;[10] yet unlike the principal narrative of *L'Astrée*, in which the male protagonist cross-dresses, most seventeenth-century transvestite narratives feature female cross-dressers. Préchac, Villedieu, fellow fairy-tale writer L'Héritier, and even Lafayette, were among the writers who depicted cross-dressed heroines in the last quarter of the seventeenth century.[11] As in the works of Villedieu and L'Héritier, cross-dressing in *Belle-Belle ou le chevalier Fortuné* at once inscribes prevailing norms of female *bienséance* [decorum, propriety] and challenges those norms by envisioning a larger sphere of activity and endeavor for women.

From the opening of the tale, the heroine is coded as the epitome of filial devotion and unselfish kindness. Her father's favorite daughter, Belle-Belle endures uncomplainingly her meager existence, worries about her father's honor, and without hesitation volunteers to abandon her feminine garb for that of a soldier. She emblematizes the ideal of civility espoused by salon society of this period, as seen in her skillful recruitment of the seven helpers.[12] The narrator prefaces Fortuné's encounter with l'Impétueux by affirming that Fortuné "savoit tout engager dès qu'il paroissoit ou qu'il parloit" [knew how to engage everyone as soon as he appeared or spoke (21)].[13] To be sure, the marvelous plays a role in these episodes inasmuch as Fortuné's speaking horse, Camarade, identifies each helper and encourages Fortuné to recruit him. Nevertheless, the fairy-tale narrator emphasizes that Fortuné's elegant discourse and "natural grace" finally persuade each helper to join him (18). Although cross-dressing violated biblical and social codes, the text reiterates that Belle-Belle disguises only to serve the crown and thereby recuperates transvestism for an indisputably worthy cause. Thus on the one hand, the heroine is the picture of female decorum, and as such she poses no threat to the established order. D'Aulnoy's transvestite heroine was at once familiar and reassuring to seventeenth-century readers. On the other hand, the representation of female transvestism is at odds with conventional understandings of man and woman in seventeenth-century France. Fortuné successfully accomplishes a series of tasks thought to be exclusively "masculine" enterprises. She traverses freely the countryside, assumes a position of authority over seven men, acts as the king's official ambassador, vanquishes a violent aggressor (the dragon), and restores to the king his wealth and honor. The narrator describes Belle-Belle/Fortuné as "la fleur de toute la chevalerie" [the finest cavalier of all knighthood (56)], and the king lauds his/her martial prowess: "vous avez tant d'adresse dans toutes les choses que vous faites et particuliérement [*sic*] aux armes" [you demonstrate so much skill in all you do, and especially in wielding arms (40)]. So accomplished is the cross-dressed Belle-Belle that her seven helpers never suspect her disguise; they address her as *maître* and *Seigneur* throughout. This depiction of the transvestite heroine thus balances "feminine" and "masculine" traits (kindness *and* military acumen, artful discourse *and* physical and moral courage, filial loyalty *and* skillful diplomacy). By virtue of the fact that Belle-Belle's masculine garb and activities fail to compromise her feminine nature and that no conflict or contradiction arises between her "masculine" pursuits and her "feminine" graces, the text suggests a far more nuanced understanding of gender and underscores the instability of gender classifications, rather than their immutability and incommensurability.

Paradoxically, if the fairy tale credits a woman with saving the kingdom, it simultaneously affirms woman's potential power to destroy it. The dowager queen embodies this destructive capacity and fulfills the conventional role of foil to the "good" heroine. The queen incarnates the worst defects of woman: "fière, violente, & d'un assez difficile accès" [proud, violent, and rather difficult to approach (1–2)], she is the antithesis of the ideal woman, distinguished by her modesty, docility, and complaisance. Extremely jealous and rejected by Fortuné, the queen conspires to send him on what she hopes will be fatal missions, since "elle aimoit mieux le voir mort, que de le voir indifférent" [she preferred to see him dead rather than indifferent (47)]. Fortuné's loyal horse Camarade equates the queen with a "monster" and warns Fortuné that she is more dragonlike than the dragon he overcame (51). Although Renaissance writers revised the Aristotelian notion of woman as monstrous and affirmed her full humanity (though she was still considered inferior to man), the assumption of power by women was nevertheless considered "unnatural," and hence monstrous, inasmuch as a powerful woman deviated from her "naturally" subordinate role. In this respect, Camarade rightfully calls the queen a monster since she has intruded into the exclusive sphere of male prerogative, political power. The queen's confidante and rival for Fortuné's affections, Florine, tells Fortuné about the "mauvais usage qu'elle faisoit du suprême pouvoir qu'elle avoit usurpé dans le royaume" [her misuse of the supreme power she had usurped in the kingdom (29)]. The accuracy of

Florine's appraisal of her rival would be dubious at best if it were not repeated almost word for word by a far more credible source, the king. When the queen clamors for the execution of Fortuné, her violence surprises even the king: "la manière dont elle parloit étonna le roi, il la connoissoit pour la plus violente femme du monde; elle avoit du pouvoir, & elle étoit capable de bouleverser le royaume" [her manner of speaking surprised the king, he knew her as the most violent woman in the world; she had power and was capable of turning the kingdom upside down (72)]. The narrator, then, draws a direct connection between a woman with power and upheaval in the kingdom. In fact, this last phrase is reminiscent of Richelieu's denigration of female rule: "le gouvernement des femmes est d'ordinaire le malheur des états" [the rule of women is usually a calamity for the state], a view Louis XIV later echoed in his *Mémoires*.[14]

Dorothy Thelander suggests that the evil queen regents of literary fairy tales evoke "the unpopular queens who had ruled France during the minorities of their sons during the sixteenth and seventeenth centuries: Catherine de Medicis, Marie de Medicis and Anne of Austria."[15] Certain elements of d'Aulnoy's tale could be cited to support such a reading. More interesting, however, are the ways in which this unflattering representation of woman functions in the tale. One might argue that the text merely reiterates the early modern association of woman and evil. Considered weak in mind and body, women were thought to be more susceptible to the influence of the devil and hence were seen as fomenters of evil. That such stereotypes inform d'Aulnoy's fairy tale is to be expected, since, as numerous latter-day theorists have emphasized, there is no position "outside" the system of power.[16] Alternatively, the unruly life and, more important, the ultimate demise of the queen may represent a necessary concession to royal censors. Wielding illegitimate power (since it was "usurped"), the evil queen of the fairy tale may have figured the monarchy's vulnerability during the Fronde.[17] But the queen's violent death acts as a kind of narrative "punishment" and symbolizes the triumph of monarchical absolutism. No doubt both of these factors—the inscription of prevailing stereotypes and the necessary acquiescence to royal censorship—as well as fairy-tale convention, are at work in the text and explain the negative portrayal of the queen. More significant, however, in terms of the textual construction of gender, the juxtaposition of the queen and the valiant heroine generates a signifying contradiction between two "opposing" images of woman, a contradiction that is regularly obscured by prevailing seventeenth-century gender *doxa*.[18] This contradiction produces in turn dissident knowledge about the perceived stability of the category of woman, in particular, and, more generally, about the underlying tension and ambivalence regarding gender in the seventeenth century.

What makes the tale's challenge to seventeenth-century gender ideologies all the more incisive is its systematic unraveling of normative myths
of masculinity. Seventeenth-century representations of female cross-dressing
implicitly call into question the "essence" of masculinity since the heroine
regularly abandons the timidity, passivity, and physical weakness inherent
in her feminine "nature" and adopts the aggressivity, martial prowess, and
mental and physical strength considered masculine attributes.[19] Far more rare,
however, given the patriarchal symbolic of this period, are representations of
male characters that deviate explicitly and remarkably from seventeenth-
century norms of masculinity.[20] From the outset, *Belle-Belle ou le chevalier
Fortuné* marks its divergence from such norms. In the opening paragraph,
d'Aulnoy suppresses the conventional fairy-tale formula—"il étoit une fois
un roi et une reine" or "il étoit une fois un roi fort riche en terres" [once upon
a time there was a king and a queen; once upon a time there was a king who
owned a great quantity of land]—and begins with a portrait of a vanquished
monarch who has barely eluded capture by his stronger enemy:

> Il étoit une fois un roi fort aimable, fort doux, & fort puissant;
> mais l'empereur Matapa, son voisin, étoit encore plus puissant
> que lui. Ils avoient eu de grandes guerres l'un contre l'autre; dans
> la dernière, l'empereur gagna une bataille considérable, & après
> avoir tué ou fait prisonniers la plupart des capitaines & des soldats
> du roi, il vint assiéger sa ville capitale, & la prit; de sorte qu'il se
> rendit maître de tous les trésors qui étoient dedans. Le roi eut à
> peine le loisir de se sauver avec la reine douairière sa soeur. (1)[21]

> [Once upon a time, there was a very kind, gentle, and powerful
> king; but the Emperor Matapa, his neighbor, was even more
> powerful than he was. They had fought many great wars against
> each other; in the last war, the emperor won an important battle,
> and after having killed or taken as prisoners the majority of
> the king's captains and soldiers, he came to lay siege to the
> capital and took it, such that he became master of all the riches
> therein. The king scarcely had time to escape with his sister the
> dowager queen.]

Structurally, this opening constitutes a paradigmatic scenario of disorder
or "lack" that will be rectified in the tale's closure, when a conventional
"happy ending" (the marriage of Belle-Belle and the king) reestablishes order
and liquidates lack.[22] On a symbolic level, however, this passage performs a
transgressive dismemberment of the king's "double body" and undermines the
ideal masculine subject incarnated by the monarch. According to Jean-Marie
Apostolidès, the concept of the king's double body reflects an understanding

of the king as a private individual and as the embodiment of the state. Apostolidès cites the late-sixteenth-century writer Guy Coquille to argue that this concept lies at the crux of political theory in the early modern period: "Le roi est le chef et le peuple des trois ordres sont les membres; et tous ensemble sont le corps politique et mystique dont la liaison et l'union est indivisé et inséparable" [The king is the head and the members of the three orders are the limbs; all together they form the mystical body politic the connection and union of which is undivided and inseparable].[23] Both the "head" of state and its populace body are integral and essential to the viability of the nation/king. The opening of Belle-Belle, then, recounts more than an isolated defeat. Rather, the imprisonment of the king's men deprives the nation of its "body" and compromises the integrity of the king. As though to emphasize the susceptibility of the king, rather than his divine and immutable essence, the narrator iterates this metaphorical sunderance:

> L'empereur transporta toutes les pierreries & meubles du roi dans son palais: il emmena un nombre extraordinaire de soldats, de filles, de chevaux, & de toutes les autres choses qui pouvoient lui être utiles ou agréables: quand il eut dépeuplé la plus grande partie du royaume, il revient triomphant dans le sien. (2)

> [The emperor transported to his palace all of the king's crown jewels and furniture: he led away an extraordinary number of soldiers, young women, horses, and all the other objects that might be useful or pleasing to him; when he emptied [depopulated] the great majority of the kingdom, he returned triumphant to his own.]

Deprived of the people (soldiers and young women)—that which the king governs and without which he cannot by definition be king—the body politic ceases to exist. In this paragraph, the narrator also reveals that the king's purloined treasures include the crown jewels ("pierreries") and palace furnishings. In other words, the king has lost the outward signs of his power and magnificence, a loss rendered even more explicit when the narrator refers to "le roi dépouillé" [the stripped [despoiled] king] in the third paragraph (2). The radical implications of this passage are twofold: the words "pierreries" and "dépouillé" evoke images of both castration and rape. The stripping of the king's "jewels" emphasizes the king's "feminine" vulnerability.[24] The adjective "dépouillé" reiterates this phallic loss, which symbolically transforms the king into a woman, who is "ravished" by the conquering male emperor. The "feminization" of the king at once causes a loss of power (the king is unable to defend his kingdom and must flee) and signals this loss.

The transgressive nature of these passages may also be understood within the cultural context of the "status" or "prestige" consumption that characterized court society of the seventeenth century. As Norbert Elias explains, over the course of the century, French noblemen lost real status and autonomy with respect to the king.[25] The monarchy gradually reduced the traditional markers of their social rank and personal identity, and in their absence, the aristocrat's social identity inhered in the ritualized display of prestige:

> An elaborate cultivation of outward appearances as an instrument of social differentiation, the display of rank through outward form, is characteristic not only of the houses but of the whole shaping of court life. . . . In a society in which every outward manifestation of a person has special significance, expenditure on prestige and display is for the upper classes a necessity which they cannot avoid. They are an indispensable instrument in maintaining their social position, especially when—as is actually the case in this court society—all members of the society are involved in a ceaseless struggle for status and prestige.[26]

Both male aristocrats and the king himself, as the chief nobleman, were implicated in this system. When the financier Fouquet outfitted a more sumptuous palace and hosted more lavish parties than those of the king, Louis XIV had him imprisoned for life, an act that testifies to the pressure exerted on the king to surpass his noblemen in extravagant self-display. Within the context of prestige consumption, then, *Belle-Belle* destabilizes the fixed image of the king, for in losing his palace furnishings and the crown jewels, the king of d'Aulnoy's tale is robbed of those signs that constitute and differentiate him as the king. Far from inviolable, the king's double body is subject to violation and despoliation, contrary to the image propagated by royal image-makers. From its opening pages, *Belle-Belle ou le chevalier Fortuné* "dethrones" the epitome of masculine subjectivity, the king.

D'Aulnoy further develops this portrait of royal vincibility by high-lighting the relationship between the king and Fortuné and by exposing the monarch's dependence on his courtiers. In fact, d'Aulnoy's fairy tale inscribes a keen awareness of the complex system of interdependences that organized and sustained the court of Louis XIV and subtended the monarch's power. By exploiting the homoerotic possibilities of the king's predilection for his handsome and courageous courtier, the disguised Belle-Belle, the tale focuses on the ways in which the monarch's dependence renders him vulnerable and complicates the distinction, as Apostolidès puts it, between "le monarque en tant qu'individu privé et le monarque comme *persona ficta*, incarnation de l'Etat" [the monarch as private individual and as *persona ficta*, incarnation of the State].[27]

Jacques Barchilon identifies the erotic complexities of *Belle-Belle ou le chevalier Fortuné* when he writes that d'Aulnoy "s'aventure courageusement dans une forêt de sentiments de plus en plus complexes et de plus en plus équivoques" [ventures bravely into a forest of more and more complex and ambiguous feelings].[28] Indeed, early modern transvestite narratives regularly exploit the erotic ramifications of cross-dressing to please and titillate readers, who are cast as voyeuristic observers of forbidden, homoerotic behavior. Transgressive pairings are formed, for instance, when a female character becomes enamored of a woman disguised as a man or, as in L'Héritier's *L'Amazone françoise*, when the prince, Cloderic, is tortured by the forbidden desire he feels for his male courtier, Marmoisan, the disguised Léonore.[29] Here the ostensible couple (Cloderic-Marmoisan) is "deviant" while the actual couple (Cloderic-Léonore) is reassuringly heterosexual.[30]

A similar plot emerges in *Belle-Belle ou le chevalier Fortuné*, for the text infuses the king's speech with conventions of amorous discourse common to seventeenth-century novels; yet because it occurs in the context of two reputedly male characters, this discourse engenders a homoerotic subtext. Upon first meeting Fortuné, the king informs him, "je me sens une affection particulière pour vous" [I feel a special affection for you (25)]. As Fortuné leaves to slay the dragon, a mission orchestrated by the queen, the king cannot conceal his distress: "aussitôt que le roi l'apperçut, il s'écria: quoi! vous êtes prêt à partir?" [as soon as the king saw him, he cried out: what! you are ready to leave? (41)]. Here both the punctuation and the lexicon signal the king's emotion as does his "profonde tristesse" [profound sadness (53)] when the queen once again seeks to endanger Fortuné, this time by sending him to confront the emperor Matapa. Far from the dispassionate agent of his superior (male) reason, the king is overcome by his (female) emotions. When the king chides Fortuné for confiding more readily in the queen than in him, his words resemble those of a jealous lover: "il me semble, dit le roi en souriant, que vous êtes assez bien dans ses bonnes grâces, & c'est à elle que vous ouvrez votre coeur préférablement à moi" [it seems to me, said the king smiling, that you are very much in her good graces, and that you open your heart more readily to her than to me (51)]. Usually found in the context of heterosexual lovers, these words lend a sexual undertone to the exchange between the king and his favorite. Another such double entendre occurs at the end of the text, when the distraught king contemplates the approaching execution of Fortuné:

> Mais, hélas! sur qui cette vengeance devoit-elle être exercée? sur
> un chevalier, qui s'étoit exposé aux plus grands périls pour son

service, auquel il étoit redevable de son repos & et de tous ses trésors, qu'il aimoit d'une inclination particulière: il auroit donné la moitié de sa vie pour sauver ce cher Favori. (73)

[But alas, from whom should this vengeance be exacted? From a knight who had exposed himself to the greatest perils on his behalf, to whom he was indebted for his peace of mind and all his wealth, whom he loved with an exceptional love: he would have given half his life to save this dear favorite.]

On one level, this passage reflects feudal notions of loyalty and service that structured the relationship of lord and vassal, ideas that still informed seventeenth-century *mentalités*, long after feudal structures ceased to obtain in court society. But on another level, the king's emphatic emotional response to the imminent death of Fortuné and his willingness to sacrifice himself for his knight intimate a bond of a different order. The word "inclination" is particularly suggestive in this regard, for it was synonymous with the word "love" in the seventeenth century.[31] This passage and those cited above challenge seventeenth-century norms of masculinity: male homoeroticism and the attendant attribution of the "female" role to one of the partners necessarily denaturalize masculinity since man is seen to abandon his "naturally" superior position.[32] Even more, Luce Irigaray contends that male homosexuality represents a subversive threat to patriarchy: "Once the penis itself becomes merely a means to pleasure, pleasure among men, *the phallus loses its power*."[33] From this point of view, the presence of homoeroticism tends to implicate royal power as well, by undermining its masculinist basis. To be sure, the text appears to conform to normative heterosexuality since the reader knows that Fortuné is really a woman; therefore the king's affection for Belle-Belle/Fortuné can be read as "normal." Yet even the narrator's reference to Belle-Belle's female identity and (heterosexual) love for the king fail to nullify the suggestion of homoeroticism evoked in these passages.[34]

D'Aulnoy also exploits this ambiguous relationship to further challenge the conflation of the private individual of the king with the abstract notion of the state, for the king's *inclination* for Fortuné eventually leads him to imperil his very kingdom. Although the king has summoned his knights, including Fortuné, for the sole purpose of engaging in battle with the emperor, the king refuses to let Fortuné endanger his life and retains him as his stable master:

Le roi lui dit après la revue, qu'il craignoit que la guerre ne fût sanglante, & qu'il avoit résolu de l'attacher à sa personne. La reine douairière qui étoit présente, s'écria qu'elle avoit eu la même pensée, qu'il ne falloit point l'exposer au péril d'une longue campagne; que la charge de premier maître d'hôtel étoit vacante dans sa maison, qu'elle la lui donnoit. Non, dit le roi, j'en veux faire mon grand écuyer. (27)

[After the military review, the king said that he feared the war might be bloody and that he had resolved to engage him [Fortuné] for his personal service; the dowager queen, who was present, exclaimed that she had had the same thought, that it wasn't necessary to expose him to the danger of a long campaign, that the position of head butler in her house was vacant. No, said the king, I want to make him my stable master.]

In this first instance of his "separation anxiety," the king insists that Fortuné remain by his side ("non, dit le roi"). The well-being of the kingdom, threatened by the loss of the *peuple* and the king's material wealth, is subordinated to gratify the king's desire for the company of his courtier. This scenario occurs in two other episodes when the king, ready to sacrifice more lives, reiterates his ardent desire to retain his favorite and only reluctantly sends Fortuné to confront the dragon and the emperor. Conceding to the queen's request, the king laments, "je consens à ce que vous voulez . . . je vous avoue, malgré cela, que j'y ai de la répugnance" [I consent to what you want . . . I confess, nonetheless, that I loathe your wish (39)]. The text, then, underscores the king's ambivalence and moral weakness. Consequently it unmasks the reputedly rational masculine subject, immune to untoward passions, and constructs a fallible and desiring male subject. While the royal symbolic stressed the statesman, d'Aulnoy's fairy tale stresses the very human foibles of the fictional monarch and the potential for national mishap when his devotion to his *favori* ("favorite") holds sway over the interests of the state. The tale suggests that the *mutual* dependency existing between the king and courtiers may compromise the king since personal whims and private considerations dictate the direction of national decisions.[35] *Belle-Belle ou le chevalier Fortuné* thus reprises implicitly the "demythification" of official history produced explicitly by Lafayette and Villedieu. Both of these writers insist that amorous intrigues, rather than great reasons of state, lie at the heart of political decision making.[36] D'Aulnoy's text is perhaps more audacious than those of Villedieu and Lafayette insofar as its love interest involves homoerotic desire. Ultimately, however, the fairy tale redeems the king and elides the potential danger inhering in his obligations toward Fortuné; finally, albeit reluctantly, the king allows Fortuné to confront the dragon and the enemy emperor, thereby privileging national interests at the expense of his personal desire. While the text thus skirts an inflammatory portrait of the king and his favorite (like those devoted to Henri III and his minions), even the king's recuperation does not completely overshadow the perils of royal dependency implied throughout the fairy tale.[37]

Even more, *Belle-Belle ou le chevalier Fortuné* includes numerous details that point to a direct correlation between the fictional court of the fairy tale and the court of Louis XIV during the sunset years of his reign.[38] Lamenting Fortuné's frigid response to her numerous sexual advances, the queen composes a love poem and has it set to music by Lully, an overt reference to Louis XIV's preferred composer of court ballets (36). The narrator also describes a palace gallery ornamented with statues, perhaps an allusion to the *Galérie des Glaces* (Hall of Mirrors) at Versailles (70). More telling is the narrator's description of the king and his courtiers: "le roi y vint avec la reine douairière sa soeur et toute leur cour; *elle ne laissait pas d'être pompeuse, malgré les malheurs que étoient arrivés à l'état*" [the king came there [to the parade ground] with his sister the dowager queen and the entire court, which was unfailingly magnificent, despite the misfortunes that had beset the state (25); emphasis added]. Although Louis's image-makers strove to dissimulate France's waning glory, the latter years of Louis XIV's reign were, in fact, plagued by economic and religious crises. In his study of the "fabrication" of Louis XIV, Peter Burke speculates that the political difficulties of the latter years of the reign, including the defeats of French armies and serious financial problems, account in part for the French government's increased production of medals, statues, and tapestries, all designed to obscure the grim reality of the sunset years.[39] The loss of the fictional king's *trésors* may allude not only to the financial straits of the nation but to a spiritual bankruptcy as well, as famine ravaged the French peasantry, aggravating its already impoverished condition; as the increased persecution of French Protestants signaled the king's moral weaknesses; and as military defeats overshadowed the enchanted and triumphant spirit of the monarchy during the early years of Louis XIV's personal reign. Furthermore, the tale calls into question the military prowess of the French monarch himself, since the fictional king never directly engages in battle against the dragon or Matapa. This detail may reflect the contemporary state of armed conflict when the king, "unaccustomed to physical warfare," did not lead his troops and when armies comprised large numbers of mercenaries and a few generals.[40] But the fictional king's absence from the battlefront may also constitute a trenchant, yet no less compelling and dangerous, criticism of Louis XIV. In reality, numerous anonymous pamphlets of the era portrayed Louis XIV as "battle-shy" and castigated him for the defeats of French troops.[41] In a direct attack on the king's courage, the anonymous writer of *Le Marquis de Louvois sur la selette* [The Marquis of Louvois on the Hot Seat (lit. saddle); 1695] sarcastically queries, "Dis-moi, pourquoi Louis qu'on nomme l'Immortel / Ne vient-il pas en Flandre attaquer un mortel? / Pourquoi ce fainéant demeure en son royaume / A-t-il peur des esprits?" [Why doesn't Louis the Immortal / Come to Flanders to attack a mortal? / Why does this loafer remain in his kingdom / Is he afraid of ghosts?][42] All too human, fearful of men and ghosts alike, according to the pamphleteer, Louis XIV oafishly and cowardly remains behind, while his troops labor to defend his empire.

Indeed, the accumulation of unflattering, even derogatory, allusions to the king suggests that d'Aulnoy's fairy tale can be read, and probably was read by some, as part of a larger wave of texts criticizing Louis XIV in the last decade of the century.[43] In her extensive study of the literary image of Louis XIV, Ferrier-Caverivière notes that after the revocation of the Edict of Nantes, repealing the religious and civil rights of French Protestants, Louis's detractors "se font à la fois plus nombreux et plus éloquents" [became at once more numerous and more eloquent (331)]. While certain seventeenth-century fairy tales, such as Préchac's allegorical *Sans Parangon* [Nonpareil; 1698], represent hyperbolic panegyrics of the king, Teresa di Scanno points out that "le merveilleux semble avoir servi souvent de masque à des allusions satiriques" [the marvelous seems to have masked satirical allusions].[44] Di Scanno identifies in d'Aulnoy's work vulgar caricatures of court habitués yet does not mention that these satirical sketches implicated the monarch as well.[45] The notion that *Belle-Belle* contains a veiled critique of the monarch is buttressed by the fact that several satiric historical novels were attributed to, among others, Mme d'Aulnoy. Specifically, Ferrier-Caverivière hypothesizes that d'Aulnoy was the author of *Le Grand Alcandre frustré ou les derniers efforts de l'amour et de la vertu* [The Frustrated Great Alcandre or the Final Efforts of Love and Virtue], an anonymous satirical novel targeting the king's sexual weaknesses.[46] D'Aulnoy's fairy tale therefore diverges from those of Murat, which, according to Apostolidès, depicted Louis's court not as it existed during the vogue of fairy tales but as it was during the early, glorious years of his personal rule.[47] Instead, d'Aulnoy targets the court during the sunset years of the reign. Her portrait of a timorous, vulnerable, and castrated monarch and a deteriorating court contravenes the image fabricated by Louis XIV's "propaganda" machine. Indeed, *Belle-Belle ou le chevalier Fortuné* prefigures the parodic and licentious tales of the eighteenth century, described by Raymonde Robert as caustically ironic and subversive in spirit.[48]

How did this veiled, nonetheless discernible, demythification pass unnoticed through royal censors? First of all, the concessions to prevailing norms and the conventional fairy tale ending shift attention away from the artful critique of the king. The supernatural denouement, in which the fairy suddenly reappears as a "second sun" leading Belle-Belle's family in a jewel-encrusted chariot, restores order and crowns both the heroine and the king in dazzling glory. Even the title of the tale, *Belle-Belle ou le chevalier Fortuné*, distracts from the unconventional (re)vision of masculinity and femininity elaborated throughout the tale: the word "or" affirms the incommensurability (either/or) of male and female and thus reflects dominant gender norms. Moreover, along with Michèle Farrell, I would suggest that the fairy-tale genre itself and the "marginality" of the *conteuses* enabled this tale to escape the close scrutiny brought to bear on other genres.[49] "Free of the censure of official esthetic restraints," writes Farrell, women fairy-tale writers "can point to the common people from whom their stories come as indicators of those stories' powerlessness and harmlessness, and as signifiers of the frivolity of their enterprise. Their activity in no way threatens the status quo and is not to be taken seriously."[50] Given this perception of the innocuousness of literary fairy tales, it is unsurprising that d'Aulnoy's narrative "passed" as inconsequential and unthreatening, arousing little interest or suspicion among those charged with creating and maintaining the image of the king's magnificence. Yet since it was never wholly divorced from historical reality, the imaginary realm of the fairy tale provided a discursive space in which "official" reality and prevailing gender norms could be challenged. *Belle-Belle ou le chevalier Fortuné* illustrates the capacity of the literary fantastic to trace, as Rosemary Jackson puts it, "the unsaid and the unseen of culture: that which has been silenced, made invisible, covered over and made 'absent.'"[51] D'Aulnoy's fairy tale discloses what the official myth of the king silenced and occulted—the fallibility and vulnerability of the monarch and the potential menace posed to the integrity of the nation/king by the complex network of interdependence that bound the king to his courtiers.[52]

By making visible what royal mythology sought to obscure, *Belle-Belle ou le chevalier Fortuné* constitutes an example of oppositional discourse, which becomes all the more apparent when considering the fairy-tale genre in relation to the Quarrel of the Ancients and the Moderns. Dating from the sixteenth century, this polemic opposed, on the one hand, those who viewed classical texts as perfect models to be imitated and, on the other hand, those who attributed to French artistic and literary production a preeminence that rivaled and surpassed that of antiquity. In defense of the moderns, Charles Perrault privileged the French fairy tale over the fables of antiquity.[53] More recently, Marc Fumaroli posits a direct connection between the tenets of the moderns and the fairy-tale genre: the genre, he writes, "naît de la Querelle et dans la Querelle, pour soutenir les théories, par ailleurs très défendables, des 'modernes'" [was born of and in the Quarrel in order to support the "moderns'" theories, which were, moreover, very tenable].[54] The product of a distinctly French, as opposed to classical, tradition and shaped by the stylistic norms refined by seventeenth-century salon society, the fairy tale was, in a sense, the quintessential modern genre. And as the title of Perrault's poem cum modernist treatise, "Le siècle de Louis le Grand" (1687), indicates, the king was aligned with the modernist side of the Quarrel. For the monarch was *the* patron of modern arts and letters: the artistic and literary excellence achieved during Louis's reign was at once the product and the reflection of the king's grandeur. According to

René Demoris, the very figure of the sun king emblematizes the relationship between the king and writing: "le pouvoir politique entend faire des écrivains son émanation et les faire servir à son illustration" [political power intends to make writers its product and to have them exemplify its glory].[55] Seen in this light, d'Aulnoy seems to resist cooptation: she appropriates the quintessentially modern genre, the fairy tale, and infuses it with meanings at variance with those "intended" by the moderns. Rather than exalt the king's image, the fairy tale tarnishes it by feminizing the fictional king and undermining his claims to authority. Within the framework of the fairy tale's sanctioned discursive space, d'Aulnoy censures the very person the genre purports to celebrate. D'Aulnoy's fairy tale constitutes an oppositional discourse because it indicates the contradictions inhering in seventeenth-century myths of monarchical absolutism. Just as the juxtaposition of the evil queen and the transvestite heroine destabilizes gender norms, so the contradiction between the fictional monarch of the fairy tale and the representation of the historical monarch challenges the "truth" of the latter. Indeed, in examining *Belle-Belle ou le chevalier Fortuné*, the pertinent question is not "if" the text is oppositional but rather to what degree it is oppositional and how it negotiates the delicate balance between subversion and the reinscription of prevailing *doxa*. The dialectic between these two potentialities confirms the role of literature in the production of social meaning and sexual difference.

Notes

1. Mary Elizabeth Storer, *La Mode des contes de fées, 1685–1700* (Geneva: Slatkine Reprints, 1972), 22. All translations from the French are my own unless otherwise indicated. Marie-Catherine Le Jumel de Barneville, countess, baroness d'Aulnoy (1650/51–1705), issued from a noble Norman family. Married at age fifteen or sixteen to a baron considerably older than she, d'Aulnoy eventually gave birth to six children during her loveless marriage. Implicated in a scandal involving an accusation of *lèse-majesté* against her husband, d'Aulnoy went to prison and afterward disappeared from Paris for approximately twenty years. Little is known of this part of her life, yet based on her extensive writings on England and Spain, Barchilon hypothesizes that she traveled and perhaps lived for a time in both of these countries. Jacques Barchilon, *Le Conte merveilleux français de 1690 à 1790* (Paris: Librairie Honoré Champion, 1975), 38. In 1690 she resurfaced in Paris where she lived in semiretreat, presided over a salon, and began her writing career. Excluded from her husband's will, d'Aulnoy died in Paris in 1705.

2. Reeditions of d'Aulnoy's tales appeared in 1710, 1711, 1715, 1725, and 1742, and her work was included in the forty-one-volume *Cabinet des fées* published in 1785. Raymonde Robert, *Le conte de fées littéraire en France de la fin du XVIIe siècle à la fin du XVIIIe siècle* (Nancy: Presses Universitaires de France, 1981), 313, 316.

3. In her discussion of cross-dressing in female-authored fairy tales, Catherine Velay-Vallantin acknowledges that sexual inversion reveals the commensurability of masculine and feminine roles and is, therefore, a form of protest in tales by women. Yet at the same time, she seems to dismiss the significance of this symbolic scrutiny of gender, for her position reflects an adherence to the containment theory of oppositional discourses, whereby any oppositional discourse is already recuperated or "contained" by the ideological network in which it is inscribed and thus merely serves to uphold the hierarchy it purports to challenge through inversion. These tales, Velay-Vallantin writes, "participent du phénomène bien connu des conduites contestatrices qui confortent l'ordre établi en faisant semblant de le critiquer, malgré la sincérité évidente de leurs auteurs" [participate in the well-known phenomenon of contestatory acts that reassure the established order while seeming to criticize it, despite the evident sincerity of their authors]. Catherine Velay-Vallantin, *La fille en garçon* (Carcassonne: Editions G.A.R.A.E./Hésiode, 1992), 11–12. See note 18 below for an alternative reading of containment theory. For analyses of the feminocentric vein in d'Aulnoy's tales, see Michèle L. Farrell, "Celebration and Repression of Feminine Desire in Mme d'Aulnoy's Fairy Tale: *La Chatte blanche*," *L'Esprit créateur* 29, no. 3 (1989): 52–64; Lewis C. Seifert, *Fairy Tales, Sexuality, and Gender in France, 1690–1715: Nostalgic Utopias* (Cambridge: Cambridge University Press, 1996); and Marcelle Maistre Welch, "Rébellion et résignation dans les contes de fée de Mme d'Aulnoy et Mme de Murat," *Cahiers du Dix-Septième* 3, no. 2 (1989): 131–42, and "Le Devenir de la jeune fille dans les contes de fée de Madame d'Aulnoy," *Cahiers du Dix-Septième* 1, no. 1 (1987): 53–62. See also Marina Warner, *From the Beast to the Blond: On Fairy Tales and Their Tellers* (New York: Farrar, Straus and Giroux, 1995), 49.

4. Seifert, *Nostalgic Utopias*, chapter 5.

5. Marie-Catherine Le Jumel de Barneville, countess d'Aulnoy, *Belle-Belle ou le chevalier Fortuné*, in *Les Contes de fées*, 4 vols. (Paris, 1697–98). Rpt. in vol. 5 of *Nouveau Cabinet de fées* (Geneva: Slatkine Reprints, 1978); subsequently cited in the text.

6. See Rosemary Jackson's study of the fantastic where she writes: "telling implies using the language of the dominant order. . . . Since this excursion into disorder begins . . . within the dominant cultural order, literary fantasy is a telling index of the limits of that order. Its introduction of the 'unreal' is set against the category of the 'real'—a category which the fantastic interrogates by its difference." *Fantasy: The Literature of Subversion* (New York: Methuen, 1981), 4.

7. Paul Delarue and Marie-Louise Tenèze, *Le Conte populaire français. Catalogue raisonné des versions de France et des pays de langue française d'outre-mer*, vol. 3 (Paris: Editions Maisonneuve et Larose, 1976), 283.

8. Ibid., 291.

9. Michèle Perret, "Travesties et transexuelles: Yde, Silence, Grisandole, Blanchan-dine," *Romance Notes* 25, no. 3 (1985): 329.

10. Teresa Di Scanno traces the presence of the marvelous in fairy tales to *L'Astrée*, which she credits with having rejuvenated enchanters, sorcerers, and druids. Di Scanno, *Les Contes de fées à l'époque classique* (Napoli: Liguori Editori, 1975),

35. Jane Tucker Mitchell contends that the literary fairy tale's focus on love and happy endings derives from allegorical novels of the early part of the century, including *L'Astrée*. Mitchell, *A Thematic Analysis of Mme d'Aulnoy's Contes de Fées* (University, Mississippi: Romance Monographs, Inc., 1978), 88. In *Belle-Belle ou le chevalier Fortuné*, intertextual references suggest that d'Aulnoy had in mind d'Urfé's pastoral novel. Toward the end of the fairy tale, the narrator describes a "fontaine des lions; il y en avoit sept en marbre, qui jetoient par la gueule des torrens d'eau, dont il se formoit une rivière sur laquelle on traversoit la ville en gondole" [fountain of seven marble lions that spouted jets of water which formed a river enabling one to cross the city in a gondola (60)]. This passage points most immediately to *bassin d'Apollon*, the ornamental pond and fountain at Versailles, yet it is also reminiscent of *L'Astrée*'s Fontaine de la Vérité d'Amour, surrounded by unicorns and lions. D'Aulnoy also exploits the dilemma of the cross-dressed character who relishes intimacy with a beloved confidante but risks losing the object of affection were his or her disguise exposed. Fortuné's lament, "quelle est ma destinée? . . . j'aime un grand roi, sans pouvoir jamais espérer qu'il m'aime, ni qu'il tienne compte de ce que je souffre" [what is my fate?. . . . I love a great king, without hope that he will ever love me, nor that he'll ever know what I've suffered (28)], echos that of Céladon: "combien de fois faillit-elle, cette feinte druide [Céladon/Alexis] de laisser le personnage de fille pour reprendre celuy de berger et combien de fois se reprit-elle de cette outrecuidance!" [how many times did this false druidess almost abandon her female persona in order to embrace that of a shepherd and how many times did she prevent herself from such impertinence!]. Honoré d'Urfé, *L'Astrée*, ed. Hugues Vaganay (Lyons: Pierre Masson), 3:549. Like many seventeenth-century readers, d'Aulnoy was probably quite familiar with d'Urfé's pastoral. And it is conceivable that, like other writers later in the century, she saw in the topos of cross-dressing a means to explore notions of masculinity and femininity.

11. Jean Préchac, *L'Héroïne mousquetaire* [The Musketeer Heroine; 1679]; Villedieu, *Mémoires de la vie d'Henriette-Sylvie de Molière* [Memoirs of the Life of Henriette-Sylvie de Molière; 1672–74]; L'Héritier, *Marmoisan ou l'innocente tromperie* [Marmoisan or the Innocent Deception; 1695], reprinted in 1718 as *L'Amazone françoise* [The French Amazon]; and Lafayette, *Histoire espagnole* [Spanish Story, manuscript published 1909]. In 1678, Jean-Marie de Vernon published *L'Amazone chrétienne ou les aventures de Madame de St Balmon* [The Christian Amazon or the Adventures of Madame de St Balmon] a fictionalized biography of an actual female cross-dresser. Cross-dressed figures predominate in memoirs as well, notably those of Madame de la Guette (1681) and la Grande Mademoiselle, Princesse de Montpensier (1718).

12. The sisters are the antithesis of this ideal. When the fairy reveals herself to Belle-Belle, she relates her encounters with the older sisters: "elles m'ont paru si dures, & leur procédé avec moi a été si peu gracieux, que j'ai trouvé le moyen d'interrompre leur voyage" [they seemed to me so harsh, and their behavior toward me was so ungracious, that I found a way to interrupt their voyage (9)]. The text emphasizes that their selfishness, rather than a telltale "feminine" behavior, reveals their

identity and disqualifies them from the good graces of the fairy. Implicitly, then, this episode disavows the notion of an innate and self-evident feminine "nature."

13. The text insists on this verbal acumen elsewhere. Welcomed by a provincial governor while traveling to the king, Fortuné/Belle-Belle "ne disoit rien qui ne fît plaisir à entendre" [didn't say anything that was not pleasing to hear (15)].

14. Richelieu cited in Wendy Gibson, *Women in Seventeenth-Century France* (London: Macmillan, 1989), 167. Louis XIV cautions the Dauphin that the only sure way to prevent women from ruining a ruler's reputation is "de ne leur donner la liberté de parler d'aucune chose que celles qui sont purement de plaisir, et de nous préparer avec étude à ne les croire en rien de ce qui peut concerner nos affaires ou les personnes de ceux qui nous servent" [to allow them to speak of nothing but purely pleasurable subjects and to prepare ourselves systematically to believe nothing they tell us that bears any relation to our affairs or to those who serve us]. Louis XIV, *Mémoires* (Paris: Tallendier, 1978), 260.

15. Dorothy R. Thelander, "Mother Goose and Her Goslings: The France of Louis XIV as Seen through the Fairy Tale," *Journal of Modern History* 54 (1982): 474.

16. See for example, Michel de Certeau, *L'Invention du quotidien, 1. Arts de faire* (Paris: 10/18, 1980); Michel Foucault, *Histoire de la sexualité, 1* (Paris: Gallimard, 1976); and Jean-François Lyotard, "Sur la force des faibles," *L'Arc* 64 (1976): 4–14.

17. The series of civil wars known as the Fronde (1648–52) took place during the minority of Louis XIV, when Anne of Austria was regent. The Fronde comprised parliamentary and agrarian factions, and some noblewomen took part in the aristocratic Fronde, although in a limited fashion.

18. Jonathan Dollimore writes eloquently about the workings of ideology and the limits of containment theory. He points out that "ideology typically fixes meaning, naturalizing or eternalizing its prevailing forms by putting them beyond question, and thereby also effacing the contradictions and conflicts of the social domain." The critique of ideology, he writes, "identifies the contingency of the social (it could always be otherwise), and its potential instability (ruling groups doubly contested from without and within), but does not underestimate the difficulty of change (existing social arrangements are powerfully invested and or not easily made otherwise)." *Sexual Dissidence: From Augustine to Wilde, Freud to Foucault* (Oxford: Clarendon Press, 1991), 87. Dollimore makes a crucial distinction that redresses one of the problems of containment theory, which posits that "resistance is *only ever* an effect of power" and thus "doomed to replicate internally the strategies, structures, and even the values of the dominant" (84, 81). He asserts that subversion and transgression "necessarily *presuppose* the law, but they do not thereby necessarily *ratify* the law" (85).

19. See Ian Maclean's *The Renaissance Notion of Woman* (Cambridge: Cambridge University Press, 1980) for a thorough discussion of this subject.

20. There is a marked asymmetry between female and male transvestism in seventeenth-century texts. Lyons's study of 244 plays featuring mistaken identity or disguise reveals that only 14 include male cross-dressers. John D. Lyons, *A Theatre of Disguise: Studies in French Baroque Drama, 1630–1660* (Columbia, S.C.: French Literature Publications Company, 1978), 81. Pollock notes a similar asymmetry

in the Baroque novel (Mordeca Jane Pollock, "Transvestites in French Baroque Prose Fiction: The Psychological Structure of Femininity," *Degré Second* 3 [1979]: 62), and this extends as well to transvestite fiction of the last twenty-five years of the century. The relative dearth of male cross-dressing suggests that it was far more threatening to the status quo, hence more disturbing than female transvestism. Zuerner, "(Re)Constructing Gender: Cross-Dressing in Seventeenth-Century French Literature" (Ph.D. diss., University of Michigan, 1993), 15–16.

21. Although d'Aulnoy's *La Grenouille bienfaisante* opens with the description of a warring king, *Belle-Belle ou le chevalier Fortuné* is the only one of her fairy tales to begin with, and thus foreground, such an unfavorable image of a king, even though he is one of the tale's protagonists. The risks involved in contravening the king's official mythmakers may account for the singularity of this tale.

22. Alan Dundes's terms "lack/lack liquidated" refer to the general structure of fairy tales, in which narrative movement advances from minus to plus, or from lack to the fulfillment of lack. Max Lüthi, *The Fairy Tale as Art Form and Portrait of Man*, trans. Jon Erickson (Bloomington: Indiana University Press, 1984), 54–55.

23. Jean-Marie Apostolidès, *Le Roi-machine* (Paris: Les Editions de Minuit, 1981), 11 and 13.

24. In *Le Parnasse satirique* (1622), Théophile de Viau's collection of burlesque poetry, the euphemism "trésor" is used to refer to female sex organs. The use of the term "jewels" to refer to male genitalia probably derives from the highly decorative codpieces worn by men in the Renaissance. See Patricia Simons, "Alert and Erect: Masculinity in Some Italian Renaissance Portraits of Fathers and Sons," in *Gender Rhetorics: Postures of Dominance and Submission in History*, ed. Richard C. Trexler (Binghamton, N.Y.: Medieval and Renaissance Texts and Studies, 1994), 169–72.

25. Compelled to live at court, rather than on their provincial estates, deprived of the governmental functions they had previously held and thus beholden to the king for their livelihood, forced to respect an elaborate system of etiquette, which alone determined their social identity, and prohibited from dueling, once the exclusive privilege of the *noblesse d'épée*, French aristocrats underwent a gradual "feminization" over the course of the seventeenth century. The eclipsing of noble prerogative first began under Richelieu, who encouraged Louis XIII to prohibit dueling, and was refined under Louis XIV, who sequestered his nobles at Versailles and, on the battlefront, replaced them with mercenaries. On this latter point, see Norbert Elias, *The Court Society*, trans. Edmund Jephcott (New York: Pantheon Books, 1983), 149; and Apostolidès, *Roi-machine*, 45–46. Apostolidès refers to Versailles as "l'espace permanent du renfermement de la noblesse après 1682" [the permanent space for the confinement of the nobility after 1682 (112)].

26. Elias, *Court Society*, 62–63.

27. Apostolidès, *Roi-machine*, 11.

28. Barchilon, *Le Conte merveilleux*, 40.

29. "Le prince ne sçavoit plus où il en étoit; toutes les paroles & toutes les actions de Marmoisan le charmoient, il ne pouvoit vivre sans lui, & il sentoit bien, que si tout le mérite qu'il lui voyoit se trouver dans une fille, elle deviendroit

pour lui le sujet d'un amour violent" [The prince no longer knew whether he was coming or going; all the words and actions of Marmoisan charmed him, he couldn't live without him, and he felt strongly that if a young woman possessed all the merits of Marmoisan, she would become the object of his violent passion]. Marie-Jeanne L'Héritier, *L'Amazone françoise*, in *Les Caprices du destin, ou recueil d'histoires singulieres et amusantes arrivées de nos jours* (Paris: Chez Pierre Michel Huart, 1718), 268–69.

30. The differentiation Michèle Perret makes between ostensible and actual couples provides a useful construct for analyzing the erotic complexities of cross-dressing. Perret refers to "rapports en apparence hétérosexuels, mais, en fait, potentielle-ment homosexuels" [relations that are ostensibly heterosexual but potentially ho-mosexual] as opposed to "rapports apparemment homosexuels, mais hétérosexuels en réalité" [relations ostensibly homosexual but heterosexual in reality (Perret, "Travesties et transexuelles," 329)]. By varying the degree of emphasis on the apparent or ostensible couple, texts amplify or block a homoerotic subtext, and variations in emphasis can occur in a single text.

31. According to the heroine of Madeline de Scudéry's *Célinte*, *l'inclination* "est plus-tost un effet d'un jugement exquis & caché, qui agit sans que nous le sçachions" [is rather the effect of an exquisite and hidden judgment, that acts without our know-ing]. Scudéry, *Célinte, Nouvelle première*, ed. Alain Niderst (Paris: Nizet, 1979), 75. This word is used interchangeably with the word *amour* in Scudéry's text.

32. The threat of male homoeroticism, and all that it implies for the notions of essential masculinity, explains in part why male transvestism was so rare in seventeenth-century literature and drama. Male transvestism gave rise much more readily to homoerotic pairings, since the cross-dressed (male) character was likely to arouse desire in an unwitting male character.

33. Luce Irigaray, *This Sex Which Is Not One*, trans. Catherine Porter with Carolyn Burke (Ithaca: Cornell University Press, 1985), 193.

34. "Fortuné ne pouvoit s'empêcher de jeter les yeux de tems en tems sur le roi: c'étoit le prince du monde le mieux fait, toutes ses manières étoient prévenantes. Belle-Belle qui n'avoit point renoncé à son sexe, en prenant un habit qui le cachoit, ressentoit un véritable attachement pour lui" [Fortuné could not stop himself from glancing at the king from time to time: he was the most distinguished prince in the world, all his manners were kind and attentive. Belle-Belle, who had not renounced her sex upon donning an outfit that hid it, felt a veritable affection for him (17)]. The presence of the masculine name, Fortuné, and the name Belle-Belle in two consecutive sentences is a recurrent semantic pattern in disguise narratives of this period.

35. The text alludes to this mutual dependence when the narrator describes the king's "obligations infinies" (76) toward Fortuné/Belle-Belle.

36. In both *La Princesse de Clèves* and *La Princesse de Montpensier*, Lafayette stresses that the disorders of love provoke political dissension and upheaval. Villedieu shares a similar understanding of history. The very title of *Les Annales galantes* [Gallant Annals] attests to Villedieu's conviction that love and history intersect. The narrator of the *Annale* entitled *La Religieuse* [The Nun] affirms "les Histoires

sont si fertiles en incidens amoureux, qu'elles nous fourniront de toutes les especes [sic]" [History books are so rich in amorous intrigues that they will provide us with all kinds of examples (38)]. Marie-Catherine Desjardins, Madame de Villedieu, *Les Annales galantes*, vol. 2 of *Œuvres complètes* (Geneva: Slatkine Reprints, 1971), 38. Later in the same *Annale*, the narrator signals the misinformation purveyed by general history: "Rome pillée, le Pape contraint d'abonner le S. Siege . . . : Tout cela . . . ont été les fruits funestes d'un amour si fatal: Mais de tant d'incidens fameux qui sont rapportez par les histoires, peu de gens se sont avisez d'en attribuer la cause à l'amour" [Rome plundered, the Pope forced to abandon the Holy See . . . : All that was the disastrous consequence of a fateful love: So many famous events recounted by history books but few people dared to attribute their cause to love (45)]. See Domna C. Stanton for a study of Villedieu's "oppositional" revalidation of the novelistic form. Stanton, "The Demystification of History and Fiction in *Les Annales galantes*," Biblio 17, *Papers on French Seventeenth-Century Literature*, 37 (1987): 339–60.

37. De Thou, L'Estoile, and d'Aubigné all described caustically the relationship between Henri III and his favorites. According to l'Estoile, "le nom de *Mignons* commença, en ce temps [juillet 1576], à trotter par la bouche du peuple, auquel ils estoient fort odieux, tant pour leurs façons de faire qui estoient badines et hautaines, que pour leurs fards et accoustrements efféminés et impudiques, mais surtout pour les dons immenses et libéralités que leur faisoit le Roy" [during this time [July 1576], the name "Minions" began to issue from the mouths of the people who considered them [the minions] truly hateful, as much for their jocular and haughty ways as for their shameless feminine rouge and getup, but especially for the immense endowments and generous gifts they king gave them]. Cited in Agrippa d'Aubigné, *Histoire universelle*, vol. 4, ed. André Thierry (Geneva: Librairie Droz, 1987), 335.

38. In general, scholars concur that fairy tales are inflected by the specific socio-historical context of their authors, but critics may perceive or define differently the nature of this dimension of fairy tales. Writing about folk and fairy tales, Zipes asserts that "tales are reflections of the social order in a given historical epoch" and that they form "alternative configurations in a critical and imaginative reflection of the dominant social norms." Jack Zipes, *Breaking the Magical Spell: Radical Theories of Folk and Fairy Tales* (Austin: University of Texas Press, 1979), 5, 18. Raymonde Robert affirms that textual references to historical context are essential for the fairy tale's efficacy: "mais dans la mesure où son objectif est d'abord le plaisir du lecteur, elle [toute littérature merveilleuse] doit s'inscrire, en contrecoup et si étroitement, dans la réalité historique que celle-ci l'informe entièrement, en lui assurant le maximum d'efficacité" [but to the extent that its objective is, first of all, the reader's pleasure, it [marvelous literature] must follow historical reality indirectly and so closely that the latter informs it entirely, thus assuring it maximum effectiveness (Robert, *Le conte de fées littéraire*, 456)]. Finally, Barchilon declares that d'Aulnoy's tales contain several political allusions, in addition to "innumerable" references to contemporary mores (Barchilon, *Le Conte merveilleux*, 47, 38).

39. Peter Burke, *The Fabrication of Louis XIV* (New Haven: Yale University Press, 1992), 132.
40. Elias, *Court Society*, 149.
41. Burke, *Fabrication*, 142.
42. Nicole Ferrier-Caverivère, *L'Image de Louis XIV dans la littérature française de 1660–1715* (Paris: Presses Universitaires de France, 1981), 345–46.
43. Both Burke and Ferrier-Caverivère discuss the literature critical of the king during this period.
44. Di Scanno, *Contes de fées à l'époque classique*, 21.
45. Ibid., 123.
46. Ferrier-Caverivère, *L'image de Louis XIV*, 342–43.
47. Apostolidès, *Roi-machine*, 142.
48. Robert, *Le conte de fées littéraire*, 231.
49. Farrell, "Celebration and Repression," 53.
50. Ibid., 52–53.
51. Jackson, *Fantasy*, 4.
52. A telling historical instance of this vulnerability is seen in the controversy surrounding Louis XIV's succession: Louis's will, naming his illegitimate son, the Duc de Maine, his successor, was contested and eventually overturned.
53. Jacques Barchilon and Peter Flinders, *Charles Perrault* (Boston: Twayne, 1981), 81.
54. Marc Fumaroli, "*Les Fées* de Charles Perrault ou de la littérature," in *Le Statut de la littérature. Mélanges offerts à Paul Bénichou*, ed. Marc Fumaroli (Geneva: Librairie Droz, 1982), 160.
55. René Demoris, "Le corps royal et l'imaginaire au XVIIe siècle: *Le portrait du Roy* par Félibien," *Revue des sciences humaines* 172 (1978): 11.

Bibliography

Aarne, Antti, and Stith Thompson. *The Types of the Folktale: A Classification and Bibliography*. Helsinki: Suomalainen Tiedeakatemia, 1961.

Apostolidès, Jean-Marie. *Le Roi-machine*. Paris: Les Editions de Minuit, 1981.

d'Aubigné, Agrippa. *Histoire universelle*. Vol. 4. Ed. André Thierry. Geneva: Librairie Droz, 1987.

Aulnoy, Marie-Catherine Le Jumel de Barneville, comtesse d'. *Belle-Belle ou le chevalier Fortuné*. In *Les Contes de fées*. 4 vols. Paris, 1697–1698. Rpt. in vol. 5 of *Nouveau Cabinet de fées*. Geneva: Slatkine Reprints, 1978.

Barchilon, Jacques. *Le Conte merveilleux français de 1690 à 1790*. Paris: Librairie Honoré Champion, 1975.

Barchilon, Jacques, and Peter Flinders. *Charles Perrault*. Boston: Twayne, 1981.

Burke, Peter. *The Fabrication of Louis XIV*. New Haven: Yale University Press, 1992.

de Certeau, Michel. *L'Invention du quotidien, 1. Arts de faire*. Paris: 10/18, 1980.

Delarue, Paul, and Marie-Louise Tenèze. *Le Conte populaire français. Catalogue raisonné des versions de France et des pays de langue française d'outre-mer*. 3 vols. Paris: Editions Maisonneuve et Larose, 1976.

Demoris, René. "Le corps royal et l'imaginaire au XVIIe siècle: *Le Portrait du Roy* par Félibien." *Revue des sciences humaines* 172 (1978): 9–30.

Dollimore, Jonathan. *Sexual Dissidence: From Augustine to Wilde, Freud to Foucault.* Oxford: Clarendon Press, 1991.

Elias, Norbert. *The Court Society.* Trans. Edmund Jephcott. New York: Pantheon Books, 1983.

Farrell, Michèle L.. "Celebration and Repression of Feminine Desire in Mme d'Aulnoy's Fairy Tale: *La Chatte blanche.*" *L'Esprit créateur* 29, no. 3 (1989): 52–64.

Ferrier-Caverivière, Nicole. *L'Image de Louis XIV dans la littérature française de 1660–1715.* Paris: Presses Universitaires de France, 1981.

Foucault, Michel. *Histoire de la sexualité, 1.* Paris: Gallimard, 1976.

Fumaroli, Marc. "*Les Fées* de Charles Perrault ou de la littérature." In *Le Statut de la littérature. Mélanges offerts à Paul Bénichou.* Ed. Marc Fumaroli. Geneva: Librairie Droz, 1982. 153–86.

Gibson, Wendy. *Women in Seventeenth-Century France.* London: Macmillan, 1989.

L'Héritier, Marie-Jeanne (Mademoiselle l'H***). *L'Amazone françoise.* In *Les Caprices du destin, ou recueil d'histoires singulieres et amusantes arrivées de nos jours.* Paris: Chez Pierre Michel Huart, 1718.

Irigaray, Luce. *This Sex Which Is Not One.* Trans. Catherine Porter with Carolyn Burke. Ithaca: Cornell University Press, 1985.

Jackson, Rosemary. *Fantasy: The Literature of Subversion.* New York: Methuen, 1981.

Louis XIV. *Mémoires.* Paris: Tallendier, 1978.

Lüthi, Max. *The Fairy Tale as Art Form and Portrait of Man.* Trans. Jon Erickson. Bloomington: Indiana University Press, 1984.

Lyons, John. *A Theatre of Disguise: Studies in French Baroque Drama, 1630–1660.* Columbia, S.C.: French Literature Publications Company, 1978.

Lyotard, Jean-François. "Sur la force des faibles." *L'Arc* 64 (1976): 4–14.

Maclean, Ian. *The Renaissance Notion of Woman.* Cambridge: Cambridge University Press, 1980.

Mitchell, Jane Tucker. *A Thematic Analysis of Mme d'Aulnoy's Contes de Fées.* University, Mississippi: Romance Monographs, Inc., 1978.

Perret, Michele. "Travesties et transsexuelles: Yde, Silence, Grisandole, Blanchandine." *Romance Notes* 25, no. 3 (1985): 328–40.

Pollock, Mordeca Jane. "Transvestites in French Baroque Prose Fiction: The Psychological Structure of Femininity." *Degré Second* 3 (1979): 61–81.

Robert, Raymonde. *Le conte de fées littéraire en France de la fin du XVIIe siècle à la fin du XVIIIe siècle.* Nancy: Presses Universitaires de Nancy, 1981.

Scanno, Teresa di. *Les Contes de fées à l'époque classique.* Napoli: Liguori Editori, 1975.

Scudéry, Madeleine de. *Célinte, Nouvelle première.* Ed. Alain Niderst. Paris: Nizet, 1979.

Seifert, Lewis C. *Fairy Tales, Sexuality, and Gender in France, 1690–1715: Nostalgic Utopias.* Cambridge: Cambridge University Press, 1996.

Simons, Patricia. "Alert and Erect: Masculinity in Some Italian Renaissance Portraits of Fathers and Sons." In *Gender Rhetorics: Postures of Dominance and Submission in History.* Ed. Richard C. Trexler. Binghamton, N.Y.: Medieval and Renaissance Texts and Studies, 1994.

Stanton, Domna C. "The Demystification of History and Fiction in *Les Annales galantes.*" Biblio 17, *Papers on French Seventeenth-Century Literature* 37 (1987): 339–60.

Storer, Mary Elizabeth. *La Mode des contes de fées (1685–1700).* 1929. Reprint, Geneva: Slatkine Reprints, 1972.

Thelander, Dorothy R. "Mother Goose and Her Goslings: The France of Louis XIV as Seen through the Fairy Tale." *Journal of Modern History* 54 (1982): 466–96.

Tuana, Nancy. *The Less Noble Sex: Scientific, Religious, and Philosophical Conceptions of Woman.* Bloomington: Indiana University Press, 1993.

d'Urfé, Honoré. *L'Astrée.* Ed. Hugues Vaganay. 5 vols. Lyons: Pierre Masson, 1925.

Velay-Vallantin, Catherine. *La fille en garçon.* Carcassonne: Editions G.A.R.A.E./ Hésiode, 1992.

Villedieu, Madame de (Marie-Catherine Desjardins). *Les Annales galantes.* Vol. 2 of *Œuvres complètes.* 3 vols. Geneva: Slatkine Reprints, 1971.

Warner, Marina. *From the Beast to the Blond: On Fairy Tales and Their Tellers.* New York: Farrar, Straus and Giroux, 1995.

Welch, Marcelle Maistre. "Rébellion et résignation dans les contes de fée de Mme d'Aulnoy et Mme de Murat." *Cahiers du Dix-Septième* 3, no. 2 (1989): 131–42.

———. "Le Devenir de la jeune fille dans les contes de fée de Madame d'Aulnoy." *Cahiers du Dix-Septième* 1, no. 1 (1987): 53–62.

Zipes, Jack. *Breaking the Magic Spell: Radical Theories of Folk and Fairy Tales.* Austin: University of Texas Press, 1979.

Zuerner, Adrienne E. "(Re)Constructing Gender: Cross-Dressing in Seventeenth-Century French Literature." Ph.D. diss. University of Michigan, 1993.

Eighteenth-Century Parodies and Transformations of the Fairy Tale

PART

III

CHAPTER 8

Fractured Fairy Tales:
Parodies for the Salon and Foire

Mary Louise Ennis

Once upon a time, in the olden days, heavy-set middle-aged men would congregate in their elitist clubs, sit in over-stuffed leather chairs, smoke air-choking cigars, and pitch story ideas and plots to each other. Problem was, these stories, many of which found their way into the general social consciousness, reflected the way in which these men lived and saw their world, that is, the stories were sexist, discriminatory, unfair, culturally biased, and in general, demeaning to witches, animals, goblins and fairies everywhere.

JAMES FINN GARNER, *POLITICALLY CORRECT BEDTIME STORIES: MODERN TALES FOR OUR LIFE AND TIMES*[1]

AS THE reader of French fairy tales will quickly note, this introduction to James Finn Garner's *Politically Correct Bedtime Stories* (1994) reveals a faulty appreciation of the first "authors" of fairy tales. In stressing their creation by men, Garner ignores their popularization by women—such as Mme d'Aulnoy, Mlle de La Force, and Mme de Murat. Moreover, he places male authors in elitist male clubs rather than in the refined *salons* of influential women—such as Mme de Lambert, Mme de Tencin, and the Duchesse du Maine.[2] In short, by disregarding the social development of the *contes des vieilles* ("old ladies' tales," as fairy tales were first called in France), Garner gaily proposes a literary heritage as sexist as the stories he "purges" of biased content!

Women's influence on fairy tales is an important topic in feminist criticism and gender studies. Likewise, the "sexist, discriminatory, unfair [and] culturally biased" content of children's stories is also addressed in popular culture research. Garner is, of course, parodying these kinds of academic texts and their language by ascribing a political agenda to every noun, verb, and adjective; every witch, goblin, and fairy. Such humorous rewriting of fairy tales for an adult public is not new, and actually dates to eighteenth-century France. As with Pierre Gripari's *Patrouille du conte* (1983) [Bedtime-Story Patrol],[3] Garner's silly anachronisms and outrageous plot twists find their predecessor in the fairy-tale parodies first written by Antoine Hamilton and continued by no less than Voltaire, Rousseau, and Diderot.

That parody should address the vogue of fairy tales is hardly surprising. Both genres are rooted in popular culture and share the dubious distinction of "paraliterature." Early French parody was considered a lesser, mixed literary genre, and therefore carried the stigma of popular (vs. official) culture during the reign of Louis XIV. At the beginning of the eighteenth century, however, there began a softening of the rigid social and aesthetic hierarchies of *le siècle classique* that would be completed during the regency of Philippe d'Orléans (1715–23). In art, the feminine curves of the rococo came to be favored over the rigid and male line of classical design. In theater, the mixed genre of comic opera was born when Comédie française and Opéra productions were parodied on the illegitimate stages of the Foires [Fairs]. Aristocrats "slumming" at the Foires Saint-Laurent and Saint-Germain-des-Prés enjoyed these carnivalesque attacks on the traditional culture with which they were familiar. Likewise, the common folk reveled in the social juxtapositions when the earthy buffoon Arlequin portrayed gods and kings.

Just as official theater provided the fodder for fair parodies, so did fairy tales inspire *Les Eaux de Merlin* [Merlin's Waters], *Arlequin, jouet des fées* [Arlequin, the Fairies' Toy], *Le Château des lutins* [Castle of the Sprites], *Arlequin valet de Merlin* [Arlequin, Merlin's Valet], *Mélusine, Arlequin, roi des ogres ou les bottes de sept lieux* [Arlequin, King of the Ogres or the Seven-League Boots], and *La Foire des fées* [The Fairies' Fair]—all penned during the Regency by Alain-René Lesage and Louis Fuzelier. Because these fair parodies were such an excellent barometer of popular culture, it follows that they would reflect another literary vogue. Accordingly, as the fairy-tale genre was transformed by Antoine Galland's translation of *Les Mille et une nuits* [The Arabian Nights (1704–17)],[4] so did the fairies cede the Foire to the "oriental" likes of *Arlequin Mahomet, Arlequin Grand Turc*, and even the cross-dressed *Arlequin sultane favorite*. Indeed, as early as 1722, one Lesage fairy complains, "On ne parle plus de nous dans le monde comme on en parloit du temps de ma Mére L'oyë" [People don't talk about us any more like they used to in the days of Mother Goose].[5]

In what ways did the fair theaters parody fairy tales and oriental tales? How did Lesage's comedies for the Foire differ from Hamilton's parodies for the salon? What did the word "parody" signify for the eighteenth-century public? In short, how did the French fractured fairy tale come to prefigure Garner's politically correct bedtime stories?

Parody and Eighteenth-Century France

Linda Hutcheon states in *A Theory of Parody* that "all historians of parody agree that parody prospers in periods of cultural sophistication that enable parodists to rely on the competence of the reader (viewer, listener) of the parody."[6]

As regards fairy-tale parodies, this observation is important for two reasons. First, fairy tales were indeed enormously popular among the cultural elite. They reveled in this "escapist literature" of bygone days so different from the seriousness of Louis XIV's court.[7] Fairy tales took the salons by storm, from the first published tale in 1690 by Mme d'Aulnoy, to the collections by d'Aulnoy, Perrault, Mlles L'Héritier, Bernard, and de La Force, the Chevalier de Mailly, and Mesdames de Murat, Durand, and d'Auneuil. The genre's popularity was compounded by the influence of *Les Mille et une nuits*, which saw its imitations in the *Mille et un jours*, . . . *faveurs*, . . . *fadaises*, . . . *folies*— to cite a few imitative titles.[8] The Comte de Caylus, himself the author of the *Contes orientaux*, commented that one hardly read anything else but fairy tales in his youth.[9] In fact, so obsessed was the public by 1755 that Frédéric-Melchior Grimm opined that just about everyone had put his hand to one.[10] Fairy tales and oriental intrigues became so popular that they influenced aristocrats and commoners alike. Accordingly, parodists could count upon the public's recognition of primary texts to decipher the encoded humor of their rewritten tales.

The second observation with reference to Hutcheon is the fact that "all historians of parody" agree on "one point"—which implies that they do not agree on others. The definition of parody itself is an example. Indeed, the words "parody," "burlesque," and "travesty" were often used interchangeably by early French critics, as a short digression will illustrate.

Boileau was the first French critic to define what we today term "parody." Author of the parodies *Chapelain décoiffé* (1665) and *Le Lutrin* (1674), he noted that Scarron's *Virgile travesti* differed radically from previous literary humor. Earlier authors had downwardly translated the style of an original text and retained noble subjects; Scarron's "burlesque" reversed this process by modifying the subjects and retaining the original style.[11]

Some fifty years later, Antoine Houdar de la Motte similarly defined "travestissement burlesque." A mediocre playwright and fabulist whose works reengaged the Quarrel of the Ancients and Moderns, he inspired more theatrical parodies than any other author save Voltaire. Several of these were printed between 1723 and 1734 and between 1729 and 1738, when the Foire and Nouveau Théâtre Italien published their respective collections of comedies. It was during this period that the merits of parody seem to have been hotly debated.

The inaugural volume of the *Parodies du Nouveau Théâtre Italien* included *Agnès de Chaillot*, a send-up of La Motte's *Inès de Castro*.[12] La Motte vigorously defended his work in his "Troisième discours à l'occasion de la tragédie *Inès de Castro*" (1730), which both defined and maligned parody for the public at large.[13]

Like Boileau, La Motte observed that parody conserved the original plot while modifying the characters. Original material was comically interpreted by adding "mots burlesques" [burlesque words] and "circonstances risibles" [amusing circumstances]. However, the greater the juxtaposition between these comic and serious elements, the greater the danger of this "buffoonery." La Motte then vented his moral and aesthetic outrage at the authors of parody, practically sputtering his charges. Not only did parodists appropriate others' works as their own, they exercised poor taste and lack of judgment by writing just anything to make the public laugh! Parody was far from being the intellectual pursuit claimed by the parodists. La Motte denied it any didactic role and declared that it corrupted the unsuspecting spectator with comic literary criticism that aimed to render virtue paradoxical and ridiculous (127–33).

Louis Fuzelier (Foire parodist, collaborator of Lesage and future coowner of *Le Mercure*) responded to La Motte's diatribe in his "Discours à l'occasion d'un discours de M[onsieur] D[e] L[a] M[otte] sur les parodies." Composed in the early 1730s, this essay was so popular that Fuzelier augmented and reprinted it in 1738, as the preface to a reedition of the *Parodies du Nouveau Théâtre Italien*.[14]

Noting that "MDLM" himself admitted to laughing at *Agnès de Chaillot*, Fuzelier ingenuously wondered why the author denied the same pleasure to the public at large. He then sarcastically commented about the "vain" and "moral" La Motte and the personal nature of his defense. The parodists never intended to offend anyone. They were merely echoing the observations of the audience in a didactic treatment of an author's stylistic faults. Far from leading spectators astray and "turning virtue into paradox" (as La Motte had charged), their literary criticism was praiseworthy: "Bien des Tragédies déguisent les vices en vertus, les Parodies leur en arrachent le Masque" [Many Tragedies disguise vices as virtues; Parodies unmask them ("MDLM," xxix–xxxj)].

Fuzelier then referred to other defenders of the genre, such as Boileau and M. l'Abbé S***—no doubt the abbé Sallier, author of the "Discours sur l'Origine et sur le Caractère de la Parodie" (1733). Although Sallier echoed La Motte's definition of parody as "intermingling" original phrases with humorous ones, he analyzed form more thoroughly and delineated five different types.[15] Championing parody, he compared it to an arrow by which truth avenges virtue and to a torch that illumines an author's weaknesses ("MDLM," xxiv and xxij).

Fuzelier also cited Luigi Riccoboni of the Théâtre Italien. Like Fuzelier, he had written a defense of parody in the 1730s that was popular enough to republish. His 1746 reprint may be situated one year before Diderot and Voltaire composed their parodies *L'Oiseau blanc, Conte bleu* and *Zadig,* and eight years before Rousseau's *La Reine Fantasque.*

Riccoboni stressed parody's didactic merits and added a precision between travesty and parody. Parody criticized a work by retaining characters and plot and modifying the style of the original, while travesty translated heroic characters into base ones.[16] This observation returns us to the distinctions raised by Boileau and La Motte, and underscores how early "historians of parody" did not agree on the genre's definition.[17] They broadly concurred, however, that it involved the downward translation of original material. And parody's partisans all supported it as didactic criticism in the literary debates that seem to have raged during the 1730s—debates that no doubt stemmed from the publication of the Foire and Théâtre Italien parodies.

As mentioned earlier, these texts occasioned La Motte's diatribe of 1730. Interestingly, this was also the year in which Antoine Hamilton's fairy-tale parodies of 1705–10 were posthumously printed. Although their belated publication has recently been questioned by Jacques Barchilon,[18] it follows that, given the renewed interest in parody, the time was finally ripe to publish those tales that had circulated for years in the salons.

Antoine Hamilton and Fairy-Tale Parodies for the Salon

Born in Ireland and reared in France, the Scotsman Antoine (Anthony) Hamilton (1646–1719) frequented the courts of both James II and Louis XIV. At the turn of the eighteenth century, both of these societies were characterized by austerity: the exiled king ruled Saint-Germain-en-Laye with a pious hand, much as Mme de Maintenon influenced Versailles. As expected, this stifling court life was countered by lighter literary pursuits. Some *salonniers* preferred to read fairy tales and oriental intrigues; others preferred to compose them. Hamilton may have done so on a wager, for the ladies at court whom he teased for their obsession with fairy tales supposedly challenged him to write one himself.[19] This practice would be repeated when later authors of fairy-tale parodies (Duclos, Caylus, Voisenon, Rousseau) accepted similar bets in 1741 and 1754.[20]

Hamilton, author of the *Mémoires de la vie du comte de Grammont* (1715), wrote so well in his adopted language that he is said to have influenced no less than Voisenon, Crébillon *fils*, Diderot, and Voltaire. They were inspired by the new genre he supposedly created: the *conte licencieux*, a "half-burlesque, half-satirical tale, Oriental in most cases, the soi-disant exotic customs depicted affording a convenient pretext for the crudest colours."[21] While this definition refers to Hamilton's *Quatre Facardins* (1710–15), certain elements are found in his earliest and more "innocent" parodies: *Le Bélier* [The Ram, 1705] and *L'Histoire de Fleur d'Epine* [The History of May-Flower, 1710].[22] Posthumously published, they were widely edited during the eighteenth and nineteenth centuries. *Fleur d'Epine* was especially popular and enjoyed thirteen French, four English, and five German editions.

It was widely acknowledged that Hamilton parodied the *contes des vieilles*, trying to "do for the fairy tale what Cervantes did for Don Quixote."[23] He sought to lighten up the stifling atmosphere of the salons while pointing out the "dullness of the *Oiseau bleu* and the *Rameau d'or*."[24] Specific references to these tales by Mme d'Aulnoy appear in the verse introduction to the *Facardins*, which the Chevalier de Mayer considered important enough to reproduce at the beginning of his discourse on fairy tales for the *Cabinet des Fées*.[25] It is a humorous epistle that opens with a pun. Dedicated to "A.M.L.C.D.F." [To Monsieur Le Comte/Conte de Fées], there is a play on words between the homophones *comte* [count] and *conte* [tale]. Hamilton goes on to sketch an account of heroic literature and describes its supplanting by fairy tales (that is, how heroes like Cyrus and Télémaque were ousted by the likes of the Renard blanc and Oiseau bleu). These "insipid readings" were, in turn, displaced by "endless volumes of Oriental allegories" whose translators embroidered upon their sources.[26]

This brief lesson in literary criticism, while not parodic in itself, does support the didactic justification of parody: to echo public opinion in humorous commentary of popular works. Some people, however, were humorless where fairy tales were concerned. The Marquise de Maintenon (the king's wife) demanded that "no Peau d'Ane" be taught the girls at Port-Royal. And at Sceaux, the Duchesse du Maine (the king's sister-in-law) dismissed them as trivial readings.[27]

A *salonnier* at Sceaux, Hamilton enthusiastically embraced fairy tales' shortcomings in *Le Bélier*. Unfortunately, in recreating their stylistic faults of lengthy and hyperbolic descriptions, abundant characters, and convoluted narrative structure, he provided far too many examples. This "Rabelaisian" accumulation risks boring the reader—a drawback noted by Raymonde Robert about parody in general.[28] But in the end, the participatory nature of decoding parody—that collusion between the reader and the writer to decipher the inscribed humor—is seductive. This complicity is strengthened by the narrator's frequent asides to the reader. Such remarks of "factitious orality"[29] address the tale's structure and content, and are reinforced by similar interruptions and commentaries by the story's fictional characters. In short, at every juncture Hamilton creates a self-conscious narrative that continuously invites the reader to question the text.

Hamilton frames his tale of a Druid's daughter and the men who love her by using a stock literary device common in eighteenth-century novels. Since at this time fiction was considered both a morally and aesthetically corrupt genre, it masqueraded as long-lost informative works (memoirs, letters, translations, and so forth) whose veracity was posited in lengthy prefaces. Accordingly, Hamilton presents the Duchesse du Maine's entourage with a didactic text, not a frivolous tale. Based on the "memoirs" of an actual acquaintance (the "learned Mabillon," author of *De re diplomatica* and the *Traité des études monastiques*), it relates how the estate of Les Moulineaux came to be known as Pontalie. The introduction's fictive historicity is reinforced by references to actual sites on the estate, which was given by Louis XIV to Hamilton's sister Elizabeth, Comtesse de Grammont. In addition to the many other local allusions, the contemporary reader may have deciphered the identities of many characters—such as the storytelling ram (Hamilton) and his fictional heroine (the princesse de Conti).[30] For these reasons, this tale is a *conte à clef* as well as a *conte de fées*.

On one level, then, *Le Bélier* is merely a fairy tale. On another, it passes as a folkloric lesson in local history—a lesson not for children but for the same aristocratic female audience addressed by the female authors of fairy tales. And a still deeper reading reveals that contemporary literary and social criticism underlie parody that is blatantly signaled by the author.

First of all, the mere title of *Le Bélier* [The Ram] is a play on words of *Le Mouton* [The Sheep], a 1694 tale by Mme d'Aulnoy. Although Hamilton does not reprise d'Aulnoy's plot, he may be poking fun at her choice of a gussied-up lamb for a metamorphosed princely lover. If so, he would then be voicing a criticism that Barchilon has made concerning d'Aulnoy's prince— that the reader "expected a stronger symbol: even a fat ram would have done the trick."[31]

D'Aulnoy's influence is found on a structural level as well, for Hamilton also uses the literary device of the intercalated tale. But where *Le Mouton* is a linear narrative that forms the middle section of *Ponce de Léon*, *Le Bélier* is a baroque "Chinese box" narrative in which many narrators recount numerous stories.

This structure is of course exploited in the *Mille et une nuits*, whose first volume of translations in 1704 would have just appeared in the courtly circles that Hamilton frequented. Seizing quickly on the voguish oriental tales, he underscores their social and literary impact in a satiric pastiche of "traditional" heroic verse. Lengthy verse. Tired verse. Verse that is so painful to read (and write!) that the narrator eventually excuses himself from his rhymes to restart his story in prose (*Œuvres*, 131–32; *Fairy Tales*, 460).

This oriental motif is introduced as early as line 29 of his 599-line prologue, when the narrator states that he has neither borrowed nor stolen his story from Schéhérazade. Later on, the impressionable heroine Alie fantasizes that she *is* Schérérazade. No doubt she has succumbed, like so many young ladies at court, to an overdose of mindless Arabian tales:

> Ells se crut, avec son aventure,
> Au beau milieu des Mille nuits;
> Car c'étoit alors sa lecture.
> Elle se crut soumise aux cruautés
> D'un époux bizarre et sauvage
> Qui, par un détestable usage,
> Epousoit chaque jour de nouvelles beautés
> Pour les immoler à sa rage;
> Et, se couchant sous un épais feuillage,
> Elle se crut à ses côtés
> Comme elle avoit dans la mémoire
> Tout le récit de ces fatras.
> Elle crut, malgré ses appas,
> Qu'il falloit conter quelque histoire
> Pour se garantir du trépas. (*Œuvres*, 128)

> [She thought herself—so strange her fate—
> A heroine of the Arabian Nights—
> A book which she'd devour'd of late;
> Imagining, that she a victim
> Had fall'n to a tyrant grim,
> Who finding out one wife had trick'd him,
> Now part from vengeance, part from whim
> A spick-span new one daily wedded.
> Whom in the morning he beheaded;
> And lying down beneath the shade
> Afforded by a wooded tuft,
> She thought her spouse beside her laid,
> And her memory being stuft
> With all this Arabian balderdash,
> She thought that she, to save her head,
> Must tell her lord some kind of trash.] (*Fairy Tales*, 456)

It is in such a state of mind that Alie recounts her life story to her lover, whom she thought was a thousand times more beautiful than the day. The words "mille" and "jour" occasion another lapse into the *Arabian Nights* mode. Imagining herself to be Schéhérazade, she complains to her sister Dinarzade that the sultan will soon leave her bed. Storytelling is over for the night, and he fears intimacy during the day: "dès qu'il est jour, je lui fais peur" (*Œuvres*, 130) [For when 'tis day I seem to scare him (*Fairy Tales*, 458)]. After this satiric yet psychoanalytic comment on the sultan's avoidance of sex, Alie falls asleep. The telling of her tale thus has the desired *Mille et une nuits* effect, and comically provides Hamilton's segue into the prose section of his story.

Le *Bélier*'s introduction, then, is a pastiche of heroic verse that pays homage to the oriental tale and to (written) popular texts of the past. Likewise, the rest of the *conte* imitates the (oral) structure and motifs of contemporary escapist literature. Unfortunately, its plot lines and chronology are particularly convoluted.

Briefly, *Le Bélier* is the love triangle formed by Alie (a druid's daughter), the giant Moulineau who loves her, and the Prince de Noisy, whom she loves. The giant is counseled by a ram, the druid is aided by a gnome. Alie, the gnome, the ram, and the druid all tell (intercalated) stories, and the characters in those narratives tell their own tales. These characters in turn interrupt each other, just as the giant interrupts the ram's tale, and the narrator interrupts his own narrative. These stories turn out to be different episodes of a legend concerning a white fox, a lovely siren, magic objects, the kingdom of Lombardy, an enchantress, and Merlin (enemy of the druid, father of the Prince de Noisy, and archenemy of the enchantress). Interestingly, those characters first presented as fictional (the enchantress and Merlin) turn out to be real players in the saga of Alie and Noisy. When poor Alie misinterprets her father's counsel and stabs the ram with a magic dagger, she finds that she has killed not a disguised Merlin but a metamorphosed Noisy. The enchantress comes to her aid, however, and revives the prince to fight Moulineau for Alie's hand. Noisy wins the battle on the castle bridge, le Pont Alie. Thus did the estate of Les Moulineaux come to be known as Pontalie.

If this synopsis is difficult to follow, it is because Hamilton is simultaneously parodying the content of the *conte* while critiquing its structure. In the interest of discussion, we shall examine the giant's reception of the ram's tale before turning to the syncretic folklore of the story itself.

Now, all readers of fairy tales know that giants are usually dull-witted. Not ours. In fact, Moulineau echoes the *salonniers* in his insightful critique of the "much despised *conte*." Constantly interrupting the ram, he attacks its willfully nonchronological order (*Œuvres*, 153; *Fairy Tales*, 474),[32] nonessential or uninteresting plot lines (157/477, 167/483, 203/508), changes in narrative points of view and illogical plot development (164/482, 168/483), tendency to abandon plot lines at the most interesting point (194/501, 203/508), and length (188/498).

Whenever Moulineau suggests a stylistic improvement, the ram either ignores the criticism, states that it is against common practice (153/474), or says that it cannot be done, given the accepted form of the fairy tale (168/484). At other times, however, the ram himself criticizes his narrative's length. He announces abridgments of lengthy passionate reunions (184/495) and eventually avoids all descriptions by referring the giant to stock elements of popular literature, such as how the swooned heroes of romances are revived in the presence of dumbfounded divinities (194/502), or how the prince's narration just happens to end at precisely the right moment (193/501). Finally, the ram refuses to finish his story, saying that the giant knows how all fairy tales end (203/508).

These structural criticisms are also echoed by Le Bélier's "narrator," who interrupts his own narrative to address the reader. For example, he relates how he wept while translating Mabillon's account of Noisy's murder (216/517), and confesses how Mabillon ought not to have switched plot lines (223/521). The most outrageous intervention, however, is the first, which occurs at the text's transition from verse to prose: Mabillon has lied in his memoirs about the hyperbolic proportions of the druid's river, the ram's bridge, and the giant's height (133/461)!

Hyperbole is, of course, a stock device in fairy-tale portraits. Used to convey the beauty of heroines or the strength of heroes, it underscores many descriptions in Le Bélier. La Motte might have noted that the humor of the following passage stems from the juxtaposition of the comic (hyperbolic description) and the tragic (Alie's preparation for suicide): "défaisant de la plus belle jambe du monde la plus belle jarretière de l'univers, elle alloit étrangler au premier arbre la créature la plus charmante et la plus désolée qui fut jamais" (Œuvres, 243) [taking the prettiest garter in the world from the prettiest leg that ever was formed, she was about to hang the most charming and the most disconsolate creature that ever existed (Fairy Tales, 534–35)]. Hamilton goes on to exploit hyperbole in the ram's story, which parodies numerous fairy-tale motifs. Here, the ugliest king in the world is married to the most beautiful queen (shades of Perrault's Riquet à la houppe). And as in most fairy tales, not only do polarities exist between these character types (ugly vs. beautiful, evil vs. good), but the people concerned are all royal.

A linear retelling of this story, one that would have pleased the critical giant, reveals that the Duke de Plaisance is under a spell of madness. A sorceress comes to the rescue. (We later learn that she is the wife of Narcissus, who had accidentally metamorphosed himself into an owl before their first meeting.) She counsels the duke's son and daughter to spend the night in a certain enchanted castle and to use the magic collar and comb she gives them. They do so and are immediately transformed into a white fox and a siren. The sorceress then gives the comb and collar to the townspeople and tells them to return when they find a man who can open the comb case and a maiden who can unbutton the collar. The enchanted objects finally arrive in Lombardy at the castle of the beautiful yet wicked queen and ugly yet good king, the duke's brother. The king's children, although persecuted by their evil stepmother, pass the tests and are magically transported to a mysterious island, where they quickly fall in love with the siren and fox. The sorceress instructs them to use the comb and collar to transform their lovers into their natural states, and all live happily ever after.

The ram's tale therefore adds a comical accumulation of marvelous motifs to Le Bélier's narrative frame. To the giant, gnome, druid, Merlin, and enchantress are added magic rings, an oracular knife, magic whirlwinds, enchanted objects, more metamorphosed lovers (the fox and siren join the ram and owl), and even a wicked stepmother.

The actions of Hamilton's stepmother allude to numerous versions of the wonder tale of the persecuted stepdaughter as defined by Antti Aarne.[33] These variations include Perrault's Cendrillon [Cinderella, folktale type #510], in which she forces her stepdaughter to wear rags, and d'Aulnoy's L'Oiseau bleu [The Blue Bird, #432], in which she practically imprisons the girl in a tower. Other allusions are to an Italian version of Snow White (#709, in which the new queen is jealous of her stepdaughter's beauty). The fact that Hamilton's characters are in Italy (Lombardy) may pay homage to Basile's tales in general and to The Young Slave in particular. Basile's evil stepmother causes her stepdaughter to die from an enchanted comb; in Hamilton's tale, it is the comb that rescues another maiden from a spell. Also released from enchantment are the king of Lombardy (whose ugliness vanishes like Riquet's) and our "animal" lovers.

The transformations of the white fox and the owl are particularly noteworthy, for they underscore the latent sexuality of the metamorphosed lover motif (#425–432). The sorceress had been overzealous in plucking owl feathers to reveal Narcissus's naked body; similarly, the princess blushes at seeing her nude lover when she remembers the caresses she lavished upon him as the fox. These scenes recall the countless stories about "animals" who immediately seduce princes and princesses. Some of them, like d'Aulnoy's Biche au Bois [The Doe in the Woods, #403], are relieved that their animal form has guarded their chastity. Others, like La Chatte Blanche [The White Cat, #402], demand that the lover destroy their "animality." Just as the prince must cut off the cat's head and tail in Mme d'Aulnoy's tale, so must the enchantress pluck the owl, and the prince burn the fish skin of his siren (#425, burning the animal skin).

The metamorphosed siren is interesting for another reason, for at times she appears with a crocodile's head—an esoteric allusion to the Egyptian divinity Sebek. Not only does this image showcase Hamilton's erudition, it also bridges the intercalated ram's tale and the plot of Le Bélier, in which Alie's castle is near Cleopatra's column on the Nile. Elsewhere in the story, however, the action occurs in France. Alie's lover strolls along the Seine, the sorceress is an Armorican princess, and Merlin (also of Breton ancestry) receives the principality of Noisy from Pépin, who (along with the inhabitants of Meudon, Saint-Germain, and Ruel) heard Moulineau roar when Alie called him a dwarf.

Pépin? Le Bélier's history is clearly as fractured as its geography! Since the Pépin in question was holding a scepter at the time, he is probably Pépin le Bref (714–768 A.D.). Without this detail, the reader might rightly think of Pépin l'Ancien (d. 639) who served under good king Dagobert, ruler of the Franks between 629 and 639 A.D. and the supposed father of our druid.[34] Hamilton has these historical kings interact with fictional characters, for Pépin remembers one of Merlin's predictions when he hears the giant roar, and Dagobert supposedly stole back from Merlin the knife of the sorceress/wife of Narcissus. Greek mythology, Frankish history, Breton folklore, and Egyptian mysticism are further chronologically jumbled in the sorceress's story, wherein magical hieroglyphics were invented by Narcissus's father, Gaspard le Savant. Gaspard, a historical figure of Asiatic birth, was one of the three magi of Christian theology. How could he have fathered a son whose folkloric history predated his own? Since when did this Christian figure invent an Egyptian language? And since when did Narcissus dabble in magic?

Since when? Since 1705, when Antoine Hamilton created the parodic fairy tale of fantastic geographies, esoteric anachronisms, and syncretic folklore—all dressed up in a Chinese box narrative to mock society's fascination with contemporary paraliterature.

The salon success of Hamilton's Bélier was eclipsed by the parody for which he is better known, L'Histoire de Fleur d'Epine. This tale's critical emphasis is the opposite of the first. Le Bélier is a literary tour de force, a didactic parody of fairy tales' faults that contains passing references to Les Mille et une nuits. The outrageousness of Fleur d'Epine, on the other hand, is primarily visual. It has a tighter structure, faster-paced plot, and political humor that stems less from literary criticism than from burlesqued fairy-tale motifs. Moreover, these carnivalesque tableaux are more suited to the Foire than the salon, and are set within a textual frame that lambastes both the structure and content of Les Mille et une nuits.

Hamilton takes "one thousand and one" literally instead of figuratively (its Arabic translation is "many"), and begins Fleur d'Epine with "the last night," the 999th since Schéhérazade married the sultan. Dinarzade, Schéhérazade's sister, is Hamilton's mouthpiece who questions and eventually deflates every vestige of the sultan's authority. She first portrays the sultan as a "ninny," "dolt," and "simpleton" who, for the past two years, has listened to Schéhérazade's tales without realizing her plan of never finishing them. Dinarzade, however, has better things to do with her nights than prompt her sister's stories. She would rather pass them with the Prince de Trébisonde, who at least won't cut off her head if she doesn't tell him a bedtime story. This flippant allusion to the sultan's life-and-death power over her sister trivializes his importance, which Dinarzade further deflates when she refers to him as a "common executioner."

Dinarzade proposes a plan to end the sultan's interminable fascination with storytelling and free up all their lives. Schéhérazade should tell a tale that will surpass all that she has recounted so far: *The Pyramid and the Golden Horse*.[35] The following night, she should plead indisposed and beg the sultan to let Dinarzade take her place. If her story isn't more extraordinary than Schéhérazade's, then the sultan should have his wife strangled first thing in the morning. On the other hand, if he interrupts her narrative, then he should grant Schéhérazade her life. Dinarzade says that the sultan will agree to this bet because he has never once interrupted Schéhérazade—no matter what trash she told him (*Œuvres*, 2; *Fairy Tales*, 367).

This proposition of course implies that the attentive yet stupid sultan will not interrupt Dinarzade, and that Schéhérazade will die. The narrator mockingly intervenes to note that such an agreement would have alarmed any other but Schéhérazade, "à qui l'étude de la philosophie avoit appris à ne point craindre la mort" [whom the study of philosophy had taught . . . to despise death]. Dinarzade is correct in thinking that the sultan will agree to her wager, and wisely makes him sign an agreement to this effect. She then prefaces her tale in the most seemingly laudatory terms whose underlying insolence escapes him.

The sultan does eventually interrupt Dinarzade, thus saving Schéhérazade's life. But the seriousness of his clemency is undermined by a Molièresque pantomime of supposed oriental customs. In a farcical scene worthy of *Le Bourgeois gentilhomme*, the vizier is busy bowing, Schéhérazade is busy kissing the sultan's little toe, and the sultan is busy pardoning everyone by rubbing their noses three times with his scepter. Finally, to complete the deflation of the august personage of the sultan, Hamilton questions his manhood. In *Le Bélier*, we remember, Alie/Schéhérazade remarked on the sultan's avoidance of sex. This observation is burlesqued in *Fleur d'Epine*, for after 1,001 nights, the amorous (and disrobed) sultan elects not to spend the night alone with his wife but instead asks the Prince de Trébisonde to tell his life story. It is this tale that frames *Les Quatre Facardins*,[36] a series of intercalated stories in which the prince inadvertently continues Dinarzade's deflation of the sultan's character. Unbeknownst to him, his tale of Crystalline la Curieuse (the ring-collecting, unfaithful genie's wife of the *Mille et une nuits* prologue) ridicules the sultan and his brother, her 99th and 100th lovers, as cowardly and inept (*Œuvres*, 358–59).

The sultan's character therefore undergoes a downward translation from august ruler to impotent spouse. This modification would have been termed *travestissement burlesque*, parody, and travesty by La Motte, Fuzelier, and Riccoboni, respectively. Turning from style to content, it may also be a political metaphor for the waning power of either Louis XIV or James II.[37] Interestingly, this same politically incorrect equation of physical impotence and inability to govern would be exploited during the Revolution in seditious pornography against Louis XVI and Marie-Antoinette.[38]

Sexual innuendo in general may well be part of Hamilton's agenda, and can be inferred from the title of Dinarzade's tale. Just as *Le Bélier* was a play on words with *Le Mouton*, so might *Fleur d'Epine* be read as "Fleur des pines" [Flower of Pricks].[39] A risqué tale from the father of the *conte licencieux* would have indeed lightened up the sober salons of both courts. As we shall see, its double-entendre subtlety would also complement the blatant scatological humor of burlesqued fairy-tale motifs.

The structure of *Fleur d'Epine* resembles that of *Le Bélier*: both share an "oriental" frame story and contain intercalated folk tales whose narratives are interrupted. Instead of a giant offering literary criticism, however, it is the sultan who questions plot development. Dinarzade tells of Tarare, who is on a quest from the good enchantress Sérène. In order to reverse a spell on the beautiful princess Luisante, whose gaze blinds and kills, he must steal an enchanted mare and hat from Sérène's evil sorceress sister, Dentue. He must also rescue Sérène's daughter, Fleur d'Epine, whom Dentue had kidnapped years ago. Before the tale's end, and in a haphazard chronological order, the characters (Tarare, his brother Phénix, Sérène) all tell their own stories. These are different episodes of a tale about a beautiful parrot (eventually identified as Phénix) and card-playing magpies (Fleur d'Epine's metamorphosed family). Because the characters recount their stories after what should be the fairy tale's happy ending—the weddings of Tarare and Fleur d'Epine, Phénix and Luisante—the reader begins to wonder when Dinarzade's story, like the thousand tales of Schérérazade, will ever end.

Compared to the baroque structure of *Le Bélier*, the plot of *Fleur d'Epine* is relatively linear since there is no extratextual mingling of "fictional" and "real" characters. There is a corresponding shift, however, between fantasy and reality, hyperbole and minimization. These juxtapositions signal the comic modifications of stock fairy-tale settings, characters, and themes, and alert the reader to Hamilton's parodic tinkering.

For example, in true fairy-tale tradition, the geographical setting of *Fleur d'Epine* is highly improbable. It takes our endurance-gifted hero but a few days to walk from Circassie (in the Caucasus, the mountains dividing Europe and

Asia) to Cachemire (the disputed territory between India and Pakistan). The fairy-tale fantastic is also evident in the most beautiful flowers and fruit trees that magically spring up at one's feet while strolling in Cachemire. But the hyperbolic enchantment is soon dispelled by preciseness, for Hamilton notes in most unfolkloric exactitude that the kingdom is "2453 leagues away." This juxtaposition of fantasy and reality signals the importance of Cachemire, also the locale of *Les Mille et un jours* (1705). Hamilton's (anachronistic) reference to a contemporary best-seller is therefore a metareferential joke, since the site of Dinarzade's tale alludes to an imitation of stories in which she is a character.

This multilayered humor and comic intermingling of fantasy and reality are accompanied by other witty displacements, such as the unexpected juxtaposition between character and name. Heroines usually have laudatory names that personify their beauty (such as the overdetermined Belle-Belle) or other virtues (such as Gracieuse and Désirée). Accordingly, Hamilton's enchantress is Sérène [Serene] and his beautiful princess is Luisante [Radiant]. The wonderment represented by Luisante's name, however, is quickly negated on two counts.

First, Luisante's beauty is introduced in a style that mimics the rhythmic orality of folktales—"Dans ce pays régnoit un calife; ce calife avoit une fille, et cette fille un visage" [Here once reigned a Caliph; this Caliph had a daughter, and this daughter a face]—and then disrupts the cadence with an unpoetic observation: "mais on souhaita plus d'une fois qu'elle n'en eût jamais eu" (*Œuvres*, 4) [but many a time did people wish that she never had one (*Fairy Tales*, 368)]. Hamilton repeats this procedure twice more. Much as his "geographical" preciseness punctured the fantasy of Cachemire, he deflates the rhythm of hyperbolic descriptions with inelegant language. Luisante was so beautiful—that nobody could stand it. Similarly, her face was a masterpiece—but her eyes spoiled everything (*Œuvres*, 4; *Fairy Tales*, 368).[40]

A second negation concerns the opposite effect expected from good fairy-tale heroines. Luisante's looks literally kill, her beauty literally blinds. Moreover, this fatal gift was bestowed upon the infant princess by the good, not the evil, "fairy." Equally backward is the description of the requisite *scène des dons* (talent-giving scene by fairies to newborns, #503): instead of appearing at the beginning of the story line, it is recounted at the end.

Sérène supposedly had a laudable motive for so cursing Luisante, and she planned to reverse her spell once her "daughter," kidnapped by her "sister," was safely returned. But we eventually learn that Sérène has been lying all along! Dentue is not her sister, nor is Fleur d'Epine her daughter. What kind of a "good" enchantress lies and causes innocent people to die? Certainly not one who is "serene."

Nor does the hero's name fit his character, for its "low" connotation does not correspond to his heroic deeds. Fairy-tale heroes are usually handsome princes named Charming who perform serious tasks. Our hero is not hand-some, is presumably of humble birth, and has nicknamed himself "Tarare." According to Furetière's *Dictionnaire*, "tarare" was a "burlesque word" such as "fiddlesticks" or "pooh-pooh" that was used as a mocking rejoinder.[41] Such a silly name is hardly heroic, and its incongruity is farcically underscored by the fact that people (and even birds) can't help repeating his name once they hear it. For example: " 'My name is Tarare.' 'Tarare??' 'Tarare' "; or, " 'Who shall undertake this task?' 'Tarare.' 'Tarare?' 'Tarare.' 'Tarare!' "

To compound the incongruous displacement of actions and name, fairy tale and parody, Hamilton disguises his hero as a smelly goatherd whose rescue of the heroine (Magic Flight, #328) occurs on a dung-covered mare. The scatological imagery of this downward translation places us squarely in the realm of the carnivalesque Foire parodies—not exactly the refined humor one would expect in the salon. Then again, it was Hamilton who introduced the bawdy fairy tale to the courts, and at least one scene in *Fleur d'Epine* has prompted a Freudian interpretation: Tarare, having discovered the shack of the sorceress Dentue [Toothy], watches as she stirs her brew with her excessively long tooth (phallus). He then spoils her spell by slipping salt (ejaculate) into her cauldron (vagina). Consequently her magic powers begin to dwindle, and disappear altogether when she later trips and breaks her tooth. Dentue's cry of "Tous mes charmes m'abandonnent" [My charms are all abandoning me], therefore announces her frigidity.[42] It is not known whether Hamilton's learned audience grasped all of this sexual innuendo, but they certainly appreciated his silly anachronisms and comic modifications of fairy-tale motifs.

Hamilton's juxtapositions of hyperbole and negation, of the serious and the comic, are clearly parodic, and conform to what La Motte termed "travestissement burlesque." The virginal Fleur d'Epine's magic flight illus-trates the contrast of the serious and comic, and her escape on the manured mare truly renders her virtue "ridiculous." There is also the ironic discrepancy between names and actions: Fuzelier might have noted that parody unmasked the vice behind the virtuous "Serene's" gift/curse for Luisante. Likewise, the relationships of the hero's name, character, and circumstances under which he must act are downwardly modified. Given the combination of "burlesque words" (like Tarare) and the strong visual and scatological humor of certain tableaux (the magic flight) it is not much of a stretch to imagine Arlequin as a "Foire Tarare." And an even better example of parodic character deflation would be Arlequin as the Molièresque simple sultan.

This type of role reversal typified the humor of pre-Regency France. As one critic has noted, where the society of Louis XIV "had wanted to elevate man to the level of the gods, [the] Regency lowered the latter to the level of man."[43] Hamilton's veiled censure of Louis XIV and/or James II therefore reflects this world-upside-down humor that was also characteristic of the fair theaters. Likewise, just as Hamilton's salon parodies adapted popular paraliterature and updated it with anachronisms, so did the Foire parodies similarly address a less-refined audience.

This is not to say that comic operas were without social commentary or literary allusions. On the contrary, send-ups of contemporary literature like Lesage's *Arlequin, roi des Ogres* reeked of the politically incorrect.

Lesage and Fairy-Tale Parodies for the Foire

Known as the "Molière of the Foire," Alain-René Lesage is generally credited with raising the literary level of comic opera. After the success of his novel *Le Diable boiteux* (1707) [The Limping Devil] and the Comédie-Française productions of *Crispin, rival de son maître* (1707) [Crispin, His Master's Rival] and *Turcaret* (1709), he had a falling out with the traditional theaters and began to write for the Foire. His more than one hundred plays and prologues, many written during the time he was composing his picaresque novel *Gil Blas de Santillane* (1715–35), influenced the "illegitimate" stage in many ways.

When Lesage arrived at the Foire, its repertory was still essentially that inherited from the commedia dell'arte in 1697—when Louis XIV banned the Italian actors for their farcical portrait of Mme de Maintenon in *La Fausse Prude* [The False Prude]. Pantomimes, slapstick gags, scatological humor, and stereotyped jokes about cuckoldry, marriage, and sex comprised the carnivalesque preoccupations of "Everyman" Arlequin and company. It was Lesage who changed the one-act fair format by offering "trilogies": either a prologue with two one-act comedies, or a three-act play (often oriental with many subplots). He also introduced more dialogue, deemphasized gestures, and eventually imparted some psychological depth to the stereotyped characters. These stylistic improvements made it possible to develop real plots that parodied the legitimate theaters and official culture.[44]

Lesage helped to edit the best of the parodies for *Le Théâtre de la Foire*. Unfortunately, the majority of the works—many of which, judging by their titles, would be useful to this study—were never published. Studies are therefore necessarily confined to what Lesage must have considered his best fairy-tale take-off, *Arlequin roi des Ogres ou les Bottes de sept lieus* (1720) [Arlequin, King of the Orges or the Seven-League Boots].[45] It is a comedy, rather than a comic-opera, in which Arlequin is shipwrecked on an island and made king of its inhabitants. Trouble is, this is an island of ogres and—as all good readers of fairy tales know—ogres eat people.

How do ogres find the tastiest humans for their dining pleasure? With the aid of the marvelous "seven league-boots of the fairy tale," as Arlequin calls them, which are worn to procure delicate morsels from around the world. Unfortunately, not only do these ogres expect their king to eat human flesh, they want to have him for dinner—literally! But help arrives at the last moment for Arlequin, who, true to his commedia proclivities, intends to use the boots to satisfy both his alimentary and carnal appetites.

The very title of this comedy would have alerted spectators to a parody of Perrault's *Petit Poucet* [Little Thumb (#327)] in which the small boy steals an ogre's seven-league boots. But this is not the only tale of Perrault's to which Lesage alludes. *Peau d'Ane* [Donkey-Skin, #510B] is invoked at the outset, for Arlequin finds and wears a wild cat skin as a disguise to protect him from predatory beasts. *La Belle au bois dormant* [Sleeping Beauty, #410], also figures in one pun-filled scene in which the ogre chef Pierrot asks Arlequin how he would like his Parisienne "dressed." Of course, Arlequin is thinking fashion, while Pierrot is discussing seasoning. When the chef asks with what sauce he should serve the girl, Arlequin replies, "belle demande"—a rejoinder alluding to the palate of Belle's/Sleeping Beauty's ogress mother-in-law. In Perrault's *conte*, the evil woman instructs her chef to prepare first her granddaughter, then grandson, then Belle herself—all "à la sauce Robert."

Literary allusions to fairy tales, however, do not provide the sole humor of this comedy. In addition to Arlequin's numerous *lazzi*, the purveyor's singsong of "Fresh flesh! Fresh flesh!" would have mimicked that of market vendors. There are also burlesque words, for an ogre chorus is constantly chanting (nonsense syllables) in their native Algonquin.[46] Silly anachronisms are also present: the king fears that Luisante will turn his entire court into Quinze-vingts (patients of the hospice for the blind), while evildoers are carted off to the Petites Maisons (the Parisian insane asylum). Finally, Arlequin's comment to newly arrived "Opera goddesses" not to worry, that ogres only ate *fresh* meat, makes use of the contemporary slang expression of "déesses d'Opéra" for prostitutes.

Prostitution is also alluded to in Arlequin's personal history. He was supposedly among the two hundred "elite men and women . . . chosen by the police" en route to Mississippi where they would establish "honest families" (scene 4). This is a direct reference to John Law's project to populate French possessions, specifically Louisiana and Mississippi. Because not enough people showed interest in the colonies, "anti-vagabond" laws like that of January 8, 1719, essentially enforced deportation. The men were usually tobacco smugglers and false salt merchants; the women were chosen from the Salpêtrière, which at that time was a "maison de force" primarily for prostitutes.[47] Interestingly, the second convoy of 1719 to which Lesage alludes in 1720 would provide the background for Prévost's *L'Histoire du chevalier des Grieux et de Manon Lescaut* (1731): there were two deported prostitutes named "Manon," and a "Marie-Anne Lescau" from Amiens, where

Des Grieux would be studying when Manon seduced him.[48] Also of historic note is Arlequin's identity as a "chevalier d'Industrie." Patterned after the Ordre de Malte, this was a true parodic order—one that Des Grieux would enter—in which "Industrie" signified the illicit means by which gamblers duped the public.

To these contemporary allusions to prostitutes, petty crooks, and colonization, Lesage adds a moral condemnation. In the tradition of what we today term the "White European Oppressor," Arlequin makes no attempt to learn the language of the natives, instructs his men to marry the females, and forces the inhabitants (now called his slaves) to renounce their dietary laws and conform to European "tastes."

Arlequin's insensitivity toward local customs primarily concerns his refusal to eat human flesh. At first, this elicits the gentle warning from the ogre counselor that his behavior is politically incorrect: "Seigneur, vous ne devriez point mépriser ainsi la chair-fraîche. La politique vous le demande" [My lord, you ought not to spurn fresh flesh in this manner. Policy requires it of you (scene 12, 155)]. When Arlequin replies that eating one's fellow man is cruel, however, the ogre becomes defensive:

> Hé, n'en faites-vous pas paroître davantage, vous autres, lorsque vous égorgez d'innocentes Bêtes pour vous nourrir de leur chair, après qu'elles ont labouré vos champs, après qu'elles vous ont donné leurs toisons pour vous couvrir? (scene 12, 155)

> [Well, don't you yourselves seem yet more cruel, when you slit the throats of innocent animals and feed on their flesh, after they have worked your fields, after they have given their fleece to clothe you?]

The ogre's attempt to educate Arlequin in cultural relativism uses what we might term today a politically correct argument for vegetarianism and animal rights. The seriousness of his cause is underscored by his passionate condemnation of man's inhumanity toward man:

> Vous, qui pensez avoir en partage toute l'humanité, comment en ûsez-vous les uns avec les autres? Vous vous querellez, vous vous chicannez, vous vous pillez, chez vous le plus fort ôte au plus foible sa subsistance; cela ne s'appelle-t'il pas se manger? Et les Ogres vous en doivent-ils beaucoup de reste? (scene 12, 155–56)

> [You, who think you've inherited all the humanity: how do you treat one another? You quarrel, bicker and fleece each other. In your world the strongest takes away from the weakest his

subsistence: isn't that called "eating each other"? And yet Ogres seem more barbaric to you than that?]

Lest this critique appear too didactic, however, Lesage adds the world-upside-down comment that it is not the ogre who is evil but man, who is obsessed by persecuting the poor ogre race.[49]

Is not this argument one that James Finn Garner could use for his *Politically Correct Bedtime Stories*? One need only add the word "ogre" to his litany of "witches, animals, goblins and fairies" toward whom fairy tales were "discriminatory, unfair, culturally biased, and . . . demeaning." Indeed, it is Lesage's cultural relevancy that makes his Ogres-Are-People-Too comment of 1720 so parodic—and so in keeping with Raymonde Robert's observation about fairy-tale parodies: those composed after 1715 treated contemporary society or politics, while pre-Regency ones did not.[50] In short, this is what our study of the salon and Foire parodies has found.

Hamilton's ludic romps through contemporary literature are pastiches of and allusions to heroic verse, the oriental narrative, and fairy tales. His silly anachronisms, baroque structure, hyperbolic descriptions, fractured chronology, and self-conscious narration recreate these genres' stylistic faults. These devices support parody's didactic role of literary criticism that was denounced by La Motte and championed by Fuzelier, Sallier, and Riccoboni.

To this comic commentary of popular paraliterature, Hamilton adds marvelous motifs from folk and fairy tales, such as the magic flight or metamorphosed "animal" lovers who quickly seduce humans. And to the stock character types of gnomes, giants, druids, sorcerers, enchantresses, handsome royalty, and wicked stepmothers, Hamilton introduces an important modification: he reverses the traditional forms of both character types (as in the burlesquely-named-yet-intelligent-not-so-handsome hero) and plot development (the scatological magic flight).

This downward transformation was noted by all eighteenth-century historians of parody. As we have seen, they used different terms to define the genre, today defined as the retention of an original text's style and modification of its subjects and characters. It is this juxtaposition of high and low elements that is particularly important in Hamilton's second fractured fairy tale. The sexual innuendo, impotent sultan, burlesque names, scatological magic flight—all are more closely associated with the humor of the bawdy Foire than the reserved salon.

Much as Hamilton straddled the two cultures at Versailles and Saint-Germain, then, so does his parody of two genres (fairy tales and oriental tales) straddle these two publics of the salon and Foire. This mixing of audiences is characteristic of the times. Just as fairy tales first seduced the salons and then the public at large, so did the upper-class begin to frequent not only literary circles but the popular Fairs. (In Hamilton's particular case, Saint-Germain-en-Laye visited Saint-Germain-des-Prés). The resulting heterogeneity incarnates pre-Regency France's defiance of the social and aesthetic hierarchies of *le siècle classique*.

It was therefore the slumming aristocrat who frequented the Foire that would have best appreciated Hamilton's Molièresque sultan and carnivalesque magic flight. Ten years after *Fleur d'Epine*'s tribute to the Foire, Lesage's *Arlequin, roi des Ogres* pays homage not only to fairy tales in general but to *Fleur d'Epine* in particular. In the play's final literary allusion, Arlequin orders "Seven-League Boots" to bring him an Asian beauty, and explains to Scaramouche that the ogre will return in a matter of minutes. The doubting Scaramouche replies "Tarare" just as the ogre arrives with a maiden who, like Fleur d'Epine, is from Circassie.

Lesage's reference to the earlier parodic text is therefore metaparodic, and complements his other literary allusions to *Le Petit Poucet*, *Peau d'Ane*, and *La Belle au bois dormant*. The resulting conceit in turn frames his stinging criticisms of colonialism and inhumanity that are masked by Arlequin's *lazzi*. In short, thanks to the ogre's parodic diatribe, the supposed virtue of European colonialism is unmasked as the vice of xenophobic expansionism.

The fact that Lesage expects his audience to understand these literary and political allusions underscores his contribution to the Foire, which he was refining during the Regency from its commedia repertory of slapstick. It also incarnates the political nature of Regency humor. Finally, it suggests how popular both Perrault and Hamilton were with the Foire public of 1720. Hamilton's inclusion is particularly interesting, considering that *Fleur d'Epine* would not be published for another ten years—no doubt in response to the renewed interest in parody during the 1720s and 1730s. Perhaps *Fleur d'Epine*'s manuscripts were widely circulated outside the salons. Or maybe Lesage's allusions are for the benefit of *salonniers* at the Foire Saint-Germain. Then again, Lesage may be paying personal tribute to his "parodic" precursor, who had died the year before, in April 1719.

From Hamilton's literary critiques for the salon, then, we arrive at Lesage's stinging parody for the Foire—a fractured fairy tale whose scathing critique is didactic in its political incorrectness.

Notes

1. James Finn Garner, *Politically Correct Bedtime Stories. Modern Tales for Our Life and Times* (New York: MacMillan, 1994), jacket.
2. For more on salon culture, see Joan B. Landes, *Women and the Public Sphere in the Age of the French Revolution* (Ithaca: Cornell University Press, 1988).
3. I am grateful to Claire L. Malarte-Feldman for the reference to the politically

correct fairy tales of Pierre Gripari (*Patrouille du conte* [Lausanne: Editions l'Age d'Homme, 1983]).

4. For the influence of this text on French literature, see Georges May, *Les Mille et une nuits d'Antoine Galland* (Paris: Presses Universitaires de France, 1986).

5. Alain-René Lesage, Louis Fuzelier, and N. D'Orneval, *La Foire des fées*, in *Le Théâtre de la Foire, ou l'Opéra-Comique, contenant les meilleures pièces qui ont été représentées aux foires de Saint-Germain et de Saint-Laurent*, vol. 5, ed. Alain-René Lesage and N. D'Orneval (Paris: Ganeau, 1724), 367. Original orthography will be observed throughout this article, and, unless otherwise noted, all translations are mine.

6. Linda Hutcheon, *A Theory of Parody: The Teaching of Twentieth-Century Art Forms* (New York: Methuen, 1985), 19.

7. Raymonde Robert, *Le Conte de fées littéraires en France de la fin du XVIIe à la fin du XVIIIe siècle* (Nancy: Presses Universitaires de Nancy, 1982), 160–70.

8. *Les Mille et une nuits* inspired *Les Mille et un jours, contes persans* (Pétis de la Croix and Lesage, 1710), *Les Mille et un Quarts d'heure, contes tartares* (Gueullette, 1715), *Les Mille et une heures, contes péruviens* (Gueullette, 1733), *Les Mille et une faveurs, contes de cour irez de l'ancien gaulois par la reine de Navarre et publiez par le chevalier de Mouhy* (Mouhy, 1740), *Les Mille et une fadaises, contes à dormir debout* (Cazotte, 1742), *Les Mille et une soirées, contes mongols* (Gueullette, 1749), *Les Mille et une folies* (Anon., 1785), *Les Mille et un mea culpa* (Anon., 1789). See Marie-Louise Dufresnoy, *L'Orient romanesque en France, 1704–1789*, vol. 1 (Montreal: Editions Beauchemin, 1946), 45–56, and consult all three volumes of Dufresnoy's study to appreciate the full impact of the oriental vogue on French literature.

9. Ruth Clark, *The Life of Anthony Hamilton* (New York: John Lane Company, 1921), 231.

10. Raymonde Robert, *Contes parodiques et licencieux du 18e siècle* (Nancy: Presses Universitaires de Nancy, 1987), 3.

11. Ibid., 16.

12. La Motte's *Inès de Castro* premiered at the Comédie Française on April 6, 1723; *Agnès de Chaillot*, by Pierre-François Biancolelli (Dominique) and Marc-Antoine Legrand, was first performed by the Comédie Italienne on July 24, 1723.

13. Antoine Houdar de La Motte, "Troisième discours à l'occasion de la tragédie d'*Inès de Castro*," in *Les Œuvres de théâtre de M. de la Motte*, vol. 1 (Paris: Gregoire Dupuis, 1730), 127–87.

14. Louis Fuzelier, "Discours à l'occasion d'un discours de M[onsieur] D[e] L[a] M[otte] sur les parodies, nouvelle édition augmentée," in *Les Parodies du Nouveau Théâtre Italien*, vol. 1 (Paris: Briassons, 1738), xix–xxxv. Subsequent references will be abbreviated "MDLM" in the text.

15. According to Sallier, parody is created 1) by changing one word of a quotation, 2) by changing one letter in a word, 3) by repeating the entire phrase, but with malicious intent, 4) by copying the style and taste of an author, and 5) by changing the subject or expression of an entire text; Valeria Belt Grannis, *Dramatic Parody in Eighteenth Century France* (New York: Publications of the Institute of French Studies, 1931), 5.

16. Ibid., 6.
17. For more on parody, see Gérard Genette, *Palimpsestes: la littérature au second degré* (Paris: Seuil, 1982).
18. Jacques Barchilon, "Antoine Hamilton and the Libertine Tale in the Eighteenth Century," keynote address of the Guthrie Workshop on Literary Fairy Tales of the Seventeenth and Eighteenth Centuries in France and Italy, Dartmouth College, Mar. 1995.
19. Clark, *Hamilton*, 232–33; Hamilton, *Œuvres*, xxxvj–xxxvij.
20. In 1741, Mlle Quinault challenged her *salonniers* Duclos, Caylus, and Voisenon to write a tale based on designs by Boucher that were originally commissioned for the Comte de Tessin (Carl Gustave, the Swedish ambassador to France). Duclos's *Acajou et Zirphile* won the bet and was published in 1744 (Robert, *Conte de fées*, 446; see Robert, *Contes parodiques*, 33–66 for a reprint of the text). Mlle Quinault may also have inspired Rousseau, for it was during the period when he frequented her salon (introduced there by Duclos) that he wrote *La Reine Fantasque* [The Capricious Queen] on the following wager: "de faire un conte de fées supportable et même gai sans intrigue, sans amour, sans mariage et sans polissonnerie" [to write a tolerable and even cheerful fairy tale that has neither plot, love, marriage nor naughtiness (Robert, *Conte de fées*, 446–47)].
21. Clark, *Hamilton*, 234.
22. Anthony Hamilton, "The Ram," in *Fairy Tales and Romances*, trans. M. Lewis, H. T. Ryde, and C. Kenney (London: Henry G. Bohn, 1849), 445–543; "The History of May-Flower," ibid., 366–444. French citations are from "Le Bélier," in *Œuvres du comte Antoine Hamilton*, ed. Antoine-Augustin Renouard, vol. 2 (Paris: Antoine-Augustin Renouard, 1812), 115–256; *L'Histoire de Fleur d'Epine*, ibid., 1–113. Subsequent references to these editions will be noted in the essay.
23. Hamilton, *Œuvres*, xxxvj–xxxvij.
24. Clark, *Hamilton*, 238.
25. Mayer, Charles-Joseph de, "Discours sur l'origine des contes des fées," in *Le Cabinet des fées*, vol. 37 (Amsterdam and Paris: Hôtel Serpente, 1786), 6–9.
26. Hamilton also makes numerous references to his own characters (Alie, Fleur d'Epine, etc.) in this introduction to the *Facardins*; ibid.
27. Clark, *Hamilton*, 232.
28. Robert, *Conte de fées*, 209.
29. Expression used by Elizabeth W. Harries in her article for this volume, "Fairy Tales about Fairy Tales: Notes on Canon Formation."
30. Clark, *Hamilton*, 238–39.
31. Jacques Barchilon, *Le Conte merveilleux français de 1690 à 1790* (Paris: Champion, 1975), 6. Barchilon posits that Mme d'Aulnoy's flower-garlanded prince might be a parody of the masculine lover type. If this is the case, then Hamilton's version would amount to metaparody.
32. References will hereafter be abbreviated with the French version first, the English, second. See an abbreviated list of comparisons in Clark, *Hamilton*, 238 n. 1.
33. See Antti Aarne, *The Types of the Folk-Tale: A Classification and Bibliography*, trans. Stith Thompson (1928; rpt., New York: Lenox Hill, 1971). Subsequent references

to these tales will be noted in the body of the essay. Some of the correspondences between French fairy tales and folktale types are noted by Robert, *Conte de fées*, 127–29.

34. There is a profusion of other potential Pépins. References to Charlemagne's son, who ruled Italy between 781 and 810, would strengthen the ties to Lombardy in the ram's tale. On the other hand, Pépin I (817–838) and Pépin II (838–852) were two kings of Aquitaine whose heritage would reinforce France as the site of *Le Bélier*'s action.

35. The last tale told by Schéhérazade is actually the *Story of Two Sisters*. *Le Conte de la Pyramide et du Cheval d'Or* was written by Hamilton for a Mlle O'Brien de Clare, born in 1697. Since the girl's "charms" described in this tale would hardly have been in evidence in 1705, the date usually ascribed to *Fleur d'Epine*, Hamilton's biographer places the composition of the parody closer to 1710 (Clark, *Hamilton*, 242–43 n. 3).

36. This unfinished work apparently influenced Crébillon *fils* and Voltaire. Crébillon's *Ah, quel Conte!* contains a character that is a "descendant of Cristalline la Curieuse" of *Les Quatre Facardins*, while Voltaire lists the *Facardins* among the tales read by his Princesse de Babylone (ibid., note 1).

37. I thank Jacques Barchilon for this last precision.

38. See Mary Louise Ennis, "The Voyage to Cythera: From Courtly Allegory to Erotic Utopia in France, 1700–1750" (Ph.D. diss., Yale University, 1989), 203–31; Lynn Hunt, ed. *The Invention of Pornography: Obscenity and the Origins of Modernity, 1500–1800* (New York: Zone Books, 1993), 301–40; and Chantal Thomas, *La Reine scélérate: Marie-Antoinette dans les pamphlets* (Paris: Seuil, 1989).

39. Barchilon, "Antoine Hamilton." The Freudian critic Alain Clerval has also posited a reading that finds that the (fairy-tale) themes of conception, mutilation, and castration underlie *Fleur d'Epine* (*Du Frondeur au libertin. Essai sur Antoine Hamilton* [Lausanne: Alfred Eibel, 1978], 207–9).

40. For a comparison of *Fleur d'Epine*'s hyperbolic style with other texts, see Robert, *Conte de fées*, 206–7.

41. Clark, *Hamilton*, 251. Hamilton may have chosen this name for his hero on a wager that he could "produce a tale in which Fiddlestick shall be the name of the principal hero" (ibid.).

42. Clerval, *Frondeur*, 207–9.

43. Robert Tomlinson, *La Fête galante: Watteau et Marivaux* (Geneva: Droz, 1981), 46.

44. For more on Lesage and the Foire, see Vincent Barbaret, *Lesage et le théâtre de la Foire* (1887; rpt., Geneva: Slatkine Reprints, 1970), and Lucette Desvignes Saint-Etienne, "La Parodie à la foire et au théâtre italien d'après les recueils de Lesage et Fuselier," *Romanistische Zeitschrift für Literaturgeschichte* 3 (1979): 297–318.

45. Alain-René Lesage, *Arlequin, roi des Ogres ou les Bottes de sept lieus*, in *Le Théâtre de la Foire, ou l'Opéra-Comique, contenant les meilleures pièces qui ont été représentées aux foires de Saint-Germain et de Saint-Laurent*, vol. 4, ed. Alain-René Lesage and N. d'Orneval (Paris: Ganeau, 1724), 123–211. Subsequent references to this text will be noted in the essay.

46. Lesage chooses a curious language, Algonquin, for his "barbaric" (French Cana-

dian?) ogres. Perhaps Voltaire was reminded of this when creating his Hurons for *L'Ingénu* (1767).

47. Erica-Marie Benabou, *La Prostitution et la police des moeurs au XVIIIe siècle* (Paris: Librairie Académique Perrin, 1987), 86.
48. Ibid., 87.
49. Says the ogre: "Nous, en mangeant des hommes nous croyons en même temps purger la terre de mauvais animaux, de monstres pleins de malice qui ne songent qu'à nous nuire" [For our part, we believe that, by eating men, we are at the same time purging the world of evil animals, of monsters full of malice that think only of harming us (scene 12, 155)].
50. Robert, *Conte de fées*, 232–34.

Bibliography

Aarne, Antti. *The Types of the Folk-Tale: A Classification and Bibliography.* Trans. Stith Thompson. 1928. Reprint, New York: Lenox Hill, 1971.

Barbaret, Vincent. *Lesage et le théâtre de la Foire.* 1887. Reprint, Geneva: Slatkine Reprints, 1970.

Barchilon, Jacques. *Le Conte merveilleux français de 1690 à 1790.* Paris: Champion, 1975.

———. "Antoine Hamilton and the Libertine Tale in the Eighteenth Century." Keynote address of the Guthrie Workshop on Literary Fairy Tales of the Seventeenth and Eighteenth Centuries in France and Italy, Dartmouth College, Mar. 1995.

Benabou, Erica-Marie. *La Prostitution et la police des moeurs au XVIIIe siècle.* Paris: Librairie Académique Perrin, 1987.

Clark, Ruth. *The Life of Anthony Hamilton.* New York: John Lane Company, 1921.

Clerval, Alain. *Du Frondeur au libertin. Essai sur Antoine Hamilton.* Lausanne: Alfred Eibel, 1978.

Dufresnoy, Marie-Louise. *L'Orient romanesque en France, 1704–1789.* Vol. 1. Montreal: Editions Beauchemin, 1946.

Ennis, Mary Louise. "The Voyage to Cythera: From Courtly Allegory to Erotic Utopia in France, 1700–1750." Ph.D. diss., Yale University, 1989.

Fuzelier, Louis. "Discours à l'occasion d'un discours de M[onsieur] D[e] L[a] M[otte] sur les parodies, nouvelle édition augmentée." In *Les Parodies du Nouveau Théâtre Italien.* Vol. 1. Paris: Briassons, 1738.

Garner, James Finn. *Politically Correct Bedtime Stories: Modern Tales for Our Life and Times.* New York: Macmillan, 1994.

Genette, Gérard. *Palimpsestes: La littérature au second degré.* Paris: Seuil, 1982.

Grannis, Valeria Belt. *Dramatic Parody in Eighteenth Century France.* New York: Publications of the Institute of French Studies, 1931.

Gripari, Pierre. *Patrouille du conte.* Lausanne: Editions L'Age d'Homme, 1983.

Hamilton, Anthony. *Œuvres du comte Antoine Hamilton.* Ed. Antoine-Augustin Renouard. Vol. 2. Paris: Antoine-Augustin Renouard, 1812.

———. *Fairy Tales and Romances*. Trans. M. Lewis, H. T. Ryde, and C. Kenney. London: Henry G. Bohn, 1849.

Hunt, Lynn. "Pornography and the French Revolution." In *The Invention of Pornography. Obscenity and the Origins of Modernity, 1500–1800*, ed. Lynn Hunt. New York: Zone Books, 1993.

Hutcheon, Linda. *A Theory of Parody: The Teachings of Twentieth-Century Art Forms*. New York: Methuen, 1985.

La Motte, Antoine Houdar de. "Troisième discours à l'occasion de la tragédie d'*Inès de Castro*." In *Les Œuvres de théâtre de M. de la Motte*. Vol. 1. Paris: Gregoire Dupuis, 1730.

Landes, Joan B. *Women and the Public Sphere in the Age of the French Revolution*. Ithaca: Cornell University Press, 1988.

Lesage, Alain-René. "Arlequin, roi des Ogres ou les Bottes de sept lieus." In *Le Théâtre de la Foire, ou l'Opéra-Comique, contenant les meilleures pièces qui ont été représentées aux foires de Saint-Germain et de Saint-Laurent*. Ed. Alain-René Lesage and N. d'Orneval. Vol. 4. Paris: Ganeau, 1724.

Lesage, Alain-René, Louis Fuzelier, and N. d'Orneval. "La Foire des Fées." In *Le Théâtre de la Foire, ou l'Opéra-Comique, contenant les meilleures pièces qui ont été représentées aux foires de Saint-Germain et de Saint-Laurent*. Ed. Alain-René Lesage and N. d'Orneval. Vol. 5. Paris: Ganeau, 1724.

May, Georges. *Les Mille et une nuits d'Antoine Galland*. Paris: Presses Universitaires de France, 1986.

Mayer, Charles-Joseph de. "Discours sur l'origine des contes des fées." In *Le Cabinet des fées*. Vol. 37. Amsterdam and Paris: Hôtel Serpente, 1786.

Robert, Raymonde. *Le Conte de fées littéraire en France de la fin du XVIIe à la fin du XVIIIe siècle*. Nancy: Presses Universitaires de Nancy, 1982.

———. *Contes parodiques et licencieux du 18e siècle*. Nancy: Presses Universitaires de Nancy, 1987.

Saint-Etienne, Lucette Desvignes. "La Parodie à la foire et au théâtre italien d'après les recueils de Lesage et Fuselier." *Romanistische Zeitschrift für Literaturgeschichte* 3 (1979): 297–318.

Thomas, Chantal. *La Reine scélérate: Marie-Antoinette dans les pamphlets*. Paris: Seuil, 1989.

Tomlinson, Robert. *La Fête galante: Watteau et Marivaux*. Geneva: Droz, 1981.

CHAPTER 9

The Reactionary Imagination:
Ideology and the Form of the Fairy Tale
in Gozzi's *Il re cervo* [The King Stag]

Ted Emery

 CARLO GOZZI'S *Fiabe teatrali*, or fairy tales for the theater,
are characterized by a strident juxtaposition of seemingly
irreconcilable elements—fantastic settings and fairy-tale
plots are brought up short by references to contemporary
Venice, serious characters speaking in verse share the stage
with the improvised *lazzi* of commedia dell'arte masks,
while exuberant stage magic and special effects get equal time with dour
diatribes against the culture of the Enlightenment in general and the plays
of Carlo Goldoni in particular. This energetic heterogeneity has given rise
to two very different lines of interpretation in Gozzi criticism. Scholars
such as Giuseppe Petronio, privileging the explicitly polemical elements
present in some of the *Fiabe*, have seen Gozzi's theatrical work as simply
one more expression of the author's rabid conservatism.[1] Other readers of
Gozzi's *Fiabe*, from the German romantics to the avant-garde Russian director
Vsevolod Meyerhold and his followers, have been struck by the extraordinary
theatricality of the plays' fairy-tale magic, and have seen them as examples
ante litteram of a modern, "pure" theater unfettered by social reference or
relevance.[2] Both approaches have serious limitations.

In his many nontheatrical writings, such as "Il ragionamento ingenuo,"
Le memorie inutili, and the prefaces to individual *Fiabe* in the Colombani
and Zanardi editions of his collected works, Gozzi explicitly declares his
polemical intentions and asserts that his plays contain a positive though
unspecified moral lesson.[3] In the *Fiabe* themselves, however, the presence of

247

an ideological motivation is not always so clear. Born in the heat of a literary *querelle*, the first *Fiaba* is a barely veiled allegorical attack on Goldoni and Chiari—but after *L'amore delle tre melarance* this specifically literary polemic disappears almost entirely from Gozzi's plays. Gozzi's overt social polemics, by contrast, are found almost entirely in the later *Fiabe*, especially *L'augellin belverde* and *Zeim, re de' geni*. Between these two poles is a long series of plays in which no ideological intention is immediately evident: *Il corvo, Il re cervo, Turandot, La donna serpente*, and so on. Such works of seemingly pure "imagination" appear to call into question Petronio's notion of Gozzi as a die-hard reactionary ideologue.

It is no less reductive, however, to privilege the "fantasy" of the *Fiabe*, disregarding the author's repeated statement of his didactic intentions. Jean Starobinski for example, sees Gozzi's plays as exuberant exercises in theatrical *écriture* in which mechanical allegorical referentiality is replaced by the pure pleasure of narrative invention, and in which any intended meaning is limited to a common-sense sagacity concerning vice and virtue.[4] What is more, even this limited meaning may not constitute evidence of an authentic didactic or ideological intention on Gozzi's part, since Starobinski believes that the *Fiabe* unconsciously reproduce the symbolic values of their original fairy tale sources:

> On l'a justement remarqué, Gozzi, dans la conduite de ses intrigues, s'est toujours montré d'une remarquable fidélité envers ses modèles empruntés à la tradition populaire ou aux sources orientales. La substance narrative—l'essence mythique—du conte est ainsi préservée. Et, pour ainsi dire a l'insu de Gozzi, les valeurs symboliques et poétiques de la fable continuent d'être agissantes. . . . Mieux encore, nous avons le sentiment qu'en quelque circonstance, Gozzi, presque inconsciemment, se laisse emporter par un élan d'imagination ingénue, dans l'esprit du rêve et du myth.[5]

> [It has been rightly observed [that] Gozzi, in the treatment of his plots, was always remarkably faithful to his models, borrowed from popular tradition or from oriental sources. The narrative substance—the mythic essence—of the fairy tale is thus preserved. And, so to speak unknown to Gozzi, the symbolic and poetic values of the tale remain active. . . . Still better, we get the feeling that in some circumstances Gozzi almost unconsciously lets himself be carried away by a burst of ingenuous imagination, in the spirit of dream and of myth.]

Edoardo Sanguineti, too, suggests that Gozzi's *Fiabe* reproduce the narrative structure and topoi of the fairy tale (for example, the rite of initiation in *La donna serpente*), thus participating in a kind of *Ur*-tale supposedly valid for all times and all societies, and which is said to be "la sola storia vera che abbiamo alla nostra disposizione, da sempre e per sempre" [the only true story at our disposition, from time immemorial to the end of time].[6] These extraordinarily ahistorical interpretations idealize the *Fiabe*'s element of theatrical play, radically compress their range of autonomous meaning, and ignore the possibility of a substantive link between Gozzi's plays and the particular historical reality of the Venetian republic in the late eighteenth century. In such a view, paradoxically, Gozzi does not so much write his plays as he is himself "written" by the fairy-tale material on which they are based.

More recent criticism does little to reconcile this split in Gozzi scholarship. A number of studies deliberately put aside the question of ideology in Gozzi's plays to focus instead on their narrative "deep structure" or their sophisticated creation of theatrical atmosphere and effect.[7] Others create a false resolution of the dichotomy between a reactionary Gozzi, critic of the real world, and an imaginative Gozzi, creator of alternative realities, by suggesting that the *Fiabe* were structured to permit a "dual reading": intellectuals and the cultured elite were in a position to decode Gozzi's allegory and receive his ideological messages, while others could experience the *Fiabe* as nothing more than entertaining fantasies.[8]

All of these studies make a very limiting assumption about the nature of ideology, equating it with the explicit polemical *content* or messages of texts. This leads us to an interesting paradox. However different the views of Petronio and Starobinski regarding the overt polemical posturing found in some of the *Fiabe*, their views of the plays' magical, fairy-tale elements and of the theatrical effects connected with them are in essence remarkably similar. For Starobinski and others the preponderance of this fantastic material in Gozzi's plays is an indication of their essential lack of ideology, while Petronio and scholars like him, however much they may stress the importance of Gozzi's overt polemicizing, have struggled with little success to show how the plays' fairy-tale material can be in any substantive way "ideological."[9]

The purpose of this study is to demonstrate that the fairy-tale material of Gozzi's plays is no less ideological than his overt polemical editorializing. To do so, it will be necessary to move away from the reductive notion of ideology that has characterized Gozzi criticism to date. Though this is not the place to undertake a systematic inquiry into the nature of ideology, the introduction of a few fundamental concepts developed by scholars such as Althusser and Jameson will help move our focus from the explicit content of Gozzi's works to their form and function. Most important is Althusser's view of ideology not as a matter of content but as a structure the defining function of which is to constitute subjects by means of closure. For Althusser, ideology naturalizes the organization of society along class lines by shutting off from consciousness those contradictions that would reveal the relations of exploitation and domination on which it is based.[10] Following Althusser, Jameson has shown that symbolic production of all kinds may have an exquisitely ideological function even when it does not explicitly propose a set of beliefs. Referring to Levi-Strauss's studies of the bodily ornamentation of the Caduveo Indians, Jameson suggests that the most basic function of symbolic production is to provide an imaginary resolution of intolerable material contradictions that cannot be resolved at the level of the real.[11] If symbolic production does indeed have this essentially comforting function, then its ideological nature is evident not only (and not principally) in the beliefs and images that individual works may specifically propose, but also (and especially) in the way those works close off thought, translating concrete material conflict to a level of abstraction at which it may be imaginarily resolved. An inquiry into the ideology of a work must not, therefore, limit itself to a survey of the explicit beliefs it contains, but must seek in its principle of organization the symptom of the ideological resolution it operates, and must trace that symbolic resolution back to the concrete social circumstances from which it sprang.

Il re cervo is an excellent test case for a reevaluation of Gozzi's fairy-tale material along these lines. When the literary *querelle* disappears as a motivating factor in Gozzi's plays, its place is taken in *Il corvo* and *Il re cervo* by the "magical" element of metamorphoses and theatrical effects. Some of Gozzi's contemporaries saw in this new prevalence of spectacular elements an indication of the plays' lack of literary quality.[12] In the preface to *Il re cervo*, Gozzi responds to these critics with evident pride in the "recklessness" of his "capricious mind," but he insists as well on the fundamental seriousness of the plot and on the presence in the text of an allegorical lesson: "Le circostanze tragiche, e robuste, ch'ella contiene, trassero delle lagrime, e 'l buffonesco delle maschere, ch'io volli sempre per le mie proposizioni tener ferme nel teatro, ed intrecciate, nulla ha levato al vigore della feroce, fantastica serietà degli impossibili accidenti, e dell'allegorica morale" [The tragic, powerful circumstances it contains moved the audience to tears, and the clowning of the commedia dell'arte masks (to which, in keeping with my project, I always strove to give a solid foothold in the theater by weaving them into the plots of my plays) stole none of the force from the ferocious, fantastic seriousness of the impossible occurrences and from the allegorical moral (154)]. But precisely what lesson does Gozzi have in mind? No "forceful" didactic intention is immediately evident in *Il re cervo*; if anything the playwright seems to give himself over wholeheartedly to the model of the oriental fairy tale, with an eye more to its abundant potential for spectacle than to its modest resources for moral instruction. Thus, despite such protests of didactic intention on Gozzi's part, *Il re cervo* may well seem to be "only" a fairy tale: nothing more than the transposition to the stage of a narrative model already rich in theatricality. To close the gap between Gozzi's declared didactic intentions and the evident predominance in many of his plays of a desire to entertain, it will be useful to compare *Il re cervo* with the sources from which it is drawn, underscoring how he transforms the original values of his sources into new and clearly ideological values.

Unlike *L'amore delle tre melarance*, *Il re cervo* is based not on an oral version of an Italian fairy tale, but on two French tales that in turn draw on various oriental sources: the inspiration for act one of the play is found in the novella "L'Histoire des quatre sultanes de Citor" [The Story of the Four Princesses of Citor] in *Les Milles et un quart d'heure, contes tartares* [The Thousand and One Quarter-Hours, Tales of the Tatars] published in 1715 by Thomas Simon Gueulette, while acts two and three are based on "L'Histoire du Prince Fadlallah, fils de Ben-Ortoc, roi de Moussel" [The Story of Prince Fadlallah, Son of Ben-Ortoc, King of Moussel] in *Les Milles et un jours, contes persans* [The Thousand and One Days, Persian Tales] written between 1710 and 1712 by François Pétis de la Croix.[13] The first of the two stories is the simplest. Bassiry, the virtuous sultan of Citor, owns a miraculous statue that laughs if anyone tells a lie in its presence. When the sultan marries, three of his new wives feign exaggerated physical or moral delicacy, and their falsity is unmasked by the laughter of the statue. Later, the sultan discovers his wives' infidelity, and takes an exemplary revenge. The first wife betrays him with a stable boy, and is killed when Bassiry leaves a wild mule loose in the stable where she meets her lover. The sultan removes a dozen steps from the dark stairway to the kitchen, and the second wife falls to her death as she slips out to visit her lover, a scullery boy. The third princess, who must cross a river to meet the fisherman she loves, drowns when the hollow gourds on which she floats are secretly pierced. Only Bassiry's fourth bride turns out to be faithful, and the sultan rewards her virtue by making her his sole wife. The theme of the story is not, however, this reward of virtue, but rather the proper method of punishing vice, and this is explicitly underscored by the final return to the novella's frame in which we see the reaction of the fictional recipient of the narration: "J'ai reçu tout le plaisir possible au récit de cette histoire, dit alors Schems-Eddin. La vengeance du roi de Citor me plaît infiniment: sans tremper sa main dans le sang de ses lâches sultanes, il trouva le moyen de les punir par l'endroit même par où elles l'avoient offensé" [I have received the greatest possible pleasure from the telling of this tale, said Schems-Eddin. The king of Citor's revenge pleases me infinitely: without dirtying his hands in the blood of his wanton wives, he found a way to make their punishment exactly mirror their crimes against him (21:516–17)].

Gozzi cuts from his source not only the least theatrical elements of the tale (for example, the long narration of the statue's discovery and presentation to Bassiry) but also the entire climax of the story in the sultan's discovery and punishment of his concubines' sexual infidelity. Eliminating the theme of crime and punishment, Gozzi concentrates on the choice of a wife, which in the original had presented no particular difficulty. The magical statue, little more than a decorative detail in Gueulette, here becomes the central element of a series of related scenes in which the author examines the "problem" of women's virtue and satirizes "female" vices.

In the first series of scenes (1.2–4) we see three candidates for Deramo's hand. Clarice is the daughter of the ambitious prime minister, Tartaglia; she secretly loves Leandro, but her father obliges her to court the king. Angela, daughter of the ex-merchant Pantalone, loves Deramo with all her heart, but can't imagine that she deserves to become queen, or that a king could possibly return her love. Smeraldina is the elderly, ugly, and far from virtuous sister of the king's valet; her foolish belief in her own attractiveness and good taste gives the playwright a springboard for a rather traditional satire on fashion, complete with topical references to popular Venetian fashion designers.[14]

Before interrogating these three characters, Deramo tells us that four years earlier he had interviewed 2,748 noblewomen, without finding an honest one among them, and only in extremis has opened the competition to non-nobles. He begs his magic statue, the gift of the wizard Durandarte, to protect him by continuing to reveal women's "insincere hearts" (1.7). In her interview, Clarice tries at first to avoid the king's questions, but then is forced to obey her father and claim she loves Deramo; the statue smiles slightly, and Deramo comments ironically afterward about how strange it had seemed to think for a moment that he had found a truthful woman (1.9). Smeraldina claims that she is an aristocrat (to the statue's amusement), that she loves Deramo passionately (the statue finds this even more laughable), and to have saved her virginity for him (overcome with hilarity, the statue gasps grotesquely for air). Deramo again condemns women's insincerity, and compares his situation to that of other men:

Oh maritati,
o padri, ed o serventi, qual ventura
sarebbe a voi l'aver simil ordigno
tutti ne' vostri alberghi, e le sorelle,
e le mogli, e le amate interrogando,
saper de' loro interni . . . (1.11).

[Oh husbands, oh fathers, and oh *cavalieri serventi* [married women's escorts], what a piece of fortune it would be for you to have such a device, all of you in your own homes, and by interrogating your sisters, your wives, and your lovers, discover what is in their hearts . . .]

Only Angela proves to be truly honest, truly faithful, and sincerely in love with the king, who bursts out in praise of her native city:

. . . Degna sareste
di monarca maggior. Veneta donna
esempio d'amor vero, che smentisce
le indegne lingue, che pel mondo vanno
predicando incostanza, ed amor finto,
e volubilità nel sesso molle,
che adorna l'Adria tua. (1.12)

[You would be worthy of a greater monarch [than I]. Venetian woman, exemplar of true love, who gives the lie to the lying tongues who go about the world telling tales of the inconstancy, and false love, and fickleness of that gentle sex that adorns your Venice.]

In the climactic action of the first act, Deramo destroys the magic statue, sure that he will never need it again.

Clearly, this is no simple staging of Geuelette's story. Discarding the greater part of the plot, the playwright makes the detail of the magic statue into the basis for a series of scenes in which he takes aim at two of his perennial "bêtes noires," women and fashion. However, the development of these themes is shot through with contradictions. On one hand, Gozzi condemns the "female" vice of fashion, repeating his frequent conflation of misogyny and misoneism, and goes on to inveigh against a universal female perfidy that excepts only Angela. Yet at the same time that Gozzi castigates women in general, he defends the honor of Venetian girls against the slander of foreigners. This was a theme with sure appeal for local audiences, and one by no means new to them: see, for example, Goldoni's *La putta onorata* [The Good Girl] of 1748.[15] In Goldoni's case, however, the defense of Venetian womanhood is integral to the playwright's stated project and to the character of his heroine, while in *Il re cervo*, after the heavy-handed satire of the preceding scenes, Gozzi's unmotivated support of the honor of his female fellow citizens strikes a decidedly jarring note.

Angela's extreme purity introduces another and even more glaring contradiction: in the ambitious villains Tartaglia and Brighella, Gozzi repeats

his often stated insistence on the "necessary subordination" of the middle
and lower classes to the aristocracy, yet the idealized virtue of the merchant's
daughter succeeds even in breaking down the barriers of class, as if Gozzi
wished to propose a moral or spiritual equivalence between bourgeoisie and
nobility. Given what we know of Gozzi's social and political philosophy, this
would be an unexpected conclusion—and in fact the text goes to great lengths
to limit and subvert any possible progressive implications in the idealization
of Angela. First, Deramo praises her in terms calculated to appeal to his
audience's municipal patriotism, presenting her virtue as the result of her
nationality rather than of her class origin. Moreover, Deramo's praise is more
contradictory than may at first appear. On taking her as his wife, the king
claims that he is only rewarding Angela's virtue, but in the same breath he
reiterates a point made repeatedly at the beginning of the act—that he is
forced to marry against his own inclination for the good of the state:

> La virtude
> innalzo al posto suo. *Necessitade*
> *di successore al regno a sceglier sposa*
> *mi sforza, ed una sposa più degna*
> *d'Angela non trovai.* (1.13; italics mine)

> [I'm raising virtue to its proper place. *The need for an heir to my*
> *kingdom forces me to choose a wife, and I have found none more*
> *worthy than Angela.*]

From an Angela rewarded for her purity, we pass with an abrupt shock to an
Angela chosen for lack of a better! Angela herself thinks she is unworthy to
become a queen, and despite her love for Deramo she tells her father that the
daughter of a poor man must not feel such an ambition (1.3). Pantalone, too,
protests his family's unworthiness, insisting in 1.3 that they have already been
"raised above their merits" by the king's generosity. He goes on to underscore
the limits of Angela's ascendancy, suggesting that her rise in social status
is unconnected to his own merits, that even for Angela it is less a reward
than a piece of good luck that fate could still take back, and that she must
therefore never presume to rise *spiritually* above her humble origins, whatever
her official change of social status:

> Ah, Maestae, no bastava, che avesse da ella tante benificenze
> senza meriti, che la vol innalzar a tanto grado una povera fiola? . . .
> Cara fia, no desmentegar mai la to nascita; no te insuperbir. Varda
> ogni momento el cielo, dal qual vien le fortune, ma vien ancora
> le desgrazie improvvise. Basta; el nostro re me farà una grazia
> de lassarme do ore a quattrocchi con ti, tanto, che te possa dar

qualche recordo, farte un'ammonizion da bon vecchio, da bon pare; ma me par ancora impossibile. (1.13)

[Ah, your Majesty, wasn't it enough for me to have received so many undeserved acts of charity from you, without your wanting to raise a poor man's little girl to such a high station? . . . My dear daughter, don't ever forget your birth, don't get above yourself. Always keep your eyes on Heaven, the source of all good fortune, but of unexpected misfortunes too. Enough of this; I'm sure our king will grant me a couple of hours alone with you so I can give you a few pieces of advice, so I can give you a proper fatherly admonition like a good old man. But it still seems impossible.]

Pantalone still can't believe it—and neither, clearly, can Gozzi, for he ennobles Angela only to foreground deliberately the exceptional and circumscribed nature of a social ascendancy so fantastic it could occur only in a fairy tale.

The first act of *Il re cervo* is thus characterized by a double contradiction: the denigration of women in general clashes with Angela's "Venetian" virtue, while the implicit proposal of a spiritual equivalence between nobles and nonnobles is immediately hedged by drastic limitations. The existence of such fault lines in the text should make us suspect that the ideology of *Il re cervo* is not primarily to be found in the satire of women's vices that appears to motivate the plot of this act. A comparison of acts two and three with their source will confirm this suspicion.

The lack of any logical relation between the two tales on which *Il re cervo* is based produces a striking thematic discontinuity: the problem of female sincerity, which seemed so fundamental to act one, is missing both from the story of Fadlallah and from the following two acts of Gozzi's play.[16] The complicated tale of prince Fadlallah occupies an interesting position as an internal narration within another novella, "L'Histoire du prince Calaf et de la princesse de la Chine" [The Story of Prince Calaf and the Princess of China], to which Gozzi would later return for the plot of his *Turandot*. Fleeing from the sack of their kingdom, Calaf and his parents arrive in the city of Jaïch, where a kindly old man, the ex-prince Fadlallah, takes them in and to raise their spirits tells the story of his own misfortunes. In the first move of the tale, the young Fadlallah refuses to marry and take on adult responsibilities until he is allowed to travel to Baghdad.[17] On his way there, he is robbed by bandits and arrives penniless. While begging, he glimpses a beautiful girl through the doors of a rich man's house and falls in love. That night he is arrested. Questioned in prison by the *cadi*, he claims to be a beggar, and confesses that he has fallen in love with Mouaffac's daughter

Zemroude. The *cadi*, Mouaffac's enemy, dresses Fadlallah as a prince and sponsors his marriage to Zemroude. On the following day, however, the *cadi's* men inform Zemroude that her husband is really a beggar. Zemroude refuses to believe it, and revenges herself on the *cadi* by tricking him into marrying a revoltingly ugly and stupid girl of the lowest class. When word of this reaches the Caliph, he dismisses the *cadi* and gives his property to Mouaffac. Restored to prosperity, Fadlallah and Zemroude return to Moussel, where they become king and queen.

In the tale's second move, a strange dervish arrives at Fadlallah's court and wins the affection of the king and his counselors. One day, while hunting, the dervish tells Fadlallah of the many great secrets he has learned in his travels, including a spell that allows him to reanimate the corpse of a dead animal and inhabit its body. Fadlallah insists that the dervish teach him the spell, but once the king has taken on the form of a stag the dervish usurps Fadlallah's inanimate body, returns to Moussel, and takes his place both on the throne and in the bedroom. Passing from the body of a stag into that of a nightingale, Fadlallah flies back to his palace, where Zemroude keeps him as a pet. Fadlallah is tortured by his inability to communicate with Zemroude, and by the fact that from his cage in her bedroom he is an unwilling witness to her false husband's conjugal visits. When the queen's lapdog dies Fadlallah takes its body, leaving the nightingale's corpse behind. Zemroude is overcome with grief at the death of her pet bird, and the dervish consoles her by taking over the nightingale's body and bringing it back to life. Fadlallah quickly takes his own body back and kills the nightingale. When Zemroude realizes that she has been unwittingly unfaithful to her husband, she dies of grief. Fadlallah gives up his crown and leaves his kingdom, finally ending up at Jaïch. Returning to the present-tense frame of the Calaf novella, the narrator draws an explicit moral lesson from his adventures: "Voilà mon histoire. Vous voyez par mes malheurs et par les vôtres, que la vie humaine est un roseau sans cesse agité par le vent froid du nord. Je vous dirai pourtant que je vis heureux et tranquille depuis que je suis à Jaïch; je ne repens point d'avoir abandoné la couronne de Moussel; je trouve des douceurs dans l'obscurité du sort dont je jouis" [That is my story. You may see from my misfortunes and from your own, that human life is a reed buffeted unceasingly by the cold north wind. And yet I will tell you that I have lived happily and peacefully since arriving in Jaïch; I do not in the least regret having given up the crown of Moussel; I find some pleasures in the kind of obscurity I now enjoy (170)].

According to Sebag the two moves of Pétis de La Croix's story are based on unrelated sources.[18] The first is the second tale of the Turkish cycle *Faraj ba'd al-shidda*, of which a Persian version exists as well. Pétis's treatment remains fairly close to the original. The second source is from the *Histoire des Quarante Vizirs*, to which Pétis adds the story's sad denouement, Fadlallah's abdication, and the moral message that is underscored in the frame. *Pace* Starobinski, it is clear that the original symbolic values of the fairy-tale sources are modified long before they ever reach Gozzi. This is not to say, however, that Gozzi does not transform the ideological message of his immediate source. In Pétis, the two moves are presented as complementary strings of picaresque adventures and misadventures, from which the narrator draws a conclusion in perfect harmony with the sort of renunciatory quasi-religious discourse that has historically bolstered feudal societies: the world and our social position in it are illusory in comparison with an afterlife (here only implied); for kings and commoners alike, life is a series of misfortunes to be stoically endured; and if a king may be most content with an "obscure" existence, why should non-nobles aspire to a higher station than they already possess? One might expect the aristocratic Gozzi to repeat without modification the ideology of his source. Instead the playwright takes the story in a new and surprising direction.

Some of the ways in which Gozzi modifies his source, and in particular the large cuts and consistent simplification of the plot, can be attributed in part to the change from prose fiction to the less flexible genre of the theater. More important, though, Gozzi's changes also correspond to a shift in the ideological perspective of the story. In the novella, the misadventures of the second move are in no way more important than those of the first—they are merely a more fantastic series of reversals of Fortune, that "north wind" that buffets the reed of our earthly lives. In eliminating the moralizing frame and concentrating exclusively on the physical metamorphoses of the second move, Gozzi not only privileges the story's most spectacular, theatrical moments, but also renders it less picaresque, reducing its stress on the vicissitudes of fortune and its stoic ideology of resignation, while instead foregrounding the specific threat of bodily *exchange* and pointing toward an entirely different sort of lesson.

Il re cervo distances itself from its source not only by the greater textual prominence of physical metamorphosis, which is here the hero's sole misadventure rather than one of many, but also by the way in which the exchange of bodies is presented. In the novella, it is the evil dervish who possesses the secret of reanimating a corpse, and who plays deftly on the prince's curiosity in order to steal his body. The thematic link between the novella's first and second moves lies in the prince's fateful curiosity: Fadlallah's initial misadventures are the result of his insistence on seeing the world before settling down to the humdrum responsibility of marriage,[19] while the second series of misfortunes is initiated by a similar, if more fanciful, desire to go beyond the bounds of quotidian existence. Having learned nothing from his first, relatively realistic set of picaresque experiences, the prince is subjected to new misadventures of a more fantastic sort, and it is only after their bittersweet result that he is capable of embracing the ideal of renunciation articulated in the novella's moralizing frame.

The playwright eliminates this theme of curiosity, and with it the character flaw that exposes Fadlallah to betrayal. In *Il re cervo* it is Deramo, not the dervish, who knows the secret incantation: political authority and magical power are combined in the figure of the sovereign. Tartaglia undergoes a radical revision with respect to the source: he becomes a bumbling, inept revolutionary who, in a mute *lazzo* repeated three times at the outset of 2.5, is nearly caught as he tries to shoot Deramo in the back. Motivated not by curiosity but by the generous desire to give Tartaglia a proof of his affection, Deramo reveals a magical secret now no longer presented as a mere game (the "si beau secret" that fascinates Fadlallah), but instead conceived as a crucial tool of statecraft:

> *Der.* Questo è 'l carme fatal, con cui passando
> talora entro ad un cane, ad un uccello,
> e in qualunque animale, o altr'uomo estinto,
> non conosciuto ribellion scopersi,
> litiganti bugiardi, e false genti,
> misfatti enormi, e portentosamente
> puniti ho i rei, tenendo questo regno
> netto dai malfattori. Ora fo parte
> col mio Tartaglia di sì raro carme. (2.5)

> [This is the fatal incantation with which, passing into the body now of a dog, now of a bird or any dead animal or man, I have discovered unknown rebellion, lying litigants, false people and enormous crimes—and I have punished the criminals prodigiously, keeping this realm free of evildoers. Now I will share this rare spell with my dear Tartaglia.]

By insisting on the political nature of Deramo's imprudence—that is, on the error of his generosity toward his subordinates—Gozzi's *Fiaba* underscores a social threat with which his source is not in the least concerned.[20] Angela may be metamorphosed from commoner to queen only because her rare virtue is linked to a strong sense of her own unworthiness; Tartaglia's social climbing is condemned not just because it is based on the betrayal of a benefactor, but principally because the villain *desires* to replace his ruler. The closed aristocracy of Gozzi's plays may be opened, in exceptionally limited circumstances, by an extraordinary stroke of fortune, but any autonomous attempt to break down the barriers of class is energetically resisted.

There is a difference, too, in the success of the metamorphosis as developed by Pétis de la Croix and by Gozzi. In the novella, the change is so completely convincing that the dervish takes possession of Fadlallah's wife and kingdom without anyone realizing that a transformation has occurred. In *Il re cervo*, the metamorphosis of commoner into king is much less successful. A stutterer before his transformation, Tartaglia has the same speech defect even in Deramo's body. He also retains his original, violent temperament, throwing his newly acquired kingdom into confusion by imprisoning his courtiers Pantalone, Leandro, and Truffaldino. This is another departure from the story of Fadlallah, in which the government of Moussel apparently functions as well under a usurper as under its rightful ruler. Unlike Pétis, Gozzi takes care to emphasize the social consequences of a revolution-by-metamorphosis.

The severity of the metamorphosis also changes in the passage from the source to its adaptation. In the story of Fadlallah, the king is changed first into a stag, then into Zemroude's pet nightingale, a metamorphosis that allows Pétis to stress the pathos of the king's situation, in which he is near his beloved but unable to communicate with her. In the earliest manuscript version of *Il re cervo*, Deramo is transformed first into a deer, then into a parrot, while the second manuscript and subsequent published versions have him change from a stag into a old man.[21] In all these versions, Deramo is able to speak to his beloved, unlike Fadlallah. The final text of the play represents an intentional shift in the theme. Gozzi eliminates the pathos of the prince's enforced silence, instead stressing the repulsiveness of Deramo's outward form and questioning whether Angela will recognize and love Deramo in an ugly body—that is, whether she will value his essence over his appearance:

> . . . Come farò, perch'ella creda,
> ch'io sono il suo Deramo, se l'infame
> ministro nel mio corpo or l'è consorte?
> E, se potessi ancor farle palese
> ch'io sono il suo Deramo, e che quell'empio . . .
> Come amerà questo deforme, e inetto
> corpo in confronto al mio? Ella è pur donna,
> e più bel corpo con iniquo spirto,
> che gentil spirto in oridezza chiuso
> vorrà, seguendo il femminil costume.
> Stanche membra, coraggio. Angela forse
> non è, com'altre son. (2.12)

[How will I make her believe that I am her Deramo, if the infamous minister in my body is now her consort? And if I could show her that I am her Deramo, and that wicked man. . . . How will she love this body, so deformed and decrepit in comparison with my own? She is a woman, after all, and as women do she will probably prefer a beautiful body with an evil soul to a noble soul enclosed in ugliness. Tired limbs, take courage! Perhaps Angela is not like all the others.]

Of course, Deramo is correct—Angela is not like other women, and certainly not like Zemroude, who notices no difference between her husband and the dervish. Zemroude has an entirely passive role in the second move of Pétis de la Croix's story; her functions are first to overlook the metamorphosis, and second, to die of shame at her involuntary faithlessness, provoking Fadlallah's abdication and retreat to a humble life. Angela, a passive subject during the king's interrogation in act one, here takes on a more active role, and her function is to "read" the difference between Tartaglia and Deramo. Pantalone's honest daughter immediately discerns the changed essence of her supposed husband, though she is powerless to explain why he now lacks the noble thoughts and dignity of spirit that had made her fall in love with him. The transformation in her supposed husband disgusts Angela and causes her to resist his physical advances, another significant alteration of the source. When Deramo appears before her, still in the form of an old man, she is at first unwilling to believe him. It is only when Deramo begs her to kill him, swearing that he cannot live if she can't love him in his metamorphosed form, that Angela recognizes his "high-minded feelings and noble soul." Her function in the second and third acts is thus to read the immutable moral essence of commoner and king, even when those differences have apparently been erased by the physical exchange of bodies. She does not do so easily or perfectly, hesitating for most of a scene before at last recognizing her true husband, but even this qualified perceptiveness is a radical alteration of Zemroude's blindness in the Fadlallah story.

Having identified Angela's reading of "moral essence" as the principal action of the second and third acts, we may now return to our consideration of act one. There, too, the principal action was one of reading inner and moral character: the "insincere hearts" of women. All that has changed is Angela's position, at first the object of a reading, later a reader herself. In the first act, too, Gozzi implicitly stresses the difficulty of such moral readings, since normal humans like Deramo himself are not sufficiently perceptive to read moral character without the aid of a magical agent: the statue that Durandarte gave him, and that represents an extension of the wizard's wisdom despite his physical absence.[22] The theme of Angela's virtue, apparently so crucial to act one, receives little further development, implying that Gozzi's intention from the beginning is less to articulate a feminine ideal than to introduce the key action of moral reading. The stress on Angela's virtue is not so much an end in itself as it is a way to justify her later uniqueness as reader and her assumption, however imperfect, of the function of the magical agent destroyed at the end of act one.

The principal activity of this reading of inner essence, common to all three acts but present in only one of the sources, and there only as a secondary element, suggests a new and intentional organizing unity. The plot assumes, significantly but predictably given Gozzi's social views, that the real value of moral essence is immutable, and therefore not subject to any sort of exchange. This assumption is then "demonstrated" in the main action of the play: the repeated readings of that immutable essence by magical agent and exceptional human (as well as by the audience, privileged in its knowledge of the plot's "truth"). The notion that such a reading is difficult may take us by surprise but is in fact essential to the allegorical moral of the story, for if everyone could discern what Gozzi considers true value it would be unnecessary for him to warn against the appropriation of that essence through any sort of exchange.

The problem of the difficulty of moral reading brings us to the last of the principal changes Gozzi makes in his source. The resolution of the play's conflict and the reestablishment of a "proper" fictional order is entrusted not to any of the main characters of *Il re cervo* but to the wizard Durandarte, found neither in Gueulette nor in Pétis de la Croix. In Propp's terminology, the wizard is a donor figure, the person from whom the hero obtains a magical agent. However, unlike the donor in Propp's folktale morphology, Durandarte has almost no function within the text. Not only does he not carry out the usual testing or interrogation of the hero, for Propp the first function of the donor; he undertakes no action whatever until the play's end: mentioned in the exposition of act one, he appears mute in the form of a parrot in 2.14, and remains in the background, a silent spectator of the play's ongoing action from 3.3 until his transformation back into human shape in the last two scenes of the play. Yet Durandarte's presence is less marginal than it may at first seem. Cigolotti's prologue in 1.1 tells us not only that it was Durandarte who gave Deramo the magic statue and the spell of transformation; we also learn that Durandarte has foreseen the "great marvels" that the possession of those secrets will cause, and that the resolution of the play's conflict will depend on his intercession. This Durandarte hovering at the margins of the *Fiaba* is a kind of super-reader who foresees the plot of the play, and who is authorized from the start to be its deus ex machina. In the view of the audience, aware of the wizard's foreknowledge and function, the entire play is projected toward his final intervention in 3.10–11, and his pronouncements there thus take on the weight of an ideal interpretation of the events to which Durandarte and the audience have been witness throughout.

As Tartaglia is about to kill Deramo, Durandarte sheds his bird body, and amidst thunder and lightning proclaims not only Tartaglia's guilt, but the exemplary quality of his offense:

Servi d'esempio, traditor ministro,
a tutti i pari tuoi, che con usurpi
prendon dei re la forma, e i lor monarchi
a' sudditi, e a' vassalli mostruosi
rendon, come Deramo, disponendo
della possanza, dell'onor, del regno.
Sappi, fellon, che gentil alma è quella
che l'uom distingue. (3.10)

[You serve as an example, traitorous minister, to all your peers, who take the form of kings, and render monarchs monstrous to their subjects and vassals, like Deramo, usurping their power, their honor, their realms. Know this, you felon: the noble soul is what distinguishes man.]

Here Durandarte clearly indicates and provides an explanation of Tartaglia's allegorical significance. The ambitious commoner is condemned not only for an act of political rebellion—not much of a danger in the Venetian world to which the allegory refers, however distantly—but for the particular manner of his *lèse majesté*. Tartaglia, like his peers in the real world, is guilty of falsifying appearances, of making his ruler look repulsive and himself attractive for purely selfish purposes. We can hardly fail to be reminded of Gozzi's criticism of Goldoni's portrait of society, thought to falsify the true essence of social classes in a mercenary appeal to "l'animo del minuto popolo sempre sdegnoso col necessario giogo della subordinazione" [the inclination of the common people, [who are] always scornful of the necessary yoke of subordination.][23] Tartaglia's punishment follows, together with a suggestive change of scene. Durandarte transforms the erstwhile prime minister into a "horrid horned monster," calls the people together, announces that Tartaglia has become a "spectacle," and pounding his magic staff on the ground transforms the internal room of the palace into the most magnificent piazza the physical capacities of the theater can allow. This is the first time since the prologue that we have seen a public space—and Gozzi underscores by means of this *apertura scenica* the social value of an appropriately public comeuppance. The spectators on stage and those in the house share the task of observing, understanding, and presumably approving Tartaglia's punishment, in a move that eliminates the distance between the fairy-tale world and the world of the audience. The return to the real world and the end of the fiction is further underscored in Durandarte's final lines to the audience, which seem to strike a false, anachronistic note. Claiming that he is no longer a wizard, he scoffs at the "magic" of modern science:

> Durandarte
> non ha mestier di regni, e sol vi dice
> ch'oggi i segreti magici hanno fine;
> ch'io più mago non son. Resti l'incarco
> alla fisica industre di far guerra
> sugli organi, e le voci, che passando
> di corpo in corpo le medesime sono. (3.11)

> [Durandarte has no need of kingdoms, and tells you only that today magical secrets have come to an end; for I am no longer a magician. Let the busy [science of] Physics now have the task of making war upon the organs and particles which pass from one body to another without ever changing.]

But this sneer at the scientific culture of the Enlightenment, clearly in Gozzi's own voice, is perhaps not really as extraneous to the text as some readers have found it, for it reaffirms, in a jocular fashion and as a matter of explicit polemical content, the message of the play's allegory, deriding any possibility of exchange and transformation even at a molecular level.

The Durandarte character is found neither in the sources nor in the initial manuscript version of the play, appearing for the first time only in the second manuscript version. The invention of this character is a logical consequence of the playwright's insistence on the difficulty of reading the moral essence beneath false appearances. In his extratheatrical writings, Gozzi makes it plain that he believes that most of his contemporaries have been taken in by the pernicious culture and philosophy of the Enlightenment—he alone remains undeceived, a taciturn observer called "Il Solitario" by his fellow members of the Accademia de Granelleschi.[24] In the same way, all the characters of *Il re cervo* save Angela are taken in by Tartaglia's falsification of appearances. Both audiences, inside and outside the fiction of *Il re cervo*, require help to perceive the essence behind appearances before they can be expected to reject the illegitimate exchange that has been foisted upon them. Rather than carrying out the typical functions assigned to the donor in folkloric tradition, Durandarte instead acts as the author's mouthpiece, providing an interpretive gloss on the allegorical meaning of the tale and an indication of its relevance to the world outside the theater. Though Gozzi had eliminated the narrative frame that underscored the meaning of his sources, he has added a frame of his own—Durandarte speaks through Cigolotti in 1.1, and again in his own voice in the last two scenes of the play—the intention of which is to underscore a new meaning: the repudiation of any exchange of social status, possible only by falsifying appearances and obscuring the true spiritual essence that distinguishes commoner from nobleman.[25] This new moral message is not only not an expression of the symbolic values of the original sources, which as we have seen are fundamentally changed in meaning as well as form during the process of theatrical adaptation, but is also substantially more complex and more explicitly sociopolitical in nature than a mere "common-sense sagacity concerning vice and virtue."

However, this does not by any means exhaust the question of ideology in the *Fiabe*, since they also necessarily incorporate an ideological horizon of which the playwright himself is not aware. In the case of *Il re cervo*, the significant exclusions and repressions of the text can best be highlighted by reference to Gozzi's principal intertexts: the plays of Carlo Goldoni, to which the *Fiabe* were in large measure a response.

Though the two playwrights' battle has often been characterized as an aesthetic disagreement between a critic and a champion of the commedia dell'arte, their substantive differences, as Petronio has shown, are ideological in nature. True, Gozzi often criticizes Goldoni on aesthetic grounds, exalting the spontaneity of the traditional masks, and deriding his rival's realistic style as a mere unimaginative transcription of daily life: "Espose sul teatro tutte quelle verità che gli si pararono dinanzi, ricopiate materialmente, e trivialmente, e non imitate dalla natura, né coll'eleganza necessaria ad uno scrittore" [He paraded on the stage all the truths that appeared before his eyes, copied out coarsely and without imagination, and not imitated from nature nor [having] the elegance necessary to a writer].[26] More disturbing than the style of Goldoni's plays, however, is their sympathetic portrayal of the lower and middle classes, which for Gozzi are far from stageworthy:

> Moltissime delle sue commedie non sono, che un ammasso di scene, le quali contengono delle verità, ma delle verità tanto vili, goffe, e fangose, che . . . non seppi giammai accomodare nella mia mente, che uno scrittore dovesse umiliarsi a ricopiarle nelle più basse pozzanghere del volgo, né come potesse aver l'ardire d'innalzarle alla decorazione d'un teatro, e sopratutto come potesse aver fronte di porle alle stampe per esemplari delle vere pidoccherie.
>
> [A great many of his comedies are nothing more than a jumble of scenes, which may contain some things that are true to life—but these "truths" are so low, so silly and base that . . . I could never manage to understand how a writer could lower himself to transcribe them in the meanest mudholes of the lower classes, nor how he could dare raise them to the dignity of a theatrical

production, nor above all how he could have the nerve to publish them as examples of true asininity.][27]

As if this were not enough, Goldoni had dared to criticize the minor nobility—Gozzi's own class. Gozzi replies, in numerous prefaces, with the explicitly political accusation that Goldoni had falsified true social appearances for purely personal gain, and that his plays constitute a social and political peril: "un pubblico mal esempio contrario all'ordine indispensabile della subordinazione" [a public bad example against the indispensable order of subordination].[28]

Gozzi clearly sees his rival's plays as a threat to his class. Surprisingly, however, he never speaks of the most substantive challenge posed by Goldoni's idealization of the bourgeoisie: the way in which economic exchange is portrayed as the basis of moral and social value. One of the most striking features of Goldoni's reform is his transformation of the commedia dell'arte mask Pantalone. As Fido and Baratto have amply illustrated, Goldoni molds the original comic figure of a skirt-chasing old Venetian merchant, alternately stingy and prodigal, into a moral paragon who is the responsible father of a family, and an honored and honorable businessman. It is in the practice of commerce that Goldoni's Pantalone is able to exercise and display his moral virtues of honesty, thriftiness, and conscientiousness. What is more, since individual commerce is thought to enrich the whole society, it is in his activity as a merchant that Pantalone can find a principle of moral if not of political equality with the nobility.[29] Commerce is energetically foregrounded in Goldoni, and an activity based on economic exchange thus becomes the vehicle by which the bourgeoisie can redefine itself, exchanging its current social status for a position of greater dignity.[30] Perhaps Goldoni's most famous expression of an economic "equalizer," and of its rejection by the nobility, occurs at the outset of La locandiera, in an argument over precedence between the impoverished but arrogant Marquis of Forlipopoli and the Count of Albafiorita, a rich ex-merchant who has purchased his title of nobility: "Mar. Fra voi e me, vi è qualche differenza. Con. Sulla locanda tanto vale il vostro denaro quanto il mio. . . . Mar. Oh basta: son chi sono, e mi si deve portar rispetto" [Marquis. There are a few differences between you and me. Count. At this inn your money is worth just what mine is. Marquis. That's enough of that: I am who I am, and people must treat me with respect (1.1)].[31]

Gozzi is clearly offended by Goldoni's characterizations of the minor nobility and resents his corresponding idealization of the non-noble classes. However, he does not seem at all to notice the thematic importance of economic exchange in Goldoni's plays, for none of Gozzi's many diatribes against his rival or against the corruption of contemporary mores even mentions the principle of economic exchange on which the bourgeoisie's challenge to the aristocracy is based. When he perceives the problem of exchange at all, it is external to the fictions themselves: for example, he takes an emphatic stance against the professionalization of literature, sneering at Goldoni for needing to write for money, and suggesting that this mercenary motivation frequently made him produce bad work. For Gozzi, the value of artistic production has nothing whatever to do with its exchange value in the theatrical marketplace. On a broader scale, Gozzi's critical writing often takes a position opposed to the widespread progressive belief that consumption, especially of luxury products, fueled commercial exchange and supplied jobs for artisans, to the advantage of the general prosperity.[32] Gozzi's condemnation of luxury goes beyond the traditional Christian view of it as an individual moral defect, to indicate in conspicuous consumption a primary source of *social* corruption:

> il perniziosissimo lusso spargendo le sue larve, altera le fantasie, e dipingendo la modestia ne' vestiti, la mediocrità negli abbigliamenti, e nelle conciature, la sobrietà, e la semplicità ne' cibi, vergognosa incoltura, e spregiabile, e villana rozzezza, fa giganteggiare le umane idee grado grado con indicibile sproporzione, nauseare tutti di tutto, e rendendo gli uomini, e le donne facete caricature col pretesto d'una immaginaria coltura, lascia indarno gemere i saggi, e va desolando le famiglie tutte del secolo se divertendo.[33]

> [scattering its phantasms, pernicious luxury alters how we perceive things. It takes simplicity in dressing, a sense of proportion in clothing and hairstyles, sobriety and moderation in eating, and depicts them as a shameful lack of culture and as contemptible, coarse ill-breeding. It inflates our human ideas unspeakably out of proportion, it makes everyone sick of everything, it turns men and women into silly caricatures on the pretext of giving them an imaginary refinement. Leaving wise men to moan in vain, it goes about ruining all the families of the century, amusing only itself.]

Here, too, Gozzi suggestively views the social threat as an illusion that makes virtues appear vices, exchanging truth for an illusory false appearance.

Gozzi's inability to come to grips on any conscious level with the notion of exchange constitutes a suggestive blind spot, and one that is reproduced in the *Fiabe* themselves. Gozzi's Pantalone is no merchant. Instead, he always finds himself in a client relationship to an aristocratic patron, and whether he is an admiral (*Il corvo*), counselor (*Il re cervo*, *Turandot*, and others) or a tutor (*La donna serpente*), he invariably takes care to note that he has been raised to a high station "beyond his merits." And if the mask of the merchant no longer engages in commerce, neither do any of Gozzi's other characters. In the *Fiabe* no one ever receives a salary or mentions the need for one. At most, Pantalone in *Il corvo* can speak vaguely of having received "favors" and "livelihood" from his patrons, never of having been properly compensated for the actual value of his work—nothing is bought or sold onstage, and we never see any money change hands. Even in the only exchange to be reported as occurring offstage, Gozzi deliberately elides the notion of *value*. In *Il corvo*, Pantalone purchases a miraculous hawk and horse for Jennaro but refuses to consider compensation for them, or even to tell the prince how much he has paid, for they are to be gifts from a grateful and loving dependent: "*Jen.* Quanto vi costarono? *Pant.* Quel che ho volesto; gnente; tre bezzi; sie milioni de zecchini. No ho mai da esser paron mi, dopo tante benificenze, che ho recevesto, de mostrar una picciola gratitudine? Le xe vostre; vogio che le ricevé; no vogio che me le paghé . . ." [*Jen.* How much did they cost you? *Pant.* Just what I wanted; nothing; three coppers; six million sequins [the highest unit of Venetian currency]. After having received so many proofs of your patronage, am I never to have the right to show a little gratitude? They're yours; I want you to take them; I don't want you to pay me for them . . . (1.5)].[34] The whole category of economic exchange as a reflection or a source of value is overlooked in the *Fiabe*, and this significant absence of something that the text cannot perceive, or cannot allow itself to perceive, is an important if involuntary indication of its ideological horizon.

This notion of an ideologically significant blind spot in *Il re cervo* does not wholly resolve the problem of exchange in Gozzi's text, however. It is useful, at this point, to refer to Fredric Jameson's reformulation of the Althusserian ideological horizon as a strategy of containment, based not just on an inability to perceive elements that contradict the coherence of a system of relations, but on an active repression of such elements by a political unconscious.[35] Whereas for Althusser the ideological horizon was a matter of passive limitation, an inability to perceive the historical realities of domination, exploitation, and alienation, Jameson suggests that a collective mind, unable to tolerate these underlying contradictions, responds by denying and repressing them in the same way that the individual conscious mind denies and represses the frightening impulses of the unconscious. The introduction of this Freudian concept leads us to speculate that those intolerable contradictions that the text structures itself so as to repress, and which are thus absent from the text in any explicit form, may nevertheless return to textual presence in transformed shape—just as for Freud psychological repression may resurface, symbolically rewritten, in the language of dreams. Something quite similar occurs in *Il re cervo*, where the category of economic exchange as social equalizer, with all the burden of anxiety this carries for Gozzi, is forced from the fairy-tale plot only to return in a more elusive, figured form as that plot's central mechanism.

What I am suggesting is that the notion of economic exchange as social equalizer constitutes an intolerable contradiction for Gozzi's aristocratic, hierarchical worldview, and is therefore repressed in *Il re cervo*, cut off from any sort of textual expression. But it does not stay cut off. Instead, the threat of exchange, reexpressed metaphorically as physical metamorphosis, is insistently foregrounded and problematized in the play, so that it may then be ritually defused. In Pétis de la Croix, Fadlallah's metamorphosis was only one of his many misadventures, and not necessarily the most important one: the actual process of the metamorphosis is barely described, and the reader's attention is instead directed away from the mechanics of the exchange of bodies and toward the pathetic situation that the transformation creates. In *Il re cervo*, not only is the audience's attention drawn to the process of metamorphosis itself—a showstopping special effect, lovingly described in Gozzi's lengthy stage directions—but the problem of exchange and its success or lack thereof becomes the principal theme of acts two and three. Moreover, we have seen that in Gozzi the disorder caused by the transformation is specifically *social* in nature: it throws the serene kingdom of Serendippo into a turmoil that can only be resolved by the miraculous intervention of the wizard Durandarte, Gozzi's mouthpiece within the fiction. Displaced from reality to the imaginary, the problem of exchange can be ever more strongly underscored until it is at last triumphantly erased by Durandarte-Gozzi in a peremptory act of authorial fiat.

Seen in this light, the ideology of *Il re cervo* is less a matter of content or message contained in the text than one of the function of symbolic production in general: to invent imaginary, formal solutions to unresolvable social contradictions.[36] Il re cervo, by displacing the problem of exchange from the concrete to the imaginary, from an economic threat to one of physical metamorphosis, allows a resolution of a problem that the playwright cannot meet head-on. However, in order to cancel the threat of economic exchange implicitly proposed by many of Goldoni's plays, Gozzi must elaborate a reply that as a condition of its functioning cannot admit into consciousness (and therefore give substance to) the concrete idea to which it responds. Simply put, the author answers a question he cannot pose. As a result, the play reveals its own contradictory ideological circularity, and Gozzi, incapable of engaging in a conscious dialogue with an opposing view too menacing to contemplate, in the end rejects exchange and idealizes immutable essence in an elaborate fantasy that does no more than repeat the comforting tautology proffered nine years earlier by Goldoni's Marquis of Forlipopoli: "Son chi sono, e mi si deve portar rispetto."

Notes

1. According to Petronio, the leitmotif of all of Gozzi's work is his hostility to the Enlightenment: "componga poemi o fiabe, discetti o polemizzi di teatro o di lingua, racconti di sé o inventi storie, Carlo Gozzi ha un solo scopo ed un solo nemico, e tutte le sue battaglie non sono che episodi di un'unica guerra lunga, tenace, che egli combatte contro la nuova cultura italiana ed europea" [whether he writes poems or *Fiabe*, argues or polemicizes about theater or language, whether he writes about himself or invents stories, Carlo Gozzi has a single purpose and a single enemy: all of his battles are no more than episodes in a long and tenacious war that he fights against the new culture of Italy and Europe]. The *Fiabe* are seen as acts more of ideology than of imagination, in that they constitute "un episodio, sotto specie letteraria, di una battaglia culturale" [an episode of a cultural battle, in literary form]. See Giuseppe Petronio, introduction to *Opere*, by Carlo Gozzi, ed. Giuseppe Petronio (Milan: Rizzoli, 1962), 9–42.

2. Gozzi's reception by the German romantics is studied by Hedwig Hoffmann Rusak, *Gozzi in Germany* (New York: Columbia University Press, 1930); Kurt Ringger, "Carlo Gozzi's 'Fiabe teatrali'—Wirklichkeit und romantischer Mythos," *Germanisch-romanische Monatsschrift*, Neue Folge 18 (1968): 14–20; and most impressively by Helmut Feldmann, *Die Fiabe Carlo Gozzis. Die Entstehung einer Gattung und ihre Transposition in das System der deutschen Romantik* (Cologne: Böhlau, 1971). The important Gozzi revival by Russian avant-guard directors and writers took place largely in a review of theatrical theory directed by Meyerhold and suggestively entitled *The Love of Three Oranges*, borrowing its name from that of Gozzi's first *Fiaba*. Meyerhold, K. Vogak, and V. Soloviov regarded the technical and compositional procedures of Gozzi as "more important than the contingent polemical *vis* of his scenarios." V. Girmunski viewed the *Fiabe* as comedies of pure exuberance, in which comic elements and alienation effects break the illusion of the tragicomic plot in order to remind spectators of the fictitious, artificially constructed nature of the theatrical experience. For V. Moculksij, the *Fiabe* incorporate "a complete autonomy of theatrical truth, which has nothing at all in common with the truth of life." On Gozzi's reception in Russia see Giorgio Kraiski, "Carlo Gozzi in Russia," *Siculorum Gymnasium* 28 (1975): 263–75, as well as Kraiski, "La fortuna di Gozzi in Russia nel Novecento," *Chigiana* 31 (1974): 137–41. See also Antonio D'Orrico and Andrea Mancini, "L'avanguardia teatrale russa del Novecento e l'idea della commedia dell'arte. Consigli per un uso gozziano di Meyerhold (e di Vaschtangov)," *Quaderni di teatro* 2 (Nov. 1979): 107–20. The notion of the "pure theatricality" of Gozzi's *Fiabe* has continued to echo in more recent criticism. See for example, Lucia Cini, "Macchina scenica ed utopia nelle 'Fiabe' teatrali di Carlo Gozzi," *Quaderni di teatro* 8 (Feb. 1986): 123–36.

3. Titles of Gozzi's works will be given throughout in Italian. "Il ragionamento ingenuo" [An Ingenuous Discourse] is Gozzi's polemical introduction to the Colombani edition of his works; *Le memorie inutili* [The Useless Memoirs] is his equally polemical autobiography. Titles of the *Fiabe* to which I make reference in this paper may be translated as follows: *L'amore delle tre melarance* [The Love of Three Oranges], *Il corvo* [The Raven], *Il re cervo* [The King Stag], *La donna*

serpente [The Serpent Woman], *L'augellin belverde* [The Green Bird], and *Zeim, re de' geni* [Zeim, King of the Genies]. Translations of quotations from these and other sources have been kept as literal as possible in the interest of purely lexical accuracy and at the expense of style. More readable and stageworthy translations of *Il re cervo* and other *Fiabe* may be found in Carlo Gozzi, *Five Tales for the Theater*, ed. and trans. Albert Bermel and Ted Emery (Chicago: University of Chicago Press, 1989).

4. Jean Starobinski, "Ironie et mélancolie: Gozzi, Hoffmann, Kierkegaard," in *Sensibilità e razionalità nel Settecento*, 2 vols., ed. Vittore Branca (Florence: Olschki, 1967), 2:436.

5. Ibid., 430.

6. Edoardo Sanguineti, "*La donna serpente* come fiaba," in Carlo Gozzi, *La donna serpente con saggi critici sul teatro di Gozzi* (Genoa: Edizioni del Teatro di Genova, 1979), 13–24.

7. The most interesting of the various structuralist analyses of the *Fiabe*, for the most part heavily influenced by the work of Vladimir Propp, is Ludovico Zorzi's "Struttura —> fortuna della Fiaba gozziana," *Chigiana* 31 (1976): 25–41. Declaring the question of Gozzi's ideology "closed" after Petronio's "penetrating" analysis, Zorzi ascribes the success of the *Fiabe* among eighteenth-century audiences to the plays' repetitive and predictable structure, which allowed the spectators to seek refuge in the security and metaphor of the dream (40). Alberto Beniscelli's excellent book undertakes a detailed and convincing study of the sophisticated "calcolo drammaturgico" of the *Fiabe*, without minimizing the importance of their author's political and social conservatism, but often without glimpsing, behind Gozzi's supposedly "theatrical" choices, the existence of an *ideological* project and an equally sophisticated "calcolo ideologico." See Alberto Beniscelli, *La finzione del fiabesco. Studi sul teatro di Carlo Gozzi* (Casale Monferrato: Marietti, 1986).

8. See Norbert Jonard, "Le Merveilleux féerique dans le théâtre fiabesque de Gozzi," *Forum Italicum* 15 (1981): 183. The idea is taken up again by Paolo Bosisio in the introduction to his splendid edition of the *Fiabe teatrali* (Rome: Bulzoni, 1984): "nelle fiabe gozziane l'ideologia conservatrice si esprime in forme mediate, ricoperte dal velo dell'allegoria e ricomposte nella struttura della parabola che lo spettatore può decodificare a suo vantaggio se non si accontenta di godere, senza pensieri, la fantasmagoria dello spettacolo. La fiaba teatrale si presenta, insomma, disponibile a un doppio piano di lettura: l'uno affatto «popolare», tutto risolto nel godimento immediato della rappresentazione fantastica fine a se stessa, della sostenuta e avvincente drammaticità della vicenda; l'altro più complesso, capace di penetrare il senso riposto degli eventi scenici, di cogliere la «morale della favola», strappando la fragile garza che la ricopre" [in Gozzi's *Fiabe* conservative ideology is expressed in mediated forms, hidden by the veil of allegory and recomposed in the structure of the parable that the spectator may decode to his own profit if he is not content to enjoy without thinking the phantasmagoria of the spectacle. In short, the theatrical fairy tale lends itself to two layers of reading: one entirely "popular," entirely taken up with the immediate enjoyment of a fantastic performance as an end in itself, and of the lofty and

compelling force of the sequence of events; the other more complex, able to penetrate the hidden meaning of the events on stage and to grasp the "moral of the story," tearing away the fragile gauze that covers it (52)]. This thesis might be acceptable if it were not linked to a decided devaluation of Gozzi's ideology, which for Bosisio (following Starobinski) is not "rigorous" from *Il corvo* on. Rather than allegories in the strict sense of the word—that is, making precise coded reference to people and institutions outside the text—the *Fiabe* were intended as "efficaci pezzi di teatro da godersi sulla scena, ricavandone un beneficio «morale» che discende dal senso latamente allegorico della vicenda e dalle frequenti massime, incastonate nel tessuto dialogico con il rilievo dell'epifonema" [effective theater pieces to be enjoyed on stage, while drawing a "moral" benefit from the broadly allegorical sense of the action and from the frequent maxims set into the fabric of the dialog, where they stand out as epiphenomena (53)]. In this way, Bosisio too ends up privileging the theatrical effectiveness of the *Fiabe* over their ideological element, reduced either to an imprecise moral lesson or to a series of heavy-handed moral maxims that are altogether too precise for the plays' own good. Indeed, it is in this too-overt expression of an ideological intention—in the "tentazione predicatoria a cui, talvolta, l'autore non sa resistere"—that Bosisio finds "il limite più significativo delle fiabe" [the temptation to preach, which at times the author cannot resist . . . the most significant limitation of the *Fiabe* (59)].

9. In attempting to delineate an ideological significance in Gozzi's fairy-tale material, Petronio suggests that the linguistic and stylistic hierarchy that the plays create among noble, fairy-tale characters, intermediate characters such as Pantalone and Tartaglia, and plebeian masks such as Truffaldino and Brighella, is a reflection of the social hierarchy, ordained by God, that Gozzi holds so dear and that he explicitly idealizes in *Zeim, re de' geni* 2.4 and elsewhere (Petronio 31–33). Unfortunately, this remains a passive and rather too generic conception of Gozzi's fairy-tale world, above all because Petronio does not identify any ideological significance in the principal magical *activities* of Gozzi's plots (for example, in the frequent metamorphoses of human beings into animals, monsters, statues, etc.). More interesting is the function that Norbert Jonard attributes to the "marvelous" in Gozzi: the playwright's fairy-tale universe is the projection to an imaginary world of a desire for social order that could not be realized outside the theater. In this suggestive view, the fairy-tale magic of the *Fiabe* has the function of punishing evil characters and of canceling, within the fiction, an illicit disorder. The role of the marvelous in Gozzi is thus to satisfy the author's unachievable desires by projecting them onto the plane of the imaginary. However, in Gozzi the "merveilleux" characteristic of the fairy tale is misappropriated: it is no longer a "dream," but a utopian construction based on the rejection of reality (Jonard, "Le Merveilleux féerique," 190–91). This is an excellent idea, but it is perplexing in several regards. While Jonard makes an important connection between Gozzi's sense of disorder in society and the disorder of his plots, he does so only in the most general terms, without ever clarifying the *specific* and *symptomatic* ways in which the *Fiabe* react to and "reorder" a *specific* sociohistorical situation—that is, how they function as ideological mediations. Further, while it is true that many of

the villains of the *Fiabe* are punished by a "colpo di magia" that reorders a disorder (see Tartaglia's transformation into a "horrid horned monster" at the end of *Il re cervo*), more often it is the innocent who undergo the torment of an involuntary magical metamorphosis. In these cases, extremely common in the *Fiabe*, magic and the marvelous are sources more of disorder than of order—nor do I think it sufficient to assign to this "negative" magic the exclusive function of creating dramatic suspense, of delaying until the last moment the magical resolution for which Gozzi and his audiences are waiting. We must ask ourselves, instead, if these metamorphoses, which constitute the most frequent expression of magic in the *Fiabe*, may have an autonomous ideological function and a concrete, substantive connection to the social reality behind the text. I have been unable to obtain a copy of a recent article that came to my attention just as this essay went to press but that would appear from its title to examine the link between Gozzi's plays and his society with particular reference to *Turandot*, and which may therefore concern itself with the issue of how a "mythic" and "spectacular" text may be "ideological." See Angelica Forti-Lewis, "Mito, spettacolo e società: Il teatro di Carlo Gozzi e il femminismo misogino della sua *Turandot*," *Quaderni d'Italianistica* 15 (1995): 35–48.

10. See principally Louis Althusser, "Ideology and Ideological State Apparatuses (Notes Toward an Investigation)," in *Lenin and Philosophy and Other Essays*, trans. Ben Brewster (New York: Monthly Review Press, 1971), 127–86. Also of interest is Althusser, "A Letter on Art in Reply to André Daspre," in *Lenin and Philosophy*, 221–27.

11. Fredric Jameson, *The Political Unconscious: Narrative as a Socially Symbolic Act* (Ithaca: Cornell University Press, 1981), 9–102, and in particular 74–87.

12. Gozzi sums up his adversaries' criticisms of *Il corvo* (but valid for *Il re cervo* as well) in his preface to the latter: "Un numero grande di persone . . . non voleva concederle nessun merito essenziale. Sosteneva colla voce, e senza cercar ragioni convincenti, che 'l faceto delle valenti maschere, che avevan pochissima parte, e 'l mirabile delle apparizioni, e delle trasformazioni d'un uomo in istatua, e d'una statua in uomo, fossero le sole cause della resistenza di quell'opera" [A great many people . . . refused to concede that it had any artistic merit. They proclaimed, without seeking any convincing arguments, that the only reasons for the work's success were the slapstick comedy of the excellent commedia dell'arte actors (who had a very small part in the play), the spectacle of the magical apparitions, and the transformation of a man into a statue and back again]. See Gozzi, *Fiabe teatrali*, 225. I will refer to this edition for all quotations from the play. As he tells us in his autobiography, Gozzi sought to outdo himself by reaching for even more spectacular effects of stage magic in *Il re cervo*: "immaginai che fosse opportuno lo spingere con franchezza oltre l'ardire, e la fantasia d'un tal genere" [I thought it opportune to push even further the daring and the imagination of such a genre]. *Memorie inutili*, 2 vols., ed. Giuseppe Prezzolini (Bari: Laterza, 1910), 2:238.

13. Both were anthologized in *Le Cabinet des Fées ou collection choisies des contes des fées, et autre contes merveilleux*, first published in 1717 and reprinted many times during the century with numerous additions and substitutions of tales. Gozzi repeatedly

cites this "gabinetto delle fate" as one of his primary sources of plot material. For Gueulette's tale, I refer to the only edition available to me: *Le Cabinet des fées,* 41 vols. (Geneva: Barde, Manget and Compagnie, 1785–89), 21:496–517. Citations of "Prince Fadlallah" are taken from a splendid modern edition of *Les Milles et un jours,* ed. with intro. and notes by Paul Sebag (Paris: Christian Bourgois, 1980), 145–70. Regarding the oral source of *L'amore delle tre melarance,* traditionally but erroneously thought to be based on a novella of Basile's *Pentameron,* see Angelo Fabrizi, "Carlo Gozzi e la tradizione popolare (a proposito de "L'amore delle tre melarance")," *Italianistica* 7 (1978): 336–45.

14. Smeraldina is paraded in a silly outfit, with a huge fan, large flowers, and ridiculous feathered plumes. She claims to be at the height of Venetian fashion, making reference to what were surely popular clothiers of the time: "Io scometto, che, se vado a Venezia vestita in questa forma, fo innamorare tutti i veneziani di buon gusto, e che i Berrettini rubano dieci mode da queste mie abbigliamenti, e vuotano in tre giorni le borse a tutte le donne veneziane" [I bet if I went to Venice dressed like this, I'd make all the Venetians who had good taste fall in love with me. The Berrettinis would steal ten new styles from my outfits, and in ten days they'd empty the purses of all the Venetian women (1.4)]. The principal source of humor here is the deliberate clash between the fairy-tale setting and the anachronistic references to an extratextual reality with which Gozzi's audiences were familiar. By contrast, in Gueulette all the matrimonial candidates had been required to dress alike in an Enlightened spirit of fairness: "Come ce monarque ne vouloit point être ébloui par des parures étrangères, & qu'il ne prétendoit consulter que la seul nature dans le choix qu'il feroit, il ordonna que toutes ces jeunes filles fusse habillés chacune d'une robe de taffetas blanc, que leurs cheveux fussent nattés d'un ruban de la même couleur, & qu'on les fît assembler à la même heure, dans la salle du divan" [Since that monarch did not in the least wish to be dazzled by foreign finery, and since he intended to make his choice purely on the basis of nature, he ordered that all these young women be attired in white taffeta dresses, that their hair be braided with a ribbon of the same color, and that they be gathered together at the same hour in the audience chamber (*Cabinet,* 21:506)].

15. Note in particular Bettina's outburst in 1.13: «Vualtri foresti, via de qua, co parlè de Venezia in materia de done, le metè tute a un mazzo; ma, sangue de Diana! no la xe cussì. Le pute de casa soa in sto paese le gh'ha giudizio e le vive con una regola, che fursi fursi no la se usa in qualche altro liogo. Le pute veneziane le xe vistose e matazze; ma in materia d'onor dirò co dise quelo:

> Le pute veneziane xe un tesoro
> Che no se acquista cussì facilmente,
> Perché le xe onorate come l'oro;
> E chi le vol far zozo, no fa gnente.
> Roma vanta per gloria una Lugrezia,
> Chi vol prove d'onor vegna a Venezia.

[When you foreigners are off in other countries, and you talk about the women of Venice, you lump them all together; but by Diana! that's not the way it is. In this country, good girls are prudent and live by strict moral standards that just maybe you can't find in some other places. Venetian girls are extroverted and like to show off, but where their virtue is concerned, I'll say what the poet says: "Venetian girls are a treasure that can't be so easily won, because they are as good as gold, and whoever wants to seduce them can't get anywhere. Rome, for her glory, can boast of Lucretia, but if you want proofs of honor, come to Venice"].

16. François Pétis de La Croix (1653–1713), the author of the Fadlallah tale, was one of the leading orientalists of his day: diplomat, royal interpreter of Arabic, Turkish, and Persian, and professor of Arabic at the Collège Royal. *Les Milles et un jours* was published in an evident attempt to take advantage of the popularity of Middle Eastern and Oriental subjects in the wake of Antoine Galland's *Les Milles et une nuits* (1704–11). Though the text presents itself as a translation of a Persian manuscript entitled *Hazâr Yek Roûz* by Dervis Moclès, *Les Milles et un jours* was at least in part the original work of Pétis de La Croix. Many of the stories are loose translations of actual Persian tales, while others are broad adaptations, and still others may be original tales in the style of the Persian material with which the author was intimately familiar. For a long time it was thought that the text had been revised prior to publication by Alain-René Lesage. Paul Sebag challenges this notion in his introduction to *Les Milles et un jours*.

17. According to Propp, fairy tales may consist of one, two, or even more discrete narrative strings called "moves." See Vladimir Propp, *The Morphology of the Folk Tale*, 2nd ed., trans. Laurence Scott, rev. and ed. Louis A. Wagner (Austin: University of Texas Press, 1968), 59 and 92ff.

18. Sebag, ed., *Milles et un jours*, 500–501.

19. "Je lui dis . . . que cela venait peut-être de ce que j'avais une extrême envie de voyager; que je le conjurais de m'accorder le permission d'aller seulment à Baghdad, et qu'à mon retour je pourrais me déterminer à prendre une femme" [I told him [my father] that I still felt no inclination to be married; that perhaps this was because I felt a terrible longing to travel; that I begged him to give me permission just to go to Baghdad, and that when I returned I would be able to resolve to take a wife (*Mille et un jours*, 145)].

20. It might be objected that as prime minister, Tartaglia cannot really represent the lower orders, and that indeed in two other *Fiabe* he is cast as a prince (*L'amore delle tre melarance*) and as a king (*L'augellin belverde*). It is true that Gozzi's use of Tartaglia is more ambiguous than his portrayal of Pantalone, always clearly middle class even when raised "beyond his merit" to high office. However, the origins of the mask as a stuttering Neapolitan lawyer are no less "bourgeois" than Pantalone's status as a merchant, and when, in Gozzi, Tartaglia is a prince or a king the tone of his role is clearly comic, far different from the *parti serie* who are entrusted with the same positions. In *Il re cervo*, the prime minister's status is evident from his discussion with Clarice in 1.2. Tartaglia tells her that this is the second time Deramo has interviewed prospective queens. Not having found an honest noblewoman, he has now thrown the contest open to "young women of any station and condition," and it is therefore now possible for Clarice— apparently a commoner, as her father must then be—to compete for Deramo's

hand. Like Angela, Clarice cannot believe that she could be chosen in preference to a noblewoman: "Lo so; né crederei, che volesse me per consorte dopo tante gran signore rinunziate" [I know that, nor could I ever believe he could want me for his consort after having refused so many noble ladies (1.2)]. Despite his position, we know from the beginning of the play that Tartaglia was not born a nobleman.

21. For an exhaustive philological study of the manuscript versions of the play and their revision for publication, see Paolo Bosisio, "Gli autografi di «Re cervo». Una fiaba scenica di Carlo Gozzi dal palcoscenico alla stampa con le varianti dedotte dagli autografi marciani," ACME 1 (1983): 61–146.

22. Propp would group the statue under the special category of magical agent as extension of the donor. See Propp, *Morphology*, 39ff.

23. Carlo Gozzi, *Il ragionamento ingenuo*, ed. Alberto Beniscelli (Genoa: Costa e Nolan, 1983), 80.

24. Typical of Gozzi's view is this passage from the *Memorie inutili:* "Le odierne novità di rovesci che ci dipingono gli Epicuri onest'uomini, i Seneca impostori, venerabili filosofi, i Volteri, i Russò, gli Elvezi, i Mirabò, eccettera, eccettera, che ci dipingono ridicoli e inetti filosofi i benemeriti nostri santi padri . . . non seducono il mio interno" [The modern reversals that depict Epicureans as honest men, Senecas as impostors, and as venerable philosophers these Voltaires, Rousseaus, Mirabeaus, etcetera, etcetera—that depict as bad and incompetent philosophers the worthy fathers of our Church . . . none of these seduce my inner man (2: 156)].

25. Gozzi himself was clearly cognizant of the novelty of his donor figures, usually the wizard of the story. In the preface to *Il corvo* the playwright remarks that "In Norando, negromante di questa Fola, scorgerà il mio lettore in qual aspetto nobile, e differente da tutti gli altri goffi maghi delle consuete Commedie dell'arte, io abbia voluto porre i negromanti, ch'entrano nelle mie Fiabe" [In Norando, the wizard of this tale, my reader will perceive what a noble character, so different from the silly magicians of the usual commedia dell'arte plays, I wished to give to the wizards of my *Fiabe*]. Carlo Gozzi, *Opere del co: Carlo Gozzi*, 8 vols. (Venice: Colombani, 1772–74), 1:120–21.

26. Gozzi, *Il ragionamento*, 79.

27. Ibid., 80.

28. Gozzi, *Memorie*, 1:214.

29. See Mario Baratto, " 'Mondo' e 'Teatro' nella poetica del Goldoni," in *Tre studi sul teatro (Ruzante-Aretino-Goldoni)* (Venice: Neri Pozza, 1964), 159–227; also Franco Fido, *Guida a Goldoni* (Turin: Einaudi, 1977), 5–47.

30. It should be remembered that this foregrounding of commerce and exchange is part of Goldoni's deliberate project of idealizing the bourgeoisie. At another level, however, Goldoni seems to retain the aristocratic notion of economic exchange as in some sense perilous, and such repressed feelings are often involuntarily revealed in the plays' organization of visual material. See Bartolo Anglani, *Goldoni: il mercato, la scena l'utopia* (Naples: Liguori, 1983).

31. In fairness, it should be pointed out that in *La locandiera*, cited here for the striking way that it focuses the issue under discussion, Goldoni's view of the middle class is

already becoming less positive: the newly rich Count is as much a figure of fun as the penniless Marquis. Four years before, at the height of his reform, Goldoni had praised commercial activity more unreservedly in *Il cavaliere e la dama* (1749), where a merchant corrects an arrogant aristocrat's view of his profession: "Un vil mercante, un uomo plebeo? Se ella sapesse cosa vuol dire mercante, non parlerebbe così. La mercatura è una professione industriosa, che è sempre stata ed è al dì d'oggi esercitata da cavalieri di rango molto più di lei. La mercatura è utile al mondo, necessario al commercio delle nazioni, e a chi l'esercita onoratamente, come fo io, non si dice uomo plebeo; ma più plebeo è quegli che per aver ereditato un titolo e poche terre, consuma i giorni nell'ozio, e crede che gli sia lecito di calpestare tutti e di viver di prepotenza" [A vile merchant, a plebeian? If you knew what "merchant" meant, you wouldn't talk like that. Commerce is an industrious profession, and far greater lords than you have practiced it in the past and do so today. Commerce is useful to the world and necessary to the intercourse of nations. An honest merchant like me cannot be called a "plebeian"—far more plebeian, rather, is the man who, having inherited a title and a few acres of property, spends his days in idleness and thinks he may run roughshod over other people and live by bullying them (2.11)].

32. For one typical Italian expression of this view, dating from the same years as Gozzi's *Fiabe*, see Pietro Verri, "Elementi del commercio," in *Il Caffè*, ed. Sergio Romagnoli (Milan: Feltrinelli, 1960), 27–32.
33. Gozzi, *Il ragionamento*, 77.
34. Ironically, Pantalone's generosity is the unwitting cause of his patron's dilemma in the following act, since the magical animals have been sent by the magician Norando to kill Jennaro's brother in revenge for the abduction of Armilla.
35. Jameson, *Political Unconscious*, 76–102.
36. Ibid., 74–86.

Bibliography

Althusser, Louis. "Ideology and Ideological State Apparatuses (Notes Toward an Investigation)." In *Lenin and Philosophy and Other Essays*. Trans. Ben Brewster. New York: Monthly Review Press, 1971.

Anglani, Bartolo. *Goldoni: il mercato, la scena l'utopia*. Naples: Liguori, 1983.

Baratto, Mario. "'Mondo' e 'Teatro' nella poetica del Goldoni." In *Tre studi sul teatro (Ruzante-Aretino-Goldoni)*. Venice: Neri Pozza, 1964.

Beniscelli, Alberto. *La finzione del fiabesco. Studi sul teatro di Carlo Gozzi*. Casale Monferrato: Marietti, 1986.

Bosisio, Paolo. "Gli autografi di «Re cervo». Una fiaba scenica di Carlo Gozzi dal palcoscenico alla stampa con le varianti dedotte dagli autografi marciani." *ACME* 1 (1983): 61–146.

———. Introduction to *Fiabe Teatrali*, by Carlo Gozzi. Ed. Paolo Bosisio. Rome: Bulzoni, 1984.

Cini, Lucia. "Macchina scenica ed utopia nelle 'Fiabe' teatrali di Carlo Gozzi." *Quaderni di teatro* 8 (Feb. 1986): 123–36.

D'Orrico, Antonio, and Andrea Mancini. "L'avanguardia teatrale russa del Novecento e l'idea della commedia dell'arte. Consigli per un uso gozziano di Meyerhold (e di Vaschtangov)." *Quaderni di teatro* 2 (Nov. 1979): 107–20.

Fabrizi, Angelo. "Carlo Gozzi e la tradizione popolare (a proposito de "L'amore delle tre melarance")." *Italianistica* 7 (1978): 336–45.

Feldmann, Helmut. *Die Fiabe Carlo Gozzis. Die Entstehung einer Gattung und ihre Transposition in das System der deutschen Romantik.* Cologne: Böhlau, 1971.

Fido, Franco. *Guida a Goldoni.* Turin: Einaudi, 1977.

Gozzi, Carlo. *Fiabe teatrali.* Ed. Paolo Bosisio. Rome: Bulzoni, 1984.

———. *Five Tales for the Theater.* Ed. and trans. Albert Bermel and Ted Emery. Chicago: University of Chicago Press, 1989.

———. *Memorie inutili.* 2 vols. Ed. Giuseppe Prezzolini. Bari: Laterza, 1910.

———. *Opere.* Ed. Giuseppe Petronio. Milan: Rizzoli, 1962.

———. *Opere del co: Carlo Gozzi.* 8 vols. Venice: Colombani, 1772–74.

———. *Il ragionamento ingenuo.* Ed. Alberto Beniscelli. Genoa: Costa e Nolan, 1983.

Gueulette, Thomas Simon. "L'Histoire des quatre sultanes de Citor." In *Le Cabinet des fées.* 41 vols. Geneva: Barde, Manget and Compagnie, 1785–89.

Jameson, Fredric. *The Political Unconscious: Narrative as a Socially Symbolic Act.* Ithaca: Cornell University Press, 1981.

Jonard, Norbert. "Le Merveilleux féerique dans le théâtre fiabesque de Gozzi." *Forum Italicum* 15 (1981): 171–95.

Kraiski, Giorgio. "Carlo Gozzi in Russia." *Siculorum Gymnasium* 28 (1975): 263–75.

———. "La fortuna di Gozzi in Russia nel Novecento." *Chigiana* 31 (1974): 137–41.

Pétis de la Croix, François. "L'Histoire du Prince Fadlallah, fils de Ben-Ortoc, roi de Moussel." In *Les Milles et un jours.* Ed. Paul Sebag. Paris: Christian Bourgois, 1980.

Petronio, Giuseppe. Introduction to *Opere*, by Carlo Gozzi. Milan: Rizzoli, 1962.

Propp, Vladimir. *The Morphology of the Folk Tale.* 2nd ed. Trans. Laurence Scott. Rev. and ed. Louis A. Wagner. Austin: University of Texas Press, 1968.

Ringger, Kurt. "Carlo Gozzi's 'Fiabe teatrali'—Wirklichkeit und romantischer Mythos." *Germanisch-romanische Monatsschrift*, Neue Folge 18 (1968): 14–20.

Rusak, Hedwig Hoffmann. *Gozzi in Germany.* New York: Columbia University Press, 1930.

Sanguineti, Edoardo. "*La donna serpente* come fiaba." In *La donna serpente, con saggi critici sul teatro di Gozzi*, by Carlo Gozzi. Genoa: Edizioni del Teatro di Genova, 1979.

Starobinski, Jean. "Ironie et mélancolie: Gozzi, Hoffmann, Kierkegaard." In *Sensibilità e razionalità nel Settecento.* 2 vols. Ed. Vittore Branca. Florence: Olschki, 1967.

Verri, Pietro. "Elementi del commercio." In *Il Caffè.* Ed. Sergio Romagnoli. Milan: Feltrinelli, 1960.

Zorzi, Ludovico. "Struttura → fortuna della Fiaba gozziana." *Chigiana* 31 (1976): 25–41.

CHAPTER 10

"Lecteur, ne vous allarmez pas"
[Reader, be not afraid]:
Giacomo Casanova and Reading the Fantastic

Cynthia C. Craig

 GIACOMO CASANOVA'S extensive body of texts ranges
from the autobiographical to the philosophical, theatrical,
poetic, mathematical, historical, and political; it includes
utopian fiction as well as literary and linguistic criticism. In
his lifetime he saw twenty-four of his works published, sel-
dom with the success he longed for; his most famous work,
a twelve-volume autobiography called the *Histoire de ma vie*, was published
posthumously.[1] An additional eight thousand pages have recently been moved
to the Státni Oblástní Archiv in Prague from the Waldstein Castle in Duchsov
(formerly Dux), where Casanova died in 1798. His last years were spent in the
enforced staticity of poverty, old age, and ill health; employed as the Waldstein
librarian, he found consolation in writing voluminously and encyclopedically.
A self-proclaimed citizen of the Enlightenment's "republic of letters," he
knew or at least met most of its other, better-known, writers: Voltaire and
Rousseau, Goldoni, (in whose troupe Casanova's mother, Zanetta Farussi,
was an actress), Gozzi, Crébillon père and fils, Da Ponte, and Haller—to
name but a few.

While Casanova is best known for his autobiographical texts, his
experimentation with the genres of the fantastic and the *merveilleux*, which,
manifested in *contes de fées*, imaginary voyages, and utopias, experienced
such popularity from the late seventeenth to the late eighteenth centuries,
merits study as well. Casanova was certainly conversant with specific works
within this tradition, inverting Voltaire's tale *Micromégas* into his own utopian

"Mégamicres," and referring to the *Princesse de Babylone* in the *Histoire de ma vie* (though mistakenly dating its publication close to his visit with Voltaire in 1760, rather than in 1768).[2]

The *Histoire de ma vie* also mentions Crébillon fils's *Le Sopha* (1742), whose premise of an animate piece of furniture is shared with Casanova's own "île des meubles animés" listed in an unpublished document from the Prague archives entitled "Mondes ou îles." We do not know if Casanova's *meubles* would have become observers of sexuality, like Crébillon's Amanzei transformed into a sofa. Jacques Barchilon does, however, note the two writers' affinity, pointing out that Crébillon, "cet observateur cynique de la sexualité, avait en lui du Casanova" [this cynical observer of sexuality, had some Casanova in him].[3] The topos of the acquisition of sexual knowledge (through the speech of a woman's body part rather than the observation of coitus) is treated in the *Nocrion* (1747), often attributed to the Cardinal de Bernis, one of Casanova's principal benefactors and patrons. Characterized by Barchilon as a *conte licencieux* (licentious tale), this tale, like Diderot's better-known *Les Bijoux indiscrets* (1748), resembles a fourteenth-century fabliau, "Du chevalier qui fist les cons parler."[4] Casanova's relationship to Bernis, including a depiction of Bernis's voyeuristic tendencies, is detailed in the *Histoire de ma vie*.

Based on his acquaintance with such texts, the popularity of the *merveilleux* and related literary forms, and the extent and variety of his own textual output, one might expect that Casanova experimented with these genres as well. Examples of the *merveilleux* and the fantastic are, in fact, not hard to find in Casanova's texts, and display, in keeping with his other writings, a wide range of narrative strategies along with a tendency to comment self-consciously upon genre and modes of reading. In particular, three of Casanova's texts demonstrate his exploration of the expressive potential of *merveilleux* and fantastic: the autobiographical *Histoire de ma vie*, whose opening episode is structured like a miniature *conte de fées*; the list of fabulous, often magical, "Mondes ou îles" found among his papers in the Prague archives, and a five-volume novel, detailing an imaginary utopian voyage to the center of the earth, entitled *Icosameron ou les aventures d'Edouard et d'Elisabeth qui passèrent quatre vingts un ans chez les Mégamicres habitans aborigènes du Protocosme dans l'intérieur de notre globe, traduite de l'anglais*.[5]

By examining the uses of the *merveilleux* and the fantastic in these texts, we can see how the richness and flexibility of their treatment permits them to play very different roles, to different effect. Taken together, they appear to explore the boundaries of the various textual strategies outlined in Todorov's definition of the fantastic and the *merveilleux*. Todorov distinguishes between three uses of seemingly supernatural elements: the marvelous, which requires an acceptance of the supernatural and cannot be explained by existing knowledge; the uncanny, in which an explanation for the marvelous phenomena is ultimately provided, and the laws of nature are reaffirmed; and the fantastic. This latter category, encompassing the zone of the reader's hesitation between the two genres, is ordinarily "evanescent," eventually revealed to be either the marvelous or the uncanny through the resolution of events. In some texts, however, such resolution never takes place. The fantastic, then, is the genre of dialectic, of questioning, of uncertainty.[6]

Casanova's several experiments with these possibilities find distinct avenues of expression, casting fairy-tale motifs in different molds primarily by exploring the limitations and potential of genre. The incorporation of these topoi into texts with various imperatives leads to conflicts with the boundaries of genre, and ultimately, through experimentation with the fantastic, to participation in a dialectic that questions modes of approaching a text. In one instance, traditional elements of the *merveilleux* occurring within the autobiographical genre coexist uncomfortably with its premise of implied veracity. In another, their placement in a list of imaginary worlds frees them from such constraints of genre. Such freedom allows the *merveilleux* to stand unchallenged, yet offers both satirical and utopian possibilities through the presumption of otherness and distance, and the juxtaposition of different worlds, which also carries an implicit comparison with our own. Lastly, in a fuller development of the utopian premise, Casanova retains the dialectic between two worlds and its inevitable moral dimension, while framing the tale with the reactions of twelve listeners. This device layers the utopian dialectic with competing modes of textual reception, which center principally on the readers' attempts to resolve the uncertainty of the fantastic elements in the narrative. Thus in his utopian fiction, Casanova appears to participate in a process described by Jack Zipes whereby the fairy-tale tradition, by the end of the nineteenth century, had acquired "different functions. As a whole, it formed a multi-vocal network of discourses through which writers used familiar motifs, topoi, protagonists, and plots symbolically to comment on the civilizing process and socialization in their respective countries."[7]

Locating this debate within the genres of utopia and the imaginary voyage allows for the use of elements of the *merveilleux* to express motifs that dominate all of Casanova's literary works: a sense of exile and exclusion, and the decentering of the prevailing culture. Within the autobiographical *Histoire de ma vie*, a similar reinforcing of otherness is achieved by a child's participation in a secret fairy-tale ritual. Furthermore, the presence of the *merveilleux* in the framed narrative of the *Icosameron* recalls such similarly structured texts as Straparola's *Le Piacevoli notti* and Basile's *Lo cunto de li cunti*, and, more generally, the literary fairy tale itself, all of which demonstrate nostalgic "attempts to compensate for a lack resulting from cultural constraints."[8]

Both the expressive potential and limitations of the *merveilleux* are explored in a compact fairy tale neatly encapsulated in the first chapter of Casanova's *Histoire de ma vie*. This tiny *conte* (approximately two pages), makes use of the fairy tale as an appropriate mode to dramatize and confront a youthful crisis, with the clash between the *merveilleux* and autobiographical discourse evoking the limited understanding, vivid imagination, and powerlessness of a child. It is ultimately portrayed as the catalyst for the development of Casanova's memory, a faculty essential to the creation and appreciation of narrative, and of autobiographical narrative in particular. The crisis described in the tale is that of a child thought to be mentally slow and unlikely to reach adulthood, ignored by his family and trapped in silence because of his dullness, the result of recurrent nosebleeds. With his grandmother, he takes a journey by gondola to the island of Murano, to a hovel inhabited by a witch ("sorcière") with a black cat. Locked in a chest, he hears magic spells recited and is aware of the creation of potions; he is later given sweetmeats, rubbed with unguents, and threatened with death should he reveal his visit. A nocturnal visit to his bedroom via the chimney from a seemingly magical figure follows: "j'ai vu, ou cru voir, une femme éblouissante en grand panier, et vêtue d'une étoffe superbe, portant sur sa tête une couronne parsemée de pierreries qui me semblaient étincelantes de feu" [I saw, or thought I saw, a dazzlingly beautiful woman come down the chimney, wearing a huge pannier and a dress of magnificent material, with a crown on her head set with a profusion of stones which seemed to me to be sparkling with fire (1.1.5/45)].

This figure, whose visit had been foretold to Casanova by the old woman, is referred to as a fairy: "la visite nocturne de la fée" [my nocturnal visit from the fairy (1.1.6/46)]. In accordance with her traditional fairy-tale appearance she performs a spell on the child: "elle vint à pas lents d'une air majestueux s'asseoir sur mon lit. Elle tira de sa poche des petites boîtes, qu'elle vida sur ma tête murmurant des mots. Après m'avoir tenu un long discours, auquel je n'ai rien compris, et m'avoir baisé, elle partit par où elle était venue; et je me suis rendormi" [she approached slowly, looking at once majestic and kindly, and sat down on my bed. From her pocket she drew several small boxes, which she emptied on my head, at the same time muttering words. After delivering a long discourse of which I understood nothing, and kissing me, she left as she had entered, and I went back to sleep (1.1.5/45)].

François Roustang, in the chapter entitled "By Magic" of his *Quadrille of Gender: Casanova's Memoirs*, has commented extensively on this episode and others dealing with witchcraft and sorcery.[9] Roustang observes that Casanova, for all that he is an "intelligent, sensible man," cannot deny that magic played a part in his recovery.[10] Casanova reasons thus: "il serait ridicule d'attribuer ma guérison à ces deux extravagances mais on aurait tort de dire qu'elles ne purent pas y contribuer. Pour ce qui regarde l'appartition de la belle reine, je l'ai toujours crue un songe, à moins qu'on ne m'eût fait cette mascarade exprès; mais les remèdes aux plus grandes maladies ne se trouvent pas toujours dans la pharmacie" [it would be ridiculous to attribute my cure to these two absurdities, but it would be a mistake to hold that they could not contribute to it. As for the appearance of the beautiful queen, I have always believed that it was a dream, unless it was a masquerade deliberately contrived; but the remedies for the worst diseases are not always found in pharmacy. (1.1.6/46)].

In instructing the reader on how to approach this departure from more conventional autobiographical discourse, this intrusion of "extravagances," Casanova's parenthetical remarks equivocate, offering various explanations: a dream, or more likely, a hoax. He acknowledges, nonetheless, that there are remedies that remain mysterious and elude logical explanation. His rationale for the mysteries of life indicates that he prefers to believe that they are most often hoaxes, which, however logically explained, undeniably have psychosomatic repercussions: "il n'y a jamais eu au monde des sorciers; mais leur pouvoir a toujours existé par rapport à ceux auxquels ils ont eu le talent de se faire croire tels" [there have never been wizards on this earth, but their power has always existed for those whom they have been able to cajole into believing them such (1.1.6/46)]. The construction of this explanation is curious, for in using the pronoun "ils" to reproduce "sorciers," unmodified by any adjective conveying fraudulence, and by the declaration in the indicative regarding their persuasive powers, the sentence seems to reaffirm grammatically the existence it claims to disprove. This ambiguity has the effect of emphasizing real power while acknowledging the subjectivity of belief.

Roustang sees this event, in which magic plays such a critical role, as a pivotal moment in the text, "the source of Casanova's later behavior."[11] It results in Casanova's conviction that "any loss of blood will signify that he has slipped in meeting his grandmother's desire," since it was her belief in the spell that rendered it effective. Furthermore, Roustang, in his psychological analysis, interprets the apparition of the beautiful fairy as a "dream about intercourse" through a "series of inversions": rather than "pulling from," one can read "putting back"; rather than "empty," "full"; and so forth. The fairy represents the grandmother, whom Roustang takes actually to represent Casanova's mother. A dream of sexual intercourse with the fairy figure enables Casanova to resolve the identification with women that the nosebleeds represent; Casanova will then be compelled "to repeat the act of intercourse with every woman possible in order to save himself from this early identification."

On the narrative level, this small tale is framed by the device, central to autobiography, of simultaneously presenting an episode from the perspective of two distinct temporal moments. These framing remarks make it clear that as a child Casanova was unaware of the episode's potential for generating narrative. At the moment of writing, however, he is aware that the crisis was responsible for stimulating the growth of his mental faculties, and therefore, by extension, made narrative possible:

> Je l'ai placée [la vision] dans le plus secret recoin de ma mémoire naissante. D'ailleurs je ne me sentais pas tenté de conter ce fait à quelqu'un. Je ne savais ni qu'on pourrait le trouver intéressant, ni à qui en faire la narration. Ma maladie me rendait morne, et point du tout amusant; tout le monde me plaignant me laissait tranquille; on croyait mon existence passagère. Mon père et ma mère ne me parlaient jamais. (1.1.5–6/45–46)

> [They made me seal it in the most secret corner of my budding memory. In any case, I felt no temptation to tell the story. I did not know whether anyone would find it interesting or to whom I might tell it. My disease had made me dull, and very poor company; people felt sorry for me and left me alone; everyone supposed that I would not live long. My father and mother never spoke to me.]

From this imposed silence and solitude emerge the promise of future narrative and audience: "ma mémoire peu à peu se développait, et en moins d'un mois j'ai appris à lire" [my memory developed, and in less than a month I learned to read (1.1.6/46)]. Indeed, the actual story of Casanova's life (the chapter opens with a family genealogy and history) begins with this very episode, since it is the first he can remember: "venons actuellement au commencement de mon existence en qualité d'être pensant . . . Je ne me souviens de rien qui puisse m'être arrivé avant cet époque" [and now to come to the beginning of my own existence as a thinking being . . . I remember nothing of what may have happened to me before that time (1.1.4/44)].

This sketch is thus undeniably linked to the creation of narrative through its treatment of the development of psychological and intellectual factors: the *merveilleux* makes its appearance as a symbolic catalyst for the passage from oblivion to memory and from silence to speech. But while it may mark an experiment in reconciling the presence of the *merveilleux* with autobiography, it cannot sustain further development and must remain safely encapsulated from the narrative, its distinctness marked by explanations and disclaimers that caution the reader. Within the confines of the autobiographical contract and its presumption of a degree of referentiality, the *merveilleux* can be granted only a very limited role, and the narrative is clearly marked as a child's recollection, which may imply contamination with oral narratives of fairy tales.

In this regard, we may apply Todorov's observations about the fantastic and fiction to autobiography. For though the presence of fictions in autobiography is undeniable, the public's presumption of a degree of referentiality governs the act of reading, making autobiography and the fantastic incompatible: "if as we read a text we reject all representation, considering each text as a pure semantic combination, the fantastic *could not appear:* for the fantastic requires, it will be recalled, a reaction to events as they occur in the world evoked . . . the fantastic can subsist only within fiction."[12] Thus autobiography's dual perspective gives conflicting reactions to the intrusion of magical or marvelous elements, reflecting the distance of some 65 years between the narration of the event and the moment of lived experience: "I saw," says the child; "or thought I saw" interjects the adult. The resulting tone is ambiguous, tinged with the adult's skepticism and the child's credulity.[13] The *merveilleux* is relegated to the realm of childhood, while the adult perceives the psychological imperatives and their conflict with the ostensibly factual recounting of events. This says more about autobiography than it does about the *merveilleux* or fantastic as genres or the narrative possibilities they possess, which are more fully explored in other texts. However, the manipulative potential of the *merveilleux* is foregrounded, and it is this treatment that comes to dominate the role of magical elements in the *Histoire de ma vie*.

In later episodes the dual perspective of child and adult, which makes possible this vacillation before the *merveilleux*, is effaced by the child's passage into a narrator who controls, indeed creates, fairy-tale scenarios and narratives for his own benefit. Their role in the text becomes mainly that of "an act staged in order to evade the law of the father (that is, of any authority) by mimicking that law through purported communication with higher powers."[14] Casanova obliquely betrays to the reader that psychological acuity and elementary logic lie behind his power to predict events: "mes oracles étaient obscurs dans tout ce dont j'ignorais les circonstances" [my oracles were obscure concerning everything whose particulars I did not know (3.11.207/209)]. While this premise clearly limits the scope of his experimentation in the *Histoire de ma vie*, no such barriers will impede explorations of the fantastic and *merveilleux* in other genres.

In other words, the intrusion of the *merveilleux* into autobiography is resolved through parenthetical instructions to the reader that preserve the text's rationality. The explanation of the *merveilleux* as children's dreams, hoaxes, or manipulations, while not denying its importance or impact, which may be as significant as if it were real, brings the text into the realm termed by Todorov as the uncanny.

This resolution of the conflict between the autobiographical genre and the *merveilleux* can cast light on a puzzling textual fragment replete with fabulous elements. Unfettered by distinctions of genre, purported referentiality, or narrative concerns, a curious list, entitled simply "Mondes ou îles," was left among Casanova's papers in Duchsov at his death, and is now held in the Casanova collection of Prague's Státní Oblastní Archiv.[15] As sketchy as it is (it contains sixty entries, though two are repeated: *malades* [the ill] and *amoureux* [lovers]), its breadth is characteristically encyclopedic. The entries betray origins that range from myth, fable, and possibly other classical sources to science, medicine, and philosophy; many consist of representative types from allegory and comedy, and as such vary from the refined to the coarse. Some order is imposed by a tendency to arrange itself by antithesis into pairs of enduring opposites: *croyans/athées* [believers/atheists]; *beauté/laideur* [beauty/ugliness]; *doutteurs/certains* [doubters/ the certain]; *aveugles/sourds* [the blind/the deaf]. Less frequently, terms are linked by affinity: *peintres/sculpteurs* [painters/sculptors]. In most cases such items fall next to each other on the list, hinting that the list was composed through a natural association of ideas and not in response to any other schema.

The largest number of terms reflects personal habits, characteristics, emotional traits, or turns of mind, ranging from the refined to the vulgar and comic: *amoureux, ivrognes, hypocrites/impies, rieurs, imposteurs, menteurs, peureux, oublieurs, fous, voiageurs, inspirés, babillards, adorateurs, avares, badins* [lovers, drunkards, hypocrites, impious, laughers, impostors, liars, the fearful, the forgetful, the mad, voyagers, the inspired, babblers, adorers, misers, the playful]. The next largest category refers to penchant or occupation, again from the most elevated to the pedestrian, the scientific and pseudoscientific to the political: *chymistes, voleurs, geometres, mechaniciens, legislateurs, musiciens, alchimistes, antiquaires, electrisants, magnetisans, architectes, peintres, sculpteurs, astronomes, cuisiniers,* and possibly *bagatelliers* [chemists, thieves, geometricians, mechanics, legislators, musicians, alchemists, antiquarians, electrifiers, magnetizers [possibly meaning mesmerizers or hypnotizers], architects, painters, sculptors, astronomers, cooks, triflers]. Many of the designations are linked by reference to religious concepts or temperaments: *le paradis sans mémoire, l'enfer sans mémoire, le purgatoire avec mémoire, croyans, athées, repentans,* possibly *esprits* [paradise without memory, hell without memory, purgatory with memory, believers, atheists, the repentant, spirits]. Philosophies or philosophical turns of mind too are represented: *penseurs, doutteurs, certains, materialistes* [thinkers, doubters, the certain, materialists]. Body imagery is marked by both idealized and aberrant characteristics as well as by gender: *chieurs, paralitiques, polyformes, malades, vieillards qui meurent à la mamelle, beauté, laideur, sourds, aveugles, femmes* [defecators, paralytics, multiforms, the ill, the old who die at the breast, beauty, ugliness, the deaf, the blind, women]. Some elude categorization: an *île des lots* [island of lots] for example. Interestingly enough, the element of the *merveilleux* is mostly provided by the governing principle of "mondes ou îles" rather than by a predominantly magical presence among the categories. Strictly magical entries are relatively few in number: *immortels, meubles animés, magiciens, possedés, parlans par écrit* [immortals, animated furniture, magicians, the possessed, those who speak by writing].

Unless and until a thorough archival search provides a context for this document or uncovers evidence linking it to a specific purpose or to a more complete text, its possible contexts can only inspire speculation. Nonetheless, its brevity belies the presence of an intriguing set of clues and intertextual connections that may be examined for relevance to the study of Casanova's interests in and experimentation with the *merveilleux*.

Despite its painstaking, two-columned structure, the page appears to have been almost an exercise in free association. Both the repetitions and the groupings of entries by affinity or disparity, with one category often leading directly to the next in a like manner, hint at an attempt to dispel tedium as much as at the possible organization of thoughts with a narrative purpose in mind. All items, however, revolve about a central motif which, positioned at the top of the page and repeated before the first three entries, establishes a governing principle of fantasy or exoticism. This motif in turn ties "Mondes ou îles" to Casanova's *Icosameron* as well as more generally to issues of genre and specifically to the related genres of utopia and the imaginary voyage.

The motif thus established by the collection's title, "Mondes ou îles," gives focus and direction to an inquiry into the possible uses of such an exercise, pointing to a particular type of marvelous or fantastic element, and uniting all, even the most banal, of the entries. The oddness of the first, "l'île des vieillards qui meurent à la mamelle," reinforces the reader's suspicion that we are in the realm of the exotic. But the motif of the island or world converts all of the varied entries, elegant and vulgar, philosophical and religious, physical and intellectual, into fantasy and exoticism, into the realm of the *merveilleux*, simply by multiplication and exclusion. For while one *ivrogne* or *chieur* is a distasteful spectacle, or at best a curiosity, an island or world of them is an anthropological phenomenon that hints of the supernatural. The differentiation between an architect and an island of architects implies—though being a list this document promises more than it delivers—a series of questions that challenge simultaneously the laws of nature and the accepted precepts of culture and society. Is such a world possible, and what phenomena, heretofore unknown, resulted in its existence and discovery? What laws, natural, supernatural, and man-made, govern it? How is it structured, geographically, legally, administratively, reproductively? Beyond the supernatural, these questions suggest utopia and dystopia, voyage, exile. "Ile" suggests isolation, "monde" suggests uniformity, exclusivity; both terms decenter our own culture and question our privileged position in the universe, implying a dialectic on culture, norms, religion, beliefs, even gender. All this is owed not exclusively to the nature of the topics on the list but to their structuring as worlds apart, a premise that challenges our accepted geographical knowledge while simultaneously resting upon principles deriving from it.

This device is a familiar one, and orients our discussion in the direction of genre, placing the topics on Casanova's list within a literary tradition. Though Casanova professed to detest Rabelais, the document perhaps recalls most closely his mixtures of the elevated and the coarse, the philosophical and the grotesque, his penchant for categorization, lists, and enumeration. It bears a particularly close resemblance to *Le Quart livre des faicts et dicts heroiques du bon Pantagruel,* in which Pantagruel and Panurge experience a violent storm at sea and then travel to a series of islands, among them the isles of the *macraeons* ("gens qui vivent longtemps" [the long-lived]), the *tapinois* ("gens craintifs" [the fearful]), the *Chaneph* (hypocrites), the *engastrimythes* ("parlans du ventre" [belly speakers]), the *gastrolatres* ("adorateurs du ventre" [belly adorers]), and the *sternomantes* ("divinans par la poitrine" [chest diviners]). The islands of book 5 continue thus: *Sonante, Triphes* ("délices" [delights]), *ferremens* ("outils en fer" [iron tools]), *cassade* ("pleine de sable" [full of sand]), and so on.[16] When answering criticism of his *Icosameron,* Casanova denies any indebtedness to Rabelais, preferring to compare his works to other utopian models.[17] Nonetheless, both the *Icosameron* and the "Mondes ou îles" join *Pantagruel* in the far older and anonymous tradition of the imaginary voyage. This genre, with its undeniable affinities to the *merveilleux* and the fantastic, and to utopia as well, links Casanova not only to Rabelais, whether he admits the resemblance or not, but to his nearer contemporaries, among them Swift and Defoe.[18]

"Mondes ou îles," though undated, seems to occupy a place somewhere in between the utopian *Icosameron* and the parenthetical, disclaimed fairy tale of autobiographical discourse. In it, the supernatural and the mundane, fairy-tale and mythological elements, exist side by side, governed alike by the principle of distance and separation. Despite its lack of a narrative component, it casts its recognizable fairy-tale elements in the structure of the imaginary voyage. This implied genre, along with the juxtaposition of opposites, holds the potential of development into utopia and dystopia, a closely allied tradition.

The inevitable debates over a precise definition of the genre of the imaginary voyage affirm its essential connections to other genres. Philip Babcock Gove has detailed both its popularity and the history of its association with the utopian and the fairy tale genres. That it experienced a period of great expansion concurrent with the dissemination of the literary fairy tale is confirmed by the first "critical recognition of the term as a literary classification," albeit in a negative cast, when in 1741 François Augustin

Paradis di Moncrif condemned the genre before the Académie Française. While it is not within the scope of Gove's study to explore the precise mechanisms of the genre's affinity with the *merveilleux*, he points out that Moncrif's discussion of the *voyages imaginaires* occurs in the same context as other related forms, particularly the *contes de fées*, as well as the *merveilleux*, the supernatural, and the imaginary voyages.[19]

Contes de fées and the imaginary voyage likewise share the same classification in the *Bibliothèque universelle de romans*, a monthly periodical begun in Paris in 1775 by Marc Antoine René de Paulmy d'Argenson: "la huitième et dernière classe, comprendra tous les *romans merveilleux*. Les Contes de Fées, les Voyages Imaginaires, les Romans Orientaux" [the eighth and final class includes all the marvelous romances: the fairy tales, imaginary voyages, the oriental romances].[20] Among the works that share this designation are *Gulliver's Travels* and *Robinson Crusoe*.[21]

Gove points out the affinities and similarities of inspiration shared by the *contes de fées* and the *voyage imaginaire*, noting that Charles Georges Thomas Garnier, editor of 1787–89's *Voyages Imaginaires, Songes, Visions, et Romans Cabalistiques*, had collaborated with Charles Joseph de Mayer on the editing of the *Cabinet des fées, ou collection de contes des fées et autres contes merveilleux*. Gove speculates that "material which Garnier had been considering for the forty-one volumes of the *Cabinet des fées* must have constantly sought admission to the later collection, for a voyage of some marvelous sort is a prevalent element in fairy tales."[22]

However, despite the sympathies and concurrent flowering of the imaginary voyage and the *conte de fées*, A. J. Tieje points out an important distinction, a special trait that may be acquired by the imaginary voyage, allying it to utopia: "The *voyage imaginaire* may outdo the nightmares of chivalric romance and the frame-work *conte de fée* . . . it may divulge scandal . . . it may explain philosophic or scientific dogma . . . it may satirize . . . fads . . . or it may be . . . reformative and Utopian."[23] In a similar vein, Sybil Goulding sees the imaginary voyage as the product of two seventeenth-century literary passions—the "fiction fantaisiste" and the truthful accounts of travel to foreign lands: "en 1727 [she is referring specifically to *Gulliver's Travels*], on est . . . assez près du xvii siècle pour être ravi d'entendre parler de la possibilité d'un roman . . . qui joindrait à la fiction fantaisiste et satirique l'intérêt d'un récit de véritable explorateur" [in 1727 we are close enough to the seventeenth century to be delighted at the mention of the possibility of a romance . . . which brings to fantastical and satirical fiction the appeal of an actual explorer's narrative]. She goes on to characterize *Gulliver's Travels* as a *conte de fées*: "Swift démontre qu'il est possible en 1726 de créer une fiction merveilleuse, un conte de fées" [Swift demonstrates that it is possible in 1726 to create a marvelous fiction, a fairy tale], attributing the popularity of such hybrid texts to the "goût inné du merveilleux dans la nature humaine de tout temps" [eternal human nature's innate taste for the marvelous], and the "tendances satiriques si prononcés à cet époque" [satirical tendencies which were so pronounced at this time].[24]

Casanova's contribution to this tradition, the *Icosameron*, demonstrates these universal and satirical traits. In this text the topoi of difference, cultural dislocation, and exile, which dominate his autobiographical texts as well, are converted by the governing principles of the fantastic and exotic into a dialectic of utopia and dystopia, and a dialectic of reading. While the heading "Mondes ou îles" imposed a genre, the document's brevity precludes any indications, other than the associations evoked by the title, as to how this curious mix of crudely physical and lofty intellectual traits is to be read. In the *Icosameron*, on the other hand, one finds a number of the fairy-tale or marvelous elements contained in the "Mondes ou îles" list combined with an interest in their potential for expanding the expressive power of narrative. This interest leads Casanova to the creation of a complex frame for a fantastic world in which these elements appear to find a fitting place, and yet are the subject of textual plays that render their status uncertain. Casanova's treatment not only questions culture but questions how we are to read the genre itself, as well as the nature of representation, which is ultimately judged to be untrustworthy. The *Icosameron* owes a variety of inspirational debts, which it questions even as it renders them homage; the various elements so casually listed in the "Mondes ou îles" manuscript are not simply reiterated, fleshed out, or incorporated into a narrative, but are infused with questioning and debate, casting doubt on the reliability of all narrative and representation.

A scathing criticism of the *Icosameron* appeared in the *Gazette d'Iéna* soon after the publication of the novel, referring specifically to several possible sources of inspiration: Klimm, Gulliver, and the *Pays des Séverambes*. The critic phrases the review's only positive note in terms borrowed from Rabelais: "on n'a jamais lu d'aventures aussi riches en péripéties simiesques et rocambolesques (pour paraphraser Rabelais) que dans ces cinq volumes" [nowhere but in these five volumes can one read of adventures so rich in simian and fantastic vicissitudes (to paraphrase Rabelais)].[25] In responding to the review, Casanova prefers to cite as his antecedents Argenis de Barclay, Robinson Crusoe, Plato, Campanella, More, Bacon, Leibniz, and Kircher. He rejects the reference to Rabelais, whom he calls "le plus sale [auteur] qui ait existé depuis la création du monde" [the foulest [author] who ever lived since the creation of the world].[26] In another reply to his critics (in the guise of an explanatory letter), he disparages Rabelais further as a writer "dont le nom même en matière de propreté ne fait pas le plus grand plaisir au goût, et à l'odorat" [whose very name in a decorous matter is not the most pleasing to taste and smell].[27] Thus, despite the evident similarities between his own

"Mondes ou îles" and those of Rabelais, Casanova, writing in the vein of literary criticism, foregrounds his text's utopian associations and downplays the grotesque.

He also minimizes as much as possible any literary indebtedness, claiming his work to be "nouveau en toutes ses parties . . . nouvelle matière, nouvelle méthode de la traiter, nouvel ordre de la narration, nouveau ciel, nouveau monde" [new in all its parts . . . new subject, treated in a new manner, new narrative design, new heaven, new world].[28] A closer examination of how the *Icosameron* questions modes of reading the *merveilleux* may shed light on the complexity of this claimed innovation, as well as on Casanova's need to emphasize his difference from other texts and certain aspects of the genre itself. The text's convergence of utopian and fairy-tale motifs is joined by extensive commentary on literary conventions, much of it dealing specifically with the *Icosameron*'s particular way of participating in the questioning and hesitation, the dialectic, inherent in the genre of the fantastic, particularly when merged with utopia. On a much wider scale, his objection to the reviewer's claims may reflect larger issues of conflict with authority and paternity, of exile and cultural dislocation, which are prevalent to a much more explicit degree in the autobiographical texts, but find expression in the utopian world of the *Icosameron* as well, with its transgressive vision of the founding of a new society.

The text's singular characteristics—its joining of narrative and commentary, as well as the dialectic of utopia and the hesitation of the fantastic—are most plainly expressed through its frame or *cornice*, indicated by the title *Icosameron*, meaning "twenty days." Casanova thus simultaneously acknowledges literary paternity and eclipses it, doubling in his characteristic encyclopedic manner the period of the *Decameron*'s narration. In Casanova's hands, the frame consists of twelve persons who listen to the tale told by Edouard and Elisabeth; this group of noble men and women and the ancient parents of the couple is joined by two scribes. The frame device links the *Icosameron* not only to the texts of Boccaccio and Straparola, among others, but also to a narrative convention typical of the imaginary voyage. It emphasizes distance and loss by constantly juxtaposing the two loci of the tale, which has the further effect of highlighting the strangeness of the fantastic elements encountered on the voyage. Casanova's manipulation of this common device signals to the reader at once that the text is a complex one, in which the frame's social aspect acquires a dialectical function as well. The frame becomes a questioning model that poses dilemmas of narrative and genre, critiquing and evaluating the *merveilleux*.

By also providing a layering of I narrators of ambiguous status—Edouard, Elisabeth, and a purported translator—who confront a skeptical public both within and without the text, Casanova ensures that the dialectic is apparent throughout the text. As Todorov points out with regard to the questioning nature of the fantastic, the I narrator "is suited to the fantastic but not to the marvelous," and in particular the "dramatized narrator," that is, one who is a character within the tale, as Edouard is.[29]

At the same time the frame and narrators form a mechanism that necessitates and excuses an oral style. This desire for a perceived authenticity confers immediacy upon the tale and, once again, gives weight to its conflicts. Such a technique is privileged elsewhere in many of Casanova's statements about narrative, as for example in his criticism of Rousseau, "l'auteur que je viens de nommer, qui n'écrit pas comme on parle" [the author whom I have just named, who does not write as people speak].[30] In the *Icosameron* the narrative design purports to preserve as closely as possible the natural flow of oral storytelling: it presents the text as a transcript of the days' conversations taken down by scribes hidden behind curtains. Their presence is kept from Edouard, so that self-consciousness will not contaminate his speech:

> Le comte de Bridgend avant que de se coucher fit appeller deux je-
> unes écrivains de sa secretairerie, et leur ordonna de se tenir prets
> à écrire toute la narration d'Edouard, placés, et assis derrière une
> mince tapisserie . . . Il [sic] possédoient l'art d'écrire tout ce qu'un
> orateur prononçoit avec une célérité égale à celle avec laquelle la
> harangue se faisoit entendre. Il ne lui en auroit fallu qu'un seul,
> mais il voulut en avoir une plus grande précaution. (1.142)

> [Count Bridgend, before retiring, had two young writers from his
> secretary's office summoned, and ordered them to be prepared
> to write down all of Edward's narration, positioned and seated
> behind a thin tapestry . . . He [sic] possessed the art of writing
> everything a speaker said at the same speed with which the
> harangue was heard. Only one was really needed, but he wanted
> to take all precautions.]

Despite the count's meticulous precautions, the *Icosameron* falls victim to the vicissitudes and uncertainties that beset all texts. Edouard, at the end of his narration, is presented with the transcript, which he corrects and "perfects," returning it to the count with the intention of having it published. Nonetheless, for reasons that are never made clear, "cette histoire ne fut jamais communiqué au public" [this tale was never revealed to the public (1.143)]. The implication is that the text now presented to the reader is this definitive text of Edouard's. It is, however, a puzzling hybrid; oral in style and claiming to be authentic, but yet mediated in the sense that it is perfected and corrected.

The reader has further cause to hesitate: the chapter that establishes the perfection of Edouard's corrected transcript concludes on a note that questions the validity of any text. The I narrator/translator informs the reader that Edouard and Elisabeth died on the same day, and that Miladi Bridgend caused them to be buried together, with an epitaph noting their ages and the date of their death. He points out, however, that the inscription stating that Edouard and Elisabeth were the same age is incorrect; Elisabeth was two years younger than her "brother-husband." The translator observes, perhaps alluding ironically to criticisms of his own lengthy texts, "ce n'est pas la première fois que dans une inscription de ce genre on sacrifie à la brièveté une circonstance importante" [this is not the first time that in an inscription of this sort an important fact has been sacrificed to brevity (1.144)].

Indeed, a sense of doubt has been imparted at the start, beginning, explicitly, with the title page. The text purports to be the translation of an English manuscript. This common conceit (the critic of the *Gazette d'Iéna* notes tersely: "fable") confers an aura combining authenticity, however unverifiable, and exoticism upon a text, while simultaneously exonerating the author whose name appears on the title page of responsibility for the text's contents and merits.[31] And in the preface, the I narrator/translator, who signs the name Casanova, is quick to establish that, because of his modesty, he will not make the original available for comparison, thus establishing the permanence of the ambiguity. He makes additional equivocal comments regarding genre:

> personne au monde n'est en état de décider si cet ouvrage est une histoire, ou un roman, pas même celui qui l'auroit inventé, car il n'est pas impossible, qu'une plume judicieuse écrive un fait vrai dans le même temps qu'elle croit l'inventer, tout comme elle peut en écrire un faux étant persuadée de ne dire que la vérité. (1.9)

> [No one in the world is in a position to decide if this work is a history, or a romance, not even he who wrote it, for it is not impossible that a judicious pen might write a true fact while believing to invent it, just as one may write a falsehood believing that one is telling nothing but the truth.]

Thus, not even the writer is in a position to judge the truthfulness of a text, and the line between truth and invention is effaced, for a text may be both invented and true. The reader's hesitation over how to approach the text is reinforced by the blurring of the boundaries between "histoire" and "roman," as well as the contents of the text's prefatory space, which consists of an address to Count Waldstein, including a lengthy discourse on the possibility of the actual existence of an inhabited world at the earth's center, and a "Commentaire litteral sur les trois premiers chapitres de la genese" [Literal commentary on the first three chapters of Genesis]. This commentary is made up of an address to the reader, "au bon lecteur" [to the good reader], and a three-chapter biblical commentary, whose purpose, Casanova concludes, is to persuade the reader not that the account is truthful but simply that it is possible: "non pas que l'histoire des *mégamicres* est vraie, mais qu'elle peut l'être" [not that the story of the Mégamicres is true, but that it could be (1.98)]. Not, of course that the reader is in actuality expected to hesitate over the possibility that a brother and sister, propelled to the earth's center by a shipwreck and the famous Maelstrom whirlpool, lived in this world for eighty-one years, married, engendered more than four million descendants, all the products of incestuous unions, and then returned to the earth's surface to tell their tale to their parents, both aged over one hundred years, and an audience of English nobles. Todorov makes clear that the reader's hesitation is not a necessary condition for the existence of the fantastic.[32] The doubt and hesitation before this fantastical premise is clearly then a play, an entirely textual matter: the reader does not know, from the instructions given in the preface, what sort of a text this is; whether Edouard and Elisabeth will be uncovered as liars, charlatans, or impostors, or whether their narrative will eventually be accepted as true by another layer of narration—the discussions of the frame characters. A third layer of narration, already mentioned, is the I narrator of the preface, who signs himself Casanova, and who never intervenes to resolve the ambiguity of the text for the reader.

That we are not yet entirely in the world of Todorov's marvelous is clear from the sense of doubt, amazement, and wonder that the frame characters constantly express. Todorov comments: "in the case of the marvelous, supernatural elements provoke no particular reaction in either the characters or the implicit reader."[33] And as noted earlier, as long as the reader hesitates before the text, unsure whether it belongs to the sphere of the marvelous, or instead the uncanny, the reader is in the realm of the fantastic.

For Irène Bessière, and significantly for the purposes of this study of the *merveilleux* in a utopian text, this hesitation has a particular focus, the "refus d'un ordre" [rejection of an order], or the "mutilation d'un monde" [mutilation of a world].[34] Where the pure *merveilleux* reaffirms order by establishing a counterorder, the fantastic "provoque une question sur la validité de la loi . . . au devoir-être du merveilleux, il impose l'indétermination. Il fait de toute légalité une affaire individuelle . . . il éfface tout article de loi" [provokes a debate about the validity of the law . . . in the place of the must-be of the *merveilleux*, it imposes indetermination . . . . it effaces every clause of the law]. The fantastic, then, is "ambivalent, contradictoire, ambigu" [ambivalent, contradictory, ambiguous], its uncertain nature making it a dialectic, and specifically a "dialectique de la norme" [dialectic on norms]. The reader's hesitation is now imbued with a purpose: the purpose of questioning, of valorizing a challenge to norms, and to the desire for order.

This dialectic is an integral part of the *Icosameron*, whose premise of the imaginary voyage places the reader's world in direct confrontation with both a utopian society founded by Edouard and Elisabeth and the supernatural world of the Mégamicres. In rendering this latter world Casanova makes use of many of the motifs from his "Mondes ou îles." Their combination of the familiar and the exotic emphasizes the ambiguity of the world he evokes: the Mégamicres employ "electrisation" as a medical practice, study the "beaux arts . . . et . . . la Physique, la Géometrie Sublime, les Mécaniques, et la Jurisprudence. Ils sont tous Géographes, et Musiciens" [the fine arts . . . and physics, sublime geography, mechanics, and law. They are all geographers, and musicians (1.22)]. Edouard also points out that "tous les chymistes sont cuisiniers" [all the chemists are cooks], possibly explaining the presence of two such disparate items on the list (1.23). And of course, young as well as "vieillards" [old], all the Mégamicres find nourishment "à la mamelle" [at the breast], one of the foundations of their social relationships and a preoccupation found in other eighteenth-century texts, shared, for example, by Rousseau. These motifs are joined by some of the most prevalent components from the *merveilleux* and the fairy-tale world: the winged beasts, the modification of time and space, the magical properties of stones that provide light, and of course, a brother and sister, lost to their parents for many years, who suffer tremendous hardship before returning home. All the discoveries and inventions of the supernatural Protocosme are subjected to the scientific, theological, and philosophical commentary of the frame characters, whose scrutiny supplies the perspective of a select contemporary public.

It is precisely this commentary that provides much of the textual dynamic. The frame characters attempt to verify the validity of Edouard's scientific explanations for all of the phenomena as they participate in an ongoing debate that touches not merely upon reality or representation, but also upon morals and law. The most transgressive subject with which they struggle is incest, a topos not only shared by Casanova's other texts and much of eighteenth-century literature but common in the genre of the fantastic as well. Citing the *Arabian Nights*, and the tales of Perrault among others, Todorov explains the prevalence of incest as one of the "most frequent varieties" of the fantastic's "several transformations of desire," most of which "do not belong to the supernatural, but rather to a social form of the uncanny."[35] The framework of the voyage, the creation of a utopian society, and the eventual return of the protagonists to our world provides multiple perspectives on these motifs and practices, making them the subject of ongoing theorizing and arguments that question, transgress, and threaten some of the most fundamental of cultural constructions.

The discussion by means of which the frame characters come to terms with the presence of incest in Edouard's society revolves around a biblical justification. Incest as the frame characters gradually come to define it fits the Enlightenment concept described by Lynn Hunt: that only premeditated, deliberate incest is evil. Couples who innocently fall into incest, as did Edouard and Elisabeth, are not considered wicked, although they are aware that they are brother and sister, and of norms that prohibit incest. In many such texts, the protagonists are ignorant of their blood relationship and possibly of the concept of incest as well, but Casanova's treatment does not efface the motif in this way; he chooses rather to bring it to the forefront of the debate. On the other hand, Edouard and Elisabeth's lack of premeditation does reflect a common feature of the motif that confers a sort of innocence. Lynn Hunt cites St. Just as an expression of this principle: "it is virtue on the part of him who gives himself over to it in innocence and is no longer incest"; and Casanova's Dunspili, going one step further and effectively removing the stigma from all heterosexual practices, agrees: "en état de pur nature il n'est aucun accouplement avec femelle de la propre espèce qui puisse faire horreur" [in a state of pure nature, no coupling with the female of the same species ought to disgust us (2.2)].[36] Here as well, however, Edouard and Elisabeth's innocence is subject to question, given that they come to accept incest as the founding principle of their race and proceed to engender millions of descendants.

All of the motifs receive treatments of similarly encyclopedic proportions, in which Edouard and Elisabeth's rational modes of discourse are juxtaposed with the frame characters' expressions of wonder, incredulity, and occasionally of disbelief. Their commentary brings the dialectic into the territory of narrative as well, eventually questioning the presence of elements of the *merveilleux*. Edouard's description of the Mégamicres' winged beasts is so lengthy it causes one of the frame characters to fear that, should all the phenomena be described in such detail, some members of the audience might not live long enough to hear the end of the story. A debate on inclusiveness in narration follows:

> Vous me pardonnerez, si je vous fais observer, que vous vous fatigueriez bien moins, si vous vous épargnassiez la peine des réflexions superflues, et de certains détails. Vous avez parlé trois jours pour nous raconter vos affaires de quinze jours, et c'est une histoire de quatre vingts ans que vous vous êtes engagé à nous communiquer . . . il vous faut précisément seize ans pour vous acquitter de votre promesse . . . quelqu'un de ces messieurs pourroit fort bien mourir, avant que d'entendre la fin." (2.67)

> [Pardon me if I point out to you that you would tire yourself much less, if you spared yourself the trouble of superfluous reflections

and certain details. You have spoken for three days in order to narrate the happenings of fifteen days, and you have undertaken to tell us the story of eighty years . . . it will take you exactly sixteen years to fulfil your promise . . . some of these gentlemen might very well die before hearing the end of your story.]

In response to Burghlei's criticism, Edouard politely agrees to abridge his narration but declines to perform the editorial task himself, asking his public to determine which details are superfluous and ought to be eliminated. Bridgend responds emphatically that nothing is to be left out; but Burghlei argues that the narrative is marred by "certain absurdities," that is, elements of the *merveilleux:* "l'histoire que nous écoutons est charmante, et elle seroit même instructive sans certaines absurdités physiques" [the tale we are listening to is charming, and would be even more instructive without certain physical absurdities], in this case the nature of the Mégamicran sun (2.69–70). Miladi Rutgland offers a resolution of this debate in the form of a scientific explanation for the phenomenon.

These incursions of science and philosophy, intertwined with the marvelous or fantastic elements, are narrated and reacted to by layers of audience and narrators; this creates an ambiguous set of superimposed narratives, all of which may be read differently. The frame permits the ambiguity of the fantastic to persist on some levels, while on others it has been resolved. Todorov tells us that most works of the fantastic "involve the reader's involvement with a character."[37] The frame of the *Icosameron* provides the reader with several choices, however; not certitude about one model of reading. Thus the reader who chooses to identify with Edouard and Elisabeth will be in the realm of the marvelous—believing in a mixture of the laws of nature as we known them and a set of laws heretofore unknown. The reader who instead believes Edouard and Elisabeth have created a hoax, as some of the frame characters maintain for a time, will be in the realm of the uncanny, believing that the commonly accepted laws of nature remain untouched by their claims. However, the reader who persists in his identification with the model of reading provided by the frame characters will pass with them through the realm of the fantastic, the realm of doubt, and gradually move with them into the realm of the marvelous, of acceptance of the supernatural.

The presence of the frame characters prolongs the hesitation of the fantastic. They serve to keep the tale from turning entirely into the uncanny, as it continually threatens to do, while they delay the arrival of the marvelous. Edouard and Elisabeth's father, Jacques Alfrède, for example, is reluctant to believe his children's tale, and when his wife Guillelmine is convinced almost immediately, he scoffs "femme, tu radotes" [wife, you are babbling

(1.109/110)]. For the reader, however, this rebuke is colored with irony, for Jacques Alfrède bases his ability to detect a hoax on the wisdom he has acquired in his 109 years of life. This in itself suggests a hint of the marvelous that somewhat undermines his status as the proponent of the "vraisemblable": "J'ai cent neuf ans, et tu en as cent sept; et après avoir vécus un aussi long tems assez sagement, nous allons nous faire dépêcher pour fous, si nous nous montrons prets à croire vrai ce qui n'est pas vraisemblable" [I am a hundred and nine; you are a hundred and seven. After living so long and so sensibly, are we going to rush into dotage by believing something that cannot possibly be true? (1.109/110)]. By Day Three, Miladi Bridgend is close to believing, but even by Day Twelve, Burghlei expresses doubts about Edouard's possible "imposture" (4.14–15). The frame contributes to the construction of a text in which the marvelous constantly argues its own plausibility, poses questions, proposes scientific explanations.

The reader is offered a choice of how to read the text: Edouard's certainty, his father's disbelief, Burghlei's uncertainty. These choices and doubts are expressed in two narratives—Edouard's tale and the frame discussions—combined with, as we have seen, a third layer of narrative provided by the "translator." But by the end of the narrative, the doubt has vanished; the frame characters have accepted the premise of the marvelous; that is, that a world different from their own exists. Despite their lengthy scientific discourses attempting to explain all of the phenomena of this world "à l'intérieur de notre globe," a leap of faith has been asked of them, and they have consented.

Does this cause the hesitation, and thus the fantastic, to vanish along with it? Only if one accepts the premise that the reader's primary identification is with the frame characters. Casanova would seem at first to propose this: in his "Esprit de l'Icosameron," he tells his readers that the frame characters have two functions: first, to clarify and explain Edouard's text, and second, to serve as a model of readership: "mon but est celui d'indiquer de quelle espèce peuvent être celles qui sont faites pour goûter cette histoire: tous gens d'élite, ou par la naissance, ou par la génie, ou par la littérature" [my aim is to point out what type of person is intended as the reader of this story: all members of the elite, whether by birth, by intelligence, or by letters].[38]

Tempting though this paradigm is, with its invitation to join a select group, ultimately the frame characters fail as a model. When they eventually pronounce their belief in Edouard's tale, they separate themselves from the reader. It would seem self-evident that the extradiegetic readers, though they may share the elite class origins or literary tastes of the frame characters, do not read the text in the same way. The doubt, the hesitation of the fantastic, has always been confined to the text and its internal audience; the reader experiences no real doubt about the text's claim to the existence of the supernatural. And so, seeking another model of reading, we turn then to the third layer of narration, and find a proposal for one in the I narrator/translator's preface. He allows the dialectic to stand, rejecting the absolute, doctrinaire solutions of either the truth or the marvelous. In their place he proposes another criterion for evaluating a text, and it is a fittingly equivocal one: "Je ne prétends pas prouver la vérité, mais la vraisemblance des propositions que j'avance" [I do not claim to prove the truth, but rather the verisimilitude of the proposals I put forward (1.5–6)].

Some of the narrator's diffident stance may be designed to deflect possible controversy stemming from his use of biblical sources. The "Commentaire litteral," in its address "au bon lecteur" [to the good reader], distinguishes in its opening paragraph between objects of faith, which are not to be touched, and history and reason, which are subject to interpretation: "celles qui regardent l'histoire, et la raison sont sujètes à interprétation, et ceux qui pensent être parvenus à les concevoir mieux qu'elles ne furent conçues par differens commentateurs peuvent sans nul scrupule les exposer au jugement des lecteurs chrétiens" [those having to do with history and reason are subject to interpretation, and those who think they have arrived at a better understanding of them than other commentators may, without hesitation, put them before the scrutiny of Christian readers (1.1)]. But the narrator has suggested at the very outset that his work may actually be, at least to a certain degree, a "roman," and has placed it outside of systems of belief: "on ne pourra sans preuve évidente ni nier un fait quelconque, ni y ajouter foi" [without obvious proof, one can neither deny nor believe in any fact (1.9)]. In this context, questions about narration and the "vraisemblable" may be regarded as more textual than theological (1.1).

The prevalence of the terms *vraisemblable* and *vraisemblance* in both the narrative and marginal spaces of the text signals its centrality to the debate on modes of reading this particular text. Lewis Seifert has ably summarized the complex history of these terms with reference to the seventeenth-century *querelle du merveilleux* in his essay included in this volume, which I paraphrase here. For the requirements of religious belief that advocates of the *merveilleux chrétien* posited as essential for *vraisemblance*, the theoreticians of the *merveilleux païen* substituted the aesthetic ideals found in myth; in other words, a system that, relying on mythological and allegorical figures, did not require belief in a religious truth. On the other hand, Seifert sees the "unmotivated marvelous" of the *contes de fées* as an example of a late seventeenth-century "crisis of *vraisemblance*." The *contes de fées* not only merge moralizing precepts with marvelous settings, but in them, *vraisemblance* often masks *invraisemblance*; the two are, in Seifert's terms, "inseparable." The utopian function of the *merveilleux* derives from this crisis.

Although Casanova's use of *vraisemblance* may seem to be complicated by his blurring of the distinction between "histoire" and "roman," as well as by his recourse to lengthy biblical arguments for the plausibility of the existence of the Mégamicres, he clearly distances his "vraisemblance" from "vérité," ultimately detaching the former from any criteria other than the aesthetic. Judging the truthfulness of a text is not, as we have seen, the province of the writer. He goes on to make it clear that it does not fall to the reader either, whose judgment is rather one of an appearance of truth and of "du bon": "L'homme qui lit doit se mettre à son aise, et croire vrai tout ce qu'il trouve vraisemblable, et faux tout ce qui choque sa raison . . . ce qu'il dit du bon ne dépend pas de l'historique" [the reader should relax, and believe to be true all that is plausible, and false all that shocks his intellect . . . the value of what is said does not derive from its historicity (1.9–10)].

Casanova has effectively effaced truth as a criterion for judging a text, separating the text's value from its veracity while valorizing the "vraisemblable." In Casanova's usage, belief and truth, ("croire vrai") derive from aesthetic judgments of *vraisemblance* on the part of the reader. Anything that is implausible ("qui choque sa raison") may be construed as false, and aesthetic principles are independent of historical veracity: "ce qu'il dit du bon ne dépend pas de l'historique." When, as we saw earlier, Jacques-Alfrède employed the term in his argument with his wife over the truth of Edouard's account, saying that they would be taken for fools if they appeared ready to believe something so implausible, he confirmed this use of "vraisemblable" to convey plausibility or likelihood: "nous allons nous faire dépêcher pour fous, si nous nous montrons prets à croire vrai ce qui n'est pas vraisemblable" (1.109).

But while Jacques-Alfrède's interests lie with ascertaining the truth of his putative son's claims rather than making aesthetic judgments about his narrative, Casanova's narrator, in the final analysis, does not care about the uncanny or the marvelous, or resolution, or truth. He is content to let the textual dialectic, the doubt, and the hesitation remain, while establishing a new standard for judging a text: the reader's enjoyment of the text, based on the persuasiveness of its art.[39] Within one text, Casanova presents a range of reading and narrative modes, but he does not advocate any of them except the independence of the artistic, of fiction, from questions of veracity. The reader, he instructs his patron and his public, should suspend the search for an absolute truth and instead believe only that which is persuasive in the text. While engaged in the act of reading, the reader must discard conventional systems of belief; deprived of this system, Casanova acknowledges, the reader may be baffled or uncomfortable, following one of his claims with a reassuring "lecteur, ne vous allarmez pas" [reader, be not afraid (1.5)]. The wise reader believes not in the truth but in literature's intrinsic potential for artistic value beyond truth or fiction, mistrusting certitude but not doubt, and thus, we may infer, not the hesitation of the fantastic:

Nous ne prétendrons pas, sottement orgueilleux, de parvenir à
la certitude, mais nous parviendrons à douter: vous savez que les
plus savans entre tous les hommes sont ceux qui sont en état de
bien douter: l'homme qui doute ne sait rien, mais en revanche il
ne se trompe jamais. (1.11–12)

[We do not claim, with foolish pride, to arrive at certainty, but we
will arrive at doubt: you know that the wisest of all men are those
who are capable of great doubt: he who doubts knows nothing,
but on the other hand is never wrong.]

Indeed, the reward may be greater than simply never to be wrong. The reader
and the writer who have the courage to doubt may find pleasure; this is a
pleasure uniquely afforded by a text that makes no claim to certainty, and one
that remains despite exile and old age: "nous pouvons néanmoins raisonner.
Heureux ceux auxquels la raison peut servir d'amusement" [we can however
use our wits. Happy are those whose wits can serve as amusement (1.12)].

Notes

*A shorter version of this study, focusing on the intertextuality of the archival document
"Mondes ou îles" and Casanova's published texts, rather than their relationship to the fantastic
and merveilleux, is forthcoming in* L'intermédiaire des Casanovistes *XIII (1996). For
their help in locating the "Mondes ou îles" document, Státní Oblastní Archiv Praha, fond
Casanova, U 16h/30, I would like to thank Mme Tarantová of the Archives, Ing. Mila
Kuhnová, and Mrs. Valerie Kopecky Craig.*

1. Giacomo Casanova, Histoire de ma vie, édition intégrale (Wiesbaden: F.A. Brockhaus, Paris: Librairie Plon, 1960). English translations are taken from History of
   My Life, trans. Willard R. Trask (New York: Harcourt, Brace, and World, 1966).
   All citations from the Histoire de ma vie are noted by volume, chapter, and page
   numbers; the English page numbers follow the French.
2. Jacques Barchilon, in Le Conte merveilleux français de 1690 à 1790 (Paris: Champion, 1975), calls Micromégas an "histoire fantastique [fantastic story]" narrated
   as if it were a fairy tale (135).
3. Ibid., 102.
4. Barchilon attributes the Nocrion to Bernis (106), though it has also been variously
   attributed to, among others, Caylus, Gueulette, J.-B. Guiard de Servigné, and
   even Diderot. See for example the entry in the Dictionnaire des lettres françaises:
   Le dix-huitième siècle (Paris: Librairie Arthème Fayard, 1960), 316–17.
5. Giacomo Casanova, Icosameron ou les aventures d'Edouard et d'Elisabeth qui passèrent quatre vingts un ans chez les Mégamicres habitans aborigènes du Protocosme
   dans l'intérieur de notre globe, traduite de l'anglais (Prague: Imprimerie de l'Ecole
   Normale, 1788; Provence: Les Editions d'Aujourd'hui, Les Introuvables, 1986):
   the latter edition, used in this study, reproduces the text of the Claudio Argentieri

edition, Spoleto, 1928. An English translation exists only in abridged form: *Icosameron, or the Story of Edward and Elizabeth Who Spent 81 Years in the Land of the Megamicres, Original Inhabitants of Protocosmos in the Interior of Our Globe*, trans. Rachel Zurer (New York: Jenna Press, 1985). Citations in French from the *Icosameron* will be listed in the text by volume number, followed by page number. English page numbers follow the French. English translations not found in Zurer's abridged version will be my own, and will appear without page numbers.

6. This paragraph summarizes the argument found in Tzvetan Todorov, *The Fantastic: A Structural Approach to a Literary Genre*, trans. Richard Howard (Cleveland and London: Case Western Reserve University Press, 1973), 25 and 41–52.

7. Jack Zipes, *Fairy Tale as Myth/Myth as Fairy Tale* (Lexington: University Press of Kentucky, 1994), 15.

8. Rosemary Jackson, *Fantasy: The Literature of Subversion* (New York: Methuen, 1981), 3.

9. François Roustang, *The Quadrille of Gender: Casanova's Memoirs*, trans. Anne C. Vila (Stanford: Stanford University Press, 1988). Translation of *Le Bal Masqué de Giacomo Casanova*, (Paris: Les Editions de Minuit, 1984).

10. Ibid., 86.

11. For the citations from Roustang's *Quadrille* found in this paragraph, see 86–88.

12. Todorov, *Fantastic*, 60.

13. The *Histoire de ma vie* was written between 1789 and 1798; the episode to which Casanova refers occurred in 1733: "au commencement d'août de l'année 1733 l'organe de ma mémoire se développa" [in the beginning of August in the year 1733 my organ of memory developed (1.1.4/44)]. However, the I narrator states "dans cette année 1798" [in this year 1798 (1.1.3/44)], implying that this first chapter or a portion of it was either written late or revised.

14. Roustang, *Quadrille*, 79.

15. A copy and transcription of this document, along with a brief description of its contents excerpted from this study, is forthcoming in Cynthia Craig, "Giacomo Casanova's 'mondes ou îles': A Microcosm of Utopia," *Annali d'Italianistica* 14 (1996): *L'odeporica/Hodoeporics*, ed. Luigi Monga.

16. François Rabelais, *Oeuvres Complètes Tome II* (Paris: Garnier Frères, 1962). Explanations of the islands' names are taken from the "Briefve declaration d'aucuns dictions plus obscures contenues on quatriesme livres des Faicts et dicts heroiques de Pantagruel," commonly attributed to Rabelais or at least assumed to have been written with his approval, 249–60, or, where no gloss exists, from the editorial annotations to the relevant chapters.

17. See Giacomo Casanova, "Confutation de deux articles diffamatoires parus dans la *Gazette d'Iéna*," manuscript, Státni Oblastní Archiv Praha, fond Casanova, BOB U23, folios 164–83 and 152–61, reprinted in Giacomo Casanova, *Histoire de ma vie suivi de textes inédits*, édition présentée et établie par Francis Lacassin (Paris: Editions Robert Laffont, S.A., 1993), 1049–76, and in particular 1064 and 1073. The Laffont/Lacassin edition is a reprinting of the Brockhaus-Plon text of the *Histoire de ma vie* with additional materials, many of them archival, appended. See also Giacomo Casanova, "L'Esprit de *l'Icosameron*," manuscript,

Státni Oblastní Archiv Praha, fond Casanova, BOB U16e, folios 21–22, reprinted in *Histoire de ma vie*, Lacassin/Laffont edition, 1076–92, and in particular 1092. Translations are my own.

18. For a history and definition of the genre, see Philip Babcock Gove, *The Imaginary Voyage in Prose Fiction: A History of Its Criticism and a Guide for Its Study, With an Annotated Checklist of 215 Imaginary Voyages from 1700 to 1800* (1941; rpt., London: Holland Press, 1961). A description of Casanova's *Icosameron* appears on 385–86.

19. Ibid., 12–13, 20, 20.

20. Marc Antoine René de Paulmy d'Argenson, *Bibliothèque universelle de romans* (Paris, 1775), 1:23f. Cited in Gove, *Imaginary Voyage*, 23.

21. Gulliver is mentioned in the publication of March 1787, 62–192, and Robinson in July 1878, ii [3]–146. This information is from Gove, *Imaginary Voyage*, 26.

22. Charles Georges Thomas Garnier, ed., *Imaginaire, Songes, Visions, et Romans Cabalistiques* (Amsterdam and Paris, 1787–1789). Charles Joseph de Mayer, ed. *Cabinet de fées, ou collection de contes des fées et autres contes merveilleux* (Amsterdam and Paris, 1785–89). Gove, *Imaginary Voyage*, 28 and 51.

23. A.J. Tieje, *The Theory of Classification of Prose Fiction Prior to 1740*, University of Minneapolis Studies in Language and Literature, 5 (Minneapolis, 1916), 64, cited in Gove, *Imaginary Voyage*, 88.

24. Sybil Goulding, *Swift en France: essai sur la fortune de Swift en France au XVIIIe siècle, suivi d'un aperçu sur la fortune de Swift en France au cours du XIXe siècle* (Paris, 1924), 74 and 80ff., cited in Gove, *Imaginary Voyage*, 110 and 111.

25. "Une critique de l'*Icosameron*," *Gazette d'Iéna, Allgemeine Literatur-Zeitung*, Aug. 22, 1789. Translated from the German by Christian Kosmacz, and reprinted in Casanova, *Histoire de ma vie*, Laffont/Lacassin edition, 1047–49. The citation is from 1049. Translations are my own.

26. Casanova, "Confutation," 1064 and 1073.

27. Casanova, "L'Esprit de l'*Icosameron*," 1092.

28. Casanova, "Confutation," 1050.

29. Todorov, *Fantastic*, 82–83.

30. Giacomo Casanova, *Mon Évasion de Venise* (retitled version of the *Histoire de ma fuite des Prisons de la République de Venise qu'on appelle le Plombs, écrite à Dux en Bohême en l'année 1787*), édition annotée par B. Melchior-Bonnet (Paris: Hachette, 1961), 39. Translation is my own.

31. "Une critique," 1047.

32. See Todorov, *Fantastic*, 31.

33. Ibid., 54.

34. Irène Bessière, *Le Récit fantastique: la poétique de l'incertain* (Paris: Librairie Larousse, 1974). The citations in this paragraph are taken from 23–24. Translation is my own.

35. Todorov, *Fantastic*, 131.

36. Lynn Hunt, *The Family Romance of the French Revolution* (Berkeley and Los Angeles: University of California Press, 1992), cites St. Just on 84–85.

37. Todorov, *Fantastic*, 33.

38. Casanova, "L'Esprit de l'*Icosameron*," 1080.

39. For a discussion of the term *vraisemblance* as it was used in novels of the seventeenth and eighteenth centuries, see the chapter entitled "Prolegomena, Theory, and Background" in Vivienne Mylne, *The Eighteenth-Century French Novel: Techniques of Illusion* (Cambridge and Melbourne: Cambridge University Press, 1981), 1–19. Mylne points out that "the words *vraisemblable*, *vraisemblance* nowadays convey concepts of probability and plausibility, qualities required for the maintenance of imaginative belief," while in the seventeenth century (and she cites examples from the eighteenth century as well), "one may need to interpret these terms in a sense much closer to their etymology: 'true-seeming,' 'calculated to give an impression of truth'—that is, the literal truth of history. Novelists therefore admit that their work may entail persuading the reader, by means of *vraisemblance*, to accept 'lies' as truths" (13). Casanova seems to have accepted both definitions of *vraisemblance*. For example, see *Icosameron* 1.13: "si Dieu a crée notre terre pour qu'il fût habitée, est-il vraisemblable qu'il ait voulu que sa partie habitable fût sa surface extérieure?" [if God created our earth in order for it to be inhabited, is it likely that he would have wanted its surface to be its habitable area?]. In this case, *vraisemblable* would seem to conform to the modern usage implying probability or plausibility. And the quotation used earlier to introduce this argument implies more of a consciousness of the writer's role in creating persuasive fictions, particularly when read in its fuller context, which refers to the text as a "dialectique": "soyez indulgent vis-à-vis de mon style; mais n'ayez aucune pitié de mon jugement ni de ma dialectique: rejettez moi avec indignation si vous me trouvez captieux, ou de mauvaise foi. Souvenez vois, je le répète, que je ne prétens pas prouver la vérité, mais la vraisemblance des propositions que j'avance" [be indulgent in the matter of my style, but have no pity on my judgment nor my dialectic: reject me indignantly if you find me captious or in bad faith. Remember, I repeat, that I do not claim to prove the truth, but rather the verisimilitude of the proposals I put forward (*Icosameron* 1.5–6)].

Bibliography

Barchilon, Jacques. *Le Conte merveilleux français de 1690 à 1790*. Paris: Champion, 1975.

Bessière, Irène. *Le Récit fantastique: la poétique de l'incertain*. Paris: Librairie Larousse, 1974.

Casanova, Giacomo. "Confutation de deux articles diffamatoires parus dans la *Gazette d'Iéna*." Státní Oblastní Archiv Praha, fond Casanova, BOB U23, folios 164–83 and 152–61. Reprinted in Giacomo Casanova. *Histoire de ma vie suivi de textes inédits*. Édition présentée et établie par Francis Lacassin. Paris: Editions Robert Laffont, S.A., 1993.

———. *Histoire de ma vie*. Édition intégrale. Wiesbaden: F.A. Brockhaus, Paris: Librairie Plon, 1960. English translation: *History of My Life*. Trans. Willard R. Trask. New York: Harcourt, Brace, and World, 1966.

————. *Icosameron ou les aventures d'Edouard et d'Elisabeth qui passèrent quatre vingts un ans chez les Mégamicres habitans aborigènes du Protocosme dans l'intérieur de notre globe, traduite de l'anglais* Praguoi Imprimerie de l'École Normale, 1788; Provence: Les Editions d'Aujourd'hui, Les Introuvables, 1986. English translation (abridged): *Icosameron, or the Story of Edward and Elizabeth Who Spent 81 Years in the Land of the Megamicres, Original Inhabitants of Proto-cosmos in the Interior of Our Globe.* Trans. Rachel Zurer. New York: Jenna Press, 1985.

————. "L'Esprit de *l'Icosameron*." Státni Oblastní Archiv Praha, fond Casanova, BOB U16e, folios 21–22. Reprinted in Giacomo Casanova. *Histoire de ma vie suivi de textes inédits.* Édition présentée et établie par Francis Lacassin. Paris: Editions Robert Laffont, S.A., 1993.

————. *Mon Évasion de Venise* (retitled version of the *Histoire de ma fuite des Prisons de la République de Venise qu'on appelle le Plombs, écrite à Dux en Bohême en l'année 1787*). Edition annotée par B. Melchior-Bonnet. Paris: Hachette, 1961.

————. "Mondes ou îles." Státní Oblastní Archiv Praha, fond Casanova, U 16h/30.

Garnier, Charles Georges Thomas, ed. *Imaginaire, Songes, Visions, et Romans Cabalistiques.* Amsterdam and Paris, 1787–89.

Goulding, Sybil. *Swift en France: essai sur la fortune de Swift en France au XVIIIe siècle, suivi d'un aperçu sur la fortune de Swift en France au cours du XIXe siècle.* Paris, 1924.

Gove, Philip Babcock. *The Imaginary Voyage in Prose Fiction: A History of Its Criticism and a Guide for Its Study, With an Annotated Checklist of 215 Imaginary Voyages from 1700 to 1800.* 1941. Reprint, London: Holland Press, 1961.

Hunt, Lynn. *The Family Romance of the French Revolution.* Berkeley and Los Angeles: University of California Press, 1992.

Jackson, Rosemary. *Fantasy: The Literature of Subversion.* New York: Methuen, 1981.

Lacassin, Francis, ed. "Une critique de *l'Icosameron*." *Gazette d'Iéna, Allgemeine Literatur-Zeitung.* Aug. 22, 1789. Trans. Christian Kosmacz. Reprinted in Giacomo Casanova. *Histoire de ma vie suivi de textes inédits.* Édition présentée et établie par Francis Lacassin. Paris: Editions Robert Laffont, S.A., 1993.

Mayer, Charles Joseph de, ed. *Cabinet de fées, ou collection de contes des fées et autres contes merveilleux.* Amsterdam and Paris, 1785–89.

Mylne, Vivienne. *The Eighteenth-Century French Novel: Techniques of Illusion.* Cambridge and Melbourne: Cambridge University Press, 1981.

Paulmy d'Argenson, Marc Antoine René de. *Bibliothèque universelle de romans.* Paris, 1775.

Rabelais, François. *Oeuvres Complètes Tome II.* Paris: Garnier Frères, 1962.

Roustang, François. *Le Bal Masqué de Giacomo Casanova.* Paris: Les Editions de Minuit, 1984. English translation: *The Quadrille of Gender: Casanova's Memoirs.* Trans. Anne C. Vila. Stanford: Stanford University Press, 1988.

Tieje, A. J. *The Theory of Classification of Prose Fiction Prior to 1740.* University of Minneapolis Studies in Language and Literature, no. 5. Minneapolis, 1916.

Todorov, Tzvetan. *Introduction à la littérature fantastique.* Paris: Editions du Seuil, 1970. English translation: *The Fantastic: A Structural Approach to a Literary Genre.*

Trans. Richard Howard. Cleveland/London: Case Western Reserve University Press, 1973.

Zipes, Jack. *Fairy Tale as Myth/Myth as Fairy Tale*. Lexington: University Press of Kentucky, 1994.

CHAPTER 11

Little Red Riding Hood as Fairy Tale, *Fait-divers*, and Children's Literature: The Invention of a Traditional Heritage

Catherine Velay-Vallantin

 THIS STUDY analyzes the points of articulation among several genres that are all too often treated separately: the fairy tale, the *fait-divers*, and children's literature.[1] I use two narratives to illustrate this approach, the fairy tale *Petit Chaperon rouge* [Little Red Riding Hood] in the many versions it appeared in from the eighteenth to the nineteenth century, and the legendary story of *La Bête de Gévaudan* [The Beast of Gévaudan], from eighteenth-century France. I will attempt to validate the hypothesis that evolving receptions of a story produce divergent understandings, according to the sociohistoric contextualization in which the story is set. What relation, then, does the fairy tale have with topical narratives? And how can a narrative, which is presented as true, develop its own margins? How do genres such as occasional works or children's literature produce readings that are at the same time unique and recurrent? What place is left for the development of the fairy tale once it is subjected to different ideological and pedagogical strategies?

I will examine several editions in this essay. I will use the least repetitive publications, those in which narrative, textual, and editorial differences reveal the intervention of an author, editor, or publisher. This type of intervention implies, we shall see, a selection of motifs, illustrations, and understandings. Any selection process revolves around a certain classification resulting in diversity; the principles that govern this classification need, however, to be grasped. I will treat the auctorial and publishing strategies that can, initially, present the disadvantage of creating the false idea that these selections were made for reasons of quality and narrative coherence. This is an argument that has been advanced by literary historians: consciously or not, most Lansonian[2] critics have, in fact, developed their analysis based on a concept that issues from the domain of biology and goes back to positivism: the idea of "natural selection." The idea of separating "good" texts from "bad" texts and that of natural selection are similar; both give a "natural" character to a process that nonetheless seems the effect of intention. Yet, this is precisely how the literary critics of Perrault's *Contes* have justified the validity of the textual transformations that the central narrative matter of the stories has undergone over the course of three centuries. I intend to show that these transformations, which highlight an effect of textual discrimination, do not seem to be the product of any fixed values inherent to the text, as if the tale carried in itself the future of its own evolution, but rather of a system of varying principles dependent upon the conceptions these subsequent authors have of literature and on contextual—historical and sociocultural—changes.

Children's literature, which from the nineteenth century onward has appropriated for itself Perrault's *Contes*, took up editorial practices already well-known in the world of booklovers and chapbook vendors, in particular the practice of printing summaries, such as appear in the 1775 *Bibliothèque Universelle des Romans* or in the "blue books" (chapbooks) of eighteenth-century Troyes publishers. The summarization process, the act of reduction or *contraction*, deserves some close scrutiny. The word *contraction* derives from the participle of the Latin verb "contrahere," to tighten, but also makes allusion to the action of engagement, of beginning something, evoking the idea of a pact, of a convention, a contract, or a transaction. The concept of reduction refers to objects put aside, rejected, or undesirable, and as such, makes a clear distinction between what is kept and what is abandoned, separated, excluded. The Latin verb "reducere" has a series of meanings that are of interest: to bring back, to return from exile, to lead back the troops, to lure in besieging troops with machines; to reconcile someone with someone else; to give way to a certain form; to make the body slim; to reestablish the behavior and clothing of the past. Restore, reestablish, and lead back, would be, thus, synonyms of "reduce."

The idea of returning, so important for the "antiquarians" of the nineteenth century and the folklorists of the twentieth, conjures forth two distinct images. To reestablish and to restore evoke the return of something or of someone, such that the subject or the situation becomes what it was before, whereas the verb "to lead" puts the emphasis more on the idea of transformation. Thus, the different meanings of this verb seem to indicate two actions that can today be considered contradictory: that of restoring an object or a state of things, and that of evolving. In effect, everything that returns, returns in a changed form. The return of texts and their reutilization in the form of "news items" fixed in place, put in writing, produces the effect of the familiar that has become foreign, of the known that has become unknown. How and why is the reader confronted with such a disturbing perception?[3]

When we approach the series of narratives deriving from *Little Red Riding Hood* we may determine the degree to which we are confronted with a literary process that seems to be governed by the revival, recycling, or reuse of a text and that nonetheless seems inseparable from another subtle phenomenon: the uprooting of a text from its context and its placement in a new context. We are in the presence of a willful intent, by an author—often anonymous—or a publisher, to manipulate the well-known corpus of versions of the fairy tale. It is undeniable that these manipulations are undertaken quite consciously, which implies that these authors and publishers had well-defined ideas and expectations about their effects. But it is not a matter of posing the problem in terms of continuity or discontinuity. Indeed, conceiving of the problem of rewriting fairy tales this way would overshadow the complexity of a process of publishing and republishing *Little Red Riding Hood* that seems devoid of valid logic. Instead of justifying or attempting to put editorial and auctorial intent into question, I will examine both the mechanisms employed by the reworking of a folkloric heritage, and the theoretical problems implied in these strategies.

Each of the authors convinced of the need to rewrite *Little Red Riding Hood* must meet the demands of a publisher, who is often presented as the sole person in control of the author's production. It is difficult to imagine, however, a strategy more marked by the will to master one's own literary creation than that exhibited by nineteenth-century authors of children's literature. The author Léo Lespès, for example, even closely managed the publication of his works. I employ the word "manage" here in the sense of administration, organization, or supervision of a cultural heritage within a cultural field, operations that concern effects, gains, and a symbolic profit. I do not believe that the strategy of authors of children's literature had as its aim economic gain in particular but rather the control, the positioning of a group of meanings, and, in this sense, the manipulation of literary works. This process had, however, commercial consequences. Each new edited version of a fairy tale was purchased by a large readership. This effect is particularly obvious in the transformations and continuations of *Little Red Riding Hood* that were the subject of the "Decadent" authors of the 1890s. This was not the only example, of course, of authors paying attention to the administrative aspect of publishing. While the management of a business is at times relegated to a manager or an administrator and that of a literary work to a publisher, an author such as Willy[4]—famous for his remunerative management—decided to assume an active role in an area most often reserved for publishers, to the point that publishers found themselves reduced to nothing more than printers.

This sort of management resulted from conceptions of literature embraced by the majority of nineteenth-century authors of children's literature.

In fact, one of the common characteristics of these authors is that they are indefatigable readers. They convey this image primarily because for them, reading launches writing; reading lies, most of the time, at the origin of their writings. Reading and rereading appear to be two activities that speak to a certain productivity. The writing of authors of children's literature puts on display its own origins and seems to convey the realization that this constitutes the best strategy for obscuring manipulations of the meaning of a text. At the same time, this concept of reading is inseparable from the rapport the author establishes with the reader and from the concept implied in publishing and republishing strategies. Indeed, the devices for establishing a text are inseparable from the conditions of its reception, although we should not define these conditions in a mechanical, absolute fashion. They direct the text by suggesting a route. The different versions of *Little Red Riding Hood* presented to the reader by nineteenth-century authors, while reflecting an intentional orientation, still deserve to be called "literary poachings."[5] A dialectical movement thus begins to appear; the next step is to present a description of it that does not freeze or immobilize the movement of this complex machine.

This process of constructing a narrative and editorial category was not the result of a single act. Rather, it was the result of many years of work, first by the clergy and the literate of the eighteenth century, then by the fashionable society of the salons and "curiosity chambers" of the nineteenth century. This process involved thought-out alterations and modifications— sometimes quite detailed—of the corpus. In addition, contrary to what a first approach might suggest, this was a richly complex system; it was not the symptom of a literature for intellectuals or for literary specialists, or for privileged young audiences. It was a literature that incessantly provoked the reader and that attacked his passivity, without calling his intellectual preparation into question. However, the presence of numerous references to authors and literary works, or to theological works, gave way among the first historians of chapbooks, such as Robert Mandrou, or literary historians such as Jacques Barchilon, to an interpretation that unanimously emphasized the "intellectual" character of this type of production. Chapbooks and children's literature, seen as editorial repetition of "learned" texts, would seem to demand a reader on the same intellectual level as the author. But it is not a matter of degree of erudition, even if historians of the book have been able to determine that most of the time, "popular" and "fashionable" readers were able to accept this intellectual challenge, having benefited from as much cultural baggage as the author. In fact, these works do demand a reader that is the intellectual equivalent of the author, but in a different sense: the works expect, prescribe, and want a particular kind of reader, an irreverent, impolite, disrespectful, and insolent reader. By defining reading as an activity, these authors impute an active quality to it, thus causing the reader to be suspicious of the norms that are imposed upon him; to be suspicious of them, to ignore them, and to subvert them.

Oral Tradition and the Printed Word: First Exchanges

In the eleventh century, the scholar Egbert de Liège published the tale, *La petite fille épargnée par les louveteaux* [The Little Girl Spared by the Wolf Cubs], which presents the central and indispensable event of *Little Red Riding Hood*, the attempt by wolves to devour a little girl dressed in a red baptismal dress. Several centuries later, while the region of Gévaudan fell prey to the terror of the "Beast," this tale resurfaced in the form of a *fait-divers*. Thus the question of narrative survival emerges: this notion, presented by nineteenth- and twentieth-century evolutionists and diffusionists as the obvious key to understanding these tales and legends, will here be examined from a different angle. A long narrative life, which too often passes as the explanation for textual energy, and which has too often been confused with the concept of continuity, will also be treated from another perspective: what if that which gave meaning to these texts, remarkable for their intermittent appearances in time, was something other than the solution of continuity?

I will examine this legend, born from a *fait-divers*, first through archival data and the meaning that they acquire by their placement in time and space, then through the "true" and plausible rewritings of the legend that appear in occasional works of the eighteenth century. The fairy tale appears as the central link between the multiple and expanded reconstructions of the *fait-divers*. But at the same time the fairy tale, reread in light of the legend, will be approached through its various editorial incarnations, from the *Bibliothèque bleue* to children's literature. One of the most significant tangents in this endeavor will regard the analysis of an originally oral tale that is subsequently conveyed by the printed word, and, then, of the creative potential that is revealed by the relationship between the text and the illustrations. I will also examine various mental attitudes toward the text, insofar as ethnologists and historians of religion permit us to reconstruct the network of meanings that justify texts that are transmitted orally and through print. This phenomenological endeavor will legitimize the multidisciplinary analyses of the two stories, *Little Red Riding Hood* and *The Beast of Gévaudan*.

Little Red Riding Hood is famous for its two endings: the first, tragic, chosen by Perrault, sees the grandmother and the little girl being eaten by the wolf, without any hope of being saved. Perrault preferred this ending in order to better illustrate the cautionary moral that sanctions his own version of the tale. The other ending, happy, has been transmitted to us by the Brothers Grimm: a hunter kills the wolf and extracts the stunned but alive grandmother and little girl from his stomach.

The oral versions collected throughout the nineteenth century are not easily divided into these two categories: the happy ending, which survived in the Moran, Touraine, and Alps regions, was relatively infrequent, for it attenuated the essential cautionary function of the tale. Oral storytellers, in fact, would vary the various happy or tragic endings of the tale's heroines depending upon their audience and the impact they hoped to make on them, particularly when children were listening. As a result, we would need to know more about the conditions under which these versions were collected, which is especially difficult for the period around the turn of the century. It is also difficult to determine the degree of influence that the literary versions of Perrault and of the Brothers Grimm (the latter was translated into French at the beginning of the nineteenth century) had. Nevertheless, it is a fact that the happy ending was not the Grimms' invention; it existed in the oral tradition, even during Perrault's life. As proof, we have the version, from long before Perrault—from the eleventh century, to be exact—in which the little girl dressed in red is spared by wolf cubs that are seized by fright and deep reverence for her baptismal dress.

In the middle of the eighteenth century, a chapbook publisher recognized the importance of the more cheerful oral tradition: Madame Garnier, publisher of "blue books" in Troyes, around 1750 published a collection entitled *Les Contes des fées, avec des moralités; par M. Perrault* [Fairy Tales With Morals by M. Perrault].[6] The texts were identical to those that appeared in the first edition of the *Contes*, published by Barbin in 1697. The illustrations above the titles, however, are older woodcuts with no marked appropriateness for the themes of the stories. Only two fairy tales, *La barbe bleue* [Bluebeard] and *Cendrillon* [Cinderella], are graced with unambiguous illustrations. In particular, the illustration above the title of *Little Red Riding Hood* merits reflection. The woodcut represents the slaughtering of a large animal standing on its hind legs that is in truth difficult to identify—wolf? ass? ox?—but that the reader cannot help but associate with the wolf to be treated at length in the pages that follow. With no apparent relationship to this story, this slaughter scene indeed alludes to the other folkloric dénouement, in which the hunter kills the wolf. Confronted by the cruelty of Perrault's ending and faithful to the uniformity of the happy endings in her own collection, Madame Garnier deliberately sought with this illustration to tone down the effect of Perrault's version.

Two remarks are necessary at this point: it is possible that we are in the presence of a new interest—undefined and uncertain, but new—in a youthful readership. Madame Garnier is perhaps one of the first *Bibliothèque bleue* publishers to anticipate the reactions, tastes, and expectations of a readership still little defined in France: the child. She knew that books could be read by children but also, and with greater probability, by an adult reading aloud, who would show the illustration to those listening, children or otherwise. It is obvious from this example that the publisher knows perfectly well the reading habits of her audience and the ways they will apprehend the meaning of her books. She knows that a reader reads a text insofar as he looks at it; that an illustration can convey meanings of a text that preceded the printed one in question; that oral tradition, omnipresent in the reader's cultural baggage, can prove to be the best source for understanding a printed text that tells a story that has already been known in other forms, for other reasons, in order to teach other lessons.

Was Madame Garnier wrong to make such assumptions? Nearly twenty years after her publication of Perrault's *Contes,* a sudden flurry of oral and printed tales recounting an atrocious and equivocal *fait-divers* showed otherwise. Indeed, a number of different narratives, with different norms and contrasting meanings, coexist in the memory and understanding of readers and listeners. The exploration and comparison of the various conclusions to these stories, however contradictory they may be, will prove to be one of the most valid approaches for analyzing the texts and the values they contained for the eighteenth-century reader.

For Perrault, but also for literary historians, ethnologists and pyschoanalysts, there is no doubt: *Little Red Riding Hood* is the story of sexual initiation. According to the harshest interpretations, it is the story of a rape, even if the act of devouring—a sexual symbol par excellence—also involves the grandmother, thus restoring to the narrative archaic ideas about a lesson in which cannibalism is indispensable. Publishers of chapbooks and of occasional works in "blue book" form quickly associated the tale with a *fait-divers,* the story of *The Beast of Gévaudan.* For this Beast only devoured little girls . . .

The Story of the Beast of Gévaudan

The story begins during the summer of 1764: a fourteen-year-old girl was discovered on July 1, in Gévaudan,[7] near Saint-Etienne de Ludgarès, half-eaten (figure 11.1). Throughout the summer, there would be more victims, young cowherds, both boys and girls, devoured not far from the Mercoire forest. When the population of the region became enraged to the point of revolt, Duhamel, the captain of the Dragoons stationed in Langogne, decided to hunt the animal with sixty of his dragoons. These first outings produced no result other than, perhaps, making the Beast escape to another area.[8]

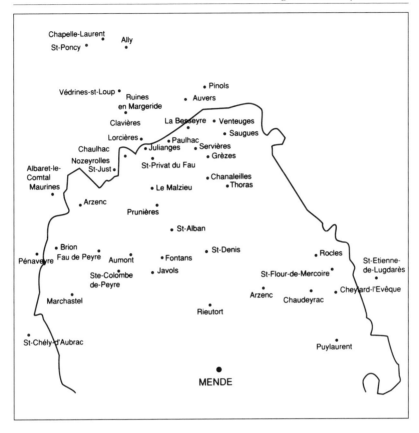

Chapelle-Laurent
St-Poncy
Ally

Pinols
Védrines-st-Loup
Ruines
en Margeride
Auvers

Clavières
La Besseyre
Venteuges
Lorcières
Sauges
Chaulhac
Paulhac
Nozeyrolles
Julianges
Servières
Albaret-le-
St-Just
St-Privat du Fau
Grèzes
Comtal
Maurines
Chanaleilles
Le Malzieu
Thoras
Arzenc
Prunières

St-Alban

Brion
St-Denis
Rocles
Pénaveyre
Fau de Peyre
Aumont
Fontans
St-Etienne-
de-Lugdarès
Ste-Colombe
Javols
St-Flour-de-Mercoire
de-Peyre
Arzenc
Cheylard-l'Evêque
Marchastel
Chaudeyrac
Rieutort
St-Chély-d'Aubrac
Puylaurent

MENDE

FIGURE 11.1 Map of Gévaudan, with locations of the Beast's attacks.

Indeed, other attacks were reported beginning in the fall of 1764 in another, bigger part of Gévaudan that covered a large part of Margeride, from Arzenc de Randon to Saint-Juéry, at the border of Auvergne. Duhamel then received orders to continue the hunt, and from November onward, he based himself in Saint-Chély d'Apcher. Lafont, a subdelegate of the quartermaster at Languedoc, organized hundreds, even thousands of peasants and hunters, but the Beast continued its attacks unhindered, killing a total of twenty people by the end of the year. Deep fear gripped the countryside, and the local newspapers began to speak of this infamous Beast who was "eating everyone in Gévaudan."

On December 31, 1764, the bishop of Mende, Mgr. de Choiseul-Beaupré, published and distributed a *Mandement* [Pastoral letter] throughout his diocese, which was read by priests in all the parishes: for the bishop of

Mende, the Beast was sent by God to punish the citizens of Gévaudan for their immoral conduct.

In early 1765, huge searches to kill the Beast were organized despite the cold and the snow, but the list of victims only grew longer; Louis XV appointed M. d'Enneval, a Norman squire and one of France's biggest wolf-hunters at the time, and his son to take charge of the hunt. The d'Ennevals tracked the Beast from spring through the beginning of summer 1765, using every method known to them: ambush, mounted hunts, and poisoned bait. They sometimes were able to enlist the help of local noblemen, such as the Marquis of Apcher, and of hunters from all over France. But they succeeded only in killing a few wolves and the Beast continued its murderous attacks from the north of Gévaudan to the south of Auvergne. All over France and at the royal court, the seemingly invulnerable Beast of Gévaudan was on everyone's lips. Louis XV then decided to dispatch his harquebus carrier, Antoine, accompanied by his son, fifteen prestigious gameskeepers, and dogs from the royal kennel.

The whole armada arrived in Gévaudan on June 22, 1765, and the hunt began anew in Malzieu. The Beast's attacks seemed by now to be occurring more and more between Gévaudan and Auvergne, around Saugues and d'Auvers. A very big wolf was killed on August 28 by one of the gameskeepers, but the massacre continued. Antoine was beginning to lose all hope of finding the Beast when he received word of some wolf attacks in the Dames de l'Abbaye Royale des Chazes forest, on the right bank of the Allier river. A hunt was organized, and Antoine himself killed a large wolf on September 20, believing that he had finally struck down the Beast of Gévaudan. For more than a month, no more attacks were reported, and Antoine was considered by all Gévaudan's savior. He returned to Paris where he was proclaimed a hero by the court.

Although the attacks began again in early December 1765, for the court the story of the Beast officially ended on September 20, 1765. In 1766, the Beast found new victims, notably near Lorcières, but many fewer in number—officially, in any case. In addition to the twenty official deaths recorded in 1764, we can add fifty-six for 1765 and only 7 for 1766. In 1766, the subdelegate Lafont was forced to hunt with limited resources and the help of only a few local noblemen. In 1767, the list of victims grew even longer. Sixteen more deaths were attributed to the Beast before his presumed death. The last attacks took place within a much smaller territory than before, near scattered villages between Mont-Mouchet and Mont-Chauvet, on the Margeride. Pilgrimages to Notre-Dame d'Estours and Notre-Dame de Beaulieu were organized to pray for an end to the killing.

Finally, on June 19, 1767, during a hunt led by the Marquis d'Apcher, the Beast of Gévaudan was killed by a peasant-poacher, Jean Chastel. We can assume that it was truly the Beast this time, for no more attacks of the sort were ever reported.

In the middle of a drama to which a whole region was subjected, came another, more specific drama—that involving the tragic death of the young Gabrielle Pélissier in 1765. How did this bloody *fait-divers* become a legend? What relationship does the legend have with the tale?

The Staging of the Tale

On April 7, 1765, in Clauze, near Grèzes, the body of seventeen-year-old Gabrielle Pélissier was found "revêtue de son vêtement de première communiante [. . .] Elle avait la tête coupée" [dressed in her first communion dress [. . .] her head had been cut off]. The death of Gabrielle Pélissier was one of the strangest to occur during d'Enneval's hunting campaign. According to the death certificate, she was eaten by the Beast on April 7 and her remains were buried the next day. But a letter from Fajolle, cited by the abbott Pourcher, "historian," of the Beast's ravages, gives the following details:

> Après avoir fait sa première communion, elle alla garder ses vaches à la Champ-de-la-Dame. Son père l'accompagna et resta avec elle tout le soir. Mais peu avant le coucher du soleil, son père lui dit: "Je ne crois pas que la Bête soit dans l'endroit. Tu diras seule tes prières; je commence de marcher; tu viendras bientôt rentrer [le bétail]." Le père la quitta en l'encourageant. Mais aussitôt que le père eut disparu, la Bête s'approcha de la fille et la tua. Probablement ses vaches voulaient la défendre, car le lendemain on les vit presque toutes tâchées du sang que la Bête leur avait soufflé.

> [After making her first communion, she went to look after her herd of cows in Champ-de-la-Dame. Her father accompanied her and stayed with her all evening. But a little before sunset, her father said to her: "I do not believe that the Beast is around here. Say your prayers by yourself and I will begin walking; bring the cows home soon." The father said a few words of encouragement, then left. But as soon as the father had left, the Beast sneaked up on the girl and killed her. Her cows probably wanted to defend her, for the next day, nearly all of them were found covered in the blood that the Beast had spat upon them.]

The end of this narrative is absolutely strange: "Lorsque la Bête l'eut mangée en partie, elle arrangea au milieu d'un bourbier si bien ses os, sa tête coupée, qu'elle couvrit de ses habits et son chapeau, que quand on vint la chercher, avant qu'il fût nuit, on la crut endormie. La Bête avait disparu" [When the Beast had partly eaten her, it arranged her bones and her severed head so carefully in the middle of a quagmire, covering them with her clothes and her bonnet, that when they came to look for her just before nightfall, they believed that she was sleeping. The Beast had disappeared].

A second letter, from Marvejols, dated April 14, gives different information: the girl was sixteen, and very pretty. One of her sisters was keeping her company and screamed, "Attention! Tu as un gros loup derrière!" [Look out! There's a huge wolf behind you!] when she first saw the Beast. The wolf had already taken hold of Gabrielle. Her sister ran screaming to the village, which was but a short distance away. As she looked back, she saw "la tête de cette aimable soeur tombant par terre, tandis que le corps était encore debout" [her dear sister's head fall to the ground, while the body was still upright]. The author of the letter adds: "Plusieurs de nos paysans ne croient pas que ce soit une bête, mais quelque diable qui en a pris la figure . . . Ils la tiennent pour un être subtilement raisonnant, immortel, invulnérable, qu'il faut chasser avec de l'eau bénite" [Several of our peasants do not believe that it was the Beast, but some devil that had taken its form. . . . They believe it to be a thinking, calculating, immortal, invulnerable being that must be hunted with holy water].

Which version do we choose? And why did these contradictory stories emerge so quickly after the death? Let us first examine the facts: Gabrielle Pélissier was killed on April 7, 1765 in Clauze, in the parish of Grèzes. Now, the Beast's last attacks in this parish were in January, and murders of April 3, 4, 5 and 8, 1765 were restricted to another zone in Margeride, fifty kilometers to the south, in a rather logical path: Fontans, Saint-Denis, Arzenc de Randon, and Chaudeyrac. The killing of Gabrielle Pélissier appears to have been atypical, given this geographic and chronological route. In addition, the details given by the father about the blood-stained cows were rather awkward coming from the mouth of a peasant: threatened, frightened cows would normally flee as far as possible. It is a good bet that the role of the father—and perhaps of the sister as well—of the pretty Gabrielle was not as clear as the letters might suggest.

Moreover, these details find a place at the heart of a subsequent narrative treatment of the story: a lament in fourteen quatrains that was composed for Gabrielle's death:

. . . d'une dent furieuse la Bête
sur la fondrière voisine
fait craquer les os de la tête,
lui déchire la poitrine.

. . . De ses habits tout est couvert
et la tête de son chapeau.
Et tout est si bien arrangé
que de loin paraît endormie.

[. . . with its furious tooth the Beast
in a nearby hole
broke the bones of her head,
and tore open her chest.
. . . Her clothes covered everything
and her hat, her head.
And everything was arranged so well
that from afar, she appeared to be asleep.]

The lament suggests a reason for this frightful trespass: in a mystical fervor, the girl apparently begged for a rapid death, in order to return as quickly as possible to "Jésus son unique bien" [Jesus, her sole good]:

Ah! sans tarder davantage,
Jésus, soyez mon meilleur sort!
Que mon corps, par un naufrage,
Rende mon âme au divin port![9]

[Ah! without waiting any longer,
Jesus, be my chosen destiny!
May my shipwrecked body
Carry my soul to a divine port!]

The author of these verses seems to suppose that this prayer was granted that same day. And it was the Beast that liberated this soul. The bishop of Mende, who played such a determining role in the making of this legend and in the creation of its meaning, had every reason to be satisfied, for according to these quatrains one could easily believe that God himself had sent the animal. But before examining the meanings of this *fait-divers*, let us examine the narrative instrumentalization put into play by the principal actors in this drama.

A Happy Version of Gabrielle's Story

There exists, in fact, a happy version of Gabrielle Pélissier's story. The tale of *La Petite Fille épargnée par les louveteaux* [The Little Girl Spared by the Wolf Cubs], a short narrative in Latin verse, composed in the first quarter of the eleventh century by Egbert de Liège, begins:

Ce que je rapporte, les paysans savent le dire avec moi,
Et il faut moins s'étonner que le croire fermement vrai.
Quelqu'un tint une petite fille sur les fonts baptismaux
Et lui donna une robe tissé de laine rouge.
Ce baptême eut lieu à la Pentecôte.
Au lever du soleil, l'enfant, âgée de cinq ans,
Marche et vagabonde, sans se soucier d'elle-même et du danger.
Un loup s'en saisit, gagna la forêt sauvage et profonde,
L'apporta comme gibier à ses petits et la leur laissa à manger.
Ils se précipitèrent sur elle, mais, ne parvenant pas à la mettre en
    pièces,
Se mirent à lui caresser la tête, loin de toute sauvagerie.
"Je vous défends, souris," dit la jeune enfant, "de déchirer cette
    robe
Que m'a donnée parrain à mon baptême!"
Dieu, qui est leur auteur, apaise les esprits sauvages.[10]

[What I recount, the peasants can recite with me,
And you must not be surprised, but firmly believe it to be true.
Someone held a young girl over the baptismal fonts
And gave her a dress made from red wool.
This baptism took place at Pentecost.
At sunrise, the child, five years old,
Walked and wandered without worrying about herself or the
    danger awaiting her.
A wolf seized her, ran to the forest, wild and deep,
And brought her, as it would freshly killed game, to its cubs and
    left her for them to eat.
They pounced upon her, but, not being able to tear her apart,
Began to caress her head, far from any savagery.
"I forbid you, little ones," said the young child, "to rip the dress
That my godfather gave me for my baptism!"
God, their almighty master, appeased the savage souls.]

A number of folklorists, notably Paul Delarue, have recognized that there is no genetic link between this story and *Little Red Riding Hood*, of which Perrault offers the oldest version known.[11] Indeed, it is incontestable that several elements of Perrault's tale are absent from Egbert de Liège's narrative: the sending of the little girl to her grandmother's house; the different paths taken by the heroine and the wolf; the scene at the grandmother's house; the child's death. The two narratives presented here have in common, however, the one scene crucial to the fairy tale: the wolf's attempt to eat a young girl dressed in red. It is true that "the marvelous element of the medieval tale *Little Red Riding Hood* (by Egbert de Liège) is still linked to the supernatural of Christian legends."[12] In fact, several elements inscribe this narrative within a strictly religious perspective. The baptism, first of all. We know that the practice of baptizing children developed during the Carolingian period and that godmothers and godfathers became important figures for the church, which wanted to inculcate children as much as possible with a basic religious education. The baptismal gift is an old practice and appears in this period more often in the form of jewelry, an animal or, as in this case, a pretty piece of clothing, than in the form of a sum of money. As for Pentecost, together with Easter, it was the usual holy day chosen for this ceremony. Then, according to Ebgert de Liège, the child escaped from the wolf cubs thanks to divine intervention. Finally, the author insists upon presenting this story as something that really happened; he does not cite the peasants as his source, but he considers their testimony as a corroboration of his own. For him, this story should not evoke a fable, but the recounting of a true story, a dazzling testimony to divine power.

The common color of the dress and the bonnet of the two young girls is not sufficient to form a genetic link between Egbert de Liège and Perrault. However, this eleventh-century narrative indeed belongs to the same sphere as the fairy tale. The little girl possesses a gift, in the form of a red baptismal dress, and before being able to define its purpose, she becomes acquainted with its function: the dress is a salvational device against the wolves. But the contextual problematics that guide this work are less a matter of a textual archeology that would have us reconstitute the history of each story, than one of reception. Indeed, the perception of works of art within a culture changes with time. The interest of this eleventh-century text, then, lies not so much in its hypothetical precedence to Perrault's tale. In fact, the curiosity that it creates comes quite clearly more from the fact that someone (a clergyman? a publisher?) knew Egbert de Liège's story, appropriated it for himself, and distributed it while reconstructing it in order better to mask what immediately appeared as a crime: the murder of Gabrielle Pélissier. Thus, the anonymous author of these 1765 narratives from Lozère decided not to abandon the work of the scholar de Liège to the whims of time and of reception, but preferred instead to create a new context for the reception of this collection of exempla. The issue is not so much to know what the use of this story was at the beginning of the eleventh century. Once we note that this story, borrowed from peasants, refers to the genre of cautionary tales aimed at warning children about external dangers, we have come to a perfectly positivist conclusion. And once we add that the little girl, far from dying for her imprudence, is saved, we come to a literary historian's conclusion, which is certainly not negligible. But we are able to reconstruct the damage done to the text if we examine the sociohistorical context that authorized such a transformation; that is, a use of the tale that is tantamount to textual murder. In the eleventh century, the little girl is saved by the power of her red dress, certainly, but most of all by means of an Egbert de Liège, preoccupied with rendering the story as orthodox as possible, through divine intervention.

A few centuries later, in Gévaudan, the same powers that de Liège's little girl enjoyed were imputed to Gabrielle Pélissier. A communicant— rather old to begin with—instructed to pray by her father, who "comforts" her before leaving her alone with the herd, Gabrielle is dressed in magical attire that paralyzes the ravenous wolf. But her adventure ends badly. The narrators charged with reconstructing the story shortly after the murder fully intended to demonstrate that she was from the outset discredited in the eyes of God. Gabrielle, pray as she might, could do nothing about the punishment that the Beast of the Apocalypse was given to inflict upon her. The letters and the lament, conveyors of the meanings given to the population of Gévaudan, go against the ambiguous distinction between magic and divine power that is innocently set forth in the eleventh-century narrative. Thus, let us risk this hypothesis: Gabrielle was, to be sure, murdered. Not by a "Beast," nor by a wolf, but probably by her father, after being sexually assaulted. Beyond the suspicions that their abundance of meanings invoke, the contradictory testimonies about the circumstances of the death, associated with the fright- ening descriptions of a dismembered and then recomposed body, attest to the circulation of an oral tale, close to the eleventh-century tale, or even more probably to a learned exploitation of de Liège's tale. What is important here is not the question of narrative permanence but rather the use of the story to highlight demonstrative and persuasive techniques that lead to one piece of evidence: a consecrated dress, in eighteenth-century, heretical Gévaudan could no longer save anyone, especially a young girl raped and killed by her father, a rich peasant from Margeride. Egbert de Liège's story, when inscribed in a new context, became an unhoped-for resource for the authorities, accomplices to the crime in their justification of it. The staging of the tale permitted the rewriting of truth. Effacing the murder with the tale opened the way for further violence: in effect, historians counted among the "Beast's" victims many unexplained incidents. And now we must consider the matter of the separation of genres: in this case, where is the fairy tale situated? Where does the detective novel begin?

The Other Story of the Beast, or On the Good Use of Narrative: Historical Testimonies in Occasional Works

Did the publishing and/or religious authorities who rewrote the story of Gabrielle consider the risks of their argumentations? Because it was said that the sacrament of communion had lost its magical powers, couldn't some credit thus be accorded to Protestant discourse? For if Gabrielle's story can be read in a manner other than that of de Liège's little girl, this is because Gabrielle lived in a Gévaudan manipulated by a religious authority of the cleverest sort: its bishop, Mgr. de Choiseul-Beaupré. He was supported by village priests but also by the royal court, whose authority took the form of sending hunters from the north—the court—to deliver the land. Everyone, in their way, participated in the legend and its creation.

The priest of Lorcières's telling, for example, was one of the principal sources of Parisian and Gévaudanian occasional writings. His belief in the version that portrayed an extraordinary Beast, which was deliberately trans- mitted through writing in order to distribute it better, as well as his knowledge of the political effects of the *fait-divers*, contributed to a seemingly unusual influence of a country priest on a publisher. In fact, the abbot Ollier, priest of Lorcières in Haute Auvergne, was one of the first to emphasize the sexual preferences of the Beast: "Ainsi un loup n'a pas cet instinct de couper si bien les têtes des personnes surtout celles du sexe de préférence" [A wolf does not instinctively decapitate so cleanly its victims, especially those of the preferred sex]. The priest's story gives an impression of authenticity, or at least of undeniable sincerity. With his testimony, the legend acquires a new strength. It is no longer simply the reflection of an oral tradition expressing the imagination of the peasantry; it is now the result of a learned, written analysis. This was clear to everyone, at least to the printers who happily took hold of the incongruous details the abbot provided. For example, the length of the monster's footprints, sixteen centimeters, is noted in the margin of their chapbooks in the form of a vertical line, as if the measurement of the Beast's paw were the same as that of the pamplet. The "historical" testimony thus delivers its hidden function: by incarnating the monster and its own diabolical metamorphoses, the pamphlet participates in magical practices, and as such produces new narrative performances, under other forms and for other audiences.

The same is true for the legend's origin. The hunters, the principal ac- tors, were for the most part noblemen and soldiers from outside the province. Through their inability to kill the beast and the supernatural explanations they gave for their failure, they contributed to the creation of a fictional story. Consider the testimony of the captain of the Dragoons, Duhamel, who was the first hunter sent to help Gévaudan in the beginning of the summer of 1764. For Duhamel, the Beast of Gévaudan was quite an uncommon animal: "Il a les pattes aussi fortes que celles d'un ours, avec six griffes à chacune de la longueur d'un doigt" [It has paws as strong as those of a bear, with six claws a paw, each claw the length of a finger], he wrote to the quartermaster at Auvergne in January 1765. He adds that "il a la gueule extraordinairement large, le poitrail aussi long que celui d'un léopard, la queue grosse comme le bras" [it has an extremely wide muzzle, a chest as long as a leopard's, a tail as thick as an arm]. And he concludes: "Je crois que vous penserez comme moi que cet animal est un monstre dont le père est un lion; reste à savoir quelle est la mère" [I believe that you will think, as I, that this animal is a monster whose father was a lion—we can only speculate as to its mother]. Duhamel's sincerity, his real desire to kill the Beast, attested to by numerous documents, and his inability to do so over a relatively long period of time (he hunted the Beast from July 1764 to April 1765) reinforces the legend of an extraordinary animal, invulnerable and endowed with a certain evilness. Duhamel was the first to offer the hypothesis that the animal was the product of cross-breeding between a wild but exotic animal, such as a lion, and another wild animal more common to the area. This hypothesis met with striking success at the time and in the long run, for it is still advanced today.

Early on, Parisian publishers took charge of the affair first by distributing handbills, then occasional writings. The wolf was described as a supernatural and malevolent beast, which explains its defeat by a mythical hunter, the peasant Chastel. But illustrations best demonstrate the didactic strategy that publishers enacted. In 1764, F.-G. Deschamps, a bookseller on Rue Saint-Jacques in Paris, offered for sale an occasional work entitled "Figure / de la bête farouche / et extraordinaire, qui dévore les filles / dans la province de Gévaudan" [The Figure of the Ferocious and Extraordinary Beast That Devours Young Girls in the Province of Gévaudan]. This booklet represents the Beast in a pen-and-ink drawing taken from a more elaborate, color engraving published by Mondhare, another bookstore on Rue Saint-Jacques. The "ferocious beast" drawn for F.-G. Deschamps holds a little girl barely bigger than a doll in its paws (figure 11.2). This representation of the massacre, linked to the title emphasizing female victims, cannot help but strike the reader, and all the more so if he knows the tale *Little Red Riding Hood*. But the bookseller went further: in a new edition of the occasional work, in 1769, he offered his Parisian public a simple representation of the "beast," whereas to Languedoc he sent a different version, which described with iconic precision the victim, her age, and her sex. This edition was distributed in the French provinces for several years.

In the meantime, Gévaudanian publishers circulated the Deschamps illustration of the little girl being devoured to their public; in addition, they sold poor imitations of the Parisian drawing. For example, the scene depicting the devouring drawn and colored for (and by?) Abraham Fontanel, in Mende, is particularly eloquent: a large wolf, bent over a naked little girl, is eating her arm while tearing with its paws at her ostensibly bloody stomach (figure 11.3). The configuration of this image is much too close to Clouzier's vignette, chosen by Perrault to illustrate *Little Red Riding Hood* in his 1695 manuscript,

FIGURE 11.2 From *Figure de la Bête farouche et extraordinaire, qui dévore les filles dans la province de Gévaudan* (Paris: F.-G. Deschamps, 1764). The Beast with a child in its paws.

FIGURE 11.3 Engraving by Abraham Fontanel. Mende, second half of eighteenth century. Beast devouring a little girl.

and again his 1697 edition of the *Contes,* to be a coincidence. From the *fait-divers* of the Beast of Gévaudan, only the slaughter of young shepherd girls was retained. Under the pen of the illustrator of Mende, the Beast's pose is identical to that of the wolf in *Little Red Riding Hood.* No reader from Gévaudan could any longer ignore the fact that the devouring of a young girl was the equivalent of rape. The Mendian illustrator was attempting to translate the occasional work chosen by the Parisian publisher for his provincial readership: for, in these parts, reading French was an arduous task, and even if the text had been translated into Provençal it would not have made any difference. The illustration distributed in Mende thus attempted to relay the meaning of this affair, such as it was suggested by Paris.

F.-G. Deschamps's plan emerged even more clearly when he learned in August 1766 that at Sarlat, in Périgord, Gévaudan-like murders had been committed. The Rue Saint-Jacques bookseller then distributed another occasional work relating the circumstances of these killings, to which he attached, perhaps for convenience, the illustration depicting the Beast of Gévaudan. But he removed the representation of the Beast's victim. F.-G. Deschamps explained it in this way: "Cet animal faisait le contraste de la

Bête du Gévaudan, car celle-ci n'en voulait qu'aux hommes, au lieu que celle du Gévaudan attaquait les femmes de préférence" [This animal contrasted with the Beast of Gévaudan, because the former attacked only men, while the latter attacked primarily women].

The Bishop of Mende's Pastoral Letter

All of these stories are indebted to one generic text: the Bishop of Mende's pastoral letter. Some extracts:

> C'est parce que vous avez offensé Dieu que vous voyez aujourd'hui accomplir en vous à la lettre et dans presque toutes leurs circonstances les menaces que Dieu faisait autrefois par la bouche de Moïse contre les prévaricateurs de sa loi: "J'armerai contre eux, leur disait-il, les dents des bêtes farouches" (Deutéronome 32:24). "J'enverrai contre vous les bêtes sauvages qui vous dévoreront, vous et vos troupeaux, qui vous réduiront à un petit nombre et qui de vos chemins feront un désert" (Leviticus 26:22): à cause que la crainte que vous aurez de ces bêtes vous empêchera de sortir pour vacquer à vos affaires. "Ils m'ont oublié," dit-il encore, "et moi je serai pour eux comme une lionne; je les attendrai comme un léopard sur le chemin de l'Assyrie; je viendrai à eux comme une ourse à qui on a ravi son petit; je leur ouvrirai les entrailles, et leur foie sera mis à découvert, je les dévorerai comme un lion et la bête farouche les déchirera." Ces textes de la sainte-Écriture que nous choisissons parmi bien d'autres suffisent pour convaincre que dans tous les temps Dieu a menacé de punir les péchés des hommes par des supplices semblables à celui dont vous éprouvez aujourd'hui toute la rigeur. Ne demandez donc plus d'où est venue la Bête féroce, qui fait tant de ravages parmi nous; ne vous mettez point en peine de savoir comment elle a pu pénétrer jusqu'à nous. C'est le Seigneur qui l'a tirée de sa colère; c'est le Seigneur irrité qui l'a lâchée contre vous; c'est le Seigneur qui dirige sa course rapide vers les lieux où elle doit exécuter les arrêts de mort que sa justice a prononcée. Tel est l'ordre immuable de cette justice éternelle, que l'homme ne puisse se révolter contre son Créateur, sans soulever contre lui toutes les créatures; sa révolte lui a fait perdre l'empire absolu qu'il lui avait donné sur tous les animaux et cette même révolte a donné une espèce de domination et de supériorité sur l'homme, puisque celui-ce est souvent livré à leur fureur en punition de ses péchés.

Pères et mères, qui avez la douleur de voir vos enfants égorgés par ce monstre que Dieu a armé contre leur vie, n'avez-vous pas lieu de craindre d'avoir mérité par vous dérèglements, que Dieu les frappe d'un fléau si terrible? Souffrez que nous vous demandions un compte de la manière dont vous les élevez; quelle négligence à les instruire des principes de la religion et des devoirs du christianisme, quel soin prenez-vous de leur éducation? Au lieu de leur apprendre de bonne heure et dès leurs plus tendres années à craindre Dieu et à s'absentir de tout péché, [. . .] ne leur inspirez-vous pas des sentiments tout opposés, d'ambition, d'orgueil, de mépris pour les pauvres, de dureté pour les misérables? On vous voit bien moins occupés de leur salut que de leur fortune et de leur avancement, pour lequel tout vous paraît légitime, et ces passions naissantes que vous auriez dû arrêter et étouffer par des corrections salutaires, vous prenez soin au contraire de les nourrir et d'en faire éclore le germe; heureux encore si vous n'étiez pas les premiers à les pervertir et à les corrompre par la contagion de vos mauvais exemples! Après cela, faut-il être surpris que Dieu punisse l'amour déréglé que vous avez pour eux par tant de sujets d'afflictions et de douleur qu'ils vous préparent dans la suite de votre vie? Quelle dissolution et quel dérèglement dans la jeunesse de nos jours! La malice et la corruption se manifestent dans les enfants avant qu'ils aient atteint l'âge qui peut les en faire soupçonner. Ce sexe dont le principal ornement fut toujours la pudeur et la modestie, semble n'en plus connaître aujourd'hui; il cherche à se donner en spectacle, en étalant toute sa mondanité et il se fait gloire de ce qui devrait le faire rougir. On le vit s'occuper à tendre des pièges à l'innocence, à usurper un encens sacrilège et à s'attirer jusques dans nos temples des adorations qui ne sont dues qu'à la Divinité. Une chair idolâtre et criminelle qui sert d'instrument au démon pour séduire et perdre les âmes, ne mérite-t-elle pas d'être livrée aux dents meurtrières des Bêtes féroces qui la déchirent et la mettent en pièces? Ce n'est pas que nous regardions comme coupables toutes les personnes qui ont eu le malheur de périr de la sorte; Dieu peut avoir permis ces tristes événements pour des raisons qui regardent leur salut et leur bonheur éternel; mais cela n'empêche pas que Dieu leur a fait subir la peine due aux péchés de leurs parents: "Je suis," nous dit-il, "le Dieu fort et jaloux qui venge l'iniquité des pères sur les enfants jusqu'à la troisième et quatrième génération" (Exodus 20:5).[13]

[Because you have offended God, you see before you the literal and nearly complete realization of the threats He made through Moses to the prevaricators of His law: "And I will send," he said, "the teeth of ferocious beasts against them" (Deuteronomy 32:24). "I will send wild beasts among you, which shall rob you of your children, and destroy your cattle, and make you few in number; and your high ways shall be desolate" (Leviticus 26:22): because of the fear you have for these beasts, you will not leave your houses to see to your affairs. They have forgotten me, He said: "Therefore I will be unto them as a lion: as a leopard by the way will I observe them: I will meet them as a bear that is bereaved of her whelps, and will rend the caul of their heart, and there will I devour them like a lion: the wild beast shall tear them" (Hosea 13:7–8). These passages from the Holy Scriptures that we have chosen among many others are enough to convince us that since time immemorial, God has threatened to punish the sins of man with torture much like what you are suffering so harshly today. Ask no more whence comes the ferocious Beast that destroys so; do not bother to wonder how it got here. The Lord took it from the treasury of His anger; the Lord, angry and upset, turned it loose upon you; the Lord leads its rapid flight toward the places where it must execute the death warrants that His justice has announced. Such is the immutable order of this eternal justice, that man cannot rise up against his Creator without raising up against himself all other creatures; his revolt made him lose the absolute power that God had given him over all other animals and this same revolt gave a sort of domination and superiority over man to the beast, since man is the victim of its fury as punishment for his sins.

Fathers and mothers who are pained to see your children's throats cut by this monster that God has armed against them, are you not right to fear that you deserved the terrible wrath that God has wrought in response to your dissoluteness? Permit us to ask questions about how you raise your children. How is it that you neglect their religious education and their Christian duties? How do you care for their education? Rather than teaching them early on, in their most tender years, to fear God and to abstain from all sins, [. . .] do you not impart to them quite opposite feelings, of ambition, of pride, of disgust for the poor, of harshness for the unfortunate? You are less interested in their salvation than in their material wealth and social advancement, which seems to you completely legitimate, and in feeding embryonic passions that you should have stopped and smothered with beneficial corrections, you make the seed burst open; if only you were not the first to pervert and corrupt by the contagion of your bad examples! After all this, should you be surprised that God punishes the negligent love that you have for your children with as many afflictions and as much pain as awaits you in the hereafter? What dissolution and what neglect in today's children! Malice and corruption shows itself in these children before they reach the age where we should harbor suspicion. Members of the sex of which modesty and reserve were always the principal ornaments seem no longer to be familiar with these; they seek to put themselves on display, make a spectacle of their worldliness, and take pride in things that should instead make them blush. They spend their time laying traps for the innocent, usurping sacrilegious flattery and inspiring adoration that is due only to the Divine. This idolatrous and criminal flesh which serves only as a demonic instrument for seducing and condemning souls, should it not be given unto the murderous teeth of ferocious Beasts to tear it to pieces? It is not that we consider all persons who have died this way guilty; God may have permitted these sad events for reasons concerning their salvation and eternal happiness; but this does not prevent God from making them endure a punishment for their parents' sins: "For I the Lord thy God," He told us, "am a jealous God, visiting the iniquity of the fathers upon the children unto the third and fourth generation of them that hate me." (Exodus 20:5)]

In commenting on this text, let us remark first on the metaphoric precociousness of the Beast's description. The bishop of Mende is one of the very first to have contributed to the emergence of the legend. The testimonies of the abbots and hunters undoubtedly comforted him in his interpretation of the killings, but the choice of images and scriptural sources was plainly his, and it was this choice that inspired publishers, storytellers, historians, and novelists from that moment to the present. The legend's creator was Mgr. de Choiseul-Beaupré. He precedes, unintentionally perhaps, what he denounces later in his text as "ces contes fabuleux dont le peuple grossier aime à se repaître" [these fantastic tales common people love to feed on].

If a long fictive tradition is indebted to the bishop of Mende's pastoral letter, it is largely due to the narrative construction of the text. The pastoral letter is laid out like an epistle, in imitation of those of Saint Paul. This influence is reflected in the text's style as well as in its rhetoric: for example, Mgr. de Choiseul-Beaupré owes his short question-and-answer argumentation and his argumentative development by rhetorical accumulation to scholastic debate and the cynical/stoic "diatribe." This pastoral letter is occasional writing, a topical response to a real, concrete situation, and not a theological treatise. The model of Saint Paul's Epistles is so obvious that the country priest, charged with reading the episcopal text, could make no mistake: he would attribute the authority of an apostle to Mgr. de Choiseul-Beaupré.

But the bishop's sermon was far from the apostolic kerygma of a crucified and resurrected Christ. Conversion of the Gévaudanian pagans, eschatological teachings, and practical exhortations owe much less to the Gospels than to Jewish and early Christian apocalyptic traditions, such as the eschatological discourses in the synoptics—Matthew's, for example. This text is inspired by biblical verses, or rather pieces of verses, often joined end to end, one leading to the other in an analogical movement. Examining the bishop's biblical citations more closely, we find that the original Latin is given in the notes to the first edition of the pastoral letter, probably meant for clergy. The citations are for the most part extracts from the Pentateuch: Deuteronomy, Leviticus, and Exodus. They refer to the same situation and the same religious story. Moses, who received the revelation of the unspeakable name of Yahweh at Sinai, led back the Israelites, liberated from servitude in Egypt; in a stirring theophany, God joined with the people and told them His laws; but the pact, barely made, was broken by those who worshipped the golden calf; God gave His pardon and renewed the Covenant; a series of orders relegated the sect to the desert. This story is retold countless times in the first five books of the Bible. The people fall incessantly into error, worshiping pagan gods, returning to ancient religions or to those of their neighbors in Assyria. The Pentateuch depicts this return to sin that causes God's wrath and His punishment as the devouring of infidels by ferocious beasts.

The story that the bishop of Mende remembered was, then, this one: Israel's refusal of God's Covenant, which is the most intolerable sin. The punishment is constantly associated with calls to return to the conditions of faithfulness, conditions set down by God himself. God gave His law to the chosen people. The laws instruct the people, regulate their conduct as prescribed by divine will and, now in the Covenant, prepare the fulfillment of His promises. The themes of promise, of election, of alliance, and of law are the guiding principles of the Pentateuch, and in a general way, of the entire Old Testament. But, in the construction of the books, they could not be understood in their totality unless they were identified as the ultimate goodness of God the Creator and were absolutely opposed to the sinful ways of mankind. Thus, repeated over and again, the motif of the ferocious beast became the symptom of the magnitude of faithlessness.

At this stage of the analysis, two facts command the reader's attention. First, it is improbable that Mgr. de Choiseul-Beaupré wrote this text himself;

he probably called upon a theologian of the episcopal court to elaborate his pastoral letter according to the customary rules of apocalyptic writings. To argue about the theme of the Beast of the Apocalypse, he needed an erudite and able scholar of biblical texts, particularly of the Old Testament. But he also needed to know which texts were read in Gévaudanian families with as much interest as the Gospels. It follows that even if Mgr. de Choiseul-Beaupré may not have been the editor of the pastoral letter, he is nonetheless its inspirer. For only the bishop of Mende could capitalize upon a *fait-divers* to condemn the past heresies of the Gévaudanians, to call them back to the fold, to evoke the hypothetical pardon of their greatest of sins: those of their fathers, those of the Camisards, that went back to the beginning of the century.[14] Recall his last biblical quote: " 'For I the Lord thy God,' " he told us, " 'am a jealous God, visiting the iniquity of the fathers upon the children unto the third and fourth generation of them that hate me.' " In 1764, or sixty years after the Cévenol incidents, the third and fourth generations are indeed targeted.

Here indeed is an odd prelate: the only biblical references that he gives are from the Old Testament. And even if he goes as far as copying certain formulas in a pastoral letter that takes as its model Saint Paul's Epistles, the reminder of Christ's pardon is nowhere in his argument. We should not, after all, be given reason to accuse Mgr. Choiseul-Beaupré or his theologian of Huguenot sympathies! It seems instead that the bishop wanted to attack the Protestants on their home territory: in the references to the "Prophets of the Desert" sermons that are abundantly taken from the Old Testament. Commentaries on the Apocalypse were found many times in the writings of religious "fanatics," who applied them to events of their own times. For the Camisards, the Catholic Church was the "Beast" or the "Great Babylon," and the Cévenols the chosen ones. The Camisards' prophetic discourse was fed by all the allusions in the Old Testament to the struggle between Israel and its enemies, the Syrians, the Philistines, the Assyrians, and the Madianites. In reality, the comparison to the chosen people was absolute for the rebels. For them, the Cévennes were the new Israel. Philippe Joutard has shown, in fact, that there was a continuity between the "Church of the Desert" phase and the other phases of the Protestant resistance.[15] Both periods shared the same idea of the sinner who had strayed from God (Camisard sermons parallel here a much older current of the Calvinist Reform), the same call to repent and to leave Babylon, the same certainty of salvation for the common people. The New Israel, the Camisard people, completely trusted prophecies that were, for them, the proof of God's solicitude, and that would give a structure to their entire organization. In addition, the Cévenol prophetic discourse was an incitement to armed resistance.

The bishop of Mende's pastoral letter quite consciously revives the same sources used by the Camisards. It uses the same scriptural exegesis. Even more cleverly, it employs the cliché used to identify the Camisards: "ferocious beasts," a formula made fashionable by Voltaire and by the Parisian circles that dared pit Catholics against Camisards. This was intolerable for the bishop of Mende. One year after Voltaire's last writings, current events gave him the occasion to respond, nearly word for word, using a clever rhetorical device: the reversibility of the narrative relationship. The Beast of Gévaudan is indeed the Beast of the Apocalypse, but it was awakened by the Cévenols for the most serious sin of infidelity: apostasy.

Demonization of the Beast grew rapidly, as the symbols and metaphors used to describe it show perfectly well. For example, the abbott Ollier of Lorcières, in his correspondence dated January 1766, calls forth typical demonic attributes to depict it: "L'animal féroce et vorace a un corps allongé, et par conséquent deux fois plus long qu'un loup ordinaire et beaucoup plus haut [. . .] avec des dents si tranchantes qu'elles séparent en peu de temps la tête d'une personne, en un mot coupantes comme des rasoirs [. . .], le poitrail beaucoup plus large quasi comme celui d'un cheval [. . .] avec une raie noire tout au long du dos" [The ferocious and voracious animal has a long body, twice as long as a normal wolf and much taller [. . .], with teeth so sharp that they decapitate its victims very quickly; in a word, they are razor-sharp [. . .], its chest, too is wide, very much like that of a horse [. . .] with a black stripe down its back]. Michel Pastoureau has demonstrated the significance of this black stripe:

> Les animaux (dans le *Roman de Renart*) au pelage rayé ou tacheté se rangent du côté des animaux à pelage roux et constituent le clan des menteurs, des voleurs, des lubriques ou des cupides. Pour la société animale comme pour celle des hommes, être roux, rayé ou tacheté est à peu près équivalent. Cette méfiance, cette peur même des animaux tachetés ou rayés a laissé des traces de longue durée dans l'imaginaire occidental. Au XVIIIè siècle, la fameuse bête du Gévaudan, qui, en 1764–1767, sema la terreur aux confins de l'Auvergne et du Vivarais, est décrite par tous ceux qui l'ont vue, ou cru voir, comme un loup gigantesque ayant le dos zébré de larges rayures. Créature diabolique, cette "bête" du Gévaudan ne pouvait pas ne pas être rayée. A sa suite, fut également rayée chacune des autres "bêtes du Gévaudan" qui, pendant plusieurs décennies, parfois jusqu'en plein milieu du XIXè siècle, troublèrent les esprits et les campagnes de France.[16]

> [Animals (in the *Roman de Renart*) with striped or spotted fur are associated with red-pelted animals, and are considered liars, thieves, lecherous, or greedy. For animals, as for people, to be red-haired, striped or spotted is more or less the same. This distrust,

this fear of spotted or striped animals is strong in the Western imagination. In the eighteenth century, the infamous Beast of Gévaudan, which spread terror from Auvergne to Vivarais between 1764 and 1767, was described by all who saw it, or thought they saw it, as a giant wolf with a back striped like a zebra. A demonic creature, this "beast" of Gévaudan *had* to be striped. As a result, every other "beast of Gévaudan" that cropped up in the French countryside over the course of many decades until the middle of the nineteenth century, was striped as well.]

This is how the Beast of Gévaudan became part of Satan's bestiary: striped, as the abbott Ollier saw it, or spotted like a leopard, as the bishop considered it.

The pastoral letter had another effect over time: it created a Camisard legend in which the Cévenol insurgent is romanticized because he revolts against the society of his time. He is even credited with the repudiation of his church officials, which before had been proof of his blameworthy pride. In the nineteenth century, the Camisards were considered first of all people who had conserved the purity of their origins. At the beginning of the eighteenth century, they rekindled beliefs dating from the beginning of humanity, those of biblical heroes; for this same reason, the Cévenols were accused of being wild and primitive. Michelet writes: "Ces populations qu'on transforma si cruellement étaient des tribus pastorales, de moeurs très pures, d'un caractère fort doux dans leur sauvagerie" [These people, so cruelly transformed, were from pastoral tribes with very pure morals, and a pleasant character in spite of their savagery]. The legend of the Beast of Gévaudan is part of a cycle of legends in which the roles of wolves and lambs, Catholics and Hugeunots are easily interchanged. And the architect of this role reversibility was the bishop of Mende, Mgr. de Choiseul-Beaupré.

Rapes in Gévaudan

"What dissolution and what neglect in today's children!" exclaims the bishop of Mende. And he goes to great lengths to unleash his wrath upon women for their impurity, worldliness, sexual provocation, and seduction. They are supposedly chosen more frequently by the Beast to be its most privileged victims; for Mgr. de Choiseul-Beaupré, women are thus the guilty party of choice. And among them is Gabrielle Pélissier, whose coming murder is legitimized, it is now clear, by episcopal texts.

First, what do the statistics show about these murders of women? Around 66 percent of the victims were women in 1764, 58 percent in 1765, 42 percent in 1766, and 68 percent in 1767. The fact that they comprised the majority of the victims is certainly significant, but of what? In any case, it is not such an overwhelming majority as the legend would have us believe.

Elisabeth Claverie and Pierre Lamaison have focused on several familial functions that remind us of a number of facts—first of all, that in a region where female shepherds occupied an important place in domestic economies, we should not find it unusual that they formed the majority of victims.[17] And what function do women have in the assignment of inheritances? Claverie and Lamaison further show that from the end of the seventeenth century onward, children who did not inherit "a little something" received a dowry "by way of legitimation" that permitted them to marry. Boys were given dowries much less frequently than their sisters; other than a few pieces of furniture, some farm implements, and some dresses, one in five girls might receive a few head of cattle or sheep, a cow, perhaps an ox, and very rarely, a horse or a mare. The difference between boys' and girls' dowries shows that these gifts made "by way of legitimation," which were supposed to be equal for all children in a family, remained at the discretion of the parents.

Young, well-to-do girls, watching over their dowries of sheep or cows would thus be in the company of other shepherd girls in fields separated from the distant villages by woods. Since the seventeenth century, the practice of collective shepherding was standard in Gévaudan; and it was while girls were tending to the animals in the fields that the rapes took place. From a very early age, these girls were in charge of the family animals—cows, sheep, or pigs—or they were hired out to other families to do the same work. In the summer months that went from May to October, they would leave the village with their animals early in the morning and stay out until late in the evening. Young female shepherds, no matter what their social condition, were alone in the fields. This childhood experience, which we can compare to an initiation, was one of solitude and fear, but also one that involved learning about ownership, boundary marking, and the husbandry and care of animals. This job has throughout history always consisted of watching over the animals so they do not stray or cross into another field to eat someone else's grass or crops; the slightest neglect was severely punished. To pass the time, girls would try to keep one another company when they had adjacent herds; and when they were alone, they would spin wool, make lace, or read their prayer books. This fear felt in childhood seems to have left its mark on Haut Gévaudan, for throughout the whole process, more than one adult admitted to not wanting to walk through the woods alone, or wander far from the village. A secret fear of the neighboring woods is found in nearly all peasant narratives.

The young shepherd girls would play games with one another when they could: "Quelquefois, en gardant les bêtes, les enfants se dénudent en badinant" [Sometimes, the children watching over the animals would run around naked].[18] This "running around" is certainly not incongruous with the reputation hired shepherd girls had. But these "games" were much different from the violence that threatened them. These children were often alone, very far from the village. A neighboring shepherd, in most cases a young single man, would surprise one of the girls, rape her, and threaten her with retaliation if she told. The shepherd girl would go home, terrorized, and say nothing to her employers or her parents for fear of being beaten, but she would go straight to the confessional box. Her mother or mistress would notice that something was wrong from the blood on her shirt and, as the case might be, would keep quiet or try to work out an arrangement.

Mgr. de Choiseul-Beaupré was thus part of this spectrum of the denial of violence. In accusing the girls of sexual provocation, he would order them, in front of his parishioners, to admit to failing in their responsibilities. Their admission, on the contrary, would touch off a chain of controlled reactions: rejection, then forgiveness, which permitted the family, the community, and the religious congregation to express all of the emotional variations of their moral stance. Furthermore, the denial of responsibility was interpreted as an open challenge to be quashed. But one element posed a problem for the bishop of Mende: the raped shepherd girls were unmarried and from all social classes. When the victims, as a group, refused to admit to any guilt, they brought the issue into the ethical realm of familial groups, who were eager to seek financial damages. The girls thus singled out and exploited the weaknesses of and breeches in the social and religious ideologies of their time. Fortunately for Mgr. de Choiseul-Beaupré and to the benefit of his authority, the Beast materialized: now he was able to regulate both the rewards and the punishments advocated by church officials.

Children's Literature: Between Rewriting and Illustration

Little Red Riding Hood, who in oral versions from Nivernais, Haute-Loire, and Cévennes, does not know whether she should choose "entre le chemin des épingles et celui des aiguilles" [the path of pins or the path of needles],[19] in training for her feminine role (as a seamstress? as a peddler of goods?), is responsible for the disclosure of sexual secrets. She is a child dressed in red, blood red, devoured by a Beast who is itself finally killed by a peasant who is in turn transformed into a mythical savior by religious and publishing authorities. All of these editorial combinations of images are well in step with the ambivalence with which the Gévaudanians regarded the Virgin Mary. It is a particularly rich example of appropriations: religious propaganda found a breeding ground in folklore, the *fait-divers* fed it, and publishers capitalized on the dense and unsettled network of multiple meanings to better justify (or denounce?) the Gévaudanian mentality. It is impossible not to think of the effigies of the Virgin that the Gévaudanians would attack, yelling, "Shopkeeper!" or of Huguenot attacks on the Virgin Mary, whom the Cévennes ridiculed with the nickname "The Redhead."

In this context, publishers used the image of the wolf better to express the meaning of *Little Red Riding Hood*. Thus, in nineteenth-century England, *Little Red Riding Hood* was unexpectedly rewritten under the title *The Wolf King; or Little Red Riding Hood*, the first in a collection of stories called *Tales of Terror* by M. G. Lewis, a successful author of crime novels. This text, published for the first time in 1801, reconstitutes the tale in verse form, in what is its most pessimistic version. It was reprinted in 1808, accompanied by a horrific yet detailed and anatomically correct engraving representing the wolf's struggle with and disembowelment of the grandmother. This engraving, which is quite representative of Lewis's literary aims, was part of a well-known narrative tradition that recounted the necessary eating of the grandmother, which contemporary oral versions routinely include. But we should note that England, like the Protestant Cévennes, permitted this theme to flourish, even in Catholic-dominated regions.

Yvonne Verdier has analyzed the versions in which the grandmother is eaten by her granddaughter, Little Red Riding Hood: "A quelle sauce la grand-mère est-elle donc mangée? Rappelons les gestes du loup: il arrive, tue la grand-mère, la dévore en partie, la saigne, met le sang de côté dans une bouteille, un verre, un plat, une terrine, une écuelle, une assiette ou un bol, et réserve la chair—c'est le terme employé—qu'il range comme provisions dans le coffre, l'armoire ou le placard" [What sauce was she covered in? Remember what the wolf does: it arrives, kills the grandmother, partially eats her, bleeds her, puts the blood aside in a bottle, a glass, a plate, a crock, a bowl, or a platter, and saves the flesh—this is the term used—for later in a chest, an armoire, or a closet]. Verdier is referring to the Tyrol version, in which the victim's intestines are hung on the door:

> On l'aura remarqué, dès le début de l'épisode, le code culinaire utilisé est sans équivoque: il n'est autre que celui du cochon depuis l'abattage jusqu'à la cuisine. Les tâches sont bien partagées: office masculin, le loup tue, saigne, réserve la chair comme s'il s'apprêtait à la saler; office féminin, la fille cuisine. Le sang fricassé directement à la poêle, ou les boudins, sont deux formes exclusives de préparation du sang tout à la fois, dans certaines régions, la technique (sauter à la poêle), le plat, préparé avec le sang, le foie et le coeur, et les portions distribuées aux parents et voisins le jour du "sacrifice": Une assiette garnie d'un morceau de boudin disposé en cercle avec au centre des morceaux de foie, de coeur,

de panse, le tout recouvert d'un peu de coiffe (péritoine). Aussi, le terme fricassée, outre le sang qui en est l'élément principal, suggère-t-il également la consommation de certains organes: foie et coeur.

[Right from the start of this episode, the culinary code is quite obvious: we are following the pig from the slaughterhouse to the kitchen. The tasks are shared: filling a masculine role, the wolf kills it, bleeds it, and stores the flesh as if he were getting ready to salt it; taking a feminine role, the girl cooks it. A pan-fricassee or a pudding are two ways of preparing pig's blood, and their consumption is associated with the "sacrifice" of the animal. In certain regions the "fricasseeing" describes both the technique (sautéing in a pan), and the dish, prepared with the blood, the liver, and the heart, of which portions are given to friends and relatives on the day of the "sacrifice": a plate garnished with a circular piece of blood sausage, which is filled in the middle with pieces of liver, heart, and stomach, all covered with a little lining (peritoneum). The term fricassee, then, other than the principal element of blood, also suggests the consumption of other organs, such as the liver and the heart.][20]

In this way, the horrifying English image says as much as the oral versions. Try as he might to conform to contemporary horror-story style, M. G. Lewis reinforces the same message as the tale: the necessity of female biological changes that help the young replace the old, even while they are alive. In conclusion, the devouring of the grandmother is acceptable. But let us not forget Gabrielle Pélissier: is she not also eaten and dismembered by the Beast? And is it not her younger sister who enjoys the fruits of her *older* sister's murder? Can we not imagine such a staging of the tale, all the more macabre because all of its symbolic components are equally exploited?

This aspect has been a source for several other texts of children's literature. One of the most striking examples is Lespès's rewriting of the fairy tale. In 1865, he published *Les Contes de Perrault continués* [Perrault's Tales, Continued] under the pen name Timothée Trimm, in Paris, at the Librairie du Petit Journal. This magnificent folio, illustrated by Henry de Montaut, is one of the great classics of children's literature, and particularly of the rewriting of Perrault's *Contes*, of which it emphasizes that it is a "continuation," a well-known tactic used by publishers of chapbooks, especially in Épinal, where the *Aventures de Madame Barbe Bleue* [Adventures of Madame Bluebeard] and other sequels were produced in abundance. Lespès justified his work in this manner: "Tous les enfants auxquels on raconte le *Petit Poucet* disent, après l'avoir écouté, ce mot charmant: encore! . . . Ils veulent une suite, comme on a fait une suite aux romans de Balzac, au *Don Quichotte* de Cervantes, aux contes arabes, à Grandisson, à *Faust* et au *Paradis perdu*" [All children to whom we read *Tom Thumb* say, after listening to it, this charming word: again! . . . They want a sequel, just as sequels were written for Balzac's novels, for Cervantes's *Don Quixote*, for the *Arabian Nights,* for Grandisson, for *Faust* and for *Paradise Lost*]. It is thus not naive to consider the child as an erudite reader, capable of undertaking, without generic or evaluative limitations, readings as diverse as Cervantes, Perrault, Goethe, or Balzac. Lespès's dream reader is as much an adult as a child, and the author looks to erase social barriers just as much as those based on age and sex. And if these barriers, whatever they are, are abolished, generic distinctions must also disappear, all the more easily because the author calls his performance an "improvisation." But no improvisation was ever so well prepared. It is clear that Lespès is playing here with the well-known fictive register of an improvisation, commonly considered a spontaneous outpouring of ideas, like the writing of an unpublished text. Yet the author, like his reader, knows that this art of spontaneity is also an art of association, where the improviser can instantaneously link a group of predetermined elements, such as words or formal structures, to an analysis of their social efficiency. Improvisation is thus a cultural practice, associated most often with oral performances—singing, storytelling—and the promise of a show. The "improvisational" author offers a form of performance that functions according to codes agreed upon by him and his audiences. This performance is often further upheld by institutions such as competing editorial series, which have a function not unlike that of popular singing contests among improvisational singers. It was not by accident that Lespès, calling upon the idea of improvisation to better define his work of "continuation," inscribed his sequel to *Little Red Riding Hood, Le Petit Chaperon rouge après sa mort* [Little Red Riding Hood After Her Death], in the initiatory vein of orality and of ritual.

Indeed, Montaut's engraving shows a smiling little girl in the wolf's belly that has been cut open by a disturbing butcher with a knife between his teeth, and the story relates that the mother, stricken with grief over the death of her own mother and child, went to consult a clairvoyant. The old woman, "who did business with the fairies," saw in her magic mirror that the wolf was holding Little Red Riding Hood, alive, in its intestines:

> En ce qui touche la grand'maman, il faut en faire son deuil. Elle avait nonante-cinq ans, et sortir à cet âge-là de la vie par une porte ou par une autre est chose assez indifférente. D'ailleurs, comme elle était grande, le Loup a dû la mâcher et la briser en plusieurs morceaux pour l'avaler; en second lieu, comme elle a

été mangée la première, elle doit être digérée à l'heure qu'il est. Ne nous tourmentons pas sur son compte.

[As for the grandmother, you should grieve her. She was ninety-five years old, and at that age, it really does not matter if one leaves life by one door or another. Anyway, since she was big, the wolf had to chew her up into a number of pieces before swallowing her and since she was eaten first, she has probably been entirely digested. There is no more hope for her.]

Lespès tells us what the oral tale teaches, as Yvonne Verdier points out: "La nécessité des transformations biologiques féminines aboutissent à l'élimination des vieilles par les jeunes, mais de leur vivant: les mères seront remplacées par leurs filles, la boucle sera bouclée avec l'arrivée des enfants de mes enfants. Moralité: les mères-grand seront mangées" [The necessity of female biological changes results in the young replacing the old, even while they are alive: mothers are replaced by their daughters, and the circle will be closed when the children of my children are born. Moral: grandmothers will be eaten].[21]

In Lespès's version, as with oral tradition, the grandmother is old, eaten, and "digested"; she belongs to the wolf through a process of biological metamorphosis that returns her to a wild, animal stage, effect of the cannibalism of which she is a victim. Lespès adds another ethnological element: the swallowed child, alive and nestled in the wolf's stomach, "n'a en réalité que sa chemisette de chiffonnée" [is wearing nothing more than her crumpled little blouse], and the clairvoyant adds, "Entre nous, avec un coup de fer il n'y paraîtra plus" [Between us, a quick iron would do the trick]. It could not be any clearer: the little girl in the crumpled blouse just had her first sexual experience. She will now have a new life, a life as a young adult woman, to whom a "quick ironing" (with a clothing iron) applied to her wrinkled dress by a masculine hand will allow her to move on, joyful but mature, to other paths. It is not a question of rape: the sexual act takes place without violence because the wolf objectively takes advantage of an apparently unexpected accomplice: the grandmother.

And the wolf? What becomes of him in the story? Verdier shows to what extent the wolf can be a "grandmother-wolf": the hairiness of the grandmother's body, present in the dialogue between the old woman and the child, is associated with deterioration, the erosion of female generative faculties. Rather than a wolf-grandmother, this is a grandmother-wolf, and the moral of the story is reversed. If little girls must eat their grandmothers (or their female elders), it is because their grandmothers want to eat them, or worse: because the grandmothers are the initiators of their first sexual relations, of their first encounters with boys who are authorized to take the role of the unmarried male with authority and brutality. In these encounters, for once the physical safety of the girls is not guaranteed by one of those adults whom they should be able to trust: grandmothers. All of the ambivalence and reversibility of the symbols in the story of the Beast of Gévaudan, read and corrected by Mgr. de Choiseul-Beaupré (and others), is there. The Beast, that is both here and there at the same time, that incessantly changes form and that dresses itself in "long silks" or scales depending on the witness and the publisher, is much like the wolf of the tale: "Sans visage à force de mimétisme, il posséderait la matérialité du miroir, renvoyant aux femmes le reflet de leurs transformations à elles, et ce serait face à ce loup-miroir que se jouerait le destin des femmes qui les fait rivales" [Without face, by force of his mimicry, the wolf has the materiality of a mirror, sending women the reflections of their own transformations, and it is in front of this mirror that the destiny of women-as-rivals is played out], Verdier writes. How could one not think of the wolf imagined by Walt Disney, disguised as a flying fairy that circles over Little Red Riding Hood in order better to seduce her?

A systematic study of foreign editions would show that there are no "traits, values, attitudes and a way of construing the world that [are] peculiarly French," as Robert Darnton has instead maintained that there are, in his study of peasant tales that opens his book *The Great Cat Massacre*.[22] In fact, if publishers were the first to advance generic classifications in their corpus, this was better to render as text, and as printed text, narratives that were originally indistinct. But authors were not deceived: Lespès, for one, ostensibly refused this artificial distinction between creation of a text and creation of a book, even if it was the best sales strategy that had been adopted (and that was still in use until very recently) to deal in the most intelligent manner possible with a multiplicity of readerships. But each of these readerships had one point in common: resistance to the imposition of dominant religious values. Beyond the idea of nation that Robert Darnton uses better to determine—and invent—a French specificity, it is useful to wonder whether publishing and religious interests in the eighteenth and nineteenth centuries symbolized struggles for cultural, political, or simply financial power.

And the cake? Who ate the cake? It is an ironic, if not facetious, question that the child never forgets to ask at the end of the story, for it is true that the cake and the pot of butter are forgotten by the storyteller. In oral versions, it is not always a cake, but something perfectly comparable: sugared bread, a cookie, a pot of cream, or cheese. But it is always something made from milk, flour, and eggs, the symbols of marriage and fertility. These cakes, traditional at wedding meals and whose presence in the eighteenth century has been substantiated by Jean-Baptiste Thiers, are once again the sign that we are reading a story about apprenticeship. The mother makes the cake and gives it to Little Red Riding Hood, who thus fills the role of intermediary between one generation and another and between one married woman and another, in the hopes of finally confronting this well-known rite of passage. This type of understanding is perfectly clear in the minds of nineteenth- and twentieth-century storytellers, who emphasize the existence of the cake, of the pastry, of the *pompe,* of the honeycake, of the waffle, or of some other sweet cake. Most remarkable is that certain authors who rewrote the tale used this theme, undoubtedly because they were familiar with its symbolic importance.

Such was the case for the anonymous author of *L'Histoire du Petit Chaperon rouge* [The Story of Little Red Riding Hood] in *Le Grand Livre des petits chérubins* [The Big Book of Little Cherubs], published in Paris by Amable Rigaud around 1860. The little girl, as in Perrault's tale, is so caught up with frolicking in the forest and chasing butterflies that she is still there when night falls. She meets a "ravenous wolf" upon her path: "'Ah! mon Dieu!' dit la petite fille, 'je suis perdue,' et elle laissa tomber le pot de beurre et la galette" ["Oh! my God!" said the little girl, "I am finished," and she dropped her pot of butter and her cake]. And curiously, as "ravenous" as he was, "aussitôt le loup dévora la galette qui lui sembla très bonne" [the wolf immediately devoured the cake, which seemed very good to him]. In 1921, André Lichtenberger presented the same story of a wolf passing up a Little Green Riding Hood in order to better savor "son petit pot de beurre et sa galette qui lui feraient un excellent petit déjeuner au réveil" [her small pot of butter and her cake, which would make a wonderful breakfast the next morning]. Of course, this is one of those examples, classic in children's literature, of "watering down" a text. But if this is the case, why not choose to copy the version of the Brothers Grimm?

Another rewritten tale provides a very elaborate version of the symbolic significance of the cake: in 1893, Emilie Mathieu wrote *Le Nouveau Petit chaperon rouge* [The New Little Red Riding Hood] published in Paris by Desclée, De Brouwer and Company. It is a long, elaborate story, set in a specific time period—March 20, 1780, to be exact—and a specific place—Morvan, in Nivernais—which confers on it the status of exemplum. The entire story consists of demonstrating how to rise up out of misery by trusting Divine Providence, the village priest, and finally, one's own resources. The resources of the family in the story are comprised, in fact, of a waffle iron that hangs on the wall, a symbol of "the good old days" when the grandmother, now the Countess's maid, was a chef's wife and "en veste blanche, coiffé de la toque traditionnelle, confectionnant d'appétissantes gaufrettes" [wore a white coat, a traditional chef's hat and made delicious waffles]. The young girl finds the old recipe and sets to selling waffles to passersby in villages and fairs. Her peregrinations put her into contact with two bear trainers who are plotting to kill and rob a rich farmer pompously named "Master Tréchaud."

The bear will of course play the role of frightening the victim. But the girl warns Master Tréchaud in time, and she has all the more merit because her gentle disposition permits her to tame the animal. The criminals are arrested and the New Little Red Riding Hood marries the farmer's son, who is as touched by her beauty as by the . . . exquisite taste of her waffles. Beyond this edifying and sentimental rewriting, the author flushes out all of the initiatory constructs of the tale in a perfect ethnological "recentering" of the tale, which seems truer than nature itself.

And as for pedagogical literature? It seems to focus primarily upon the terrifying lessons of the *fait-divers*. Let us look at the case of alphabet primers of the late nineteenth century, which presented, following the alphabet, illustrated stories that served the purpose of teaching to read. As Ségolène Le Men specifies, these illustrated stories were the precursors of the modern comic strip.[23] With their narrow and particular association between text and image, these stories have their origins neither in the illustrated book nor in the album. The page is divided into uniform sections, under which a few lines of text may be printed. The sections are linked together from left to right and from top to bottom, as if one should read the text through the series of illustrations, which are responsible for producing the narrative. In precluding the possibility of illustrating the alphabet itself, this narrative quality of the stories, which issues from the domain of popular imagery (and, indeed, the primers are published by Pellerin and Pinot of Épinal), reflects the cultural and ideological norms of the day. However, even if we can sometimes establish a link between a story and a close source, it is nonetheless true that the alphabet primer allows for new developments in page layout, which coincide with the opening of new sources of inspiration. The child can thus build a more autonomous culture for himself.

Regarding *Little Red Riding Hood*, the version published in Épinal in 1874 by Pellerin as part of *l'ABC des enfants sages* [The ABCs of Good Children] illustrates the epilogue to the child's death by reviving the legend of the Beast of Gévaudan. Clouzier's aforementioned vignette is followed by a devouring scene that owes its existence to the occasional works written about the Beast of Gévaudan. And in *Le Livre des enfants sages* [The Book of Good Children], published by Pinot and Sagaire in Épinal following publication of *Nouvel Alphabet de l'enfance orné de gravures et suivi de l'histoire du Chaperon-Rouge* [New Children's Alphabet Decorated With Engravings and Followed by the Story of Little Red Riding Hood] in 1869 by Ch. Thomhs in Metz, we find a terrifying representation of the wolf associated with the presence of a font hung on the bedroom wall, and on it a quite visible crucifix (figure 11.4). Now, this cross had quickly become indispensable in the occasional works treating the Beast of Gévaudan. It was often situated at an angle in the vignette, as in a late-eighteenth-century Clermont-Ferrand woodcut, as

FIGURE 11.4 From the alphabet primer *Le Livre des enfants sages* (Épinal: Pinot et Sagaire, n.d. [1873–74?]). Little Red Riding Hood and the wolf, with font and crucifix.

an autonomous and stereotyped iconical sign which points to the analogy between the Beast of Gévaudan and the Beast of the Apocalypse (figure 11.5). This configuration is thus found again in an illustration for a children's fairy tale. What was in the eighteenth century a publisher's specialty usurped by religious authorities had now become part of the iconical protocol used in an alphabet primer. Beyond this frightening representation of Little Red Riding Hood is, in reality, the attempt to eclipse Perrault's moral, which is nonetheless ostensibly restated:

> On voit ici que de jeunes enfants,
> Surtout de jeunes filles
> Belles, bien faites, et gentilles,
> Font très mals d'écouter toute sorte de gens,
> Et que ce n'est pas chose étrange,
> S'il en est tant que le loup mange.

> [We see here that young children,
> Above all young girls,
> Who are pretty, well-formed and nice,
> Are very wrong to listen to everyone,
> And that it is not a strange thing,
> If they do and the wolf eats them.]

When taken literally, the illustrators and publishers erased every inde-cent reference to sexuality or to rape in both the text and the entire story.

FIGURE 11.5 Woodcut, Clermont-Ferrand, late eighteenth century. Beast of Gévaudan as Beast of the Apocalypse.

This was achieved by appropriating the tale's strongest symbols, such as the reciprocal devouring of the little girl and the grandmother, and the initiation of Little Red Riding Hood into her role of woman and wife, and by making reference to a *fait-divers* claimed to be banal, that of a ravenous, devouring wolf. For even if the general configuration of these illustrations is similar to Clouzier's, there is nonetheless a crucial difference: the reader finally sees what happened under the covers; and what a relief! the child is purely and simply eaten (figure 11.6).

In the twentieth century, a publisher of children's literature uses the image of the Beast devouring little girls for the same end. In the case of *Les Contes de Perrault*, published by Henri Laurens in 1931, the job of inserting the terrifying devouring scene at the heart of *Little Red Riding Hood* was left to the illustrator Vimar (figure 11.7). This version was reprinted with no changes to Perrault's text, but Perrault's wolf is nowhere to be found; on the other hand, the Beast is there, as evidenced by the presence, once again, of the font and crucifix. It is unlikely that the urban bourgeois child for whom this book was meant recognized the "scourge of God" or that he had ever heard of the frightened shepherd girls of Margeride.

Conclusion

No process, no matter how complex, permits a systematic analysis of all the editorial and narrative production of a corpus of tales. Any attempt to

FIGURE 11.6 From the alphabet primer *Le Liver des enfants sages* (Épinal: Pinot et Sagaire, n.d. [1873–74?]). Little Red Riding Hood devoured by the wolf.

grasp in one argument the various auctorial and editorial practices that come into play seems destined to a reduction and impoverishment that goes against the principles set down by this heritage. This study is not an investigation of "structures," "primary cores," or "matrices" that are supposed to contain the essence of the functioning of narrative invention. For I believe that this type of reading presupposes the existence of a hierarchy among writings. But this cannot be true, for the foundations of this corpus of tales is based on the rejection of the idea of a definitive text. Rewritings, even those that are judged to be less than perfect by literary historians, can only produce more rewritings. To print a narrative demands that a choice be made, but it is only momentary: a text's form corresponds to a precise occurrence, and its reedition produces a new version of the writing.

The stories in this corpus do not stagnate in any one literary genre. The displacements from one genre to another become, for authors as for their publishers, a norm in their production, or more exactly, a norm of production. In effect, these displacements are produced within the texts themselves, preventing the literary critic from classifying them, as he is always tempted to do. These unresolved tensions, that result in a questioning of literary genres, engender writing. The corpus of rewritten tales is not a transgression of genres, of which the conventional quality is never completely forgotten. But authors explore the possibilities of mixing techniques and principles of different genres. In reality, the uneasiness that these displacements present for literary historians can be explained by the fact that the productive aspect of this generic cross-breeding is constantly highlighted. Let us take the example of the oral tradition "rediscovered" by André Lichtenberger in

FIGURE 11.7 From Vimar, illustrator, *Les Contes de Perrault illustrés* (Paris: Henri Laurens, 1931). Wolf with font and crucifix; wolf and Little Red Riding Hood.

his *Petit chaperon vert et autres contes* [Little Green Riding Hood and Other Tales], in whose epilogue we find a child disoriented by the new stories offered him by the author: " 'N'est-ce pas qu'elles ne sont pas si vraies que les autres?' " ["Aren't they just as true as the others?"], asks little Jacques, in "une petite voix chevrotante, le menton tremblant" [in a quavering voice, his chin trembling]. The author, "atterré" [dismayed], reassures the little boy, who is suddenly doubtful: " 'Mais alors, les autres histoires? Celles qui sont dans le livre? Peut-être qu'elles ne sont pas vraies non plus?' " ["But what about the other stories? The ones in the book? Maybe they are no longer true?"]. And the author responds to him: " 'Elle sont tout à fait vraies, mon petit Jacques, et tu le sais bien, voyons, puisqu'elles sont imprimées tandis que les autres, ce sont des histoires en l'air que l'on raconte seulement' " ["They are all quite true, my little Jacques, and you know it. Come now, *these* were printed, whereas the others were all just stories that people told"]. We have here the fiction of an overestimation of the printed word, but at the same time as the epilogue is used as an advertisement for a new edited collection based on "oral" tales: the readers are obviously being manipulated through this salvaging and exploitation of oral tradition and its possibilities. For an author who does not believe in the reproduction of spoken language, this leads to the need to translate certain oral forms through techniques that belong to the realm of written language. This exercise is artificially disqualified, according to a classic procedure of seducing the reader, and illustrates quite clearly the problems involved with different versions, rewritings, and revivals of a story. As time passed, none of these authors gave up this concept of rewriting, which was structured as much by sociocultural changes in the field of literature as by translation techniques.

After Roland Barthes wrote that the *fait-divers* was "the unorganized discard of news" and that each story could be seen as "total news" that is "immanent; it contains all its knowledge in itself,"[24] it appeared, until very recently, that "les faits-divers sont des écrits clos dans le sens où, comme les contes, ils contiennent en eux-mêmes toutes les informations que leur compréhension nécessite" [the *faits-divers* are closed writings in the sense that, like tales, they contain within themselves all the information needed to comprehend them]. It has been further advanced that "Structure fermée, fonctionnant d'une manière autonome, le fait divers est naturellement prédisposé à n'accorder d'attention qu'à ce qui paraît universel, permanent, fondamentalement humain" [as a closed structure, working autonomously, the *fait-divers* is naturally predisposed to pay attention only to what appears universal, permanent, and fundamentally human].[25]

In reality, the analysis of texts and their materiality shows that the meaning of the *fait-divers* and the tale depend upon their sociohistoric identification. Yet from one passage to another, the stories seem to lose this historical mooring. And if it is true that the context in which they were released and received by the public is erased, it is no less true that this is to the benefit of a new context. When a story becomes inscribed in a specific historical period, discussions arise about genre, in part because of the ambiguity of certain texts, but also because through the construction of their meanings, authors and publishers attempt to accentuate the oscillations between fiction and reality. In some cases, publishers go as far as exploiting the effects of their own distribution to question the genre of their texts: F.-G. Deschamps, for example, traced a route that went from Paris to the countryside, from the real to the romanticized. A good number of occasional works published about the Beast of Gévaudan have strong ties to political events of the day. The subject, the vocabulary, and even the syntactic organization of these texts leave a mark that allows us to date them with precision. At first glance, then, these texts would hardly seem to lend themselves to a contextual uprooting. Yet this is exactly what happened: it turned out, in fact, that publishers foresaw, beginning in 1764, variations in the publishing medium, in different understandings of history, and in what they anticipated to be ulterior reappropriations. Was this not the surest way of putting the generic identity of their texts to the test?

Why not present the problem differently? Instead of trying to classify texts, why not examine how the management of texts by publishers demonstrates that the genre constitutes an important element in the production of these works? Publishers of occasional works, alphabet primers, or children's books, beyond any primary intentionality on the part of the authors, impute great importance to literary tradition, even at a time when it is agreed upon to present only new works. Thus, they seem to proceed as if they did not know about traditional classifications in fiction or in reality. Identifying and evaluating the tangle of strategies used by publishers to remove stories from the contexts in which they were first presented and received and to resituate them in new contexts is not always easy. For this editorial approach presents a dialectic between the move to return to a previously published text and the move by which the text is placed in its new collection, which makes it a different text, even if it is otherwise unchanged. This editorial manipulation is realized thanks to the exploitation of the great confusion of the reader's affects, without, on the other hand, trying to efface the totality of traces of this violence imposed on the texts, to which we can refer as proof. The results are greater than the publishers' expectations: the ideological efficiency of these fictional narratives, considered to be true even when facts prove otherwise, is obvious. Consequently, debates on the universality and the invariance of tales no longer have reason to exist.

And since Roland Barthes's writings have too often been used to justify every kind of mechanical approach, let us take a closer look at the terms of his argument:

> *La défection des origenes* / The abandonment of origins
>
> His work [Barthes's own] is not anti-historical (at least, so he intends), but always, persistently, antigenetic, for Origin is a pernicious figure of Nature (of Physis): by an abusive interest, the *Doxa* "crushes" Origin and Truth together, in order to make them into a single proof, each reinflating the other, according to a convenient swivel: are not the human sciences *etymological*, in pursuit of the *etymon* (origin and truth) of each phenomenon?
>
> In order to thwart Origin, he first acculturates Nature thoroughly: nothing natural anywhere, nothing but the historical; then this culture (convinced as he is, with Benveniste, that all culture is only language) is restored to the infinite movement of various discourses, set up one against the other (and not engendered) as in hand-over-hand choosing.[26]

347

Notes

Translated by Joey R. Hood.
An earlier version of this essay appeared in Gradhiva *17 (1995): 111–26.*

1. Translator's note: Roland Barthes defines the *fait-divers* this way: "A murder is committed: if political, it is news, otherwise, we French call it a *fait-divers*." It is a term that derives "from a classification of the unclassified, it would be the unorganized discard of news; its essence would be privative, it would begin to exist only where the world stops being named, subject to a known catalogue (politics, economics, war, amusement, science, etc.)" ("Structure of the *Fait-Divers*," in *Critical Essays*, trans. Richard Howard [Evanston: Northwestern University Press, 1972], 185).

2. Editor's note: Gustave Lanson (1857–1934) developed a form of literary criticism that applied historical and comparativist methods to the study of literary works.

3. Here I draw on Freud's concept of the uncanny.

4. Editor's note: Willy was the pen name of the writer Colette's first husband. He was a music critic and a novelist, and Colette's first works, the Claudine novels, were written in collaboration with him and published under his name.

5. Concerning the concept of *braconnage* [poaching], I refer the reader to Michel de Certeau, *The Practice of Everyday Life*, trans. Steven F. Rendall (Berkeley and Los Angeles: University of California Press, 1984), ch. 12 ("Reading as Poaching").

6. See Catherine Velay-Vallantin, "Le miroir des contes. Perrault dans les Bibliothèques bleues," in *Les usages de l'imprimé*, ed. Roger Chartier (Paris: Fayard, 1987), 155–57 and 165–68.

7. Editor's note: Gévaudan was an old *comté* [county] between the Margeride mountains and Mount Aigoual, now in the department of Lozère.

8. The story of the *Beast of Gévaudan* has given rise to a number of works, including: Félix Buffière, *La Bête du Gévaudan, une grande énigme de l'histoire* (Toulouse: Buffière, 1987); Véronique Campion-Vincent, *Des fauves dans nos campagnes. Légendes, rumeurs et apparitions* (Paris: Imago, 1992); Guy Crouzot, *Quand sonnait le glas au pays de la Bête* (Clermont-Ferrand: C.R.D.P., 1985) and *Requiem en Gévaudan* (Clermont-Ferrand: C.R.D.P., 1992); Jean-Marc Gibert, *La Bête du Gévaudan. Les auteurs du XVIIIè, XIXè, XXè siècles: historiens ou conteurs?* (Mende: Société des Lettres, Sciences et Arts de la Lozère, 1993); R. Mazauric, "Mandement de Mgr. de Choiseul-Beaupré, évêque de Mende," *Lou Païs* (June 1960); Gérard Ménatory, *La Bête du Gévaudan* (Mende: Chaptal, 1976); Abbé P. Pourcher, *Histoire de la Bête en Gévaudan* (Saint-Martin-de-Boubaux: Pourcher, 1889); Henri Pourrat, *Histoire fidèle de la Bête en Gévaudan* (Paris: de l'Epervier, 1946, and Marseille: Lafitte Reprints, 1982); Rudy Scohy, *La Bête du Gévaudan, Manifestations littéraires d'un phénomène historique mal connu* (thesis in romance philology, Université Libre de Bruxelles, 1984–85); Bruno Soulier, *Le Loup dans l'imaginaire contemporain du Gévaudan* (master's thesis in ethnology, Université Paul Valéry-Montpellier III, 1988).

9. The text of the lament, as well as the previously cited letters, can be found in "Fille de La Clause, Gabrielle Pélissier," in *Histoire de la Bête du Gévaudan, véritable fléau de Dieu, d'après les documents inédits et authentiques*, ed. Abbot P. Pourcher (Saint-Martin-de-Boubaux: Pourcher, 1889), 467–73.

10. Text translated and commented by Jacques Berlioz, in Jacques Berlioz, Claude Bremond, and Catherine Velay-Vallantin, *Les formes médiévales du conte merveilleux* (Paris: Stock Moyen Age, 1989), 133–39.
11. Paul Delarue, "Les contes de Perrault et la tradition populaire," *Bulletin folklorique d'Ile de France* (1951).
12. Hans-Robert Jauss, *Untersuchungen zur mittelalterliche Tierdichtung* (Tübingen, 1959), 67.
13. See R. Mazauric, "Mandement de Mgr. de Choiseul-Beaupré, évêque de Mande," *Lou Païs* (June 1960).
14. Editor's note: The Camisards were Huguenots of the Cevennes Mountains. After Louis XIV revoked the Edict of Nantes and banned Huguenot worship, they rebelled against his government (1702–10). After 1715, the Camisard Church of the Desert, which operated in clandestinity, held synods.
15. Philippe Joutard, *La Légende des Camisards. Une sensibilité au présent* (Paris: Gallimard, 1977), 44–48.
16. Michel Pastoureau, *L'étoffe du diable. Une histoire des rayures et des tissus rayés* (Paris: Editions du Seuil, 1991), 45–46.
17. Elisabeth Claverie and Pierre Lamaison, *L'impossible mariage. Violence et parenté en Gévaudan, 17è, 18è et 19è siècles* (Paris: Hachette, 1982), 59ff.
18. Ibid., 61.
19. See Yvonne Verdier, "Le Petit Chaperon rouge dans la tradition orale," *Le Débat* 3 (July–Aug. 1980): 31–61.
20. Yvonne Verdier, "Grands-mères, si vous saviez. Le Petit Chaperon rouge dans la tradition orale," *Cahiers de littérature orale* 4 (1978): 30–31 and 33–37. For more on the ethnohistorical approach, see Yvonne Verdier, *Coutume et destin. Thomas Hardy et autres essais* (Paris: Gallimard, 1995), and Claudine Fabre-Vassas, *La bête singulière. Les juifs, les chrétiens et le cochon* (Paris: Gallimard, 1995).
21. Verdier, "*La Petit Chaperon rouge*," 185.
22. Robert Darnton, *The Great Cat Massacre and Other Episodes in French Cultural History* (New York: Vintage, 1985), 63. For a critical analysis of Darnton's approach to *Little Red Riding Hood*, see Jack Zipes, *The Trials and Tribulations of Little Red Riding Hood*, 2nd ed. (New York: Routledge, 1993), 1–15.
23. Ségolène Le Men, *Les abécédaires français illustrés du XIXè siècle* (Paris: Editions Promodis, 1984), 39–41.
24. Barthes, *Critical Essays*, 185 and 186.
25. Catalogue of the exposition "Le fait divers," organized by the Musée des Arts et des Traditions populaires, Nov. 1982–Apr. 1983, 50 and 56.
26. *Roland Barthes by Roland Barthes*, trans. Richard Howard (New York: Farrar, Straus and Giroux, 1977), 139.

Bibliography

L'ABC des enfants sages. Èpinal: Pellerin, 1874.
Barthes, Roland. *Critical Essays*. Trans. Richard Howard. Evanston: Northwestern University Press, 1972.

————. *Roland Barthes by Roland Barthes*. Trans. Richard Howard. New York: Farrar, Straus and Giroux, 1977.

Berlioz, Jacques, Claude Brémond, and Catherine Velay-Vallantin. *Les formes médiévales du conte merveilleux*. Paris: Stock Moyen Age, 1989.

Buffière, Félix. *La Bête du Gévaudan, une grande énigme de l'histoire*. Toulouse: Buffière, 1987.

Campion-Vincent, Véronique. *Des fauves dans nos campagnes. Légendes, rumeurs et apparitions*. Paris: Imago, 1992.

Certeau, Michel de. *The Practice of Everyday Life*. Trans. Steven F. Rendall. Berkeley and Los Angeles: University of California Press, 1984.

Claverie, Elisabeth, and Pierre Lamaison. *L'impossible mariage. Violence et parenté en Gévaudan, 17è, 18è et 19è siècles*. Paris: Hachette, 1982.

Crouzot, Guy. *Quand sonnait le glas au pays de la Bête*. Clermont-Ferrand: C.R.D.P., 1985.

————. *Requiem en Gévaudan*. Clermont-Ferrand: C.R.D.P, 1992.

Darnton, Robert. *The Great Cat Massacre and Other Episodes in French Cultural History*. New York: Vintage, 1985.

Delarue, Paul. "Les contes de Perrault et la tradition populaire." *Bulletin folklorique d'Ile de France* (1951).

Fabre-Vassas, Claudine. *La bête singulière. Les juifs, les chrétiens et le cochon*. Paris: Gallimard, 1994.

Le fait divers. Catalogue of the exposition organized by the Musée des Arts et des Traditions populaires, Nov. 1982–Apr. 1983.

Figure de la Bête farouche et extraordinaire, que dévore les filles dans la province de Gévaudan. Paris: F.-G. Deschampes, 1764.

Gibert, Jean-Marc. *La Bête du Gévaudan. Les auteurs du XVIIIè, XIXè, XXè siècles: historiens ou conteurs?* Mende: Société des Lettres, Sciences et Arts de la Lozère, 1993.

Jauss, Hans-Robert. *Untersuchungen zur mittelalterliche Tierdichtung*. Tübingen, 1959.

Joutard, Philippe. *La Légende des Camisards. Une sensibilité au présent*. Paris: Gallimard, 1977.

Le Grand Livre des petits chérubins. Paris: Amable Rigaud, n.d. [1860?].

Le Men, Ségolène. *Les abécédaires français illustrés du XIXè siècle*. Paris: Editions Promodis, 1984.

Lespès, Léo. *Les Contes de Perrault continués par Timothée Trimm*. Illustrated by Henry de Montaut. Paris: Librairie de Petit Journal, 1865.

Lewis, M. G. *Tales of Terror*. London: Balmer, 1801.

Lichtenberger, André. *Le Petit Chaperon vert et autres contes*. Illustrated by Joseph Hémard. Paris: Grès, 1921.

Le Livre des enfants sages. Épinal: Pinot et Sagaire, n.d. [1873–74?].

Mathieu, Emilie. *Le Nouveau Chaperon rouge*. Paris: Desclée et De Brouwer, 1893.

Mazauric, R. "Mandement de Mgr. de Choiseul-Beaupré, évêque de Mende." *Lou Païs*. June 1960.

Ménatory, Gérard. *La Bête du Gévaudan*. Mende: Chaptal, 1976.

Nouvel Alphabet de l'enfance orné de gravures et suivi de l'histoire du Chaperon rouge. Metz: Thomhs, 1869.

Pastoureau, Michel. *L'étoffe du diable. Une histoire des rayures et des tissus rayés.* Paris: Editions du Seuil, 1991.

Perrault, Charles. *Les Contes des fées, avec des moralités.* Troyes: Mme Garnier, n.d.

———. *Les Contes de Perrault illustrés.* Illustrated by E. Courboin, Fraipont, Geoffroy, Gerbault, Job, L. Morin, Robida, Vimar, Vogel, and Zier. Paris: Henri Laurens, 1931.

Pourcher, Abbé P. *Histoire de la Bête en Gévaudan, véritable fléau de Dieu, d'après les documents inédits et authentiques.* Saint-Martin-de-Boubaux: Pourcher, 1889.

Pourrat, Henri. *Histoire fidèle de la Bête en Gévaudan.* Paris: de l'Epervier, 1946; Marseille: Lafitte Reprints, 1982.

Scohy, Rudy. *La Bête du Gévaudan, Manifestations littéraires d'un phénomène historique mal connu.* Thesis in Romance Philology, Université Libre de Bruxelles, 1984–85.

Soulier, Bruno. *Le Loup dans l'imaginaire contemporain du Gévaudan.* Master's thesis in Ethnology, Université Paul Valéry-Montpellier III, 1988.

Velay-Vallantin, Catherine. "Le miroir des contes. Perrault dans les Bibliothèques bleues." In *Les usages de l'imprimé.* Ed. Roger Chartier. Paris: Fayard, 1987.

Verdier, Yvonne. *Coutume et destin. Thomas Hardy et autres essais.* Paris: Gallimard, 1995.

———. "Grands-mères, si vous saviez. *Le Petit Chaperon rouge* dans la tradition orale." *Cahiers de littérature orale* 4 (1978).

———. "*Le Petit Chaperon rouge* dans la tradition orale." *Le Débat* 3 (July–Aug. 1980): 31–61.

Zipes, Jack. *The Trials and Tribulations of Little Red Riding Hood.* 2nd ed. New York: Routledge, 1993.

Contributors

ANTONELLA ANSANI, assistant professor of Italian at Barnard College, specializes in Italian Renaissance literature, and is working on a book on magic
and rhetoric in Renaissance theater. Her previous works include studies
of Pico della Mirandola, Ariosto, and Bandello.

NANCY L. CANEPA is assistant professor of French and Italian at Dartmouth
College, where she teaches and researches early modern Italian literature and the history of the literary fairy tale. She is currently completing
a book entitled *From Court to Forest: Giambattista Basile's "Lo cunto de li
cunti" and the Birth of the Literary Fairy Tale*, and has previously published
articles on Basile, Tomaso Garzoni, and Arcangela Tarabotti.

CYNTHIA C. CRAIG is associate professor of Italian at Michigan State University, where she specializes in the literature of the Enlightenment, Middle
Ages, and Renaissance. She has published articles on Casanova's autobiographical and fictional texts, as well as on Tasso and Ariosto. She
has recently completed a book-length study, *Casanova and the Art of
Narrative*, which focuses on issues of genre, narrative strategy, gender,
and exile.

TED EMERY teaches Italian at the Universidad de Puerto Rico, Recinto de
Río Piedras. He is author of the book *Goldoni as Librettist: Theatrical
Reform and the "drammi giocosi per musica"* (1991), is the coeditor and
translator of *Carlo Gozzi: Five Tales for the Theater* (1989), and has
published articles on Chiari, Goldoni, and Gozzi.

MARY LOUISE ENNIS is visiting assistant professor of Romance languages at Wes-
leyan University, where she specializes in eighteenth-century French
literature. Her research and teaching interests include literary art criticism, imaginary voyages, sexual politics in the novel, and political
pornography of the Revolution. She has published articles on gardens

and erotic utopias, and is finishing a book-length study entitled *The Voyage to Cythera: From Allegory to Erotica in Eighteenth-Century France*.

ELIZABETH W. HARRIES is professor of English and comparative literature at Smith College. She is the author of *The Unfinished Manner: Essays on the Fragment in the Later Eighteenth Century* (1994), and has published articles on Sterne, Hogg, Freud, Richardson, and French women fairy-tale writers. She is now at work on a book-length study of women writing and rewriting fairy tales, from the 1690s to the 1990s.

CLAIRE-LISE MALARTE-FELDMAN is associate professor of French at the University of New Hampshire. She is the author of an annotated bibliography on Charles Perrault as well as a series of articles on his *Contes*. After several years dedicated to the analysis of their multiple versions and subversions in the field of contemporary children's literature in France, she is currently working on a full-length study of their iconography. She has also guest-edited a special issue of *The Lion and the Unicorn* devoted to French children's literature.

LEWIS C. SEIFERT is associate professor of French studies at Brown University. He has published articles on seventeenth-century French literature and culture and especially the *contes des fées*. He is the author of *Fairy Tales, Sexuality, and Gender in France, 1690–1715: Nostalgic Utopias* (1996), and is currently working on a book about masculinity and civility in early modern France.

CATHERINE VELAY-VALLANTIN teaches at the École des Hautes Études en Sciences Sociales in Paris. Her research interests include folk narrative and literature, popular literature, hagiography, and the literary fairy tale, on which she has published numerous articles. She is the author of *L'Histoire des contes* (1992) and *La Fille en garçon: Classiques de la littérature orale* (1992), and coeditor of *Pensées chrétiennes de Charles Perrault* (1987) and *Formes médiévales du conte merveilleux* (1989).

JACK ZIPES is professor and chair of the German department at the University of Minnesota. His research interests include twentieth-century German literature and the European fairy tale. He is the author of the critical studies *Breaking the Spell: Radical Theories of Folk and Fairy Tales* (1979), *Fairy Tales and the Art of Subversion: The Classical Genre for Children and the Process of Civilization* (1983), *The Brothers Grimm: From Enchanted Forests to the Modern World* (1988), *Fairy Tale as Myth/Myth as Fairy Tale* (1994), and *Creative Storytelling: Building Community, Changing Lives* (1995). He has also translated and edited numerous fairy-tale collections, including *The Trials and Tribulations of Little Red Riding*

Hood (1983), *Don't Bet on the Prince: Contemporary Feminist Fairy Tales in North America and England* (1986), *The Complete Fairy Tales of the Brothers Grimm* (1987), *Beauties, Beasts, and Enchantment: Classic French Fairy Tales* (1989), and *Spells of Enchantment: The Wondrous Fairy Tales of Western Culture* (1991). He is currently working on a book on the origins of the literary fairy tale.

ADRIENNE E. ZUERNER, assistant professor of French at Skidmore College, received her Ph.D. from the University of Michigan and specializes in seventeenth-century French literature. She has published on Tallemant des Réaux and Corneille and is working on a book-length study of cross-dressing and gender politics in seventeenth-century French literature.

Index